TESTING THE LIMITS OF TEAMS

HOW TO IMPLEMENT SELF-MANAGEMENT IN HEALTH CARE

■ ■ ■

Elizabeth D. Becker-Reems
Daniel G. Garrett

AHA press
American Hospital Publishing, Inc.
An American Hospital Association Company
Chicago

Library of Congress Cataloging-in-Publication Data

Becker-Reems, Elizabeth D.
Testing the limits of teams : how to implement self-management in health care / by Elizabeth D. Becker-Reems and Daniel G. Garrett.
p. cm.
Includes bibliographical references and index.
ISBN 1-55648-215-9
1. Health care teams. 2. Self-directed work teams. 3. Health services administration. I. Garrett, Daniel G. II. Title.
R729.5.H4B43 1998
362.1'068—dc21 97-53189
CIP

Item Number: 169113

Contents

PART III TEAMS IN ACTION

About the Authors

Elizabeth D. Becker-Reems, MS, is director of Human Resource Development, Mission+St. Joseph's Health System, Asheville, North Carolina. With over 20 years experience in personnel management and human resource development in health care, Ms. Becker-Reems provides internal and external consultation in areas of organizational effectiveness, self-managed work teams, customer service, leadership development, organization culture, and change management. She is a frequent speaker on these topics at national meetings and has consulted with hospitals, nursing homes, retirement communities, and physicians' offices. She is the author of the book *Self-Managed Teams in Health Care Organizations,* published by AHA Press in 1994. Ms. Becker-Reems hold a bachelor's degree in Spanish and Political Science from Michigan State University, and a master's degree in Human Resource Development from Western Carolina University.

Daniel G. Garrett, MS, FASHP, is director of Pharmacy, Mission+St. Joseph's Health System, Asheville, North Carolina. He is also the president of the North Carolina Center for Pharmaceutical Care. He consults with hospitals and pharmacy organizations throughout the United States on implementing self-managed work teams and innovative pharmacy practices. He is a graduate of the Ferris State University School of Pharmacy and has a master's degree in administration from Central Michigan University. He has over 15 years experience as a pharmacy director. He has published articles on pharmacokinetics, productivity systems, quality improvement, and other related topics.

Preface

Self-managed teams are complex organizational entities. They are difficult to create and implement, and yet they are an extremely popular and successful organizational structure. Why do workers and their managers pursue self-management? How can it be so complex? What have self-managed teams achieved? Should it be tried in your organization? This book answers these questions and many more, and can serve as a guide for those who wish to explore the mysteries and complexities of self-managed teams. It provides a catalog of experiences that enable both the novice and experienced team member to delve into structures that help teams function in an environment that is more commonly hierarchical and to learn the secrets that help teams achieve the highest levels of performance.

This book is designed for managers and staff who are innovative and entrepreneurial. It will help them create a self-managed work environment to unleash the spirit, intelligence, and experience of their organization. Today many leaders are moving away from the passé concepts of a single all-knowing boss who holds all the intelligence and wisdom necessary to manage a group, toward the concepts of collaboration in which effectiveness comes from the collective wisdom of the workers.

For those who seek detailed and specific information on the "how to" of self-management, this book provides a road map sprinkled with actual experiences of self-managed teams. This book can be used by staff members who are interested in creating a democratic management structure in which leadership is truly shared among the staff, rather than vested in a single superior. Through the information in this book, it is possible to establish a self-managed team and guide it through its development stages. It is possible to reduce costs and reduce the number of management-level positions in an organization. It is ultimately possible to create a highly motivating work environment where a normal group of employees becomes a team of outstanding performers who work together to meet and exceed the needs and expectations of their customers.

Organization and Content

The book is divided into three parts: Getting Started, Work Design, and Teams in Action. Each section is described below. The book is a manual that answers questions, provides advice, and guides the design and implementation of self-managed teams. Each chapter contains examples from actual health care self-managed teams that have had experience in the phases and stages of self-management.

Part I: Getting Started

In this section, the concept of self-management is introduced, along with the societal changes that have provided a fertile ground for their development and success. Self-managed teams are not unmanaged. This section explains what self-managed teams are, the boundaries they generally operate within, and the role transitions that occur when self-management begins.

In chapter 1, Introduction to Self-Managed Teams, the authors begin their discussion of self-managed teams with a definition and by providing examples of teams that exist in health care organizations today. They provide tips on how to start teams and present a "readiness survey" to help work groups determine if they are prepared to embark on self-management.

Chapter 2, Reasons for Teams, explores the reasons that teams have formed in various health care organizations. Sometimes teams are formed as a matter of workplace philosophy; other times they are formed in response to a change in management or a merger of departments or organizations. Not every group should become a self-managed team. There are basic requirements that a work group must meet if it wants to become a team. These requirements are outlined and supported with examples from existing health care teams. The authors describe structures that do not support teams and address barriers to teams that exist in all organizations. This chapter also includes a simple-to-use format for justifying a team that can be adapted to any organization.

When teams are created they must operate within the boundaries of authority and structure that exist within the organization. In chapter 3, Development of Team Boundaries, the authors define areas for boundaries and give examples of boundaries for teams that have been implemented in health care organizations. A process for setting boundaries is described.

The conversion to self-management is not easy. Chapter 4, Transitions in Work Roles, describes the agony, resistance, and metamorphosis that occurs when self-management is implemented. The people in the organization who are directly impacted by the change include the staff and management of the group who become a self-managed team. But they are not the only ones who must change. Many people in the organization are impacted by self-managed teams. They experience resistance to the need to form new habits and new relationships. Many systems of operating in a traditional work environment must change, and others remain untouched. This chapter deals with the changes that are experienced. It contains tips from team members, managers and others who have lived through these transitions.

The final chapter in the first section—chapter 5, Introduction to Work Design—describes the design process and serves as an introduction to part II, Work Design. In this chapter, the authors provide an overview of work design. They introduce the concepts of technical and social systems, and describe the importance of involving the self-managed team in the design process. The chapter concludes with design tips from self-managed health care teams.

Part II: Work Design

Every team will need to go through a design phase. When designing large teams, or multiple teams, it is advisable to use a representative design team. In chapter 6, The Design Team, the authors describe a design team in detail. They include information on how to select design team members, the role of the facilitator, design team goals, the importance of communication, and recognition of the design team. The practical approach that the authors use will help the reader create a successful design team and a successful launch to the design process.

The design process is further described in chapter 7, The Design Timeline. This chapter provides a road map for the design of a self-managed team and offers a glimpse of the complexity of the design. The chapter gives examples of timelines from several self-managed teams and discusses the likelihood that the team will get off track on occasion. Barriers to successful design are described as are solutions to problems that are encountered during the design process.

One of the most important work and communication mechanisms that teams have is the team meeting. Chapter 8, Holding Effective Meetings, is a nuts-and-bolts approach to team meetings. It describes agendas, ground rules, roles, and techniques for managing meetings that will benefit any meeting facilitator or participant. The authors include model formats for meeting agendas and meeting minutes, as well as techniques for handling meetings that get out of hand.

The first challenge that the design process undertakes is the design of the work that the team is responsible for accomplishing. This challenge is described in detail in chapter 9, Technical System Development. In this chapter, the authors describe the process of drawing macro flow diagrams of their work and consulting with customers to determine their needs. A simple customer survey tool is described. Teams that use this tool, and redesign their work processes based on the information they gather, will make great strides toward significant performance improvement.

In chapter 10, Social Systems Design, the authors present a laundry list of social systems that must change to reinforce the team process. Social systems include systems such as communication, hiring, discipline, conflict resolution, performance reviews, reporting, and recognition. Most social systems have been designed to support individuals who function under the control of supervisors. Considerable redesign of social systems is needed to enable them to be supportive of self-managed teams.

One of the most important structural elements of high-performing self-managed teams are the roles that team members perform. Roles are an integral part of shared leadership and a foundation of self-management. Chapter 11, Team Roles, describes the roles that are typically found in self-managed teams. The roles are outlined in detail, along with a brief overview of the knowledge, skills, and behaviors that team members will need to develop to fill those roles effectively. Part of the self-development that occurs in teams comes from accepting the responsibility of a role and then changing roles routinely to develop a full complement of new knowledge, skills, and behavior. This self-development process is one aspect of teams that benefits individual teams members as much as it benefits the organization. The authors also describe options for selecting which team members will fill which roles and for role rotation alternatives.

In order for teams to accomplish great things, they must work together in a concerted and forward-thinking manner. Chapter 12, Planning Systems, describes a planning method that teams can easily adapt for their use. This system will enable the self-managed team to be creative and energized as they work toward future performance. Sample mission statements, visions, and values are presented in this chapter, as well as tips on how to develop them. The process for creating team goals is also described.

Although health care organizations utilize measurement effectively to gauge clinical performance, it is not used as effectively to measure people performance. In chapter 13, Measurement Systems, the authors describe how to develop team performance measures. Sample measurement systems and display boards are presented in this chapter. Teams can model their measurement systems and their performance measures from those presented in this chapter. Teams can learn how to develop a customer survey tool, how to establish performance targets, and how to report their progress. When a team measures its performance, it is more likely to take action to continuously improve that performance.

In chapter 14, Human Resources Management Systems, the authors provide a guide for developing the hiring, orientation, performance evaluation, discipline, and recognition systems that will work in a team environment. This chapter also gives tips to team members on how to address and overcome the people problems that teams invariable must address from the outset.

Chapter 15, Team Communication Systems, describes the most important of the social systems that teams must develop. This chapter gives a simple five-step process for developing the team communication system. It introduces the team to simple phrases and techniques for team and relationship building. It provides a conflict resolution process. The chapter also outlines the communication responsibilities that each role needs to assume in order to ensure effective communication within the team and to the team's customers.

In chapter 16, Daily Operations Systems, the authors describe staff scheduling and how to make it work in a self-managed team environment. In addition, this chapter provides a team decision-making process and tips for handling conflicts between team members and the daily crises that arise and must be handled by the team. This chapter provides very practical advice as well as simple techniques for dealing with daily problems that teams encounter.

Part III: Teams in Action

The final section of the book—part III, Teams in Action—presents the reader with actual examples of team meetings, team building exercises, education programs, and team celebrations. In this section, the flavor of team work is clearly expressed, and team members can learn practical techniques for establishing or improving their performance.

In chapter 17, The First Team Meeting, the authors help teams set the tone for their future through a detailed outline on how to plan and conduct the first team meeting. A sample agenda for the first meeting is included. Team meetings must be highly structured to ensure their efficiency. In this chapter, the structure and roles in an effective meeting are outlined and explained.

Team building is an exercise that receives as much criticism as it does praise. In chapter 18, Team Building, the authors note that teams will never achieve the highest levels of performance if they fail to achieve a highly cohesive work group. There is a simple chart that teams can use to assess how close and cohesive they are, or how far they are from true team cohesiveness. Several team building exercises are outlined and can be easily implemented by any team seeking to improve its cohesiveness.

Teams do not start out functioning at top performance levels. In chapter 19, Team Education, the authors describe competencies for self-managed teams. Using a baseball analogy, learning needs are outlined from spring training through the World Series. Methods for obtaining education and resources that are available to all teams are described. One of the fatal errors that organizations make is to skimp on the training that team members receive. High-performing teams will be involved in education continuously.

Self-managed teams do not experience smooth sailing all the time. As is clear to all who have participated on teams of any kind, it is hard work and unreasonable to expect calm waters throughout the life of the team. In chapter 20, Bumps in the Road, the phases of team growth and development are described. The authors give tips that will help the team through difficult times.

Acknowledging that teams and individuals seek recognition from the organization and will extend themselves to achieve outstanding results providing they get occasional feedback, the authors address recognition and celebrations in chapter 21, Team Achievements and Celebrations. In this chapter, the authors describe the feedback systems that are needed in health care organizations and the methods that teams use to ensure team and individual recognition. The authors review currently held beliefs about motivation and describe "REST" (Recognize, Encourage, Share, Trust), a method for ensuring a motivating work environment. Teams that take time to celebrate and reflect on their accomplishments will likely learn from their achievements as well as develop motivation to continue their endeavors.

In chapter 22, Maintaining Team Excellence, the authors provide a comprehensive list of the characteristics that are deemed necessary for team excellence. They elaborate on the characteristics in order to help team members understand their importance. They describe frequent causes of team performance problems and methods that teams can use to solve the performance problems they are likely to encounter. For readers who are interested in focusing on the vital few aspects of team performance that are critical to success, this chapter provides a valuable listing.

The final chapter in the book—chapter 23, Beyond Teams: Adapting to the Future—takes the reader to a time in the future of health care, describing the impact of the external environment on team and other organizational structures. The authors look at the impact of communities working together to improve health care, managed care and mergers, multidisciplinary and multiorganizational networks, and the impact of technology on the structures that are so familiar now. They discuss ways that teams can become aware of the need to change their structures to adapt to their changing environment. This chapter encourages teams to look to the future and to see their present structure as temporary. It presents a practical strategy for responding to the need to change.

In an appendix, the authors provide brief profiles of self-managed teams in hospitals, a retirement community, and a physicians' practice. These profiles provide a snapshot of many different types of teams and how they are structured. Each profile lists a team advocate or participant who can be contacted for further information.

Acknowledgments

It is with deep appreciation that we recognize Robert F. Burgin, President, Mission+St. Joseph's Health System, for creating an environment that allows empowerment, innovation, and self-managed teams to flourish. If not for him, we would not have been able to experiment with self-managed teams nor have the support throughout the organization that permitted teams to flourish.

We value the contribution that Glenn Yokoyama, Pharmacy Manager at Huntington Memorial Hospital, Pasadena, California, has made to the development of self-management on the West Coast and thank him sincerely for introducing us to other devotees of self-management in a Southern California health care setting.

We would also like to acknowledge the contributions of pioneers in workplace change: Moe Jones for her entrepreneurial interest in self-managed teams in Little Rock and her efforts to bring her dream of team compensation to reality. Ken Partin, Executive Director of Givens Estates Methodist Retirement Community, who can truly envision and lead a workplace in which all employees work in a spirit of community and self-actualization. Randy Johnson, MD, who had the confidence in the abilities of the office staff in his general surgery practice and who gave them the opportunity to become a highly successful self-managed team. Dean Strahm and Ellen Williams, members of the Mission+St. Joseph's pharmacy coaching and leadership team, for their excellent design and implementation of 13 high-performing self-managed pharmacy teams. Rose Spittle, a Top 100 Nurse, who led the self-managed and cross-functional wound team to exceptional performance. Graham Skinner, Cooperative Laundry, who had the confidence in his staff and the commitment to providing a better work environment that led to the creation of three self-managed teams and a highly productive laundry. Gail Williams and Dianne Hill, One Day Surgery, for their leadership skills and willingness to carry the one day surgery team to the next level of team performance. Wil Bowler, Debbie Vargo, and Dee Gabbard, who, along with all the dietitians, continue their emphasis on excellence through the freedom and responsibility that are theirs in a self-managed environment. MaryAnn Aelmans-Digman, COO, Memorial Medical Center, who took a calculated risk, knowing that her patient care services department directors could easily rise to the challenge of self-management and pave the way for other management teams.

We would also like to acknowledge the valuable input and editing services of Rose Morford, Anna Garrett, and Sally Lordeon, and the endurance and support of the members of the Mission+St. Joseph's Health System

Pharmacy and Human Resource Development departments while the book was being written.

The book itself was improved and enhanced by the efforts of the staff at AHA Press and Rick Hill, Senior Editor, who supported our endeavors.

> Until one is committed, there is hesitancy, the chance to draw back. . . . There is one elementary truth, the ignorance of which kills countless ideas and splendid plans: that the moment one definitely commits oneself, then providence moves too, and all sorts of things occur to help one that would never otherwise have occurred. A whole stream of events issues from the decision, raising in one's favor all manner of unforeseen events, meetings, and material assistance which no one could have dreamed would have come their way. Whatever you can do or dream you can do, begin it.
>
> Boldness has genius, power and magic in it. Begin it now!
>
> *—Goethe*

Part 1

Getting Started

This section introduces you to the concept of self-managed work teams in health care organizations. It will give you a solid foundation in the "basics" of self-managed teams—what they are, why people have formed them, how teams fit into the larger organization, and whose roles teams affect.

In chapter 1, you will find a definition for self-managed teams, case examples of teams that are operating in different health care settings, and profiles of the people who started them. Chapter 2 describes the compelling business and philosophical reasons that motivated these groups to make the transition to self-managed teams.

Before groups become self-managed, certain preliminaries must be addressed. An early step is to establish "boundaries," such as team purpose and goals. By defining the parameters in which they will operate, teams clarify their responsibilities and pave the way to acceptance by the larger organization as a whole. In chapter 3 you will find examples of boundaries that different self-managed teams have set as well as a process for defining and establishing team boundaries.

The transition to teams is a major one that requires significant changes in the roles that management and staff traditionally play. Chapter 4 describes these role changes and provides tips from those who have successfully made the transitions. Chapter 5 complements chapter 4 by providing an overview of the team design process and the systems involved in team design.

Part Contents: Getting Started

Section contents: Getting Started

Chapter 1

Introduction to Self-Managed Teams

Chapter Preview

"When you come to a fork in the road, take it."

—*Yogi Berra*

At Memorial Mission Hospital in Asheville, North Carolina, most pharmacy staff would have described their work as fast paced and ever changing. Many felt as if they couldn't keep up. Management always seemed to be planning new tasks for staff members to do and didn't understand why they didn't rush to embrace every new idea. Adding to the stress was the supervisory situation. The supervisor of the technicians was a pharmacist who wanted to be a clinician, not a boss. The technicians felt that their efforts were not appreciated by the pharmacists, while the pharmacists, busy trying to meet increasing clinical demands, felt that they didn't have time to keep track of the technicians. *Something had to change . . .*

Huntington Memorial Hospital in Pasadena, California, was facing stiff competition and mounting pressure to hold down costs. The director, busy planning for the future, kept losing ground in his struggle to keep up with day-to-day activities. The pharmacy staff had been decentralized, clinicians' demands on staff were growing, and communication was sorely lacking between the two groups. As a result of these situations, the pharmacy staff felt as if they were being pulled in different directions. Although everyone was committed to excellence, under these conditions, excellence was difficult to maintain. *Something had to change . . .*

At Baptist Health Preschool in Little Rock, Arkansas, teaching staff struggled to meet conflicting demands. Parents wanted the teachers to meet the individual needs of each child, while management wanted the teachers to follow standard rules and procedures. Many on the teaching staff felt frustrated. Because the school had numerous layers of management, staff lacked the autonomy that they needed to meet day-to-day multiple demands. As a result, turnover was high, and the continuity of the curriculum was suffering. After completing a national accreditation process, the preschool received a recommendation that addressed turnover. *Something had to change . . .*

The supervisor of the staff at the One Day Surgery Center of St. Joseph's Hospital in Asheville, North Carolina, was out on leave. During this time, the staff, a group of seasoned veterans, had learned to be flexible to meet patient and physician demands. Staff were feeling anxious about what would happen when the supervisor returned and a layer of management was restored to a system that was working well without it. *Something had to change . . .*

At Givens Estates Methodist Retirement Community in Asheville, North Carolina, a question gnawed at the back of the executive director's mind: If Givens truly had a progressive environment, then why were hierarchy and bureaucracy still used to control the staff? *Something had to change . . .*

In each of the preceding case examples, the "something" that had to change was the group's organizational structure. Although the circumstances that led to the need for change varied from organization to organization, all the organizations suffered from the same basic problem—a management or supervisory system that failed to meet the work needs of a group or groups of staff and, by extension, the organization as a whole. To solve this problem, the groups turned to a structure that better met their needs: the self-managed work team.

This chapter is intended to be the starting point in your quest to implement teams in your health care setting. Based on the team-building experiences of others in health care, the chapter defines self-managed work teams, describes common barriers to teams, outlines techniques for overcoming these barriers, and provides a team activity for assessing your environment's readiness for teams.

Chapter at a Glance

In this chapter, you will find

- A definition of self-managed work teams
- Case examples of real health care work teams
- Tips for readying a group for self-governance
- A tool to assess your group's readiness for teams
- Discussions of barriers to teams and ways to overcome them
- An activity for identifying and overcoming barriers in your environment

Definition of Self-Managed Work Teams

"Self-directed work teams increase productivity and morale by empowering employees. These teams do not maintain individual leaders or hierarchy. Rather, members work as a team toward care for the patient."

—The Advisory Board Company

Most health care organizations have management teams. They may also have teams that carry out quality improvement activities or task teams that work to solve specific problems. This book is *not* about those kinds of teams. It is about self-managed work teams; that is, permanent self-managed groups of about five to fifteen employees who work together to produce a product or service. This basic definition contains four key ideas that explain what self-managed work teams are and what qualities are essential to their success.

Four Key Ingredients of Teams

There are four key ingredients for successful self-managed work teams:

1. Permanence
2. Appropriate size
3. Shared work
4. Production of product or service

The first key ingredient of self-managed work teams is permanence. To form the relationships needed for team success, the team must stay together. This quality separates the true self-managed work team from ad hoc temporary teams that form to fulfill a specific task and then disband when the task is completed.

The second key ingredient of self-managed work teams is appropriate size. Although a team can have as few as three members or as many as eighteen, both extremes in size can present problems. Teams that are too small do not have enough members to effectively share leadership. Teams that are too large cannot work together efficiently.

The third key ingredient is that the members of a team work together. In this context, "working together" does not mean that team members must be physically grouped in the same area of the workplace (although they certainly may). "Working together" means doing the same or similar work, such as covering the same area or function. Although team members do not need to do exactly the same work, their work must be similar enough that they can offer support to each other and share responsibility for getting work done. No team member should have more responsibility or authority than any other. All must have the authority to make decisions to meet their customers' needs.

The last key ingredient of self-managed work teams is that they exist for a purpose—to produce a product or service. The purpose is defined by identifying the customers, customer needs, products, or services that the team is responsible for. The team must also define how its purpose helps fulfills the purpose of the organization as a whole.

Mistaken Ideas about Teams

Notice that the definition of self-managed work teams stresses the importance of shared work and responsibility. Although people sometimes mistakenly think that teams are loose coalitions of employees in related jobs, this is not the case. Take, for example, the risk management department of a large hospital. While the members of this department share a common purpose—to control risk and prevent loss for the organization—none of the professionals who fulfill this purpose can perform the work of the other. They do not collaborate on projects or fill in for each other during absences, and they cannot answer requests for information in each other's areas of responsibility. In short, because the risk management staff do not work together, they cannot form a self-managed team. The single most important ingredient of the self-managed team is that it be a group of people who work together to achieve a common purpose. A team is *not* any of the following:

- *A collection of specialists who can't or won't do the work of other team members when needed.* The members of a self-managed team must share some work and learn each other's roles. In this way, they will gain an understanding of what each team member contributes to the larger group and how members can support each other.
- *A regrouping of a supervisor and his or her staff in a participative management scheme.* For a self-managed work team to succeed, every employee must share in and equally feel the weight of the group's collective responsibility. Employees should not be given merely the illusion that they have input.
- *An assortment of "free agents."* Every team member must understand that fulfilling the stated purpose of the team is more important than meeting personal agendas.

"Real-Life" Examples of Self-Managed Teams

"When you have seen one self-managed work team, you have seen one self-managed work team."

—Self-managed work team observer

Self-managed teams of all shapes and sizes can be found in a variety of different health care settings. In fact, almost any existing work group that has the four key ingredients—permanence, appropriate size, shared work, and shared production of a product or service—can become a self-managed team. For clarification, consider the following "real-life" self-managed teams.

Pharmacy Department, Mission+St. Joseph's Health System

Beginning in December 1993, the pharmacy director of Memorial Mission Hospital in Asheville, North Carolina, started to educate the staff of his department about self-managed teams. In September 1994 a design team was commissioned, and teams were officially started on "T Day" in May 1995. To coordinate the department's activities, the teams were organized around the various clinical lines that the department served. These teams used a shared leadership philosophy, rotating team roles every four months. The teams ranged in size from three to eighteen members, and each team had a coach.

In March 1996 Memorial Mission Hospital partnered with St. Joseph's Hospital to form the Mission+St. Joseph's Health System. A design team was commissioned in August 1996 to plan teams for St. Joseph's pharmacy and combine these with teams from the Mission Hospital pharmacy.

Today the pharmacy of Mission+St. Joseph's Health System is organized into 12 teams. Each team has a specific customer(s) to serve and a common set of products or services to provide. For example, one team provides pharmacy services to surgery, another for heart services, and a third for outpatients, among others. In addition, there is a small office support team, an inventory team, and a large central production and distribution team. Although the size of the teams ranges from three employees to almost twenty employees, most of the teams have five to seven employees. Within each team, employees work together to provide the services their customers need. Not all team members can perform each other's tasks. For instance, the pharmacy technicians cannot perform the functions that, by law, must be performed by pharmacists. However, all team members can work together to meet their customers' needs.

Joint Laundry, Mission+St. Joseph's Health System

There are three self-managed teams in Mission+St. Joseph's joint laundry. Each of these teams is composed of from five to fifteen members. Although these teams share a joint purpose—to produce clean laundry for the health system—each team performs one segment of the work process. One team picks up dirty laundry from the system hospitals, transports it to the laundry, washes, and dries it. The next team irons, folds, and stacks small pieces. The third team irons, folds, and stacks large pieces of laundry and prepares the clean laundry for delivery. Despite these different work assignments, members of different teams can fill in for one another when someone is absent or when a team member's work volume is extremely high.

Givens Estates Methodist Retirement Community

In 1995 the executive director of this progressive retirement community of 200 employees sought out expertise on starting self-managed work teams. The philosophy of integrating stewardship ideals and service to residents seemed to fit with the implementation of self-managed teams for the employees. The executive director empowered the personnel director and administrator to begin the process of implementing teams in 1995.

Givens Estates staff members are organized into 16 teams, each of which provides an essential service or group of services to the residents. For example, there is a nursing services team, a food services team, a housekeeping team, a transportation team, a grounds team, and a maintenance team. The teams vary in size from three to fifteen members. Within each team, employees work together to provide their designated service. Although certain services can be provided only by licensed staff, all the team members work together to make sure that the service is provided.

Pre-Op/Post-Op/PACU, St. Joseph's Hospital

In 1995 the supervisor of the Pre-Op/Post-Op/PACU areas of the One Day Surgery Center at St. Joseph's Hospital had to take extended leaves of absence. Upon the supervisor's planned return, the supervisor and the staff approached the vice president responsible for the area and asked to form a self-managed work team. With the vice president's support, the approximately 30 staff members received team training and formed a self-managed team. Although the vice president serves as the team coach, the team of nurses, assistants, and unit secretaries runs the outpatient surgery activities with minimal involvement of senior management.

The team's primary purpose is to provide all the one-day surgery services other than those provided in the operating rooms. Team staff is a mixture of registered nurses who work full-time, part-time, and on a PRN, or occasional, schedule. Each team member can work in any of the three areas of service as the need arises, although all team members have specific assignments. Team members work a specific area and assignment unless there is a need to cover an absence or help out in another area experiencing a higher than usual volume of duties. When either of these events occurs, team members move to meet the need and are capable of functioning in any assignment within the Pre-Op/Post-Op/PACU area.

Baptist Health Preschool, Baptist Health System

In January 1994 six teams were implemented in the Baptist Health Preschool in Little Rock, Arkansas. The team model, which assigned each team a different age group of children, was developed in the spring of 1993. After five months of training, the teams were fully functional, with the former director of the preschool serving as the head coach. They now provide a full-service preschool for the children of hospital employees and others in the community.

Team members work together, consult with each other and with parents, and collaborate on business activities and issues. The teams have an average of seven staff members each. All members of a team can perform each other's duties. Although each team has specific assignments based on the age group it serves, staff help each other provide services and fill in for each other when a team member is absent.

Barriers to Teams and Ways to Overcome Them

"The harder you push, the harder the organization pushes back."

—*Margaret Wheatley*

Learning about actual self-managed teams, such as those just described, is helpful because established teams can serve as models for groups thinking about making the transition. However, looking at just the "finished product" can be deceptive. Although these teams are now successful, the transition to teams took hard work and planning, and the groups had to overcome plenty of "roadblocks" along the way.

Some barriers that teams are likely to encounter lie within the organization as a whole. Others lie within the department or unit in which the team may be formed or within the minds and hearts of the employees who have been asked to consider forming a team. Understanding that barriers are likely to occur and developing ways to overcome them are important parts of preparing for teams.

Organizational Barriers

Organizational barriers are those obstacles that arise from the customs, habits, and beliefs of the health care setting. More specifically, organizational barriers fall into three main categories: those related to structure, those related to channels of communication, and those related to policies.

Hierarchical Structure Today most organizations are structured as a hierarchy, with layers of management at the top of the organization and staff members at the bottom. The hierarchy serves the purpose of establishing a "chain of command." It lets everyone in the organization know who is in charge, who makes decisions, and who holds key information. The hierarchical structure is a barrier to self-managed teams because teams are "flat" structures in which information is shared with all and everyone is involved in decision making.

How does a self-managed team overcome the barrier of a hierarchical organization? It adapts to it and learns how to exist within it. The team learns how to get information and sets an example for others by sharing it. The team learns the types of decisions it can make and the extent of its authority. In short, the team identifies its place within the hierarchy and operates within those boundaries.

Chain-of-Command Communication Another barrier to teams and one that arises from hierarchical structure is chain-of-command communication. When an organization needs to communicate something to those in charge, it generally communicates through this channel, disseminating information to a list of directors and supervisors. The organization sends the information to people on this list with the expectation that information will be shared with staff if they need to have it. Chain-of-command communication can be a barrier to self-managed teams because they may not have a director or supervisor who can gather information and disseminate it to them. To ensure that the team stays within the information loop, they should get approval to have the team leader or a team communicator placed on the official organization "director list" for purposes of communication. This individual should be included in organization communication meetings, such as meetings for department directors, and should be placed on circulation lists. When the team has access to interoffice memos, reports, and meetings, the barrier of chain-of-command communications is overcome.

Traditional Personnel Policies Traditional personnel policies are a more difficult barrier to overcome. In many organizations, the policies that govern hiring, discipline, performance review, confidentiality of employee information, and compensation were set up for a hierarchical structure rather than a flat structure like self-managed teams. To overcome personnel-related barriers, the self-managed team needs to create new policies that will work for the self-managed team yet be acceptable to personnel decision makers. The best way to do this is to involve the director of human resources or another representative of the human resources department in creating self-managed team policies. It also is helpful to research policies that other organizations have developed for self-managed teams and to make this information available to team members and human resources staff. Although the policies may need modification, they are a good starting point and, if need be, can be implemented on a trial basis.

Another key to overcoming the barrier of personnel policies is to recognize the resistance that may be encountered and not push too hard against it. In the end, small steps can move the team forward just as effectively as large leaps.

Department or Unit Barrier

The concept of shared leadership is likely to seem as strange to the smaller group as it is to the larger organization as a whole. Therefore, it is not surprising that barriers to the formation of teams may also arise within a department or unit. Traditionally, work groups have written job descriptions that define roles and instill the department director and supervisors with ultimate authority over group members. As a result, many workers rely on an authority figure to make decisions and enforce rules, a deeply ingrained habit that can be a difficult obstacle to self-governance.

When self-managed teams are implemented, team members need to seek counsel from each other, from the total team, and from experts anywhere within the organization. Even though team members know this, they will still fall into the old habit of asking permission, approval, and advice from the person in charge. Team members can break this habit by learning how to make decisions and resolve conflicts for themselves, by forgiving each other's mistakes, and by giving each other friendly reminders that they are now part of a team.

Barriers within the Minds and Hearts of Employees

Finally, it is common for barriers to arise within the minds and hearts of potential team members. Some of these barriers are rooted in a lack of knowledge; others, such as resistance to change, stem from fear of the unknown.

Lack of Understanding of the Team Concept Many people fail to support the team concept because they do not understand what a team is or how it works. These individuals are not resistant to teams; they just truly don't understand how they work. The best way to overcome this barrier to self-governance is education. The self-managed team needs to explain what it is, what its purpose is, and how it will work within the organization as a whole. Clarity about the team concept decreases fear and increases understanding. With education, individuals generally come to understand that the team structure can successfully exist within a hierarchy.

Resistance to Change Although education about teams can help dissipate confusion, many people who clearly understand the team concept may still initially resist making the transition. After all, most people feel some degree of fear when faced with adjusting to a major change. What helps overcome this barrier? There are several techniques that can be used. First, team members should listen carefully to resistant staff members in order to understand their concerns. Once resisters have been given a chance to voice their reservations, they can be given information about ways that teams in other organizations have successfully addressed similar areas of concern. In addition, change-resistant staff members should be given time to adjust. Many people feel the need to mull over initiatives before implementing them, and this need should be respected. Finally, team supporters should ensure that resistant staff members are involved in developing the self-managed team for their unit, section, or department. Often, involvement leads to buy-in.

Time Restrictions As staff think about how they will function as members of a self-managed team, another barrier inevitably arises—concerns about time restrictions. Being a member of a self-managed team does require people to allocate time to self-management. Employees—particularly those in clinical departments—are naturally concerned about how they will perform their patient care duties while participating in meetings, making decisions, solving problems, and doing all the other tasks formerly done by management. Unfortunately, there is no simple solution to time barriers. Procedures will have to change to allow time for staff members to meet and solve problems together. Work may need to be reorganized. People will have to cooperate with each other more than they may have in the past.

When a team is just beginning, staff members must attend meetings and educational sessions to learn how to function as a self-managed team. These meetings can be time-consuming. As a result, some employees may have to work overtime, and some staff may have to pitch in and cover for another when he or she must attend to a team responsibility. Team members should be assured, however, that meetings will become less frequent and lengthy as the team becomes accustomed to communicating as a group. Over time, team members also often find ways to create new efficiencies that allow them to attend to both "team work" and their usual duties.

Group Analysis of Barriers

The barriers that were just described are representative of the obstacles that teams typically encounter. The barriers covered are not, however, all-inclusive. Just as organizations, departments, and individuals may vary, so may the obstacles that a group must overcome. As a result, groups that are contemplating self-management should analyze the barriers in their own environment and brainstorm ways to overcome them. The first team activity at the end of this chapter, the Force-Field Analysis tool, will help team members do just that. To prepare for the analysis, the group might skim the barriers previously described and the summary box of solutions below.

Techniques for Overcoming Barriers

- Change policies and procedures to accommodate teams.
- Involve human resources in self-managed team policy development.
- Make sure that a team member is included in the information loop.
- Change old patterns of behavior; learn methods of self-governance.
- Give friendly reminders that team members should take initiative.
- Listen and try to understand those who resist change.
- Take small steps.
- Involve others in creating the new structure and systems.
- Share the team's story with others in the organization.
- Schedule time for the team to be together.

Team Readiness

"Planning is everything."

—*Dwight D. Eisenhower*

Analyzing barriers and planning ways to overcome them are important steps toward readying groups for teams. However, they alone are not enough. For teams to succeed, the environment and team members themselves must be ready to make the transition. Consider the conditions that are needed to build a snowman. The temperature must be just right so that the snow is almost melting. Then comes the hard part—getting the initial amount of snow packed into a small ball that will eventually "roll itself." Starting self-managed teams is a similar process. The internal conditions must be right, and the people must be willing "to get the ball rolling." Here are some questions to ask to see if workplace conditions are conducive to starting teams:

- *Is it the right time to start?* Teams cannot be started at just any time. Start when you have personal commitment and freedom to try something new.
- *Do you have a core of supportive staff?* The critical mass for starting the mindset shift to teams is about 25 percent of staff. Don't expect everyone to jump for joy when you start teams. Know who can be counted on to help build teams.
- *Are people prepared for a cultural shift?* During the initial start-up phase, it is critical to develop an understanding of workplace environment and culture—the unspoken values, beliefs, and customs that influence how people in an organization work and behave. Many organizations are structured around a hierarchy and believe that a chain of command is necessary to ensure that employees work efficiently and effectively. As teams form, this culture will change. Everyone must be aware that there will be a cultural shift; everyone must be sensitive to the effects of this change on himself or herself and on other team members.
- *Does the organization have time and money for team training?* When teams do not succeed, the failure is usually caused by a lack of training. Team members must be taught team skills. Invest in the time it takes to learn how to share leadership.
- *Are managers and supervisors willing to stay out of the way?* Perhaps the most difficult thing for managers and supervisors to learn is a "hands-off" attitude. The more the "ex-boss" interferes in the team process, the more the old command-and-control paradigm is reinforced, and the more likely that the team will fall apart. Once the decision to form self-managed work teams is made, the teams must be allowed to manage themselves.
- *Is everyone willing to be patient?* Starting teams is hard work. There will be mistakes. Without these mistakes, team members will not learn the skills necessary to work as a team. There will be times when each member of the

team will want to throw in the towel. Team members must remember that the transition to teams is a long-term commitment, not a quick fix.

In short, readiness for teams requires participation, team behaviors, knowledge of teams, and resources. Many work environments encourage participation of staff in decision making; therefore, some staff members may exhibit team behaviors already. If these skills are present and the group has management's support to provide resources, such as team training and help to work through barriers, then the conditions for teams are ripe. To further gauge the group's readiness for teams, group members should complete the Self-Managed Team Readiness Survey, the second team activity at the end of this chapter.

☞ **Team Tip:** *Celebrate small first steps in big ways.* Harold Kushner points out that the greatest harm that we do to people is to criticize their failures rather than celebrate their successes.[1] When infants are learning to walk, we do not scold them when they fall. Instead, we celebrate every step and encourage them to try to walk again. We must recognize initial team efforts in big ways.

Chapter Wrap-Up

Self-managed teams are forming where conditions are right and where people are willing to try something different. Self-management is a way for people to share leadership, do work, and provide for patient and customer needs. Team start-up requires proper timing, supportive staff members and a supportive culture, education, and patience. Team members also must anticipate barriers to team formation and plan ways to overcome them. When all these factors are combined, self-managed work teams develop and thrive.

Reference

1. Harold S. Kushner, *How Good Do We Have to Be?* (Boston: Little Brown, 1996), p. 79.

Suggested Readings

Drucker, Peter F. *Post-Capitalist Society.* New York: Harper Business, 1993.

Lipnack, Jessica, and Jeffrey Stamps. *The Age of the Network.* New York: John Wiley and Sons, 1994.

Riley, Pat. *The Winner Within.* New York: Berkley, 1993.

Wheatley, M. J. *Leadership and the New Science.* San Francisco: Berrett-Koehler, 1994.

Team Activity 1

Force-Field Analysis

Purpose: To provide a simple way to identify potential barriers to an idea, a plan, or a concept. The force-field analysis tool is also used to help brainstorm actions that can be implemented to overcome the barriers.

Instructions:

1. Brainstorm a list of barriers that your team might encounter when it implements a plan, a decision, or a new concept.
2. Using the force-field analysis graphic that appears below, write each barrier in a box in the left-hand column.
3. Starting with the top box, brainstorm techniques or actions that the team can take to overcome the first barrier. List these in the box directly opposite the first barrier on the right-hand side of the page.
4. Continue this process until actions have been written in the right-hand side of the page for all the barriers listed on the left-hand side of the page.
5. Review the actions listed to overcome the barriers. Identify those that would be most likely to work. Circle them.
6. Develop a plan to implement the circled actions: describe specific actions to be taken, assign people to do them, and determine deadlines for each action.

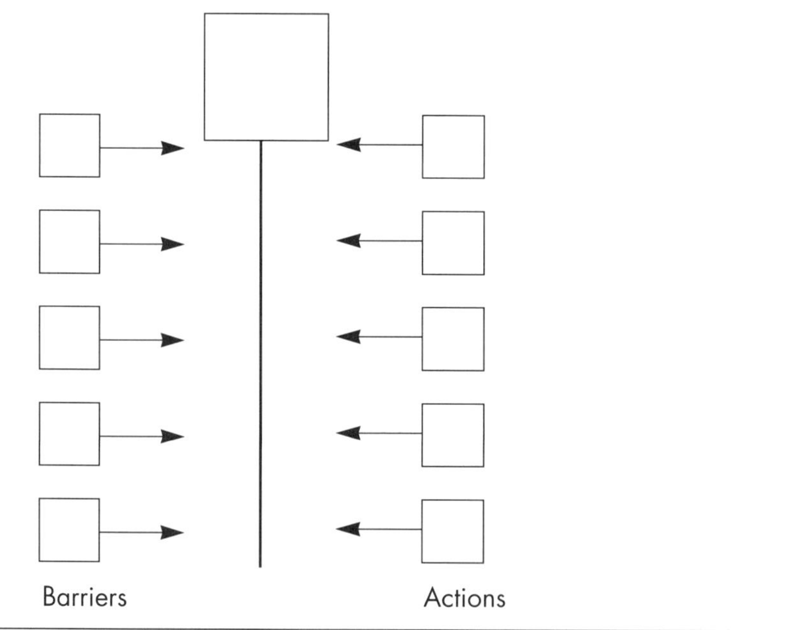

Team Activity 2

Self-Managed Team Readiness Survey

Purpose: To determine whether a group of employees, a department, or a unit is ready to accept the opportunity to develop as a self-managed work team.

Instructions: Have individuals considering formation of a team complete the survey on their own, then meet as a group to compare answers and come to a consensus on team readiness and perception of barriers. The group discussion is best when facilitated by an outsider and when staff members and managers are treated as equals in the discussion.

Readiness Criteria	Percent Estimate
Percentage of staff that actively participates in staff meetings, communications with other departments, decision making, planning, problem solving, and measuring performance	
Percentage of staff that performs group work by working on projects together, working on committees or task forces, serving on quality improvement teams, sharing the same work	
Percentage of time that staff members work in groups (working jointly or sharing work they are responsible for as a group) vs. working on their own (working independently on jobs for which they are personally responsible)	
Percentage of time that employees exhibit team behaviors, such as supporting each other's ideas, asking for help, offering help, celebrating together, sharing information, planning together, solving problems together	
Percentage of time that management exhibits team behaviors with staff, such as supporting staff members, seeking input, offering help, celebrating with staff, sharing information, planning together, solving problems together	
Percentage of employees and managers who have gained knowledge about teams by reading books or articles, completing team skill training, participating on quality improvement teams, or attending workshops	

(Continued on next page)

Readiness Criteria	
Are there strong advocates for teams in the department?	YES / NO
OVERALL ASSESSMENT OF TEAM READINESS: In your opinion, can teams be implemented in your department?	YES / NO

Resources: To what degree are the staff time for meetings and education, information on customer and employee satisfaction, and information on cost, quality, and productivity available?

Barriers: What barriers do you see to self-managed teams? What barriers would other staff and/or management perceive to starting teams? Can actions be taken to overcome these barriers?

Conclusion and Recommendations: Summarize the degree to which you believe this group of employees will be able to make the transition to teams. Based on this assessment, what is your recommendation about the possible success of implementing a self-managed team with this group?

Chapter 2

Reasons for Teams

Chapter Preview

"Teams were started because they are the way of the future."

—Martha Ballard, a service worker

Groups who are thinking about making the transition to teams should carefully consider their reasons for making the change. As chapter 1 points out, most groups can expect to encounter barriers related to organizational structure or misconceptions that people have about self-governance and teams. One of the best defenses against these obstacles is to have strong justifications for self-management. The stronger the group's reasons for changing to the team structure, the more likely that barriers will be overcome and that the team will succeed. This chapter describes events that have triggered actual groups' transitions to the team structure and the business reasons that motivated these groups to become teams. Learning about other groups' reasons for "crossing the bridge" is useful to staff who are considering making the transition themselves but are unsure whether they have sufficient justification.

The chapter also discusses performance expectations—the measures that management creates to evaluate the success of a self-managed team. The chapter explains why performance expectations should relate closely to business goals and gives examples of "real-life" team performance expectations, explaining how they were generated. In addition, the chapter examines the role that performance expectations play in providing guidance and structure to the team and the important links that performance expectations create among management, the team, and the organization as a whole.

The team activity for this chapter is a simple-to-use tool that will help groups write a proposal to implement self-managed teams. The tool guides groups into thinking about five major concerns:

- The current situation in the group's unit or department
- The event that has triggered the group's desire to become a team
- The business reasons underlying the change
- The projected cost of implementing teams
- The benefits that the organization will derive from the change

The resulting proposal, appropriate for a variety of audiences—staff, management, and other interested parties—can do much to educate and persuade those who have reservations about self-managed teams. Moreover, working on the proposal will help groups clarify their own understanding of the team concept and its implications for the organization.

Chapter at a Glance

In this chapter, you will find

- "Real-life" reasons for forming teams
- The functions of performance expectations
- A tool for creating a proposal to implement self-managed teams

"Real-Life" Reasons for Forming Teams

"We were having problems with the supervisory role. The person in the role and the staff were not satisfied with how it worked. This was the trigger event that caused us to look at self-managed teams."

—*Graham Skinner, Joint Laundry Director*

There are a number of reasons why staff and management may contemplate implementing self-managed teams. Sometimes the transition to teams is triggered by a pivotal event, such as a merger or a manager's conversion to a new management style. Other times, groups make the transition to teams for "hard" business reasons, such as to increase productivity. The reasons that follow are based on the experiences of the teams that will be profiled throughout this book. As you read about their experiences, you're likely to find situations and reasons that mirror those in your organization.

Trigger Events

A "trigger event" is a situation that provides an impetus for groups to look seriously at becoming self-managed teams. These events may be related to workplace changes in management or organizational structure, or they may be related to philosophical changes within an individual.

Events Related to Management The staff members of the Pre-Op/Post-Op/PACU department of the One Day Surgery Center at St. Joseph's Hospital in Asheville, North Carolina, decided to form a self-managed team because they had managed themselves successfully during their supervisor's long family leaves of absence.

According to Peggy Carlson, team leader, "The staff were confident that we could be truly self-managed based on our recent experience without a supervisor. In addition, after being on leave, our current supervisor really did not want to resume that role. She was ready for reduced stress on the job."

The vice president of the area, Tim Johnston, described his willingness to embark on teams this way: "The unit performed extremely well in patient and staff satisfaction as well as budget management. We had excellent team facilitation resources available to us. I was confident that there was little risk and the opportunity for continued excellent performance. The staff was very competent."

A similar event triggered the transition to teams in the general surgery unit of Memorial Mission Hospital in Asheville. When the director of the unit resigned, staff members were given the option of forming a self-managed team by their vice president, and they voted to try it. The vice president saw the resignation of the manager as an opportunity to empower the patient care staff. His management philosophy was one of involvement and empowerment. He trusted that the patient care team would be successful.

A director's decision was the impetus behind change at the newly merged Mission+St. Joseph's laboratory. The lab had a new director, who proposed adding a supervisor to oversee the functions of the night shift. Before hiring the new supervisor, the director offered the cross-functional group that performed prior lab functions on the night shift the opportunity to become a self-managed team. He had experience with informal self-management and believed it would work in his new department. The group decided to take it.

Change was triggered in the joint laundry of Mission+St. Joseph's Health System, in Asheville, for a different reason: a supervisor position that was not functioning effectively. The poorly defined position was eliminated, and roles and duties were reassigned to staff. To perform their new duties effectively, staff formed self-managed teams.

Events Related to Mergers In the midst of the chaos that surrounds mergers, opportunities may arise for departments, units, and groups to seek self-management. Such was the case for a newly consolidated respiratory care unit that was formed after the merger of Memorial Mission and St. Joseph's Hospitals. The resulting combined respiratory care unit ended up without a director, and when the staff educator in the department proposed that the respiratory care unit form self-managed teams, the vice president concurred, even though a search was underway for a new director. The respiratory care unit ultimately formed a self-managed team.

Similarly, when the decision-support staff of Memorial Mission Hospital and St. Joseph's Hospital were joined during a hospital merger, the vice president decided to restructure the groups into self-managed teams rather than add a frontline manager. This move eliminated the need for supervisory positions.

Events Related to Work Philosophy Personal philosophies may also motivate people to implement self-managed teams. Every organization has a few visionaries who see a picture of the future that differs from the conventions of the day. These individuals hold the belief that staff have the capacity to manage themselves, perform better under a system that is not based on hierarchy, and define their own futures. In short, self-governance is part of these visionaries' human philosophy.

Take, for example, Moe Jones, of the Baptist Health System in Little Rock, Arkansas. The system, which has a solid reputation as a quality health care provider, is also known to be conservative, studying and evaluating major changes carefully before implementing them. Moe, the director of the preschool and formerly director of the nursing school, was a high-control, autocratic manager—a style consistent with the traditional culture of Baptist Health. Her philosophical transformation came in 1992, when she studied a plan created by human resources. Moe believed that the plan, which included self-managed work teams, presented a better way of getting work done. She also felt that the innovative work structure would be better for the children, better for the staff, and, ultimately, better for Baptist Health. Moe is now Baptist Health's internal consultant on team development, providing support to other departments interested in adopting the team approach.

Another firm believer in innovative management is Dan Garrett, pharmacy director of Memorial Mission Hospital. Dan, an inveterate reader who enjoys examining new management philosophies, has a large network of friends and associates who help him stay abreast of cutting-edge management theories. When Dan first learned about self-managed teams, he believed that they were not just a fad but the way work would be done in the future. He saw how self-managed teams would complement his goals of decentralizing the pharmacy and increasing his staff's ability to be self-reliant. The pharmacy implemented self-managed teams in 1995.

Glen Yokoyama, of the hospital pharmacy of Huntington Memorial Hospital in Pasadena, California, also implemented self-managed teams in his area. Looking back at the reason he embarked on teams, Glen stated, "I could see the potential for the staff and for Huntington. The time was right."

Mark Gordon, vice president of operations at Mission+St. Joseph's, had a similar reason for implementing teams in his organization. Summing up his work philosophy, Mark said, "I've always believed that staff have the capacity to perform all the work of their unit with only occasional guidance and the benefit of a management 'sounding board.' Too many management layers interfere with a smooth operation. They lead to confusion and impede performance."

Cliff Carlin, a director of hospital housekeeping at Memorial Mission Hospital who was nearing retirement, thought about hard work and commitment, two things that his staff had given the hospital over the years. He also thought about what the hospital had given his staff. Housekeepers, generally considered the bottom of the totem pole, were given little respect in an organization that focused on clinical skills and clinical contributions. To change this situation, Cliff decided to leave his staff the opportunity to become self-managed. Explaining that he wanted "to leave a legacy to [his] staff," Cliff formed the teams in 1992 and retired in 1994.

Ken Partin, executive director for the Givens Estates Methodist Retirement Community for more than ten years, also wished to empower staff. One secret to Givens's success is the link between its ministry's mission and the almost 200 employees who work there. Ken expects staff to exhibit a sense of service and mission in their daily work. When Givens opened its doors in 1979, it sought staff who could be part of the ministry, staff who had a commitment and calling to serve others. The workplace philosophy at Givens is that staff can be relied upon to know what to do for the residents and how to do it. Self-managed teams were implemented to provide a work structure in which the philosophy would flourish.

☞ **Team Tip:** When a staff member needs to develop a justification for changing to self-managed teams, it is in his or her best interest to focus on the business benefits of the change rather than just the practicalities or the philosophies.

Business Reasons

Although trigger events are often the impetus behind self-managed teams, trigger events alone may be insufficient to capture the attention and support of senior management. This group is more likely to be persuaded by "hard" business reasons; that is, measurable reductions in cost or measurable improvements in quality, customer satisfaction, or productivity. As Steven Kerr has pointed out, "In high-performance organizations, you can never sell the soft stuff on its own merits. You have to make the connection to the bottom line."[1]

Business reasons generally focus on critical success factors—areas of performance that are vital to the health of the organization. In addition to cost, quality, and productivity, critical success factors may include intangibles that can have a tangible impact on the organization's success, such as physician and staff satisfaction. The business reasons behind the teams profiled in this book are described in table 2-1.

Notice that the business reasons easily translate into performance expectations, or goals. The establishment of clear and compelling business reasons aids in the articulation of clear and compelling performance expectations. These, in turn, build senior management support for teams.

The Functions of Performance Expectations

"Only when you challenge people to deliver performance outcomes that are relevant to their mission can you engage them in the change process."

—Douglas K. Smith

When a self-managed team holds its first meeting, it should be given a challenge, charge, or list of expectations from upper management. This list of team performance expectations should directly correlate with the business reasons for starting the team. For instance, among the business reasons for starting self-managed teams in the respiratory care unit at Mission+St. Joseph's was the need to reduce overtime below 2 percent. This need was made a team performance expectation for the respiratory care teams. (See table 2-2.)

Team performance expectations fulfill two major functions. First, they form vital links between management and team members, as well as between the team and the organization as a whole. Second, performance expectations guide the team in its structuring of roles, responsibilities, measures, and procedures.

Table 2-1. Teams' Critical Success Factors

Teams	Cost	Quality	Productivity
Pharmacy, Huntington Memorial Hospital, Pasadena, CA	Reduced cost and increased flexibility during restructure	Improve service to nursing units	
Pharmacy, Mission+St. Joseph's Health System, Asheville, NC	Drug cost per patient day	Reduce turn-around time from prescription order to delivery on the unit	
Baptist Health Preschool, Baptist Health System, Little Rock, AR	Achieve a subsidy reduction	Improve customer satisfaction	Enhance enrollment
Respiratory Therapy, Mission+St. Joseph's Health System, Asheville, NC	Eliminate management positions and one staff educator; reduce overtime below 2%	Improve satisfaction in nursing units; improve physician satisfaction	
Joint Laundry, Mission+St. Joseph's Health System, Asheville, NC	Eliminate annual salary of one supervisor		Increase pounds per productive hour
Pre-Op/Post-Op/PACU, St. Joseph's Hospital, Asheville, NC	Eliminate annual salary of one supervisor	Maintain excellent customer satisfaction level	
Regional Surgical Specialists, Asheville, NC	Eliminate annual salary of one manager	Improve customer and staff satisfaction	
General Surgery Unit, Memorial Mission Hospital, Asheville, NC	Reduce cost of management positions	Improve quality of patient care	Reduce confusion and time by reducing layers of management
Givens Estates Methodist Retirement Community, Asheville, NC	Reduce cost through employee innovations	Improve resident satisfaction and staff retention	

Table 2-2. Sample Performance Expectations

Team Performance Expectation	Goal	Performance Measure	Team Roles and Responsibilities
Reduce overtime below 2%	By July 1, develop and implement a system to reduce overtime so that it falls below 2% in each succeeding month.	Months in which the hours of overtime fall below 2% of total hours worked	*Role:* Team Scheduler *Responsibility:* Develop the team schedule; monitor overtime; report overtime rate on a monthly basis; maintain overtime records on an annual basis for the last three preceding years; identify and report problems and successes *Role:* Reporter *Responsibility:* Report overtime rate monthly to team and to director; report quarterly to vice president

Performance Expectations as Critical Links

Many managers who are unfamiliar with self-managed teams fear that self-governed groups will become "loose cannons" in an otherwise orderly hierarchy. Performance expectations help dispel this fear by creating these critical linkages:

- *Link with management:* When management formulates performance expectations for the self-managed teams and says, "These are our goals for you," the team is expected to react by taking action to meet those expectations. This influence link leaves managers with the positive feeling that they have control over the focus of the team's efforts as well as plans and goals that the team may establish and actions that the team will take.
- *Link with the department or organization:* Performance expectations also provide a critical link between team goals and the goals and strategies of a department and/or the organization as a whole. This link ensures that the efforts of the team are in harmony with the direction the organization is taking.
- *Link of commitment:* The final link that team performance expectations establish is to create a sense of commitment for the team concept. When

managers see that the team is working toward achieving expectations that the managers established, they feel a sense of involvement and ownership in the team. This sense of ownership leads to buy-in and support for the team.

Performance Expectations as Providers of Structure

Team performance expectations serve another vital function. They help the team establish its structure for accountability and responsibility. Performance expectations let the team and other employees know the boundaries of the team's authority and responsibility and the deadlines by which teams are expected to realize goals.

Teams use these expectations to establish goals and performance measures. Expectations also help the team decide what roles it needs to fill and what responsibilities are associated with these roles. For example, if the team is expected to achieve a reduction in overtime rates, then the team knows that its members will be monitoring and reporting overtime and that all team members will be working toward solving the problem of excessive overtime. The team will also know that it must report progress on this goal. As a result, the team will have to decide who will report overtime, what format the report will be in, and to whom the report will be distributed.

In short, the business reasons for teams eventually become business objectives. When managers charter, initiate, or start a self-managed team, they share their business reasons for wanting a team in the form of team performance expectations. These expectations form links between the managers and the teams as well as guide the structure of the teams.

Development of a Proposal to Implement Self-Managed Teams

"The more participants we engage in this participative universe, the more we can access its potentials and the wiser we become."

—*Margaret Wheatley*

Organizations typically require departments that are contemplating a structural change to present a written report explaining why the change should be made. These reports, or proposals, present facts and figures in support of the initiative. Because self-managed teams represent a major change in structure, groups or managers contemplating the transition would do well to put together a proposal in support of the change. If possible, all potential team members should participate in putting together the proposal and/or in discussions leading to it, so that everyone is provided with practice in "thinking like a manager."

Developing a proposal is not difficult, but it does require time and thought and may require some research. Teams can greatly facilitate the development process by using the template in Creating a Proposal to Implement Self-Managed Teams, the team activity at the end of this chapter. The sections that follow are based on the sections of the proposal template provided in this activity.

Current Situation

A good first step in preparing a proposal is to think about the current situation within the affected department or unit. Questions to answer include

- What is the purpose of the unit?
- What is its current staffing, including management, in full-time equivalents (FTEs)?
- What statistics about the unit's performance can be obtained? (The accounting and human resources departments and/or a management engineer are good sources of information.)

In analyzing the current situation, it also is valuable to calculate the ratio of management positions to staff positions. If there are three management people (directors and/or supervisors) and 24 staff, for example, the ratio is one manager to eight staff.

The manager and/or group should also discuss problem areas that the unit is facing and that self-managed teams might solve, such as undesirable activity levels, decreasing revenues, rising costs, declining customer satisfaction, or increasing complaints.

Events and Reasons

In addition to considering the unit's current situation, the group should consider the trigger event and/or business reasons behind the desire to form teams. Although most of the teams described in this chapter were initiated as a result of a trigger event, it is not necessary to have one in order to convince management or staff of the need to implement self-managed teams. It is, however, important that the group be able to clearly articulate its business reasons. These reasons should answer the management question "Why should we invest time and money to create self-managed teams?" Senior managers will be looking for a return on their investment expressed in terms that are important to them. Therefore, the proposal must include information on potential cost reduction, productivity improvement, and/or quality improvement.

Projected Cost

Developing the projected cost for implementing self-managed teams is relatively simple. The group can get an estimate of the average rate the organization spends per hour on unit salaries from the human resources or accounting department, or each group member can round his or her own hourly rate to the nearest fifty cents so that the group can calculate its average hourly rate. The average is then multiplied by the number of hours needed to design the self-managed team and the number of people who will be on the design team. For example:

Design cost:	$15.00/hour x 20 hours x 5 people =	$1,500
Training cost:	$15.00/hour x 20 hours x 20 people =	$6,000
Total cost:		$7,500

Note that if the group implementing self-managed teams is small and only one team will be implemented, the design process and the training process should be combined, so that only three to five hours will be needed specifically for design.

Benefits to the Organization

Finally, the group should consider the benefits that the organization is likely to realize as a result of implementing self-managed teams. Again, these benefits should be expressed in terms that are persuasive to management: that is, in terms of potential cost reduction, productivity improvements, quality improvements, and customer and staff satisfaction improvement. When numbers and statistics are available, they should be used to help demonstrate, in specific measurable terms, how the organization will benefit from implementing a self-managed team.

To continue the previous example, in which the implementation cost was estimated to be $7,500, the dollar value of some benefits might be as follows:

- If one management position is eliminated at a savings of $40,000 and overtime is reduced from 3 percent to 2 percent for a department with an annual payroll of $1,500,000, then self-managed teams will save the organization $40,000 plus $15,000, or a total of $55,000.
- If turnover costs $5,000 per position and turnover is reduced by three positions per year, then the organization will save another $15,000. Expressed numerically, the sum total of benefits to the organization now looks like this:

Manager's salary	$40,000
Overtime reduction	$15,000
Turnover reduction	$15,000
Total savings	$70,000

Compared to a cost of $7,500, the benefits of $70,000 are outstanding.

The $70,000 benefit does not include the benefits to be derived from "intangibles," such as improved patient satisfaction and improved staff morale. To compute the value of improved patient satisfaction, the group might ask risk management (RM) to estimate the average cost of following up on a patient complaint or settling a lawsuit and include that figure as a savings that self-managed teams might realize.

In short, it is not difficult to accumulate a compelling financial argument for self-managed teams. The group need only consider its contribution to the organization's critical success factors and attach a dollar amount to those factors.

Chapter Wrap-Up

Groups may form self-managed teams for a variety reasons. Some of these reasons are practical and expedient, while others stem from visionary work philosophies. Whatever the impetus, the group should be prepared to justify the move to teams with hard business reasons. Organizations do not implement the dramatic change that a self-managed team brings without a careful review of the business implications of the decision.

The group's business reasons should closely relate to the performance expectations that the team will be held to. Clear performance expectations link the team to management and to the organization as a whole.

Reference

1. Steven Kerr, "GE's Collective Genius," *Leader to Leader* (no. 1): 30.

Suggested Readings

Smith, Douglas K. "Making Change Stick," *Leader to Leader* (no. 2): 24–29.

Wheatley, M. J. *Leadership and the New Science.* San Francisco: Berrett-Koehler, 1994.

Team Activity

Creating a Proposal to Implement Self-Managed Teams

Purpose: To provide groups with a template for creating a proposal to implement self-managed teams.

Instructions: Potential team members should discuss each of the sections in the first column of the template and the accompanying items in the second column. The third column provides space for discussion notes. To gather information for the template, the group should actively seek out the help of others, such as human resources, so that the finished proposal will be based on authentic numbers.

After completing the template, the manager and/or a group member should create a formal proposal based on the information. (Each of the items in the first column represents a section of the proposal.) The proposal should be written as a narrative (rather than just a listing of items), should be word processed, and should document sources of information included in the report. In addition, the group may wish to attach articles or a bibliography of books and articles to show that it has researched the concept and to provide evidence that other people in reputable organizations have successfully implemented self-managed teams.

Subject	Information Needed for Justification	Notes for Team Justification
Current Situation	■ Purpose of Department/Unit ■ Total Staff (FTEs) ■ Total Management (FTEs) ■ Current Performance/ Statistics ■ Budget, Cost per Unit of Service ■ Productivity Rate ■ Quality Performance ■ Customer Satisfaction Rate ■ Staff Turnover Rate ■ Problems Department/Unit Is Facing	

(Continued on next page)

Subject	Information Needed for Justification	Notes for Team Justification
Trigger Event	Management Philosophy Merger Other	
Business Reasons for Team	■ Cost Reduction ■ Productivity Improvement ■ Quality Improvement ■ Satisfaction ■ Physician Satisfaction	
Projected Cost	■ Design Process (Average hourly rate of design team x 20 x number of staff on design team) ■ Staff Education (Average hourly rate of staff on team x 20 hours x number of staff)	
Benefits to the Organization (Use projected numbers as much as possible)	■ Reduced Cost ■ Improved Productivity ■ Quality Improvement ■ Customer Satisfaction ■ Staff Satisfaction	
Summary	Highlights of information above	
Recommendation	Implement self-managed work teams beginning (date)	

Chapter 3

Development of Team Boundaries

Chapter Preview

"What lies behind us and what lies before us are tiny matters compared to what lies within us."

—*Ralph Waldo Emerson*

When an organization, department, or unit decides to implement self-managed teams, one of the first actions it must take is to determine the boundaries within which the teams will operate. Boundaries consist of the visible and invisible restrictions that are placed on teams. Boundaries act as "property lines" to help organizational members differentiate between their areas of responsibility and authority and those areas that belong to others. For most self-managed teams, boundary setting is a formal process. Management is asked to clarify what the team can do on its own, what the team will need approval to do, and what is outside the team's responsibility.

A team needs boundaries so that it—and the organization—clearly understands the scope of the team's authority and the decisions it can and cannot make. For example, boundaries let the team know if it can commit and spend budget dollars and what those budget amounts are. Boundaries also let the team know what it can and cannot control and serve as guides to acceptable behaviors. Examples of boundaries that exist within any organization include the following:

- Safety rules
- Mission and vision statements
- Laws and regulations

- Organizational values
- Budgets
- Job descriptions
- Policies and procedures
- Licensing requirements
- Ethics
- Organizational goals and strategies

A team is also bound by the role, functions, and culture of the department or unit in which the team is located.

Many times when a self-managed team is implemented, boundaries are established and then extended in a phased approach. Much as a dimmer switch can be turned to create a brighter and brighter light, so the "switch" that controls the number of restrictions placed on the team may be "turned" to allow more and more authority to the team as it acquires new skills. In short, the boundaries placed on teams are often initially restrictive, then become broader and broader over time, until the team has full authority to function like any department in the organization.

This chapter describes the types of boundaries within which teams in health care organizations operate. The chapter also guides the new self-managed team through a process for defining boundaries and discusses the influence of work theories on boundary setting in organizations.

Chapter at a Glance

In this chapter, you will find

- Descriptions and examples of types of boundaries
- A discussion of the benefits and drawbacks of boundaries
- A discussion of the mechanistic and organistic theories of organizations and their impact on boundary setting
- A four-step process for setting boundaries
- Three decision-making scenarios and the pros and cons of each

Types of Boundaries

"The need for team boundaries should surprise no one. Every member of a well-run organization, from the CEO on down, functions within a framework that both requires and prohibits certain actions."

—J. D. Osburn et al.

Boundaries serve many useful purposes. They provide clarity to teams and to those who work with the teams. They let people on the team know which tasks to spend their time and efforts on and which problems and challenges to let others, outside the team, handle. Boundaries also help team members connect, form a cohesive group, and develop a culture and identity. In short, boundaries help create comfort zones for people.

Self-managed teams in health care organizations generally work within three types of boundaries: geographic, functional or clinical, and administrative.

Geographic Boundaries

Geographic boundaries define the team's "physical turf"—those areas within the health care organization in which the team works. For example, the three floors on which heart patients are located are within the geographic boundaries of the heart services pharmacy team of Mission+St. Joseph's Health System. Also within the team's geographic boundaries is the central pharmacy at Memorial Mission Hospital, in which team technicians and pharmacists work.

Functional or Clinical Boundaries

Functional or clinical boundaries define the formal responsibilities that a team fulfills for the health care organization. For example, the aforementioned heart services pharmacy team is responsible for ordering, distributing, and evaluating drugs. It is also within the team's functional boundaries to provide information and advice to help physicians and nurses ensure the best outcomes for heart patients. Like all teams, the heart services pharmacy team also has team administrative boundaries.

Team Administrative Boundaries

Team administrative boundaries define the routine organizational tasks that the team may perform, such as work scheduling, progress reporting, goal setting, and training. Often, these are the administrative tasks that were formerly performed by supervisors or directors. Team administrative boundaries also define the organizational tasks that the team may *not* perform. Notice, for example, that table 3-1, the heart services pharmacy team chart, states that the team may schedule staff to cover heart services needs and develop work processes, but may *not* perform most budgeting functions.

Differences in Boundaries

Because each group may have its own work areas, functions, and structures, the extent of boundaries may vary from team to team. For example, the

Table 3-1. Heart Services Pharmacy Team

Category	Boundary
Daily Work	Schedule staff to cover heart services needs; make assignments; develop work processes; resolve conflicts within team
Communication	Schedule team meetings; submit triannual progress report to leadership
Personnel Management	Orient and train staff; conduct 360-degree performance evaluations; administer the first step of the disciplinary process—the verbal warning; maintain tardy and absentee records; do not have access to salary information, pay systems, and personnel files; hire new employees in conjunction with leadership team
Planning	Set goals; develop plans; report progress. Work with pharmacy leadership team to develop strategic plan for pharmacy. Work with heart services leadership to develop strategic plan for heart services
Budget and Purchasing	Team receives continuing education and travel allotment; team decides how to distribute it. All other budget functions are performed by leadership team.
Equipment	Maintain the pyxis system for heart services; ensure cable lines are in place for pyxis support; maintain ATC machine
Customer Contact	Responsible for all interactions with patients, nurses, physicians, and managers in heart services
Quality Improvement	Perform all QI activities for pharmacy in heart services; ensure JCAHO, ASHP, OSHA, state, and federal requirements are met
"Fire fighting"	Solve daily work problems. Problems involving other teams must be resolved by all involved.

Pre-Op/Post-Op/PACU nursing team has the geographic boundary of the One Day Surgery Center within St. Joseph's Hospital. It has the functional or clinical boundary of providing nursing care in the preoperative, recovery, and postoperative arenas for patients who are scheduled for outpatient surgery. Within the team's administrative boundaries are scheduling and conducting team meetings, submitting a quarterly progress report to the vice president, and developing long-range plans for its area. (See table 3-2.)

As is apparent from reviewing the boundaries listed on the chart, the Pre-Op/Post-Op/PACU team has more authority and fewer restrictions, or boundaries, than the pharmacy team, even though both teams work within the same organization. The differences in boundaries depend, to a great extent, on the conditions at the time that the teams were formed, the culture of the organization, and the team's functions and skills.

Benefits and Drawbacks of Boundaries

"[My vision is to create] a new corporate culture based on empowerment, accountability, and boundarylessness."

—Jack Welch

Boundaries, like virtually any aspect of work structure, can be a double-edged sword. While boundaries provide many benefits, too many boundaries—or boundaries that are unnecessarily restrictive—can create problems. An understanding of the benefits and drawbacks of boundaries can help organizations strike an effective balance between total freedom and total restriction.

Benefits to Management, the Team, and the Organization

Boundaries act as "safety nets" for both the team and management. Boundaries give the team the feeling of security in a new environment, while giving management a sense of security about the team's limitations. Managers feel secure knowing that the team won't venture into areas it considers "off-limits," and the team feels secure in the knowledge that management will take responsibility for what occurs outside the boundaries.

Boundaries also facilitate good working relationships between the team and others in the organization. When the larger organization is first apprised that a group within it has formed a self-managed team, managers and staff in other departments need to know how to interact with the new organizational unit. A clear description of the team's function, purpose, and responsibility helps the organization fit the team into its systems and processes.

Table 3-2. Pre-Op/Post-Op/PACU Team

Category	Boundary
Daily Work	Same as preceding pharmacy example
Communication	Schedule and conduct team meetings; submit quarterly progress report to vice president
Personnel Management	Perform all personnel functions; limited access to personnel files and salary information
Planning	Same as preceding pharmacy example. Work with vice president and the One Day Surgery OR to develop long-range plan for One Day Surgery and Pre-Op/Post-Op/PACU
Budget and Purchasing	Develop, implement, and monitor entire budget; has department director–level purchasing authority
Equipment	Recommend equipment for purchase; maintain and order replacement equipment
Customer Contact	Responsible for all interactions with patients, nurses, physicians, and managers
Quality Improvement	Same as preceding pharmacy example
"Fire fighting"	Solve work problems at all levels in the organization; may involve vice president if team wishes to

Drawbacks to Management, the Team, and the Organization

Although boundaries are generally viewed as helpful, those who remember their teenage years will agree that when too many boundaries are imposed, people's creativity, growth, and development may be stifled. For teams to perform well, a balance must be struck between restrictions and freedoms. Teams are effective because they have the ability to be flexible, change, and respond as situations and needs demand. Limitations on team action imposed by the artificial boundaries of hierarchies, bureaucracies, and confining job descriptions can create problems for teams, setting up barriers between people and the organizational problems and issues they must confront.

This drawback has been noted by many of today's visionary leaders, such as Jack Welch, chairman of General Electric. Welch, who has gained fame as an excellent and forward-looking thinker, wants his organization to be creative and capable of responding quickly to customers and to changes in the environment. As a result, he sees boundaries as slowing down results and inhibiting communication, collaboration, and change.[1] It should be noted, however, that not all business leaders share Welch's views. As chapter 1 points out, many other managers believe that a hierarchical structure is needed to prevent chaos and help the organization perform efficiently. This dichotomy in management thinking reflects two major theories of work that have long influenced organizations in the United States.

Two Major Work Theories

"If organizations are machines, control makes sense. If organizations are process structures, then seeking to impose control through permanent structure is suicide."

—*Margaret Wheatley*

Most managers' approach to work is grounded in either the mechanistic theory or the organistic theory. Because these theories affect how management views teams and their boundaries, groups contemplating self-governance should be familiar with them.

The Mechanistic Theory

The mechanistic theory grew out of the work of Henri Fayol, a nineteenth-century French business leader and author, and Frederick Taylor, a nineteenth-century American engineer. Fayol was one of the first to define and extol the virtues of the chain of command, the functions of management, and the hierarchical structure of the typical business organization. Taylor performed time-and-motion studies to determine the most efficient way to achieve high production rates. He also developed the theory that piece-rate incentives would motivate workers to increase their production rates. The theories of Fayol and Taylor, collectively known as the scientific or mechanistic theory, continue to influence many managers in the United States.

According to the mechanistic theory, organizations and people can function like well-oiled machines if given the right conditions. These conditions include the proper lighting, temperature, energy source, and linear "assembly-line" form of production. In mechanistic organizations, work is organized in narrow tasks, spelled out in specific job descriptions, and confined in "silo-like" departments and divisions. "Mechanistic managers" believe that employees have a productive capacity of eight hours per day and need timed and scheduled breaks to maintain their energy level. They also believe that employees must be closely supervised so that their mistakes can be corrected before production is harmed. Sensitivity, caring relationships, lateral processes, and teams are anathema to mechanistic managers. They believe that monetary rewards such as salary and bonuses are the chief motivating forces behind high productivity. Flexible teams operating with few boundaries and constraints have little place in a mechanistic-based organization.

The Organistic Theory

At the opposite end of the spectrum is the organistic theory, which is rooted in the work of American business theorist W. Edwards Deming. Deming rejected the mechanistic theory, arguing that what is wrong with American business is not the worker, but the numerical quotas, inspectors, incentives, and piece rates under which they work. Deming introduced the idea of lateral processes that go beyond the artificial functional boundaries that organizations are built around. He supported the concept of teams and challenged the measures and controls that management had relied on for years.[2]

Building on Deming's approach to work, Peter Senge, in his book *The Fifth Discipline,* suggests that managers need to step back and take a systems view of their organizations; that is, realize that a slight change in one arena has a broad and generally unknown impact throughout the whole organization. In Senge's approach to work, the concept of control is challenged because it assumes a narrow field of impact.[3]

Margaret Wheatley, in her book *Leadership and the New Science,* sees organizations from a slightly different angle—that of quantum physics. Wheatley believes that once a picture or vision is drawn and the organizational unit understands its purpose, "employees can be trusted to move freely, drawn in many directions by their energy and creativity. There is no need to insist, through regimentation or supervision, that any two individuals act in the same way."[4] According to this organistic theory of work, organizations—like organisms—are self-regulating: they have the inherent capacity to respond to the forces in their environment and remain true to their purpose. Organistic organizations are ideal environments for self-managed teams.

The Impact of the Theories on Boundary Setting

Although few organizations are purely mechanistic or organistic, most do show a tendency to favor one approach over another. Self-managed teams should be aware of the end of the spectrum toward which their organization leans because their organization's approach to work greatly influences the boundaries it is likely to impose. The more mechanistic the organization, the more restrictions on teams. This does not mean that teams cannot succeed in organizations that tend toward the mechanistic style of management. What it does mean is that teams in these organizations must strive to work within a structured and controlled system.

At the Baptist Health System in Little Rock, a certification process provides the structure and boundaries that make teams more palatable to the organization. This systematic process guides the group through periods of learning and development, slowly expanding the team's boundaries once they have demonstrated competence in designated skills. For example, the team does not have to make decisions until decision making is taught, or deal with conflict or customers until skills in those areas are added, taught, and certified.

The certification process is helpful because it allows both the team and the organization to move toward self-management in comfortable steps, rather than in one fell swoop. While this approach to self-managed teams is mechanistic, in that it assumes that a team can function effectively in a linear development plan, it is not so restrictive that the self-managed teams cannot function at all.

☞ **Team Tip:** To tell what approach your organization favors, consider your organization's culture—"the way things are done around here." Are there set work schedules and break times, or does the organization permit "flextime" where appropriate? Is communication generally from the top down, or does senior management have an "open-door" policy? Does senior management regularly make major decisions without input from workers, or is their input actively sought?

The Case for Fewer Boundaries

In today's competitive and volatile environment, when the ability to anticipate and quickly respond to change can spell the difference between success and failure, a strong case can be made for keeping boundaries to a minimum. When team members are allowed to operate outside the limits of the hierarchy, they can communicate directly with their customers and with other people in the organization. This direct communication obviates the need to wait for a request to travel through layers of the hierarchy for approval, thereby enabling the team to respond to problems and customer needs quickly. Moreover, the team can more easily develop strong working relationships with people in the organization who can help them, such as clinical and support personnel in other departments. To work effectively, team members should be on a first-name basis with "support individuals," such as their purchasing agent, housekeepers, and storeroom assistants. Operating outside the hierarchy facilitates building close ties with individuals like these.

It will take time for team members and the rest of the organization to learn how to operate without the structure and familiarity of the supervisor and director. Initially, team members may seek permission to do something that they already have the authority to do. As mentioned in chapter 1, team members tend to revert to the hierarchical structure with which they are familiar and comfortable. Likewise, organizational members unaccustomed to dealing directly with employees at the staff level may question a staff member's authority to commit resources or request them from other departments. In the early days of self-managed teams at Memorial Mission Hospital, for example, a member of the engineering department refused to take action on a work order requested by a member of the housekeeping self-managed team, explaining: "We need a supervisor's signature before we can process this, ma'am."

In summary, although boundaries can provide clarity and comfort, they also can hamper a team. For this reason, boundaries should be carefully drawn and regularly reviewed to ensure that they serve worthwhile purposes. In addition, to get a team started on the "right foot," the boundaries within which the team will operate must be made clear to both the team and the organization in which it exists.

A Four-Step Process for Setting Boundaries

"It is not enough to do good. One must do good in the right way."

—*John, Viscount Morley of Blackburn*

The major task in boundary setting is to assign responsibilities. Decisions must be made regarding which authorities and responsibilities management will retain and which will be transferred to the team. Before these decisions can be made, team members and the unit or department director should make a list of potential responsibilities. This list should include tasks that the staff usually performs as well as tasks that are usually done by the supervisor or director. Notice, for example, that the sample team boundary list (table 3-3) contains many management-level responsibilities that staff will probably be excluded from performing, such as the review of personnel folders. Even though the team will not perform "management tasks" like these, the tasks have been listed to ensure that all duties will be assigned.

This list should then be reviewed so that every item on the list can be assigned to either management or staff. The review can be handled in one of three ways: Management can review the list and decide which responsibilities should be given to the teams; team members can review the list and decide which responsibilities they are comfortable assuming; or management and staff can review the list together and decide which responsibilities will be given to teams. (The pros and cons of each review method are described later in this chapter.)

Whether management, staff, or a combination of management and staff determines the boundaries for the team, the process is basically the same. Participants must assign responsibilities, reach a consensus on these assignments, transfer responsibilities in an orderly fashion, and communicate decisions about the team to the rest of the organization.

Step 1: Assignment of Responsibilities

During this first step in the boundary-setting process, participants should select responsibilities that they believe management should retain. An easy

Table 3-3. Sample Team Boundary List

Category	Boundary
Daily Work	Schedule staff Make daily work assignments Monitor daily work and adjust assignments to meet needs Find replacements for absences Grant vacations Authorize overtime Keep daily records Keep work environment clean
Communication	Schedule team meetings Develop agendas for team meetings Conduct team meetings Prepare memos, letters, and reports Communicate with other departments Communicate with top management
Personnel Management	Select and hire new employees Create job descriptions Orient new employees Provide staff education Coach and give feedback on work Request additional staff Control absenteeism, tardiness, and behavior problems Administer discipline Set performance standards Give performance reviews Fire an employee Review personnel files Manage compensation
Planning	Set goals Develop plans Delegate work to accomplish goals Develop and implement a new department service Give quarterly goal update reports
Budget and Purchasing	Work directly with vendors Evaluate new products Complete purchase requisitions for supplies Authorize purchases Develop the budget Monitor budget performance; adjust expenditures
Equipment	Maintain equipment Evaluate new equipment Teach staff how to use the equipment Purchase equipment

(Continued on next page)

Table 3-3. (Continued)

Category	Boundary
Customer Contact	Interview customers to identify customer needs Resolve customer problems Monitor performance with customers Conduct customer surveys Improve customer performance
Quality Improvement	Develop and improve work systems and processes Meet licensing and accreditation requirements Utilize QI process and tools to make improvements
"Fire fighting"	Solve daily problems Respond to emergencies and crises Respond to last-minute requests for service

way to complete this step is to give each participant a copy of the team's boundary list and ask him or her to circle those items that team members should never be held responsible for. Most participants would agree, for example, that team members should never have firing privileges or be given access to each other's confidential personnel files.

Step 2: Reaching of Consensus

The goal of the second step in the process is for participants to reach an agreement about the responsibilities that management should retain. During this step, participants meet as a group and discuss the items that they circled on their own. Items that everyone agrees should be kept as management responsibilities are then clearly marked on a separate master list.

Most managers are quick to exempt teams from firing and purchasing. Some also exempt teams from the personnel responsibilities of approving overtime and administering discipline. Staff, in turn, usually select discipline and firing as responsibilities they never want to assume. However, it is not unusual for management and staff to disagree on a number of items. For example, the first time that the Mission+St. Joseph's Health System pharmacy managers looked at the team list, they believed that about two-thirds of the items should be reserved for management and one-third reserved for the teams. Team members, on the other hand, responded very differently. They thought about one-fifth of the items should be retained by management, with the remaining four-fifths transferred to staff.

In reality, the number of items that the team should never do should be small. By limiting restrictions to a small but necessary minimum, management shows confidence and trust in staff members' capabilities.

Another possible outcome of the review process is that management and the team decide to share certain responsibilities. A number of tasks that are not solely the responsibility of the team or management may be better accomplished with input from both. For example, the pharmacy teams at the Mission+St. Joseph's Health System determined that they will share responsibility with management in the following areas:

- Strategic planning
- Discipline
- Hiring
- Overtime approval
- Safety
- Budget preparation

Step 3: Transfer of Responsibilities

After clarifying which items the teams should not do, participants must decide whether to transfer the remaining responsibilities all at once or in phases. If the new responsibilities are to be phased in, then priorities must be set: participants must decide which new responsibilities the team will assume first, second, and so on. No magic formula exists for deciding which new responsibilities should be given to the team first; the order depends upon needs, circumstances, and management's work attitudes. As pointed out earlier in this chapter, some teams work within the boundary of a "certification" process, which prescribes the order in which new skills are to be learned, the training that team members must undergo to learn the skills, and the competencies that team members must demonstrate before they are allowed to handle certain duties. Other teams have a core group of responsibilities to learn first but may assume other duties without formal training.

Step 4: Communication of Decisions

During this final step, decisions regarding management and team responsibilities are communicated to the rest of the organization. Also to be communicated are the dates upon which the team will assume certain responsibilities (if they are to be phased in gradually) and the specific authorities that the team will have. By keeping the rest of the organization apprised of team developments, management and staff help ensure that the transition to self-managed teams goes as smoothly as possible.

Selection of Decision Makers

As mentioned earlier, decisions regarding "who does what" may be made by management, the team, or both. To determine which scenario to use, participants should weigh the pros and cons of each scenario and determine which best meets the needs of management, the team, and the organization as a whole.

Management as Decision Maker

In this scenario, the department director, the vice president, and any supervisors meet to review the list of responsibilities and authorities that could be transferred to the self-managed team. These individuals then make the decision about which responsibilities to retain and which to transfer.

There are several advantages to having management make the decision:

- *Heightened comfort for management:* When management makes the decision about which authorities and responsibilities will be transferred to teams, it has total control over the results.
- *Assurance that teams will be assigned appropriate tasks:* Management is unlikely to transfer items to teams that teams are unprepared to handle.
- *Good organizational fit:* Intuitively, managers will be able to assess which items that the organization will support transferring to a self-managed team and which items should not be transferred. As a result, the team's new responsibilities and authorities are more likely to be supported by the organization.

Drawbacks of having management make the decision include the following:

- *Appearance of a lack of trust in staff:* If management makes this decision for teams, it is launching self-managed teams without a vote of confidence. Furthermore, it sends the message that teams need not be responsible for themselves because management will continue to act as "caretaker." When managers make decisions for staff, they miss an opportunity to demonstrate their trust in the team.
- *Possible lack of knowledge of team capabilities:* If management believes that it knows best what the team is capable of, it is not giving team members credit for knowing what they can and cannot handle. It is a rare manager who knows the team players as well as the players know each other.
- *Failure to take risks:* Managers know the culture of the organization and are conditioned to know what the organization considers to be acceptable. This knowledge can be a hindrance when starting something new because it can keep managers from taking initiatives and making positive changes.

The Team as Decision Maker

When team members make the decision regarding which duties the group will be responsible for, they should review the list independently and then meet to reach consensus about items that they *don't* want to be responsible for. As mentioned earlier, the number of items is usually very small and includes the personnel responsibilities of discipline and firing.

Advantages to having team members make the decision include the following:

- *Increased staff commitment:* When the team decides which responsibilities it will assume and which it won't, it starts to develop a commitment to fulfilling its new responsibilities. Staff members cannot complain that management unfairly restricted their freedom.
- *Assurance of team competence:* When the team members decide what they are capable of and what they want responsibility for, they are beginning self-management and starting the process of defining their accountability. In short, they are learning how to be a self-managed team. Moreover, they are likely to try to prove that they made good decisions.
- *Initiation of team building:* Deciding where to start with new responsibilities and authorities is a major decision. When team members decide together, they have begun the process of team building. Opportunities for team building strengthen the team and help it become more effective.

A danger of having team members make the decision is that they may unconsciously underestimate their own capabilities. For example, because purchasing, overtime, and budgets are perceived by staff as always being reserved for management, some prospective teams give up those responsibilities without ever asking for them. Other drawbacks of having team members make the decision are the potential for

- *Management discomfort:* When team members decide, they may select responsibilities that management would never have transferred to them, thereby making management feel uncomfortable. Management may imagine what could go wrong if the team has these authorities and may worry about losing control.
- *Team errors:* If the team decides it can handle a responsibility that is beyond its capability, it could stumble in fulfilling it, thereby creating problems that management may have to resolve later. Moreover, making mistakes early on could erode the team's confidence.
- *Team timidity:* Because most of the responsibilities on the list will be new to team members, they may "play it safe" and choose only a few, thereby limiting their ability to be a high-performing team by failing to accept a full range of responsibilities.

Management and Team as Joint Decision Makers

When management and the team decide together, they should have a dialogue, not a debate. Management must avoid the urge to dictate the outcome rather than let it evolve through open discussion, and the team must make every effort to listen to and acknowledge management's ideas and concerns. When management and staff truly listen to and respect each other, they build the kind of strong work relationship that both need to succeed.

Other advantages of joint decision making include

- *Heightened comfort:* When management and the team decide together, they get to know each other. They learn why management is hesitant about a particular new responsibility and why the team believes itself capable. As a result, any decisions will be better informed than they would have been if one group made the decisions independent of the other.
- *Assurance of team competence:* The discussion that managers and staff have about what is involved in meeting new responsibilities and what capabilities are present within the team helps ensure that the team will have the competence to perform in the areas that are selected.
- *Improved relations and development of trust:* When the team and management decide together, a new relationship is being forged. The team and management are speaking as equals, and this parity builds the confidence of the team, its team spirit, and an improved relationship with management. It also builds trust, because management shows that it has faith that staff members can govern themselves.
- *Increased team commitment:* Team members are likely to feel a greater commitment to fulfilling their new responsibilities if they participate in selecting them.

Disadvantages of joint decision making include

- *Greater time expenditure:* The meeting to make the decisions may take more time than if just management met or just the team met to decide which responsibilities the team will assume.
- *Greater potential for conflict:* When management and the team are in the same room discussing the new responsibilities, there will be differences of opinion and opportunities for conflict and hurt feelings.
- *Lack of honesty:* Managers may feel uncomfortable giving an honest assessment of team capabilities while the team is present. Likewise, team members may feel uncomfortable about appropriating management duties while management is present.

After reviewing the pros and cons of each method of decision making, most organizations would agree that the benefits to be derived from joint decision making far outweigh the drawbacks. Although other scenarios may, of course, better meet a particular organization's needs, management should not underestimate the power of joint decision making to build mutual respect and trust. For this reason alone, it is the preferred choice.

Chapter Wrap-Up

Team boundaries are helpful tools for the team, management, and the organization as a whole. Teams have geographic, functional or clinical boundaries, and administrative boundaries. When a self-managed team is first created, establishing boundaries is a priority.

Setting boundaries is a four-step process: assign responsibilities, reach consensus on assignments, transfer responsibilities, and communicate decisions to the organization as a whole. The most effective way to assign responsibilities is for management and staff to discuss boundaries before they are set. Once the outer limit of the boundaries is set, teams can go through a certification process or an evolutionary process to move from tightly confined boundaries to broad boundaries.

Regardless of the type of organization, the most important reason for boundaries is to clarify the purpose of the team and the behavior patterns the organization considers to be acceptable. Setting and clarifying boundaries is a simple—but essential—process.

References

1. Jack Welch, as quoted in Steven Kerr, "GE's Collective Genius," *Leader to Leader* (no. 1): 32.
2. M. Walton, *The Deming Management Method* (New York: Perigee, 1986), p. 77.
3. P. Senge, *The Fifth Discipline* (New York: Doubleday, 1990).
4. M. J. Wheatley, *Leadership and the New Science* (San Francisco: Berrett-Koehler Publishers, 1994), p. 36.

Suggested Reading

Weisbord, M. *Productive Workplaces.* San Francisco: Jossey-Bass, 1978.

Chapter 4

Transitions in Work Roles

Chapter Preview

"A man I know owns a meatpacking plant in the Midwest. His company's motto is 'People don't make sausages; sausages make people.' That is, the purpose of the company is not to manufacture a product. The purpose is to give the people who work there the sense that they are competent, valued men and women."

—*Harold S. Kushner*

Physics teaches us that it takes 1 calorie to raise the temperature of 1 gram of water 1 degree. The transition for 1 gram of water to ice and of ice to water requires 80 calories each for freezing, then melting. To change 1 gram of water into steam requires 540 calories. Clearly, it takes much more energy to produce major changes than marginal changes within a current state of matter. The same is true of people. The change from bureaucracy to self-managed teams is a significant one that requires a tremendous amount of energy. Every person, every system, and every relationship will be affected by team formation. The amount of effort required to make these types of transitions is much greater than that required by incremental changes in bureaucracy. With a clear understanding of the transitions that are required, teams will succeed. Without this appreciation, bureaucracy will prevail. Many people are involved in implementing self-managed teams, each of them with different roles to play during the transition to teams. Team members go through a significant transition as they learn to play new roles and help change existing systems to accommodate a team-based work environment.

Figure 4-1. It Takes Energy to Make Worthwhile Transitions

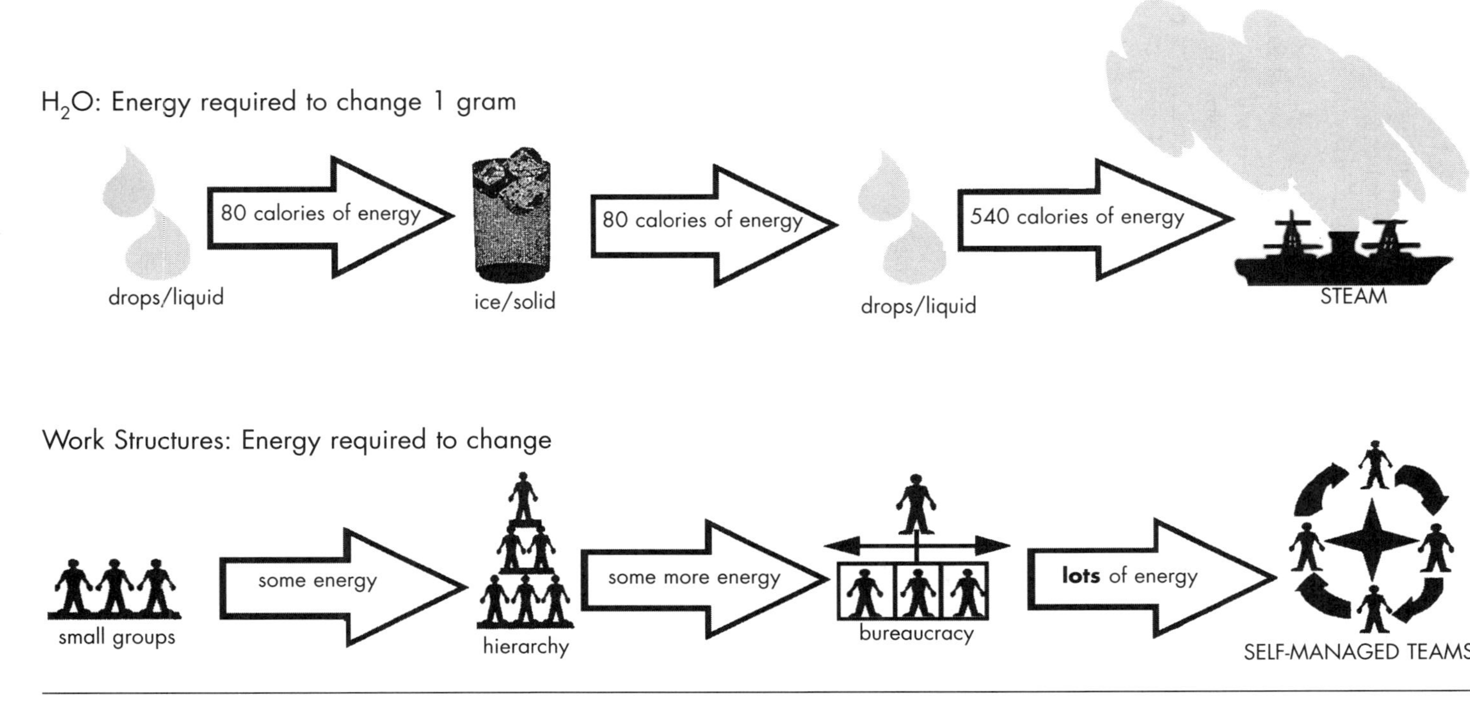

This chapter helps prepare future team members for the emotional metamorphosis they will need to make to be effective in the self-managed team environment. Role transitions require significant changes. This chapter describes the energy, anguish, and personal commitment required to make this transformation. Critical to taking on a new role is the shedding of old habits, old dreams, and old ways. Therefore, this chapter reviews the difficult process of "unlearning." Because role changes create the need for systemic changes, this chapter also presents an overview of changes that will need to take place in management and human relations systems. (These systems issues are covered in more depth in section 2.) The chapter concludes with two team activities that can be used to help groups anticipate and plan for role changes and the losses and gains that they entail.

Chapter at a Glance

In this chapter, you will find

- A discussion of role changes that occur during team implementation
- An examination of the changes that teams bring to the management systems
- An examination of the changes that teams bring to human relations systems
- A description of the emotional changes that people typically undergo during the transition to teams
- Two team activities to facilitate discussion about change

Changes in Roles

"Do not ask people what the problem is. Instead, ask them what they need."

—*Camile Wade Maurice*

What changes do people undergo when self-managed teams are implemented? This question is best answered by contrasting the roles that people play in the typical bureaucracy with the roles that they play in a team-based culture. It is critical to recognize that the change from bureaucracy to self-governance is a substantial one. It will affect not only staff but also the supervisors and managers who work with them.

The role transitions chart (table 4-1) provides an overview of the role changes that must take place. Based on interviews with many team members in a variety of health care settings, we have concluded that the changes boil down to a simple truth: When the behavior changes identified on the chart

Table 4-1. Role Transitions

Role before Teams	Role after Teams	Role Behavior Changes
Vice president	■ Mentor	■ Don't issue commands; ask questions
Director	■ Mentor ■ Coach	■ Don't issue commands; ask questions ■ Don't give orders; listen
Supervisor	■ Coach ■ Team member ■ Department specialist	■ Don't give orders; listen ■ Don't give orders; contribute ■ Don't give orders; offer support
Staff	■ Team member ■ Department specialist	■ Don't keep quiet; contribute ■ Don't keep quiet; offer support
Human resources staff	■ Team facilitator	■ Don't teach; facilitate learning
Clinical expert, department educator, quality improvement coordinator	■ Department specialist ■ Team member	■ Don't hoard knowledge; share it ■ Contribute

occur, other behaviors fall in line and the team system works. To better understand how these transformations occur, it is helpful to examine each of these role changes individually.

Vice President to Mentor

In a hierarchy, the vice president is responsible for all the people in a large division of several departments. Vice presidents command a large number of people, their authority is based on control over their divisions, and their power is determined by the number of people and resources they command. Vice presidents' effectiveness is judged by the wisdom of their commands and the success with which these commands are executed by the people who work for them.

In contrast, in an organization of self-managed teams, the people on the teams are responsible for their work, and the authority and power that once resided in the vice president are transferred to the division teams and their members. The vice president's effectiveness is judged by the effectiveness of the teams. In short, the vice president's major role in the self-managed team setting is to develop people and team effectiveness. This role is best played by being a mentor rather than a commander. Instead of issuing commands, the vice president must help teams think through their actions by asking the right questions.

☞ **Team Tip from a Vice President Who Became a Mentor:** "Provide the education and organizational commitment to assure the team's success. This commitment must be long term, six months or more. Generally, I would say that managers and supervisors are very hesitant to give up power and authority to teams. You must provide the teams freedom to make mistakes and create the work environment they desire."

—Tim Johnston, Mission+St. Joseph's Health System

Director to Mentor/Coach

The director in a hierarchy is responsible for all the people in a department. Directors give orders based on the vice president's commands; their authority is based on control over their department. The director's power is based on the size and scope of the department. The effectiveness of the director is judged by the success with which he or she implements the orders of the vice president and by the degree of compliance demonstrated by the staff in carrying out those orders.

In a self-managed team setting, the people on the teams—not the director—are responsible for their work. The authority and power that once belonged to the director now belong to the department teams and team members. The effectiveness of the director is judged by the success of the teams. To make the director's transition effective, the director must help teams take the right actions and make good decisions. The director's role is now to listen to team members and help teams make good decisions. This is best done by being a good coach. When people are given the opportunity to talk about their options and share their thoughts, they not only come up with good decisions but also "own" the decisions that they make. When teams own the process, they make decisions they can implement.

☞ **Team Tip from a Director Who Became a Coach:** "Flexibility, flexibility, and flexibility! One must be able to accept change and adjust to one's new role accordingly. Have trust, faith, and take a global view of our new environment. I had thought my role was going to be diminished. My role changed and expanded to systemwide responsibilities beyond my expectations."

—Paul Chu, St. Joseph's Hospital

Supervisor to Coach/Team Member/Department Specialist

In a hierarchy, the supervisor is responsible for a group of people within a department. Supervisors are the "boss" for a few people, and their power and authority are based on the number and skills of the people they supervise. In an organization of self-managed teams, people are responsible for their work. Thus, there are no supervisors.

It is not surprising that supervisors experience the most uncertainty when teams are implemented. The role that supervisors used to fulfill no longer exists, leaving them with four options: become a coach, a team member, a department specialist—or quit. Of these four options, perhaps the most difficult course is to go from being a supervisor to a team member. The individual used to being judged on the basis of how well his or her group carried out the director's orders will have a hard time adjusting to performance evaluations based on contributions to the team. Nevertheless, a number of supervisors have successfully made the transition. The toughest behavioral change is to avoid the urge to give orders. The former supervisor must seek to help fellow team members contribute by being a role model for open discussion and participation.

☞ **Team Tip from a Supervisor Who Became a Team Member:** "Have an open mind, be willing to accept change and be optimistic. You have to know your own faults and be willing to accept the faults of others."

—Jim Humble, Memorial Mission Hospital

Staff to Team Member

In a hierarchy, staff members are at the bottom of the totem pole. They are responsible for carrying out the orders given to them by the supervisor. They have little authority or personal responsibility.

In an organization of self-managed teams, staff are responsible for their work. The authority and power of the organization, division, and department now reside within them and their teams. This radical shift in roles is one that many staff members find to be both uncomfortable and challenging. The role shift is particularly difficult for staff who are used to "doing as they're told" and not speaking up. Self-managed teams require every team member to take responsibility for his or her team's effectiveness. To make this transition, staff must be encouraged to contribute their thoughts and opinions.

☞ **Team Tips from Staff Members Who Became Team Members:** "Be yourself, be honest, be open, and most of all, be willing to adjust to changes."

—Donna Gwyn, Givens Estates

☞ "Take it one step at a time, with a happy attitude."

—Melissa Hutchinson, Givens Estates

Human Resources Support to Team Facilitator

In a hierarchy, the human resources staff are responsible for seeing that the wisdom of management is taught to staff in all departments. Human resources employees have little formal authority; their power in the organization is determined by how effectively they teach other employees what management dictates. In an organization of self-managed teams, in which teams are responsible for their own effectiveness, the role of the human resources department is to help teams learn the skills necessary to be effective. Human resources personnel must help teams identify the skills they need and integrate the experiences of the teams to help them learn how to work together. The best way to get people to learn is to find out what they want to know, then help them obtain the resources and experiences to learn it. This is best done by being a facilitator of learning rather than a teacher.

☞ **Team Tip from a Human Resources Educator Who Became a Team Facilitator:** "The more I facilitate, the less I am needed to teach."

—Gwen Marvels, Memorial Mission Hospital

Subject-Matter Support Staff to Department Specialist/Team Member

Subject-matter support staff, such as clinical experts, department educators, and quality improvement coordinators, are included in the hierarchy to add knowledge of new methods or processes to the department. To do their jobs, these experts have access to information and databases outside the organization. Their authority is based on the knowledge that management perceives them to possess and on their ability to successfully implement new programs.

In an organization of self-managed teams, the team members themselves are responsible for acquiring and applying new knowledge. Subject-matter support staff work as department specialists, facilitating teams' adoption and implementation of new and innovative methods. To make this transition, subject-matter experts must share their knowledge and resources and help their fellow team members identify opportunities for expansion of services. The department specialist's main role is, then, to offer support to teams.

☞ **Team Tip from a Subject-Matter Specialist Who Became a Team Member:** "Don't lose sight of the big picture or forget about the endpoint, and focus on the expected outcome of your services. You need to have good communication and personal interaction skills. These skills are needed to deal directly with people on your team to solve problems and resolve conflicts."

—Scott Crawford, Memorial Mission Hospital

Selection of Roles

Although the role transitions chart (table 4-1) describes the usual roles that people in different job positions take when making the transition to self-managed teams, it is likely that future team members will still wonder, "Who should do what?" Groups that have made the transition would probably answer: "Ask the potential team members themselves which roles they would like to assume." Experience shows that when employees are given a choice about their roles, they will choose roles that they find comfortable. Most people choose to do what they do best. When people are given the chance to do what they want, the results can be truly amazing—not only for the team, but for the organization as a whole.

Changes in Management and Human Relations Systems

"The Golden Rule is just the beginning. The advanced course teaches: Do unto others as you would have them do unto you if you were in their particular, unique and different shoes. It is not an easy learning."

—*M. Scott Peck*

Management and human relations systems are inexorably intertwined with work roles. Team relationships encourage people to share openly with each other and this leads to a cocreation of new ideas and work processes that enhance organizational effectiveness. Thus, when work roles change, management and human relations systems must change with them.

Fayol's Five Functions

As pointed out in chapter 3, nineteenth-century author Henri Fayol was one of the first to define the functions of management in a bureaucracy. Fayol's model, which continues to influence managers today, consists of five major functions: planning, organizing, commanding, coordinating, and controlling. Together, these functions make up an organization's management system.

In every organization, the five functions need to be fulfilled. However, they do not necessarily need to be fulfilled by management. Recall from chapter 3 that during the boundary-setting process, decisions are made regarding which responsibilities will remain with management and which will be transferred to teams. When self-managed teams are implemented, the functions do not change. What changes are the people who fulfill the responsibilities associated with each function and the manner in which the functions are fulfilled. Table 4-2, Management Systems Transitions, summarizes these changes.

Early in the implementation process, it is helpful for teams to discuss changes in the five functions. The first team activity at the end of this chapter, What Changes and What Stays the Same, is designed to facilitate this type of discussion.

Four Components of Human Relations Systems

Role changes affect not only the organizational management systems, but also its systems of human relations; that is, those procedures and methods that influence work relationships between people. When bureaucratic organizations switch to self-managed teams, changes must occur in all four major components of the human relations systems—communication channels, expectation setting, performance review and compensation, and methods for carrying out strategic change.

Communication Channels

In a bureaucracy, formal communication channels include policy and procedure manuals, memos that may or may not be shared with staff, and meetings scheduled and conducted by management. In contrast, formal communication channels in a team-based environment include general team guidelines, E-mail messages sent to all team members, and meetings scheduled and conducted by the team. When the need for immediate communication arises, team members are responsible for ensuring that the appropriate people are kept informed.

Notice that traditional formal communication channels become less formal and more flexible in a team-based environment. Instead of people serving

Table 4-2. Management Systems Transitions

Management Systems	What Stays the Same	What Changes
Planning	Big picture from top management and planning support staff	Teams define goals for their own areas of responsibility
Organizing	Boundaries for action set by top management	Teams make their own decisions and integrate actions with other teams
Commanding	Organizational strategies are defined by top management	Teams develop and implement their own tactics
Coordinating	Top management establishes general timelines and provides resources	Teams act instantly to meet customer needs and share new developments rapidly with other teams
Controlling	Information systems resources are provided by top management along with a free flow of data	Information is accessible to all and shared freely, teams are trusted to use information as basis for necessary action

the needs of the system, the system serves the needs of the people. Moreover, information is usually communicated more rapidly, because staff members do not have to wait for management to hand down decisions.

Informal communication channels also change during the transition to self-managed teams. In a bureaucracy, management tries to control "grapevine communications." Nevertheless, the grapevine continues to thrive, and staff use it to find out what is really happening, what ulterior motives may exist, and how to "cover themselves." In the self-managed environment, the grapevine is encouraged because informal networks are used to share information and coordinate the activities of teams.

Expectation Setting

In the traditional organization, staff members often have to guess what management expects of them. Second-guessing performance expectations is difficult and stressful. The more staff members speculate, the more anxious they are likely to become. Moreover, expectations may vary from supervisor to supervisor and manager to manager, causing both conflicts among staff members who hold similar positions and a lack of uniform quality. In an organization that has self-managed teams, staff and management are respected as equal contributors. Expectations are clearly defined and are based on customers' expectations, not on the expectations of supervisors and managers.

Performance Review and Compensation

Bureaucratic organizations are based on the command-and-control model. "Bosses" define department goals and standards and penalize staff when they do not meet them. Staff members' focus is therefore on avoiding mistakes and pleasing their bosses. In the self-managed team environment, performance reviews and compensation are handled quite differently. Teams and individuals set their own standards and goals. Accomplishments are celebrated, and mistakes are viewed as opportunities to learn. Because teams are rewarded for outstanding service to their customers, staff focus on pleasing them rather than bosses.

Implementation of Strategic Change

The transition to self-managed teams also influences the manner in which strategic change is implemented. In traditional organizations, plans for change are carefully drawn up by management and then implemented by staff. In the self-managed environment, expectations for outcomes of change are shared with teams, which are then encouraged to be creative to meet or exceed the expected outcomes. To do so, teams plan their own changes in their work systems.

The Emotional Impact of Change

"When teams were started, I was afraid that I could not handle all the responsibilities expected of me. Now that we have teams, it is better than I ever expected it to be."

—Donna Gwyn, Givens Estates

In considering changes in human relations systems and staff roles, it is important to consider the emotional impact of change. Although human relations is often referred to as the "soft side" of management, human relations issues are the toughest that teams will face. Because management systems issues are concrete, they can be written in policy manuals or drawn on flow charts. In contrast, human relations systems are abstract and difficult to capture on paper because they are based on people's feelings and perceptions.

When the decision to implement teams is announced, emotions will run the gamut, from anticipation and excitement to worry and anguish. Eventually, however, people will feel a sense of joy and triumph as new roles are established and implemented. To understand the emotional impact of the transition to teams, consider the first time you rode a roller coaster. Recall the excitement of waiting in line and the emotions you felt before you started the ride. Remember the anticipation and anxiety of the long climb to the top and then—*whoosh,* down the first big hill you went, your stomach rose to your throat, and you felt as if you were flying. As you recovered from the speed of the hill, you were abruptly turned and wedged into the side of the car. The ride continued, and you wondered if the tracks would hold and get you safely to the end. After the ride was over, if you were asked how it was, you may not have known how to describe the experience. These are the same feelings that you may experience during the changes brought about by the formation of self-managed teams. At the beginning of the process, you don't know quite what to expect. During the process, you experience many highs and lows—moments of exhilaration and moments of doubt. At the end of the process, you will probably find it difficult to describe.

Gains and Losses

The first step toward becoming used to a new role is "losing" the old one. "Unlearning" is very difficult because in a bureaucracy, roles and behavioral rules are well encoded and deeply entrenched. When moving away from these roles and rules, people will experience losses. Vice presidents will lose a sense of command. Directors will lose a sense of control. Supervisors will lose a sense of status. Staff will lose a sense of protection. Subject-matter experts will lose a sense of unique value.

It is critical to identify losses and discuss them. Potential team members need to speak to others about their feelings of loss. At the same time, team members should discuss the gains they are apt to realize. Team activity 2, Losses and Gains, can be used to facilitate discussion.

Key to surviving the transition to new roles and relationships is understanding that you are not alone: other team members are also going through this gut-wrenching process. By talking and listening to one another, team members can identify sensitive issues, learn one other's perspectives, and eventually come to feel comfortable sharing fears and hopes. It is important to remember that people want to be understood from their point of view. Dialogues on role and systems changes will result in a common understanding of the significant emotional changes that each team member faces when teams are formed.

The Creation of a New Culture

It also is important to remember that the formation of self-managed teams is the creation of a new culture. When a new culture is formed, a few old traditions survive, others must be forgotten, and new traditions will be developed. The transition to a new culture is similar to the challenge that stepfamilies face when preparing for a holiday. Stepfamilies that are successful at including everyone and making them feel welcome are those that openly discuss their traditions and value the importance of each person's preferences. Taking the time to identify and recognize the loss of some traditions and being open to establishing unfamiliar traditions is what enables individuals to come together to form a new culture.

The transition to the new culture of self-managed teams is dependent on how well individuals adapt collectively to their new roles. Recognizing the emotional roller coaster that each person will be going through and understanding the situation from multiple perspectives is a key to implementing self-managed work teams.

Chapter Wrap-Up

Tremendous energy is required to make the meaningful role transitions necessary to implement self-managed work teams. The changes in roles will happen on a very personal and emotional level for every future member of a self-managed work team. Management systems and human relations systems need to change simultaneously to support the role changes that people must make on all levels. Support from top management and the transition of vice presidents and directors to the roles of mentors and coaches is crucial to the success of other role transitions. A key to team implementation is unlearning the old rules of bureaucracy and hierarchy. The use of outside facilitators to establish dialogues among all the people going through these role changes will help staff and management share their perspectives and the challenges they are facing.

Suggested Readings

Belasco, J. A., and R. C. Stayer. *Flight of the Buffalo.* New York: Warner, 1993.

Kushner, H. S. *How Good Do We Have to Be?* Boston: Little Brown, 1996.

Peck, M. S. *In Search of Stones.* New York: Hyperion, 1995.

Schein, E. H. "How Can Organizations Learn Faster? The Challenge of Entering the Green Room." *Sloan Management Review* (winter 1993): 28.

Wheatley, M. J. *Leadership and the New Science.* San Francisco: Berrett-Koehler, 1994.

Team Activity 1

What Changes and What Stays the Same

Purpose: To facilitate discussion about changes in management systems.

Directions: Participants should work in small groups. Together, group members should complete the chart below based on the changes they anticipate in their own organization.

Management Systems Transitions

Management Systems	What Stays the Same	What Changes
Planning		
Organizing		
Commanding		
Coordinating		
Controlling		

Team Activity 2

Losses and Gains

Purpose: To facilitate discussion about losses and gains.

Directions: This activity is most interesting when it is done in a "mixed group" that contains both managers and staff. When discussing losses and gains, managers should project themselves into the roles of staff, and staff should project themselves into the roles of managers. The discussion will then yield insights not only into losses and gains, but also into different frames of reference and perspectives.

Losses	Gains

Chapter 5

Introduction to Work Design

Chapter Preview

"The functions of design are rarely visible; they take place behind the scenes. The consequences that appear today are the result of work done long in the past, and work today will show its benefits far in the future."

—Peter Senge

In *The Fifth Discipline,* Peter Senge poses the following question: "Imagine that your organization is an ocean liner, and that you are 'the leader.' What is your role?"[1] Senge reviews the common responses—captain, navigator, steward, and engineer. Then he challenges readers to consider the role of the ship's designer. Senge contends that it is the designer who has the most significant role because it is the designer who creates the systems required for a successful cruise and who ensures that all the systems work in harmony. In Senge's opinion, effective systems design is the most essential leadership role because systems have the greatest impact on people's ability to do their jobs successfully. As Senge puts it, "What good does it do for the captain to say, 'Turn starboard thirty degrees,' when the designer has built a rudder that will only turn to port, or which takes six hours to turn to starboard?"[2] Clearly, the design of work systems can make or break an organization. Work design also plays a major role in the success of self-managed teams.

This chapter is an overview, or "bird's-eye view," of self-managed team design. The chapter describes the critical nature of the design process, introduces the technical and social systems included in work design, and contrasts proven design principles with shortcuts that are to be avoided. Because changes in work design necessitate changes in people, the chapter also examines the emotional impact of changes in work duties and responsibilities. The systems and processes examined in this chapter will be presented in greater depth and detail in section 2 of this book. This chapter is intended to pave the way for the "how-to" material to follow.

When learning something new, it is helpful to observe and listen to others who are more experienced. In this chapter, you will find design suggestions derived from the experiences of actual team designers. Learning from their experiences will help you draw up your own successful "team blueprint." Interspersed throughout the chapter, you also will find team tips. These "voices of experience" will help you avoid some of the bumps in the road on the way to self-managed teams.

Like the design of an ocean liner, the work design of self-managed teams should be a group effort. Although larger groups will need to create a design team made up of group representatives, every team member should be given opportunities to contribute to the team's overall work design. It is the team members themselves who are in the best position to know what designs will work best. Team members are also more apt to be motivated to improve the systems that affect their work and more open to new ideas than the managers who designed the traditional work systems.

Chapter at a Glance

In this chapter, you will find

- An examination of the two major work systems involved in team design
- An analysis of five major principles of team design and their outcomes
- A discussion of design teams and their physical and emotional makeup
- "Design Lessons from the Field," a collection of tips from experienced team designers

Major Systems in Work Design

"It is the social systems that have the greatest impact on human creativity, teamwork and motivation. The social systems impact the performance of people at every moment of every day."

—Lawrence M. Miller

When groups make the transition to self-managed teams, they typically begin by identifying technical systems. Teams are formed, and people select work roles suited to their skills and interests. Social systems are then designed to manage the relationships required for team members to work together. Team design thus involves two basic systems—one technical, or work oriented, and the other social, or people oriented.

Technical Systems

Technical systems include those work processes that involve tools, technology, and job-specific skills. Technical systems are generally organized around the work that needs to be done. For example, the work of acute care hospitals involves curing or controlling the ailments presented by their patients. To produce these outcomes, hospitals typically organize their technical systems around patient care needs. In the case of self-managed teams, staff members operate in groups that are organized around the work processes needed to produce the products or services that their customers need. Recall, for example, that each of the self-managed teams in the Givens Estates Methodist Retirement Community is organized to provide an essential service or group of services to the residents. Thus, there is a nursing services team, a food services team, and a housekeeping services team, among others.

In analyzing technical systems, designers look at the following aspects:

- The flow of work and materials
- The interface between people and machines
- The number and nature of work steps
- The availability and use of information systems
- The physical arrangement of equipment, tools, and space
- Work procedures and policies [3]

Groups planning to become self-managed teams review the design of their technical systems to ensure that their teams will work in an efficient way. Staff who produce work that is tangible and fairly predictable generally find the review relatively easy to perform. Pharmacy technicians, for example, can count the number of doses dispensed or the IV admixtures prepared in a given time period. The review process is more complex for clinical staff, who must try to measure intangibles such as the impact of a patient medication counseling session. (Chapter 9 provides an in-depth explanation of technical systems review and design.)

☞ **Team Tip:** Drawing process flow diagrams can be hard work. Celebrating milestones like these will encourage the team to move forward.

Social Systems

Of equal importance to work design are social systems—those processes that enable people to work together and contribute to the organization as a whole. Social systems include processes for

- Hiring, training, and development
- Communication
- Decision making and conflict resolution
- Planning
- Performance feedback for team and individuals
- Discipline
- Compensation and celebration[4]

For self-managed teams, social systems design entails making the transition from hierarchical/bureaucratic systems to systems that support democratic teams. As you saw in chapter 4, staff members relate to one another under self-management in a totally different manner from that experienced under hierarchies and bureaucracies. (Chapter 10 provides more detailed information on social systems and their design.)

☞ **Team Tip:** The design of social systems touches on sensitive issues, such as procedures for resolving conflicts and for hiring and firing. To avoid overwhelming new teams, it is best to have teams take on these responsibilities gradually.

Technical and social systems work hand in hand. Most departments of health care organizations do both "manufacturing work" and "knowledge work." For example, in the pharmacy, technicians compound intravenous admixtures and pharmacists advise physicians on which admixtures are most effective. Thus, the design of self-managed work teams in health care organizations must balance the technical and social systems required to accomplish both process and clinical work.

Balance between the Systems

J. Richard Hackman and Greg R. Oldham, authors of the landmark 1980 book *Work Redesign,* were among the first to analyze the relationship between technical and social systems.[5] In examining the need for modern organizations to redesign themselves, Hackman and Oldham identified two routes that could be followed: Fit jobs to people (redesign work systems to better accommodate people), or fit people to jobs (make people accommodate existing work systems). The authors concluded that even though the first route made more sense, most organizations would follow the second. Their reasoning was that management would find it easier and more comfortable to rely on old methods and "the way things have always been done." The authors proved to be prophetic: Most organizations are still bureaucratic and still continue to fit people to jobs.

A strong argument can be made that this "design route" is outdated. Although it may have been efficient during the industrial age of mass production, when many people labored in standardized, unskilled manufacturing jobs, it makes much less sense in today's information age, when most jobs require specialized knowledge and people depend on a complex set of relationships to do their work. As table 5-1, the Balance of Systems, shows, the pendulum has swung, and we are returning once again to a time when social systems and relationships are as important as science and technology.

In today's world, the two routes have become one—paradoxically, we must fit jobs to people *and* fit people to jobs. In designing self-managed teams, equal attention must be given to technical and social systems.

Principles of Design

"The great leader is he who makes the people say, 'We did it ourselves.'"

—*Lao-tzu*

The design process, like work design itself, might follow one of two routes. Route 1 is to follow standard design principles born of the experience of others. This route enables teams to repeat their predecessors' successes and avoid their mistakes. Route 2 circumvents established principles of design in an attempt to save time and avoid "making waves." Unfortunately, as is true of many shortcuts, people are likely to get lost along the way.

Route 1, the recommended design process, consists of five major design principles. Experience has shown that following each of these principles will yield positive outcomes. Route 2, which is *not* recommended, has its consequences as well. The following sections present the five design principles and their corresponding "shortcuts," contrasting the likely consequences of each.

Principle 1: Use a Design Team Composed of Staff

The first principle—use a design team composed of staff—provides many advantages. Staff participation encourages employees to feel empowered and provides them with practice in exercising that power wisely. Staff participation also fosters a sense of ownership in the team design and team concept. This sense of ownership builds team support—and helps sell the team concept to those who have yet to buy into it.

Table 5-1. Balance of Systems

Era and Type of Organization	Degree of Reliance on Relationships, or Social Systems "Fitting Jobs to People"	Degree of Reliance on Work Processes, or Technical Systems "Fitting People to Jobs"
Nomadic (small groups)	++++	
Agricultural (hierarchy)	+++	+
Industrial (bureaucracy)	+	+++
Information (self-managed teams)	++	++

The shortcut is, of course, to have management design the teams *for* staff. The negative consequences of this approach are many: Staff members are apt to resist designs in which they have no say, and the design itself is apt to be faulty without the input of the front-liners who have firsthand knowledge of how day-to-day tasks are actually performed. Moreover, having management design the teams perpetuates the hierarchical structure that is anathema to the team concept.

Principle 2: Use a Trained Facilitator from Outside the Team

Stating that staff should be allowed to design their own teams does not mean that staff should be left completely on their own. To ensure that design standards are met, it is important that staff work under the guidance of a trained facilitator. This individual should be an "outsider" who is skilled at leading discussions and soliciting the participation of all group members.

Groups who are tempted to bypass this second principle are urged to reconsider. Without a facilitator, the design team is likely to be dominated by a few outspoken individuals who will serve their own agendas. The negative consequences of this are obvious.

Principle 3: Begin with the Technical Systems Review

Many people—particularly managers—are inclined to begin the design process by setting rules for team behaviors. This approach puts the cart before the horse. As mentioned earlier in this chapter, the first real step in the design process is to perform a standard review of technical systems (which is covered in chapter 9). This type of review requires team members to analyze their work in light of their customers' needs. Thus, it helps staff learn work-flow analysis skills and leads to process improvements that have a direct impact on customers. Beginning the design process by setting behavioral rules fails to yield work improvements. Because behavioral rules seek to solve problems that occurred in the past, they have no measurable impact on work processes of the future.

Principle 4: Make Necessary Changes in Social Systems

After team members review technical systems, they must review the social systems that make technical systems work. Allowing the design team to develop new human relationship systems will encourage self-managed teams to take responsibility for their new work processes and develop their "people skills." The alternative—forcing teams to follow bureaucratic personnel policies—is sure to cause problems. These policies stifle teams' interest in taking charge of their own work, thereby fostering their natural inclination to rely on management. Moreover, they hamper teams' ability to build the new work relationships that they will need to succeed.

Principle 5: Have Staff Define Roles and Responsibilities

The final principle—allow staff to define their own roles and responsibilities—is, perhaps, the most important of all. Because of the nature of work design, staff roles will, in part, be dictated by systems requirements, team goals, and organizational expectations. Given these boundaries, it is important to provide opportunities for individuals to fulfill their need for personal and professional growth. Allowing staff members to decide "who does what" gives them a chance to take on new responsibilities and help educate others about team members' roles.

The shortcut—having management assign people roles—is likely to cause resentment. The predetermined roles will be resisted, and staff members will learn how to work around the new roles or fall back on the old hierarchy.

☞ **Team Tip:** The simple truth is that the more management seeks to control and make decisions for team members, the more likely that the teams will fail.

The Design Team

"Shakespeare wrote his plays, and Mozart his symphonies, to earn money to feed their families, but they also did it to be creative, to make use of their talents, to leave something of themselves behind when their lives ended."

—*Harold S. Kushner*

Having presented the arguments in favor of a staff-based design team, we turn to some of the specifics of the design team itself. Although every group that plans to become self-managed needs to go through the design process, not every group needs to form a design team. If the group is small and plans to form only one team, then that group can do its own design. Larger groups that plan to reorganize themselves into two or more self-managed teams will benefit from a design team.

In creating the design team, it is essential to get the right "mix" of staff. It is also essential to create the right organizational climate. The composition of the design team and the atmosphere in which the design team operates will have a great deal of influence over the future success of the group as a whole.

☞ **Team Tip:** Adults do not like to be told how they should act; they need to be themselves and discover what behaviors work best for them.

Composition of the Design Team

For work team designs to be effective, the design team must include representatives of all major job functions and job classifications within the affected department. Part of the design team's job is to analyze team technical systems and team members' roles, and an accurate analysis of work processes cannot be performed without the input of everyone involved.

The design team should also include a variety of personality types. Usually, the design process is started by a courageous few who are champions for self-managed work teams. Their zeal is helpful as the design team works through obstacles in the technical and social systems analyses. Because these visionaries see the light at the end of the tunnel and keep the group moving forward at difficult points, they are indispensable. As self-managed teams are implemented, it is the visionaries who serve as role models for future team members who have not yet had the opportunity to work as part of the team.

At the same time, however, the design team should include a few healthy cynics. Their gimlet-eyed view ensures that the sometimes tedious task of analyzing work processes and social systems remains focused on the details of daily operations. The "reality checks" that cynics can provide also help the design team anticipate and plan for the realities of life in the self-managed system.

Organizational Climate

Perhaps the most important step in creating the proper environment for design teams is to help the designers find their own way. The design team will be breaking new ground, creating new work systems, new social systems, and new behavioral expectations. This means that the members of the design team must be given broad latitude to discuss alternative ideas for technical and social systems. As pointed out earlier, the best way to ensure that the design team "looks beyond the horizon" is to use the services of a trained facilitator. The best facilitators create a sense of trust and safety. They encourage members to brainstorm even the craziest of ideas, because they know that people who stretch their imaginations also begin to stretch their capacity to take on new roles.

A side benefit of the design process is that it helps the design team discover the positive feelings of creating something new. At the same time, groups should realize that team designers typically experience moments of anxiety. These conflicting emotions are to be expected: excitement and anxiety go hand in hand when people work through a new process. The thought of blazing a new trail fills the adventurer with the anticipation of discovery. But the trailblazer also senses unforeseen obstacles and worries whether he or she will be up to meeting new challenges. The dynamic tension between hope and fear will always be present during the design process. For this reason, it is essential to celebrate progress every step of the way. Success builds upon itself. Acknowledging the designers' "baby steps" will enable them to develop the strength they need to walk on their own and eventually jump the hurdles in their way.

While celebrating design team accomplishments presents the opportunity for positive feedback on a job well done, it also fulfills another important function: Communicating the design in small pieces also allows other staff members to learn about the design and begin to adjust to the principles of self-management. Feedback from staff members on the design team proposals and alternatives are also a big help in anticipating the "bumps in the road." It is important that issues on which staff members have different perspectives, such as whether work processes should be centralized or decentralized, surface early in the process. In addition, staff members usually have concerns about assignments—"who should be on what team"—and the manner in which conflicts between different personalities will be addressed. Tough issues such as these are most easily resolved when they surface early and all team members have a say in the resolution.

In sum, energy—both positive and negative—will be created by the tension between technical and social systems designs. Key to the success of the design process is to use this energy to further the team. Negative comments and behind-the-scenes developments must be acknowledged rather than squelched. For the team to operate smoothly in the future, all team members must feel free to express their opinions. Such freedom builds trust. The design team should actively seek out different opinions and acknowledge that dissidents may have good ideas. In fact, when naysayers' energy is channeled from problem seeking to solution seeking, they often become champions of the team concept.

Design Lessons from the Field

"If I could go through this transition again, I would read and share with the department everything I learned about teams."

—Sandi Ducker, pharmacy technician, Memorial Mission Hospital

When blazing new trails, it is helpful to talk to other explorers who have made successful journeys. The suggestions that follow are based on the experiences of the teams profiled throughout this book. Tips from others are a good place to start, because learning new concepts and improving on the ideas of others add to the texture of design, helping team members to create systems tailored to their work situations.

Start with a Core of Staff Committed to the Team Concept

When the staff members of the outpatient surgical unit at St. Joseph's Hospital decided they wanted to try self-management, they were committed to the team concept. The personal motivation of individuals on this unit to work as a team was the key to their ultimate success. This motivated group of employees made the design process seem like fun rather than a mandatory task. Involving staff members who want to make a difference is crucial in implementing self-managed work teams.

Look at Work Processes from the Customer's Perspective

When the pharmacy design team at Memorial Mission Hospital began the design process, their first step was to survey their customers. These customers included patients, nurses, and doctors in every patient care area. The simple question the design asked was "What would we have to do differently for you to consider our service outstanding?" Customer responses were then used to focus the design team on essential work processes. The result was a "lifesaver design" that consists of teams focused on customer needs. This design enables pharmacy personnel to work closely with patient care areas, providing high levels of service and enhancing job satisfaction of staff members.

Help the Designers Learn about Teams

Before the respiratory care unit at the Mission+St. Joseph's Health System began the work design process, the entire staff was educated on the concept of self-managed work teams. From the staff came a group of motivated volunteers to work on the design. This core group then searched for a respiratory care department that had already implemented self-managed teams. They found such a department and invited its members to share what they had learned about teams. Learning about the specifics of teams for individual departments helped the designers gain confidence and move forward with self-assurance.

Keep Management out of the Design Process

When pharmacy services of the Mission+St. Joseph's Health System were combined into one department, staff were concerned that one hospital would dictate its traditional management models to the other. This situation was handled by turning the design process completely over to staff members representing all areas of the departments being merged. An outside facilitator worked with the design team, and the final design recommendations were shared with management at the end of the process. It is hard for management to stay out of the way, but it is essential to establishing the culture of self-management.

Let Teams Ease into the Tough Social Issues

The Baptist Health Preschool in Little Rock took careful steps when it came to implementing the social systems needed for teams. The teams' first "social task" was to assume responsibility for work scheduling—a relatively innocuous duty. Next, the teams tackled daily operational issues. Finally, under the guidance of their coach, they began to take on hiring and performance evaluation tasks. Teams that jump right into conflict resolution or discipline without first learning to work together will find themselves enmeshed in draining personality issues. Teams need to learn to walk before they can jump.

Allow Ample Time for Team Design

Observers and the coach of the outpatient wound care team for the Mission+St. Joseph's Health System were concerned that the team would never get off the ground. The team was composed of diverse professionals from different disciplines who had previously worked as independent clinicians. Patience, perseverance, and dialogue resulted in a team of interdependent staff members who use their skills to complement the roles of one other. The lesson to be learned from their experience is that some things just take time.

Communicate with Staff Every Step of the Way

The design team for pharmacy services of the Mission+St. Joseph's Health System faced the challenge of combining cultures from two hospitals that had previously been competitors. Compounding the difficulty were future team members' concerns about how the implementation of systemwide self-managed teams would affect them personally. To alleviate these concerns, the design team communicated with staff members during every step of the design process. The questions that staff asked and the suggestions they made helped the design team develop new approaches. By including ideas from many sources, the design team was able to create self-managed teams that laid the groundwork for a new organizational culture.

Chapter Wrap-Up

Creating self-managed work teams is an exhilarating and challenging process. Use of technical and social systems design principles results in self-managed work teams that meet customer needs and enhance job satisfaction for team members. Teams can ensure success and avoid pitfalls by following design principles and avoiding shortcuts. People involved in design experience change, and the energy they generate can be used to motivate others to help implement the design they have created.

By learning lessons from other teams, self-managed work teams save time and are better equipped to create systems that fit their teams' unique situations. Careful design of self-managed work teams is the starting point for creating the work environment needed to thrive in the information age.

References

1. P. Senge, *The Fifth Discipline* (New York: Doubleday, 1990), p. 341.
2. Ibid.
3. L. M. Miller, *Design for Total Quality: A Workbook for Socio-Technical Design* (Atlanta: The Miller Consulting Group, 1991), p. 155.
4. Ibid.
5. J. R. Hackman and G. R. Oldham, *Work Redesign* (Reading, MA: Addison-Wesley, 1980), p. 260.

Suggested Readings

Hackman, J. R., and G. R. Oldham. *Work Redesign.* Reading, MA: Addison-Wesley, 1980.

Kushner, H. S. *How Good Do We Have to Be?* Boston: Little Brown, 1996.

Miller, Lawrence M. *Design for Total Quality: A Workbook for Socio-Technical Design.* Atlanta, The Miller Consulting Group, 1991.

Senge, P. *The Fifth Discipline.* New York: Doubleday, 1990.

Part II

Work Design

The purpose of this section is to provide an overview and practical examples to follow in the team design process. This section enhances the reader's awareness of the complexity of self-managed teams and of the stages of design that must be completed to ensure the success of teams. Teams need to have their own organization structure and specific roles for shared leadership. Generally, the design process takes six months. Sample design timelines are included in chapter 7.

The design process includes redesigning how the work is done to make sure it is both team based and customer focused. It also includes designing the social systems in which the employees on teams operate. Social systems are the ways that people work together—for example, how decisions are made, conflicts are resolved, hiring and discipline occur, and what communication needs and methods will be necessary in a team environment. Very few processes that are effective in a hierarchical system can work exactly the same way in a team-based structure.

As the chapters in this section unfold, they help to clarify the ways that teams operate. The examples and structures described in this section help clarify how teams work and remove the mystery of team methods. The chapters in this section also illustrate the many ways that teams differ from the standard work group.

Part Contents: Work Design

Chapter 6

The Design Team

Chapter Preview

"The desire to create is not limited by beliefs, nationality, creed, educational background or era. The urge resides in all of us."

—*Robert Fritz*

Once a group has decided to become a self-managed team and has been given the okay to do so, it typically wants to begin the implementation process immediately. It is important to recognize, however, that implementation cannot take place that quickly. Planning and design must be done before the self-managed team can start operating effectively.

As pointed out in chapter 5, all groups must go through the design process to analyze and plan team members' roles, technical systems, and social systems. As was also pointed out, it is useful to create a multifunctional team of staff members to carry out these purposes, particularly when the group planning to become self-managed is large (20 or more members) and will form two or more teams. In fact, for large groups, creation of a design team is a virtual necessity. In health care institutions, it is almost impossible to find a time at which all department or unit staff can meet weekly for the four to six months that the design process typically takes to complete. Moreover, it is inefficient to make decisions in a large group when a smaller, representative group can make them just as well. The key is to ensure that the group is truly *representative:* The design team should be a vehicle for balanced participation in the design process. For this to occur, the design team must include one or more representatives of every function, area, and shift that plans to become self-managed.

The many facets of the design process are described in detail throughout part II of this book. This chapter focuses on the goals and composition of the design team and on the qualifications and skills design team members need. The chapter also looks at the pivotal roles played by the design team facilitator.

Chapter at a Glance

In this chapter, you will find

- A discussion of the design team's early steps
- An analysis of the design team as a prototype for self-management
- An examination of the roles and qualifications of the team facilitator
- A look at the communication skills used by design team members

Early Design Steps

"Begin at the beginning."

—Lewis Carroll

The design team has two major goals: (1) to redesign work processes and create the structure and systems needed for self-managed teams to operate and (2) to learn to function as a self-managed team. To fulfill these goals, the design team performs a variety of preliminary tasks.

Definition of Purpose

As pointed out in chapter 1, self-managed teams don't operate in a vacuum. They help fulfill the mission of the department and the organization as a whole by providing products or services to customers. One of the tasks of the design team is to identify the customers, customer needs, and products or services that the team is responsible for. The team must also define how its purpose helps fulfill the missions of the department and the organization as a whole. Design teams must keep those greater purposes in the front of their minds throughout the process.

Figure 6-1 illustrates how the respiratory care design team of the Mission+St. Joseph's Health System defined the important relationship between the self-managed teams and the customer they serve—the patient.

Figure 6-2, the Lifesaver Plan, illustrates how the design team at the Mission+St. Joseph's Health System mapped out the teams' focus on providing pharmaceutical support to the service lines of the health system.

Throughout the design process, the design team should maintain its focus on meeting the needs of the customers. Keeping this focus helps ensure that the teams will be successful.

Application of Boundaries

Within the first several meetings, the design team also learns the boundaries within which the self-managed teams will operate. As described in chapter 3, management and prospective team members should work together to define the scope and nature of the responsibilities the teams will have. The design team takes the master list and incorporates the items into the team design. For instance, if the design team learns that the self-managed teams will be responsible for tracking absenteeism and tardiness and giving verbal warnings but not issuing written warnings or firing employees, the team will design the discipline process accordingly.

Application of Performance Expectations

The design team also incorporates the teams' performance expectations into the design. For example, when the team learns the financial performance expectations, it includes them in the roles, goals, measures, records, and reports for all teams. When the team learns the quality performance expectations, those, too, are incorporated in the roles, goals, measures, records, and reports the teams will be responsible for. In other words, each performance expectation that is given to the design team is included in the design process.

The Design Team as Prototype

"To produce things but not to take possession of them, to act, but not to rely on one's own ability, to lead them, but not to master—this is called profound and secret virtue."

—*Lao-tzu*

Figure 6-1. Respiratory Care Self-Managed Teams

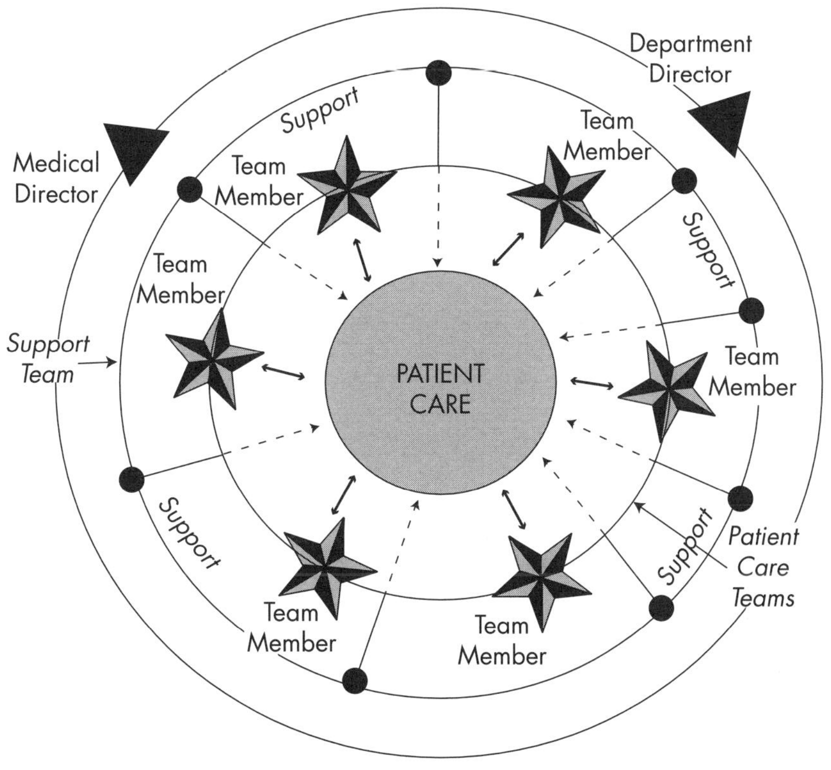

The design team plays an important role in the successful launching of teams. As the first subgroup to form during the transition to self-governance, the design team is the prototype for all the teams to follow. To serve this function, the designers must themselves be structured as a self-managed team and must operate as one. They must learn how to play team roles such as leader and record keeper (discussed in chapter 8), how to make group decisions, and how to resolve conflicts between team members. All team members must share responsibility for the tasks of the design team, and all may have assignments. In this way, team members learn to be a self-managed team at the same time that they create the work design, the team structure, and the social systems within which the teams will operate. Typically, the whole department is curious about how the design team works and what progress it is making. Seeing members of the department function as a self-managed team is reassuring to future team members.

Design Team Size

The ideal size for a design team is the same as that for any self-managed team: five to ten members. To guarantee that all future self-managed team

Figure 6-2. The Lifesaver Plan

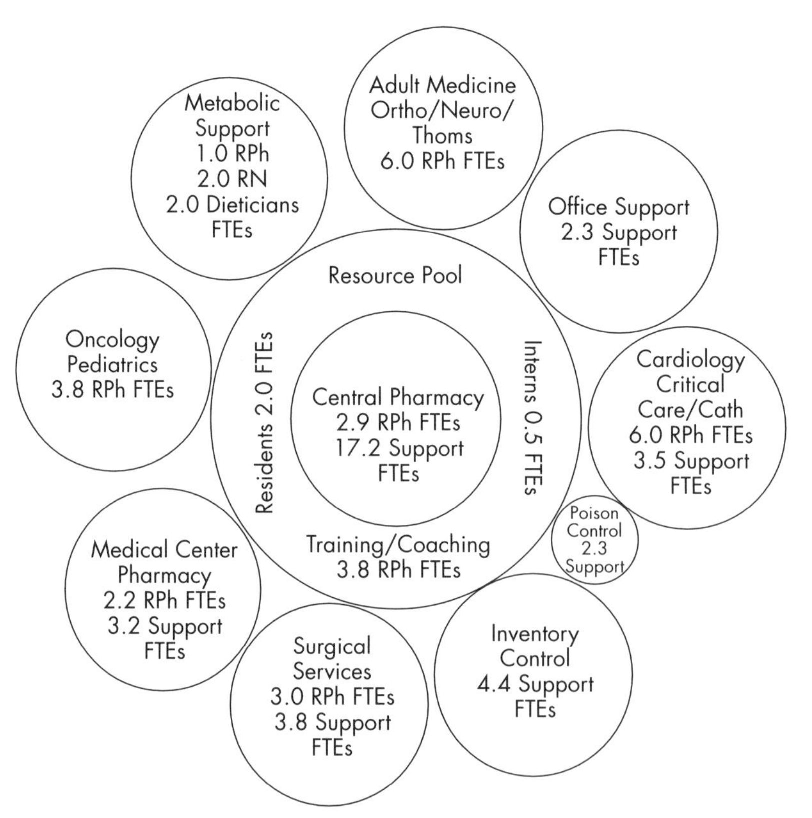

members have a voice in team design, it is essential that the design team include representatives of all the functions, job classifications, and shifts that the teams will cover. For balance, the team should also include both people who are new to the department and "old-timers," both people who have traditional ideas and those who pursue innovation and new ways of looking at things. At the same time, it is in everyone's best interests to restrict membership to the required minimum. The larger the design team, the more burden placed on other staff, who must cover team members' regular duties during team meetings. Moreover, the larger the design team, the less likely that every representative will have an opportunity to voice opinions during team meetings.

Design Team Membership

To ensure that design team members develop new skills, department managers should exclude themselves from the design team. If self-governance is to succeed, staff must learn how to function without the direct involvement of management-level personnel, and the design team is the logical place to start. Though the team loses the benefit of management's knowledge and experience, it gains something even more important: the opportunity to take sole responsibility for an important function. If the team creates a design that works beautifully, then the team gets credit for making wise decisions. If the design team makes poor design decisions, then team members learn how to own up to their mistakes and correct them. Either way, the organization "wins."

☞ **Team Tip:** *All* self-managed team members should remember that team decisions are not written in stone. If a team makes a faulty decision, it can always be reversed.

Selection of Members Just as management should exclude itself from the design team, so should it exclude itself from the team selection process. The night shift should select its representative, the clerical staff its representative, the technical staff its representative, and so on. If a group of staff is not represented—a slip-up more likely to occur when management selects the design team—the "missing" group's perspective may not be heard until the design process is well underway, necessitating the unhappy task of working through previously made decisions to ensure that all groups are included. For the sake of efficiency as well as self-management, staff members should be allowed to make their own choices, either by nominating representatives for the design team and holding a vote or by asking for volunteers.

Qualifications for Membership Before selecting representatives, staff members must give careful consideration to the qualities and characteristics they would like their representatives to have. Design team members must be willing to speak up and voice the perspective of the group they represent. They must have patience and be willing to stay with the design process for four to six months. They must be open to different views and capable of voicing their honest reactions to other people's ideas. It also is helpful if design team members already have a commitment to meeting customer needs and a strong commitment to work.

An additional qualification for design team members is that they can make the time to attend meetings, do homework, and communicate with the group or groups they represent on the design team. Members of the design team may need to do research about other teams and organizations, and they may need to survey customers. They will definitely need to spend time keeping the staff in their areas up to date on the design team's progress and "next steps." Design team members must also be willing to take the time to ask coworkers for input on upcoming decisions or design options.

Design team members work hard at the design team meetings, learning new concepts and assessing ways to apply them in their work environment. They also deal with differing opinions of what will and will not work. Working through the conflicts that inevitably arise during the design process helps team designers develop the conflict management skills that they will need to handle clashes of opinion back in their work areas. Staff who aren't members of the design team are not privy to all the debate that can occur during design meetings. As a result, they may not fully understand the rationale behind some team decisions and may criticize or second-guess decisions that the design team struggled to reach. At times like these, the designer cannot look over his or her shoulder and say, "That was management's decision and I don't like it either." The designers face the reality that self-managed teams face on a daily basis: *There is no one to blame but ourselves.* For this reason, it is helpful to choose team designers who have previously held a leadership role and are accustomed to dealing with "shots" fired by staff members. Although leadership experience does not make the shots any more comfortable to take, most people who have been in leadership roles know not to take them personally.

Team Members as Leaders Whether or not staff members were informal leaders before joining the design team, they will have leadership abilities at the end of their experience. Because the designers have to learn a lot about how teams and organizations work, because they have to make difficult decisions, and because they have to face coworkers with difficult news, members of the design team develop leadership abilities. After participating as design team members, these staff members know how to conduct and participate effectively in meetings, how to make consensus decisions and resolve conflict, how to juggle multiple priorities, and how to set goals and measures and develop plans. They also will have a clearer understanding of personnel policies and practices.

☞ **Team Tip:** When the department or larger group finally divides itself into teams, it is helpful to ensure that each team includes at least one design team member. As experienced team players, the "ex-designers" can help other staff make the transition to teams.

The Design Team Facilitator

"The facilitator says only what is needed at each point in time. The artistry of dialogue lies in experiencing the flow of meaning and seeing the one thing that needs to be said."

—*Peter Senge*

Stating that the design team should function without managers does not mean that the team should be left to struggle without resources. As pointed out in chapter 5, the design team should have the benefit of a trained facilitator to help it on its journey to self-management. At the beginning of the process, the facilitator is heavily involved in guiding the design team. As the design team progresses and develops skills and knowledge of the design process, the facilitator's role changes from guide to coach. Eventually, the team will find that it rarely, if ever, needs the facilitator's help. It is at this point that the design team is truly operating as a self-managed team.

Roles of the Facilitator

The facilitator plays several important roles during the design process. He or she helps the team obtain resources—such as in-house experts, contacts with other organizations, meeting rooms (on and off site), and articles and books relating to the specific topic the team is discussing—and may serve as a "teacher," helping the team learn the processes and methods it needs to know to create self-managed teams. The facilitator works closely with the team leader, helping this individual develop agendas for design team meetings and skills in managing the meetings. Because meetings are where the work of the design team is done, the management of meetings is an extremely important skill.

The facilitator provides guidance but does *not* direct the team or make decisions for it. The facilitator is more concerned about *how* the team makes its decisions than about what decisions the team makes. The facilitator is not the design team's liaison with management. Either the team leader or another member of the design team is assigned the responsibility for keeping management informed of the team's progress and obtaining input from management. The facilitator stays removed from the internal workings of the department and does not serve as management's voice.

Qualifications of the Facilitator

The facilitator should be knowledgeable about the process of designing self-managed teams, about team structures, about work design for groups, and about social systems design. The facilitator also should have knowledge of group processes and be a skilled conductor of meetings so that he or she can help the design team establish its own meeting structure and timeline for the design of self-managed teams. It is extremely unlikely that a staff member from the area that is implementing self-managed teams possesses the knowledge needed to be a facilitator. It also is unlikely that a staff member would be able to remain neutral and objective throughout the design process. For these reasons, the use of a properly trained individual from outside the department is a necessity. A human resource professional who has facilitated quality improvement teams, reengineering teams, or other groups is an ideal candidate to play the role of design team facilitator. Because the human resource person is an "outsider" to the group, he or she finds it easier to remain neutral and help the team reach effective decisions than does someone from within the group.

Design Team Meetings

"Many things, having full reference to one consent, may work contrariously, as many arrows, loosed several ways, fly to one mark; as many ways meet in one town."

—William Shakespeare

Meetings of the design team are conducted like any other meeting of a project team. They have a structured agenda, ground rules, and time frames for addressing issues and making decisions. (See chapter 8 for instructions on how to set ground rules and develop agendas.) The design team leader conducts the meeting, the facilitator observes and supports, and members of the design team may be on the agenda along with people from outside the design team who have been invited to address a topic. A timekeeper keeps the meetings on track, and a record keeper takes notes for the minutes. The design team follows a timeline that outlines the process and what needs to be decided. The timeline can be established to coincide with specific meeting dates of the design team, or it can be more general. (Chapter 7 provides more detailed information about timelines.)

As the sample agendas in figure 6-3 show, the typical design team meeting focuses on the design process rather than on general self-managed team concerns, such as conflict resolution or reassigning of group roles.

Internal Communications

To hold successful meetings, members of the design team must exercise a variety of interpersonal communication skills. Team members must be willing to speak freely—exposing their ignorance and assumptions as well as sharing their knowledge and expertise—so that the design team as a whole

Figure 6-3. Two Sample Design Team Agendas

Sample Agenda 1
Decision Support and Audit Services

Objectives

1. Determine best method to set up team structures, that is, representatives or the whole group.
2. Review self-managed team definition and clarify how it applies to the decision support and audit services department.
3. Begin determination of what teams will do (create check sheet).
4. Learn principles of meeting effectiveness.

15 minutes	*Welcome and Introductions* Facilitator introduction Team member introductions Objectives of today's meeting Plan overview: Self-managed team definition review Objectives of self-managed team development Divisions of teams	Team and facilitator
5 minutes	*Team Structure* Design team made up of representatives Each team constructs and then collates results	Team
20 minutes	*Self-Managed Team Questionnaire* handout	Team
15 minutes	*Meeting Effectiveness* Roles Ground rules	Team
3 minutes	*Meeting Evaluations*	Team
2 minutes	*Summary/Next Meeting*	Team

Sample Agenda 2
Respiratory Care Department

1. Welcome and Introductions	Team leader, 5:00–5:05
2. The Team Conversion Process	Member, 5:05–5:15
3. The Timeline	Member, 5:15–5:25
4. Teams	Member, 5:25–5:35
5. Team Assignments	Member, 5:35–5:45
6. Accountability and Reporting Hierarchy	Member, 5:45–5:55
7. Mission and Values	Member, 5:55–6:00
8. Expectations	Member, 6:00–6:10
9. Questions/Summary	Team leader, 6:10–6:25
10. Adjourn	6:25–6:30

is able to make informed decisions. Team members must also learn how to "discuss the undiscussable." Problems that have been buried, tolerated, or hidden by the entire department must be unearthed and resolved.

Design team members must also be good listeners, ensuring that everyone has a chance to be heard. Like all groups, the design team may have a tendency to ignore or give short shrift to minority opinions. When the majority of team members agree on an issue, they may not want to take the time or make the effort to work through dissenting points of view. Yet to rush to a decision without fully considering all viewpoints is a mistake. For this reason, most decisions that the design team makes must be consensus decisions—ones in which the minority view is incorporated in the final outcome. It takes good listening skills to understand different perspectives and creativity to negotiate consensus. Design team members will build these communication skills over time. (See also chapter 8.)

Design team members also need to develop clarifying and confirming skills so that they are clear about their assignments when they leave design team meetings and about the feedback and input they received from staff. (Chapter 15 covers these communication skills in detail.)

External Communications

Team members must communicate not only with each other but also with the rest of the staff, including those outside the department who have a stake in the success of the self-managed teams. For example, physicians who work with pharmacy specialists making the transition to self-management have a stake in the pharmacists' success because the work of the pharmacists affects physicians' ability to provide good care to their patients. It is up to the design team to plan and implement formal and informal communications with stakeholders outside the department.

Methods of Communication Time is at a premium for most people, design team members included. As a result, regularly scheduled face-to-face discussions with other staff about design team work may not be possible. There are a number of other ways that the design team can communicate team business to staff. The teams profiled in this book used the following methods:

- *A communication book.* The design team compiled a notebook consisting of minutes of meetings and draft designs. Copies of the book were left throughout the department so that staff could read them and record their questions or comments. Staff comments were then reviewed at the beginning of each design team meeting.
- *Reserved meeting times.* Time was allotted during routine staff meetings for the design team to inform the department about its actions. During a staff meeting, the design team representative discussed upcoming decisions and asked for staff input. Staff had the opportunity to ask questions and engage in dialogue about the issue being addressed.

- *Bulletin board.* Space was reserved on a departmental bulletin board for design team updates and display of the design timeline. One design team managed to solicit feedback on its draft of a work design process by placing a supply of "sticky notes" nearby. Staff then put their written comments directly on the design, anonymously.

Ideally, the design team will take design options to the staff before making final decisions. As much as possible, staff input is to be obtained on changes in any system, structure, or process that the design team develops. If the design team can create alternatives for the staff to review and evaluate, the alternatives help generate enthusiastic discussions. When only one option is presented to staff members, they may feel that they are being told what to do rather than being allowed to participate in the decision.

Barriers to Communication Of course, problems will sometimes arise in even the best communication systems. Because people interpret messages based on their own experiences, needs, and interests, miscommunication will undoubtedly occur. For example, different design team members may interpret the same discussion or decision differently and therefore communicate different messages about it. Staff, in turn, will provide input based on their interpretation of the design team member's understanding of what occurred. To take the chain one step further, consider that the design team member who gathers input may interpret it differently from the staff member's intentions. One design team learned the lesson of misinterpretation so well that it checked to make sure "yes" did not mean "no" and vice versa.

Another major barrier to communication is time. Staff should remember that design team members have full-time work responsibilities in addition to the time they spend at design team meetings. This double workload means that team members may not have extra time to talk to staff one-on-one or make elaborate presentations to staff about design team business. Some design team members may "take the easy way out" and just share meeting minutes with staff, asking them to provide feedback. Other design team members may prefer to get permission from their supervisor or director to spend some time each day or several days a week talking to staff in order to share information and get input.

The End of the Design Team's Work

Social scientists who specialize in group behavior have pointed out that groups that have worked closely together tend to want to extend the life of the work group beyond the point at which it serves a purpose. Design teams are no exception. Team designers typically become close to one another and develop a true collegial spirit. They develop an appreciation for each other's background, knowledge, and experience. And they learn to console and reassure each other during times of discord with staff who are not design team members. As a result, some team members may want to continue meeting even after all the design tasks are done. To guard against unnecessary meetings, the organization should ensure that the team's progress and performance are periodically assessed.

Several techniques can be used to ease the design team into the end stages of its existence. One technique is to let the team know from the start that it is needed for only four to six months. Another is to create a timeline, or schedule, that shows right from the beginning when the design process will end. (Chapter 7 covers the subject of timelines in detail.) Toward the end of the process, the facilitator or a member of the design team can also remind the group how many meetings are left.

Because the work of the design team is difficult, stressful, and time consuming, it is recommended that the team be rewarded with a celebration at the end of the design process. In this celebration, design team members can be formally thanked for their efforts, time, and commitment. This formal ending for the design team also helps brings closure to the meetings and the process.

Chapter Wrap-Up

For larger groups planning to reorganize themselves into two or more self-managed teams, the design team plays an integral role in the transition to self-management. The two major goals of the design team are to (1) redesign work processes and create the structure and systems needed for self-managed teams and (2) to operate and to learn to function as a self-managed team. As the first self-managed group in the department, the design team may be viewed as a prototype of self-management. Design team members will serve as role models for others moving toward self-management.

Although the design team should operate as a self-managed team, it should not be expected to make the journey to self-management alone. A trained facilitator who is knowledgeable about work systems, processes, and small group interaction should be there to help guide the way.

Design team members must learn to communicate effectively with each other, with other staff in the department, and with stakeholders throughout the organization. As a result of their experiences, design team members will further develop their ability to listen without rushing to judgment, to negotiate compromises among people with differing points of view, and to explain work processes.

Suggested Readings

Fritz, R. *The Path of Least Resistance.* New York: Fawcett-Columbine, 1989.

Senge, P. *The Fifth Discipline.* New York: Doubleday, 1990.

Chapter 7

The Design Timeline

Chapter Preview

"I'm late, I'm late, for a very important date!

No time to say hello. Goodbye. I'm late, I'm late, I'm late!"

—*White Rabbit in* Alice in Wonderland

At this point in the process, research on self-managed teams has been done, and the decision to implement teams has been made. Boundaries have been set, and a design team has been established. It's now time to get off to an official start on the road to self-managed teams, yet important questions remain to be asked and answered: How long will the design process take? When design is complete, how long will it take to implement self-managed teams? And once these time estimates are made, how can design team members keep their work on schedule? This chapter presents the time-honored answer these questions: develop and use a timeline (pun intended).

This chapter explains the purpose of the timeline and outlines group exercises for establishing a timeline. More important, it describes how to use the timeline as a tool for keeping the design and implementation of self-managed teams on track. There will often be forces that cause the team to fall off the pace set by the timeline. Tips are given on how to use these "challenges" as "opportunities" for making design and implementation progress. This chapter concludes with examples of timelines, from simple to sophisticated, that can be adapted to help design and implement self-managed teams.

Chapter at a Glance

In this chapter, you will find

- A definition of the timeline
- A four-step process for creating the timeline
- Team uses of the timeline
- Possible barriers and delays along the timeline
- Examples of timelines
- A team activity that produces a timeline

Definition and Functions of the Timeline

"Time is the measure of movement."

—*Medieval proposition*

Organizations use timelines as planning and implementation tools for major projects or new programs. There is no magic to a timeline. The timeline is simply a listing of planned steps in a project, along with a target time frame for completing each step. After a timeline is generated, it is then possible to estimate how long it will take to complete the entire project.

In addition to their usefulness in planning and scheduling, timelines serve as communication tools. A timeline can communicate to those involved in the process what steps or tasks are expected, when to expect these steps or tasks to be completed, and, when the project is ongoing, how much progress has been made and what remains to be done to reach the goal.

Because timelines work by simplification—turning a complicated project into a series of steps—it is important to guard against oversimplification when using them: keep in mind that work is not always a linear process. It is also important that the timeline itself not become the focus of attention, rather than the quality of work. Nor should the timeline be considered sacred: the team must always adapt to changes in the environment of work.

People use timelines daily, though the timelines aren't always written. Table 7-1 presents the timeline that Anna, a busy mother, uses to get ready to leave for work in the morning:

Anna's timeline for getting ready for work is very tight. Even though her timeline isn't posted on the refrigerator door, you can bet that on any given morning at any given time Anna knows whether she is on schedule. Her daughter understands these time frames as well. The stress that Anna and her daughter are under every day to get out the door at 7:00 A.M. is reduced because they have a timeline. Having a timeline lets them know where they stand and keeps them on track. It is easy to appreciate what happens when something occurs on a morning when there is a break in the timeline. Tempers can grow short, and there is pressure to get caught up. A simple exercise you can do to appreciate the use of a timeline is to outline your own routine for getting ready for work. That timeline will probably be as stringent as Anna's.

Development of the Timeline

The principles for creating a timeline are similar to those used by Anna in setting up her morning routine. The starting point is the endpoint. Anna knows what time she needs to leave for work and what needs to be accomplished by the time she walks out the door. She has a mental list of all the steps that need to be done, and she knows how long each step should take.

Table 7-1. Timeline for Anna to Get Ready for Work

Step in Process	Target Time
Alarm sounds	5:30 A.M.
Start coffee machine	5:40
Complete shower	6:00
Wake daughter; get coffee	6:05
Finish makeup	6:15
Help daughter start preparing lunch	6:20
Get dressed	6:30
Help daughter finish lunch and get started eating breakfast	6:35
Dry and arrange hair	6:45
Prepare own lunch and eat breakfast	6:55
Brush teeth; grab purse and leave	7:00

Anna works backward from 7 A.M. to determine that the alarm should sound at 5:30 A.M. if she is to meet her deadline for leaving.

The endpoint of a self-managed team's timeline may not be as specific as Anna's. And teams don't always have complete control over their starting points. The boundaries established by management, for example, will affect the expected date for team formation. Part of team timeline development, therefore, is negotiating with top management over the starting date and the target date for formation of self-managed teams.

It is important that the design team be responsible for the timeline once there is agreement regarding a target completion date. Anna's boss has an expectation about when Anna should be at work, but it is Anna's responsibility to get ready for work. The only difference with self-managed teams is one of degree. To some extent, the design team will play the role of "boss," determining where the endpoint should be set. The team activity at the end of this chapter leads a design team through the creation of a timeline.

The timeline will go through several drafts and will require much discussion among design team members. All design team members must speak up at this stage. It is a common mistake to let one or two people set the path based on their limited perceptions. If the timeline is to be an effective tool, all members of the design team must work to meet its deadlines. They are more likely to make the effort if they contributed to setting those deadlines.

Team Uses of the Timeline

Having a timeline does not ensure design and implementation of teams. Self-managed team implementation depends on the performance of the design team. The timeline merely offers an outline for members of the design team. Anna's timeline for getting ready for work is a tool she uses help her accomplish her goal of getting to work on time. The design team uses the timeline as a tool to help implement self-managed work teams in many ways.

Timeline as a Plan Listing and ordering the steps anticipated for self-managed team design and implementation is a starting point. Remember, though, that all plans get changed. The purpose of any plan is to give those involved an idea of where they are headed and what needs to be done to get there. The focus is not on how closely the plan is followed but on how well processes are executed to achieve the desired outcome.

Timeline as a Responsibility Assigning responsibility for steps on the timeline is the first step in establishing accountability. The power of making public who on the design team is in charge of what step cannot be overestimated. Everyone on the design team wants to contribute. Design team members need to volunteer for the steps they want to work on. Responsibilities should not be assigned. The timeline serves as a notice of recognition for design team members. Everyone likes to get credit for what he or she accomplishes.

Timeline as an Organizer Order comes from disorder. The timeline serves the design team as a reference point for the processes needed to create a team environment. At the end of the design process, the team will not look back to see how well they followed the plan or how well organized they were. Instead, the design team will look at the self-managed team system they have developed. This is what people will remember. The timeline will be forgotten, but if it is was used to help organize the design team it will have served part of its purpose.

Timeline as Task Master Procrastination is a well-ingrained human trait. Many people do their best work when they have a deadline. Some people *only* do work when they have a deadline. Using the timeline to display deadlines will create peer pressure on design team members to complete their respective tasks in a timely manner. Everyone wants to look good, and people will not let the other design team members down.

Timeline as Communications Device Letting the stakeholders know how the design process is progressing is critical in maintaining the freedom needed for the design team to work on their own. Management will stay out of the way if it knows work is being done. Customers will participate if they know when they will be included. Staff members will provide constructive input if they know they will be given the chance to share their ideas. People are afraid of what they don't understand. Using the timeline to communicate what the design team is doing helps reduce fear and encourage acceptance of the self-managed team system the designers are creating.

Timeline as a Cause for Celebration Designing self-managed teams is hard work. The timeline needs to include causes for celebration.

More important, the timeline needs to schedule pauses for celebration. People need to take a break every once in a while to reflect on what they have accomplished and enjoy the moment. Western culture does not usually allow us time to "smell the roses." The design process is difficult, and we need to encourage the designers to stop often on their journey to celebrate their progress.

Timeline as Means to an End The timeline is a means to an end. When Anna and her daughter are ready to walk out the door in the morning, they don't look back and say, "Wow, we really stuck to the timeline this morning." Instead, Anna's daughter will look at her mom and say, "You look very pretty today"; and Anna will give her daughter a big hug and tell her how much she loves her. The design team will be proud of its eventual accomplishment as well.

Barriers to Timeline Development

"Failure is not an option."

—*Buzz Aldrin,* Apollo 13

Three major drawbacks to the use of timelines were pointed out earlier in this chapter. These drawbacks are the source of barriers and delays along the timeline. But, in fact, these problems are functions of the timeline. They are functions of the real world. Human beings exist in living systems that are dynamic. The problems of sticking to the timeline arise from the basic incompatibility between the timeline's stringent order and a world that seems out of order. Because the natural order of the workplace is organic and not mechanistic, the timeline must be flexible. The three drawbacks of using a timeline are described below. The key to dealing with all of them is maintaining flexibility.

Assumption That Work Is a Linear Process

People live in complex social systems where relationships are the source of power, energy, and innovation. When Anna and her daughter get ready for work in the morning they do not follow a strictly linear path each day. They will have multiple interactions and conversations and will support or conflict with each other differently each morning. An outside observer would probably view the process that Anna and her daughter use as one of disorder and chaos. But this seeming chaos reflects the complexity of human relationships.

The design team must realize and take advantage of the multiple relationships they each have during the design process. Self-managed team design requires input from all stakeholders with whom the teams will interact. Team members will need to have conversations with many people in their individual networks and with each other as the design for teams is developed. *Listening to people takes time.* Accepting this fact is critical to understanding why design and implementation of teams takes so long.

In hierarchical/bureaucratic processes, management tells people what they should do. Self-managed teams do just the opposite, listening to stakeholders. The complex nature of relationships can seem like a barrier to timeline development, but the design team's ability to tap into these relationships will be a key to self-managed team success.

Focus on Time versus Focus on Quality

Anna has to focus carefully when putting on her mascara in the morning. This is a very delicate task, and if she is distracted she will smear the mascara or poke herself in the eye. The design team needs to focus on each specific design step. Having a timeline puts pressure on people to meet deadlines, which can create healthy stress. But when the focus changes from the task at hand to the ticking clock, the "rush job" that results invariably leads to poor performance.

The timeline is a guide, and once it has been created it almost needs to be forgotten. Design team members who created the timeline will know their specific goals and targets. Nobody likes to be nagged, and a key factor in keeping focus on the task at hand will be the absence of nagging. This point is especially important for top management. Leaders in the 1990s are often told to "create a sense of urgency." And historically, as well, management has looked at timelines and focused on what has not been completed.

In the design process, management has an opportunity to change from the controlling mode to the encouraging mode. The timeline needs to be used to remind the design team of how much it has accomplished and what a great job it's doing. The timeline should remind those outside the design team of the hard work it takes to design self-managed teams. Focusing on what a good job the design team is doing will support the design team, and they will be inspired to keep up the good work. Tapping into the human drive to do a good job will ensure that the job is done right the first time. People feel good when they know they have performed well, and this sense of accomplishment will build on itself, leading to more success.

Failure to Adapt to Change

Think about what would happen to Anna and her daughter if one morning they had no electricity. Anna's options might be to (1) not go to work and sit home in the dark; (2) muddle through on the normal schedule, frustrated by the darkness; or (3) think through options for adapting to the lack of power. Sitting home in the dark would accomplish little. Muddling through without the hairdryer would result in a "bad hair day." Anna can adapt and go to her mother's house to get ready for work and stop at McDonald's for breakfast. She may arrive at work a few minutes late, but she would be there and in a better mood than if she refused to adapt.

Mergers, buyouts, CEO turnover, legislative changes, nursing unit moves, and new computer systems can change the work environment overnight. These events are significant and cause disruptions in the system. What can the design team do when major changes happen in the middle of its work? Its choices are like Anna's: (1) stop the design and revert to bureaucracy; (2) bulldoze forward with the design as planned; or (3) reflect on the change and adapt the design to anticipated system changes. Options 1 and 2 will lead to failure. Option 3, adaptation, is the path to successful design.

Self-organizing systems have an innate capacity to adapt to the environment. The design team has the ability to process the impact that changes will have on the team design. All the design team needs is information. The sooner top management shares information on impending changes with the design team, the sooner the design team will be able to develop and assess options. The key will be for management to trust the design team to meet change demands on its own, and for management to stay out of the way.

The following true story illustrates the capabilities of a design team. Five months into the design of teams for the pharmacy at Mission Memorial Hospital, it was announced that virtually every nursing unit in the hospital would be moving. The pharmacy self-managed team design was built around decentralized clinical support for service lines, and the pharmacy director knew that the team plan on the table would need to be altered drastically. The director had attended the initial design team meeting five months before and decided to attend another meeting. At the meeting the director shared the new hospital bed plan, then he stayed for the rest of the meeting.

Two members of the design team visited the director the next day. They thanked the director for the information on the bed plan then politely informed him that he had interrupted their meeting and that it was not appropriate to come to design team meetings unannounced. The design team members suggested to the director that future information of this nature could be shared in written form. The design team could then follow up with questions or could complete their own research. The team easily revised the pharmacy self-managed team design. The lesson learned by the director and demonstrated by the team is that when people know the facts, they will act accordingly.

Working with design teams in many settings has taught us that what are big deals to top management can be accommodated by design teams if the facts are shared and the opportunity for adaptation is given. It may take a little longer to reach the target, but the simplicity of the solutions are surprising.

Nonlinear thinking, focusing on the task at hand, and having the information needed to adjust to changes are the keys to overcoming the barriers encountered on the timeline. There will always be obstacles that cause delay. The design team will succeed when it turns challenges into opportunities.

Examples of Timelines

"You won't know when you get there, unless you know where you were going."

Anna's timeline for getting ready for work is not written down. The timeline used by NASA for its launches is itemized to the millisecond and represented by sophisticated computer graphics. Timeline displays for self-managed team design fall somewhere between. Table 7-2 provides a range of sophistication for timelines and the pros and cons of each level of complexity.

This tongue-in-cheek view emphasizes the need for balance between practicality and functionality. The design team must be able to display the timeline efficiently. Use of the timeline as a communications tool for the design process requires a display that will be meaningful to the stakeholders. Design teams commonly use a combination of steps outlined on a word processor and a spreadsheet. See table 7-3 and figure 7-1 for examples.

The respiratory care department at Baptist Hospital in Little Rock, Arkansas, used a graphic display for their "learning curve" (see figure 7-2). The learning curve display was a very effective way to share progress on design with members of the department and administration.

Table 7-2. Timeline Options

Timepiece	Display Format	Advantages	Disadvantages
Sundial	In your head	Can make it up as you go along	People have to read your mind
Hourglass	Drawn in sand	Quick and dirty approach	Sometimes gets washed away
Pendulum	Handwritten	Accomplished quickly	Appears messy when edited
Mechanical	Word processor outline	Commonly available and easily changed	Limited to text display of steps
Quartz	Spreadsheet chart	Displays summary of steps and time frames	Requires some technical expertise
Digital	Computer graphics	Provides visual picture and high-tech appearance	Sophisticated software and hardware needed

Table 7-3. Self-Managed Team Implementation Schedule: Mission+St. Joseph's Health System, General Surgery Unit at Mission

Week	Date	Content
1	3/13/97	Review design team role and responsibilities; review role of facilitator; time commitment; team boundaries.
2	3/20/97	Learn meeting effectiveness; learn meeting roles; select design team members to fill meeting roles.
3	3/27/97	Review/develop General Surgery mission, vision, values, and goals for 1997. Decide on number of teams, team roles, and role rotation.
4	4/3/97	Finalize team roles and role rotation; role education needs.
5	4/10/97	Develop team communication plan; plan design process communication.
6	4/17/97	Learn consensus decision making; decide on next series of meetings or retreat.
7	4/24/97	Define team performance measures; measure display.
8	5/1/97	Develop team conflict resolution process.
9	5/8/97	Develop team discipline process.
10	5/15/97	Develop team hiring process.
11	5/22/97	Develop team performance review process.
12	5/29/97	Develop macro flow diagram of key customer processes; do they need to improve or be modified for teams or customers?
13	6/5/97	Design customer survey; conduct survey.
14	6/12/97	Develop scheduling process.
15	6/19/97	Develop budget, cost reduction, financial management process.
16	6/26/97	Develop recognition process and celebrations calendar.
17	7/3/97	Develop orientation for new team members.
18	7/10/97	Plan staff education on teams; implement education.
19	7/17/97	Implement teams.
20	7/24/97	Celebrate!

Figure 7-1. Self-Managed Work Team Implementation Plan

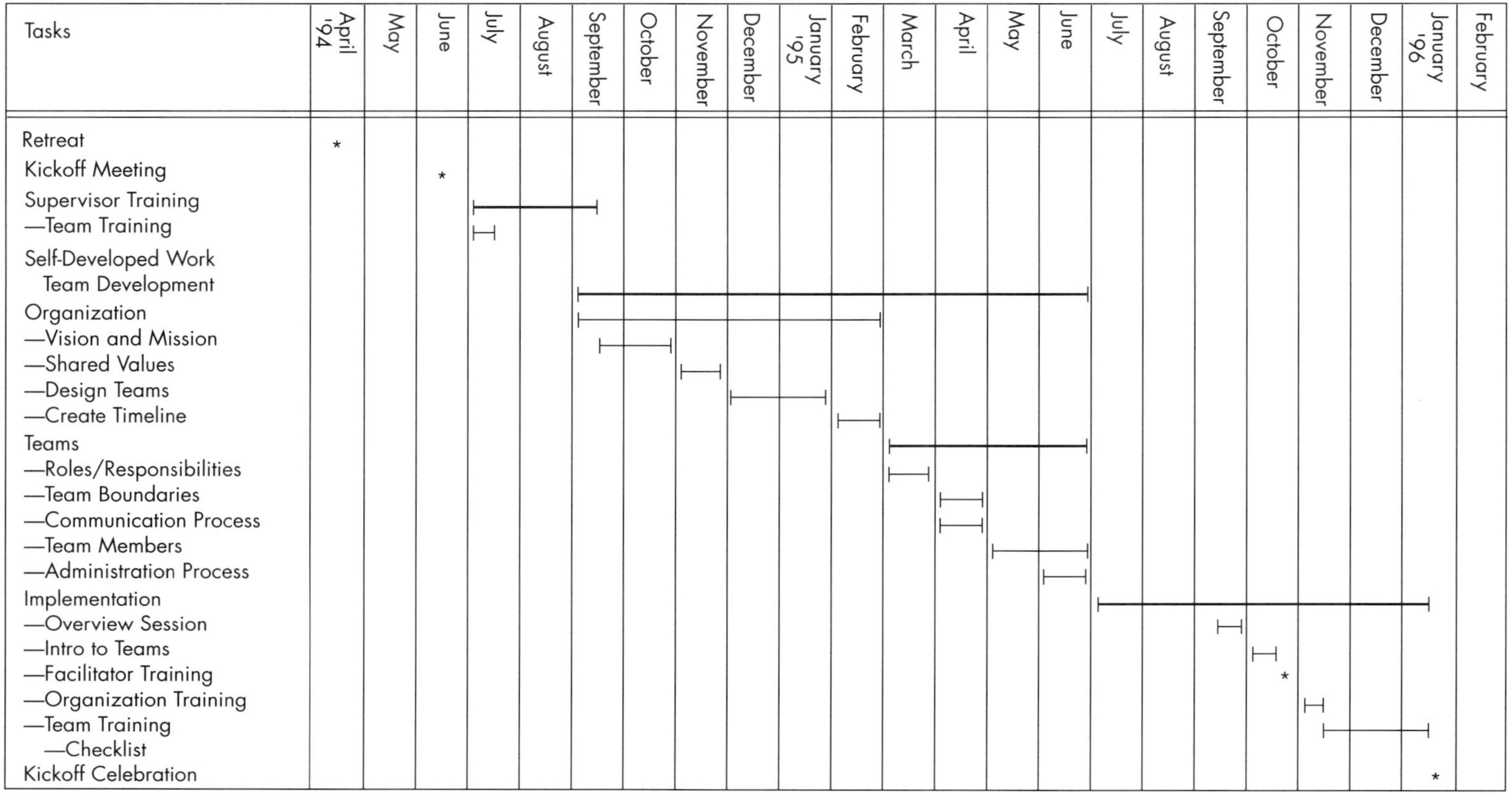

Tasks	April '94	May	June	July	August	September	October	November	December	January '95	February	March	April	May	June	July	August	September	October	November	December	January '96	February
Retreat	*																						
Kickoff Meeting			*																				
Supervisor Training																							
—Team Training																							
Self-Developed Work Team Development																							
Organization																							
—Vision and Mission																							
—Shared Values																							
—Design Teams																							
—Create Timeline																							
Teams																							
—Roles/Responsibilities																							
—Team Boundaries																							
—Communication Process																							
—Team Members																							
—Administration Process																							
Implementation																							
—Overview Session																							
—Intro to Teams																							
—Facilitator Training																			*				
—Organization Training																							
—Team Training																							
—Checklist																							
Kickoff Celebration																						*	

Figure 7-2. Timeline for Conversion to Teams: Respiratory Care Department

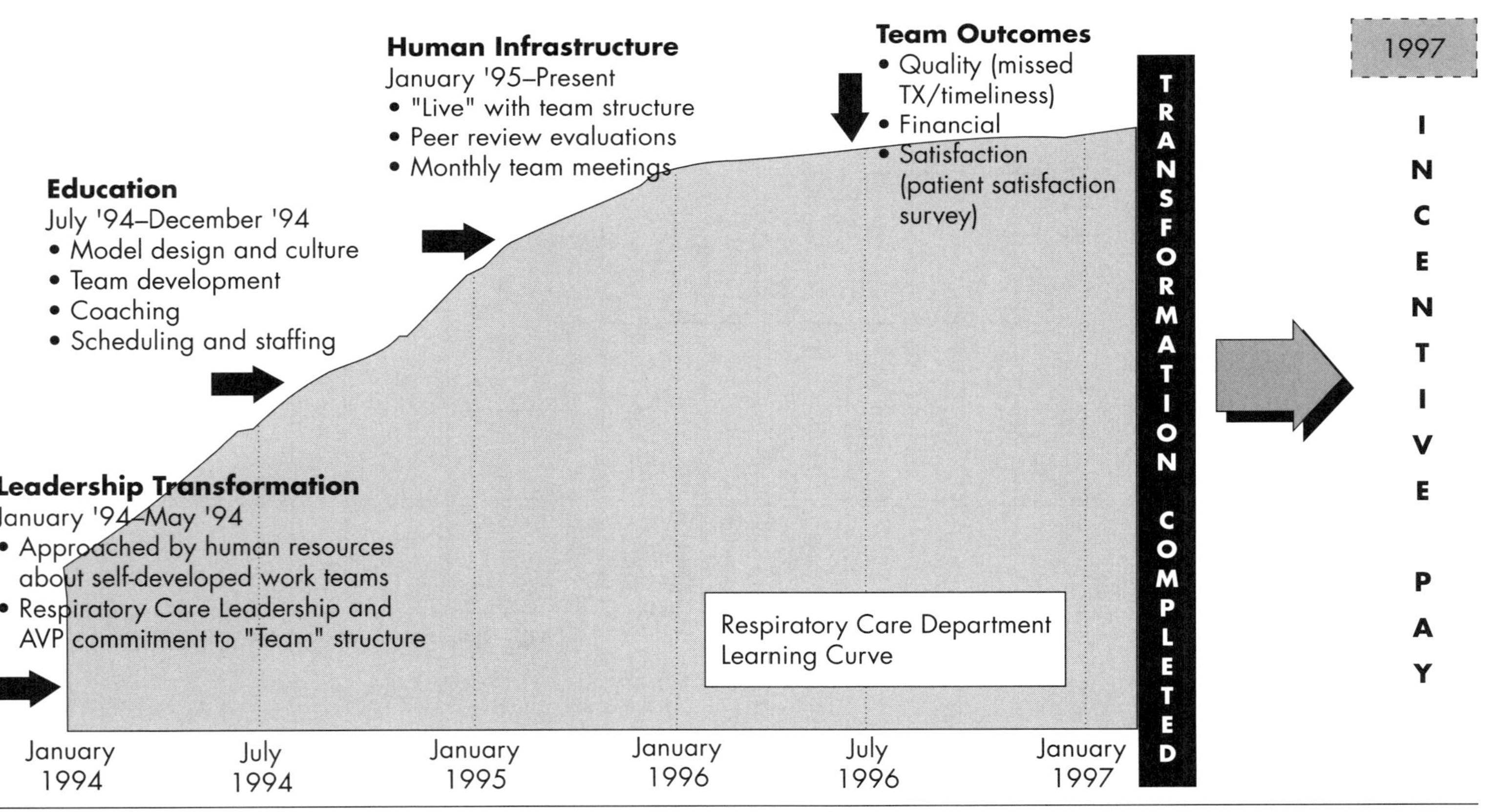

Timeline display must be adapted to the abilities of the design team and the needs of the stakeholders. The design timeline is displayed to let everyone know what the steps in the design process will be, who will be involved on each step, and when the design is expected to be completed. Different circumstances require different timelines, from sundials to digital.

Chapter Wrap-Up

One of the first questions people ask about the implementation of self-managed teams is, How long will this take? A discussion of timelines could attempt to answer this question, but this chapter has not. Design and implementation of self-managed teams has taken anywhere from three months to over two years. The variation is large enough that any estimate would really be a guess, and possibly a dangerously misleading one.

Using a timeline will help the design team identify the steps needed for self-managed team development and implementation. The timeline is a tool. Realizing that there will be challenges along the way helps keep the design process in perspective. Displaying the progress the design team has made is a key function of the timeline. Effective use of a timeline will enable the design team know that they got where they were going.

Team Activity

Creating a Team Timeline

Purpose: To create a timeline for team formation; to encourage input for all design team members.

1. As a group, review the expectations of top management for a target date for team formation. Brainstorm a list of positive and negative forces that will affect completion by the desired date. Come to consensus on an end date, and develop a rationale for adjusting the date if it differs from top management's. Top management then needs to accept the design team's end date. This is the first critical step in allowing the design team to control the process. (Design teams commonly choose a time frame shorter than they will actually need.)
2. Brainstorm the major steps that need to be completed in order to form teams. Place these in the order in which the team wants to work on them.
3. Make a time estimate for each step. Determine the total time for the process by adding up all the individual time estimates. If the total time needed is less than the time allowed for implementation, consider which steps might benefit from more time, or move the implementation date up. If the total time needed is greater than the time allowed, consider which steps can be accelerated, or move the implementation date back.
4. Assign responsibility for each step to a design team member, and develop a tool that will display progress along the timeline. The design team reporter will eventually use this tool to report on the team's accomplishments.

Chapter 8

Holding Effective Meetings

Chapter Preview

"We meet because the knowledge and experience needed in a specific situation are not available in one head."

—*Peter Drucker*

Teams accomplish the majority of their "team" work in meetings. For that reason, the ability to have effective meetings is of paramount importance in team-based organizations. This chapter reviews the components of effective meetings, including agendas, roles, minutes, team member responsibilities, meeting facilitation, and ways of evaluating how effective a meeting has been. There are role descriptions, checklists, and sample formats.

Since the design team goes first, it sets the example for meeting effectiveness. Staff pay attention to the way the design team manages, conducts, and communicates its meetings. This chapter includes sample agendas and information from a first design team meeting. The *first* meeting of the design team is of particular importance because it sets the stage for the design process, as well as for the implementation of self-managed teams. This chapter will help the reader develop a clear plan and agenda for a first meeting and will provide a methodology for all team meetings.

Chapter at a Glance

In this chapter, you will find

- A description of measures to achieve meeting effectiveness
- A description of goals for a first meeting
- Techniques for meeting facilitation
- Techniques for managing conflict and disruptive behaviors
- A team building activity for a first meeting

Meeting Effectiveness

"We all had to follow the meeting rules. You know, have an agenda, take minutes. . . . I thought it was a big waste of time, but then I saw how efficient we were. . . . We got everything done in a short period of time."

—Teleda Waldrip, pharmacy team member, Mission+St. Joseph's Health System

Whether team members are from a clinical or an administrative area, they usually have little patience for long and unproductive meetings. Meetings must be planned and scheduled. Their content must also be planned—that is, they must have an agenda. In addition, group roles must be assigned to ensure that leadership and note-taking tasks are accomplished. By following a few simple measures, meeting planners and meeting participants can help assure that team meetings are models of efficiency and effectiveness.

Meeting Planning

A meeting planning checklist should include the following items:

- Meeting objectives set
- Agenda developed and copies distributed
- Attendees notified
- Guests notified
- Location reserved
- Supplies ordered—for example, flip chart, markers, white board, overhead projector, and slide projector
- Refreshments ordered

Effective meeting planning can be achieved by asking and answering basic questions of who will plan meetings, what will be discussed, when and where the meeting will take place, and how long it will last.

Who? The important players in planning team meetings are the team leader, the note taker, and the meeting facilitator, or coach. The department director, supervisors, and vice president do not attend team meetings and therefore do not need to be involved in planning those meetings.

What? Teams use meetings for communication, updates, clarification of roles and responsibilities, delegation and assignment, goal setting, advocacy, problem solving, decision making, and obtaining input and creative ideas. In planning the meeting, the first question that must be addressed is "What does this meeting need to accomplish?" In order to determine meeting objectives and desired meeting outcomes, the planners will want to review the overall team implementation plan or timeline, as well as what was accomplished at the previous meeting and what was left undone at that meeting. The planners then use this information to develop a meeting agenda.

When? At the very beginning, it helps to decide how often the team will meet and how long each meeting will last. Some teams decide to meet weekly, biweekly, or monthly. They specify a time and location and reserve that space for six months or a year. Once the meeting schedule for the future is arranged, it does not have to be discussed and resolved before each subsequent meeting. To ensure good communication and team spirit, meetings need to occur at least once a month.

Where? Meeting planners must make sure there is a meeting place. The location must have enough seats and any necessary equipment, such as a flip chart or white board. Some teams plan refreshments; others do not.

How Long? Depending on what teams need to accomplish, they may meet in an informal "huddle" for a few minutes at the start or end of the shift, or they may hold a formal meeting with an agenda. Formal meetings usually last one hour. However, there are teams who plan less frequent meetings of one and a half or two hours. Routine team meetings are best when they are kept short. That way the emphasis of the meeting is on being efficient, and team members are not kept away from their work too long.

Meeting Scheduling

It is important that as many team members as possible attend all meetings. Depending on the type of work that the team performs, however, it may be difficult to find a regular meeting time that accommodates everyone's needs. For example, there are some staff—whether clinical or administrative—who cannot leave their work areas to attend a meeting. In such situations, the team needs to find the best time to meet, taking into account all the barriers and working around them when possible. Depending on the constraints, several team members may have to come to work early or stay late. Some team members may have to come to meetings on their days off. Coverage for team meetings may need to be provided by staff members who are not on the team. In some cases, management should be prepared to incur overtime expenses. To emphasize the value and importance of meetings, team members need to know that the time they spend at meetings is compensable as worked time. For example, when team members give up some time off to attend a team meeting, they should be compensated for the time as though they had worked it.

Even with the best planning, sometimes a team member will have to miss a meeting. To help keep absent team members up to date, many teams assign buddies for meeting communication. A person who attends the meeting volunteers to be the buddy of a person who could not attend. After the meeting, the buddies find a time to meet with each other, either by phone or face-to-face, to discuss and review what occurred at the meeting.

Meeting Agenda

At its most basic, a meeting agenda is a list of topics to be discussed or acted upon at the meeting. Every team meeting should have an agenda to provide structure and to ensure that the meeting serves a purpose consistent with the overall implementation plan. Teams can create their agendas on word processors, write them on white boards or flip charts, or handwrite them and then distribute them to all meeting participants. Ideally, the agenda is distributed to team members well before the meeting. Advance knowledge of the agenda gives team members the opportunity to think about particular agenda items and to prepare for the meeting. When it is not practical to distribute agendas in advance, a discussion of the next meeting's topics can be incorporated into the end of each meeting. This will serve as advance notice.

Agendas have certain standard components, such as items for opening and closing the meeting:

- Opening the meeting
  —Reviewing the meeting roles
  —Reviewing the minutes of the last team meeting
  —Refreshing everyone on the meeting ground rules
- Closing the meeting
  —Summarizing decisions and assignments
  —Planning the next meeting
  —Evaluating the effectiveness of the meeting

In addition, the agenda can include meeting objectives, as well as individual items. While the agenda is being developed, it is helpful to estimate the time that each agenda item will consume. Old business from the previous meeting is placed on the agenda before new business. The name of the person who will lead the discussion of each agenda item is included next to the item. If the team wants to hear reports from team members who have role responsibilities, or from team members who are working on goals or projects, these reports are placed on the agenda before new business. (See figure 8-1 for a sample agenda format and figure 8-2 for an example.)

Group Roles

Self-managed teams depend on shared leadership. This means that everyone has a role to play at meetings. Nevertheless, in order for a meeting to be effective, there are primary roles that must be formally designated. These roles are the meeting leader, or team leader, the note taker, and the timekeeper. In addition, there are secondary roles that can be filled or not.

Figure 8-1. Sample Agenda Format

Hospital/System
Meeting Name/Group:
Date:________
Time (start to end): __________
Place:__________________________

AGENDA

1. **Welcome** ■ The purpose of our meeting today ■ Our meeting roles Team Leader:_____________ Note Taker:____________ Timekeeper:_____________ ■ Minutes review ■ Ground Rules Review	Team Leader
2. **Old Business** ■ Why this item is on the agenda ■ What we hope to accomplish today ■ Discussion or Input/Information Only/ Decision ■ Summary before moving to next agenda item	Topic Leader
3. **Old Business** ■ Why this item is on the agenda ■ What we hope to accomplish today ■ Discussion or Input/Information Only/ Decision ■ Summary before moving to next agenda item	Topic Leader
4. **New Business** ■ Why this item is on the agenda ■ What we hope to accomplish today ■ Discussion or Input/Information Only/Decision ■ Summary before moving to next agenda item	Topic Leader
5. **Summary, Evaluation, and Adjourn** ■ Review of topics discussed, decisions made, input received ■ Review of assignments made ■ Scheduling and topics for next meeting ■ Evaluation of meeting	Team Leader or Summarizer

Figure 8-2. Example of an Agenda for a Design Team Meeting

Respiratory Care Department Self-Managed Teams
Design Team Meeting
June 19, 1996 5:00–6:30 P.M.
Private Dining Room 1

OBJECTIVES

1 Develop an understanding of the role and responsibilities of the design team.
2. Create a communication process for the design team and the rest of respiratory care.
3. Learn meeting effectiveness techniques.
4. Practice some self-managed team skills.
5. Identify meeting schedule and meeting requirements.

AGENDA

1. Welcome Review of meeting objectives	Liz Becker-Reems 5:00–5:05 P.M.
2. Getting Acquainted	The Group 5:05–5:30 P.M.
3. The role of the design team Design team customers Design team services Design team effectiveness 1. Learn about self-managed teams 2. Practice self-managed team skills 3. Learn about technical and social system design 4. Design self-managed teams for the department 5. Design technical and social systems for self-managed teams 6. Develop the education plan 7. Develop the team implementation plan 8. Develop the team effectiveness evaluation process 9. Implement the evaluation 10. Make revisions to the self-managed teams based on the revisions 11. Communicate	Liz and Group 5:30–6:00 P.M.
4. Meeting Effectiveness Team leader Note taker Timekeeper	Liz and Group 6:00–6:15 P.M.
5. Schedule for our meetings	Group 6:15–6:25 P.M.
6. Summary, Evaluation, and Adjourn	Liz 6:25–6:30 P.M.

Meeting Leader The meeting leader, or team leader, is responsible for opening the meeting, conducting the meeting, and closing the meeting. The leader follows the agenda carefully, keeping his or her eyes on the time frames allotted for each agenda item and trying to adhere to those time frames. The leader encourages discussion and participation but brings discussions to a close when team members start to lose their focus or when time runs out.

> Meeting Leader
>
> - Plans the meeting
> - Develops the agenda
> - Conducts the meeting
> - Manages participation
> - Closes the meeting

Since the agenda serves as a road map for the meeting, team members know what they are supposed to accomplish, in what order, and how long they have to accomplish it. It sounds simple, but in reality conducting the meeting is very complex. Team leaders and team members can get sidetracked. Discussions can stretch the time limits. Someone who is on the agenda may fail to attend the meeting.

The team leader navigates these bumps in the road by focusing on the agenda, being flexible, and managing the participation of the team members. The team leader tries to provide an opportunity for everyone to share thoughts and input. He or she makes sure that the meeting isn't dominated by one or two people and that quiet people get a chance to participate. The team leader helps control conflicts and disruptive behavior while demonstrating respect for all team members.

Note Taker The note taker makes a written record of the meeting—the minutes. On some self-managed teams, the note taker role rotates from member to member, meeting by meeting; on others, it is a permanent role that rotates only when all other roles rotate. For continuity and follow-through, the latter is the better arrangement.

Because the note taker must document any conclusion reached about an agenda item, he or she often asks questions to clarify. In this way, the minutes become an accurate summary of the meeting. In addition, the note taker's

> Note Taker
>
> - Notes attendance
> - Documents decisions and assignments
> - Summarizes discussions
> - Notes future events and plans
> - Summarizes at the end of the meeting
> - Writes the meeting minutes and distributes them

questions may help clarify the outcome for other team members who were not sure what conclusion had been reached on the topic.

The note taker also works with the team leader to put together the agenda for the next meeting. From the note taker's minutes, it is easy to determine which items need to be included on the next agenda.

Timekeeper The timekeeper helps everyone keep track of the time. He or she documents the start and end times of a meeting and shares that information with the note taker. The timekeeper uses the time frames noted on the agenda as a guide and reminds the team when the time allotted to a particular agenda item is almost used up, or when the end time of the entire meeting is drawing near. The timekeeper must be assertive; when the team becomes engrossed in a topic, they may not respond to gentle reminders that it is time to move along.

Timekeeper

- Notes start and end times of the meeting
- Keeps track of agenda topic times
- Gives a warning when time is almost up

Secondary Roles Secondary roles include the cheerleader, the goal getter, the devil's advocate, and the summarizer. These roles can be assigned, but they are usually merely discussed so that team members understand that they are expected to exhibit these behaviors.

- *Cheerleader:* The cheerleader gives the entire team positive feedback and encourages individual team members. Cheerleaders are sensitive to how the group is behaving and how group members seem to feel. By commenting on what they observe, cheerleaders reduce tension and help resolve disagreements. Comments that cheerleaders might make during meetings include:
  —Positive feedback: "Good idea!"
  —Encouraging other's involvement: "Let's hear from Mary; she hasn't had a chance to speak yet."
  —Expressing feelings: "It looks like we are all comfortable with that method."
- *Goal getter:* The goal getter tries to keep the team focused on its tasks. Goal getters warn the team when it starts to stray off the topic. They summarize in the middle of discussion to clarify points of agreement and disagreement. They help maintain a steady pace in the meeting and move the team toward the completion of meeting objectives by the end of the meeting.
- *Devil's advocate:* The devil's advocate takes the opposite point of view from the one being expressed by the majority. This role is important because it

helps the team look at a decision from all directions, before the decision is made. Devil's advocates help improve the quality of thinking that occurs at team meetings. Rather than attacking an individual or a viewpoint, however, devil's advocates focus on alternatives. They usually say, "Let's look at it from a different point of view."

- *Summarizer:* The summarizer makes sure that each agenda item is summarized before the team leader moves to the next agenda item. Summarizers may ask for everyone's attention before summarizing by saying, "Let's see whether we all understand what was just decided." They then proceed with the summary. If team members are confused, or if their interpretations vary, it comes out before the team has moved to the next agenda item.

All the secondary roles help the team leader manage the meeting. They serve as extra eyes and ears, noting when the team is struggling and when the team is perhaps moving too fast and not hearing from all team members. All roles—primary and secondary—exist to help manage the meeting and make it as effective as possible.

Steps in the Meeting

The first part of conducting the meeting is starting it on time. The team leader needs to decide whether to start before all members arrive in order to start on time, or whether to start late and wait for everyone to arrive. If it is a ground rule to start on time, then the team leader starts the meeting on time whether everyone is there or not.

At the start of the meeting, the team leader reviews the objectives of the meeting, the roles, and the ground rules. The team leader then calls on the note taker to present minutes from the previous meeting.

During the meeting, the team leader introduces each agenda item, explaining why it is on the agenda, specifying what the team needs to do, and asking for discussion and input when appropriate. The team leader uses meeting facilitation skills to obtain and manage participation. The leader clarifies and summarizes discussions and checks frequently for group consensus.

Meeting Evaluation

At the close of the meeting, the team leader asks the note taker to summarize the decisions and assignments made during the meeting. The team plans the agenda for the next meeting, including items that were not concluded during the current meeting and that must be raised again. If the team wishes to hear reports from team members who were given assignments, the reports are added to the agenda for the next meeting.

Finally, the team evaluates how well they managed the meeting. Although the team leader leads the meeting, it is the responsibility of every team member to help manage the meeting. The team evaluates whether the agenda was followed, whether the meeting started and ended on time, whether the goals of the meeting were accomplished, whether everyone participated, and whether the team sought consensus for decisions and summarized decisions during and at the end of the meeting. A standardized form can be a helpful guide for meeting evaluation. (See figure 8-3).

Meeting Minutes

In writing the minutes, note takers do not make a word-for-word record as the meeting progresses. Instead, they try to capture the key discussion points and summarize them. For each agenda item, the note taker documents the

Figure 8-3. Team Process Evaluation

GOAL GETTING

1 2 3 4 5 6 7 8 9 10

Team has no agenda; team does not follow.
Team has structured agenda; team stays on track.

PARTICIPATION

1 2 3 4 5 6 7 8 9 10

Meeting is dominated by a few members; others don't participate; few enjoy meeting.
Everyone contributes and participates; members all involved in decisions. Group has fun; smiles evident.

LEADERSHIP

1 2 3 4 5 6 7 8 9 10

Meeting started late; goals and rules not clarified; team roles not assigned.
Meeting started/ended on time; goals, rules, and roles were clarified.

SUMMARIZING

1 2 3 4 5 6 7 8 9 10

There was no checking for group consensus, no clarifying opinions, and no review at meeting's end; confusion exists.
Meeting leadership is shared; group helps manage meeting; meanings/decisions are clarified and restated for understanding.

conclusion or outcome. They do not need to record who said what. They look for a brief way to tell what happened in the meeting—a summary.

The note taker starts the minutes with a list of who is present and who is absent. Following along with the agenda, the note taker writes down the topic and what happens with it. The note taker follows the discussion and notes any decisions that are made. If there is an update or report on a previous assignment, the note taker may write down key points that are raised. In addition, the note taker always documents new assignments and items that are tabled until the next meeting.

Depending on the team, the meeting minutes may be prepared on a word processor or typewriter. The minutes may also be handwritten. The method is not important as long as the result is legible. The minutes need to be completed shortly after the meeting and distributed to the attendees. Since the minutes serve as formal documentation of the team's actions, they form a permanent record and a history for the team. Note takers often become the team's historians.

The format shown in figure 8-4 is effective for team meeting notes. It identifies the agenda topics in one column, key elements of the discussion in a second column, and decisions made about the action needed in a third column. If assignments are made, they stand out, in this third column, separated from the text of the discussion.

Figure 8-4. Minutes Format

Regional Surgical Specialists
Self-Managed Team
MINUTES FORMAT
(Date)
(Meeting Location)

AGENDA	DISCUSSION	ACTION NEEDED
Welcome	Liz Becker-Reems opened the meeting.	
Self-Managed Teams		
Meeting Effectiveness		
Team Roles		
Baseline Survey Results		
Next Meeting	The next meeting is scheduled for January 29, from 8–9 A.M.	

The First Design Team Meeting

"We were all there and excited about our first design team meeting. Some of us had to make baby-sitting arrangements; others had to come in early or stay late. We felt like we were embarking on an adventure."

—Debbie Frisbee, RN, general surgery design team

The first meeting of any group sets the tone for future meetings. If it is poorly planned and poorly conducted, the group or team loses energy and enthusiasm. If the meeting is well structured and well managed, the team gains energy and develops momentum for future meetings and interactions. First meetings are organizational meetings. They help the group define who they are, what the meeting purpose is, and how their meetings will be conducted.

At the first meeting, group members look around to see who else is there. They make judgments about how effective they expect the meetings and the process to be, based on their past experiences with the individuals who are there. There is energy and excitement in the first meeting, as well as a sense of anxiety. Group members wonder whether they will be successful, whether they have the knowledge they need, whether they will have the courage to speak up when they disagree. They may wonder what kind of pressure they will get from coworkers who are not a part of the team. There is usually a sense of pride at being asked to participate in the team's project or goal. Team members are interested in helping with the project and look forward to sharing their knowledge and ideas.

The group may also have a degree of cynicism. There may be participants who are skeptical about how successful the group will be given barriers and constraints that have derailed groups before. As the team leader looks around the room, he or she is looking at the raw material and resources that are available to accomplish the task the group has accepted. To get the group started right, the team leader will first want to spend a little time on team building. (See the team activity at the end of this chapter.) When the group feels comfortable as a group, members are more likely to participate, to be honest and open, and to share agreements, disagreements, and wild or very creative ideas. The group will be more ready to discuss issues important to its life as a team: its purpose, goals, and roles as a team and standards, ground rules, and a schedule for its meetings.

Clarification of Purpose, Goals, and Roles

When the airline hostess announces to the passengers before the plane takes off: "This is flight 242 to Chicago," she is clarifying for the group their purpose and goal. When any group gets together for the first time, it helps to check that everyone clearly understands why they have gathered together. The meeting leader may include a statement of purpose on the agenda for everyone to read and contemplate. Or the leader may open a discussion of the purpose of the group, asking group members why they think it has been formed. In either case, the group should decide what its purpose is, and what it is not. For example, "We are here to develop a plan for approval by administration. We are not expected to implement the plan."

When a group gets together for the first time, it should also define its role in relation to the role of the facilitator and in relation to the role, needs, and expectations of management. A member of management may attend the first meeting of a group to help clarify its purpose and to define management's expectations. (See table 8-1.)

Review of Meeting Standards

At the first meeting, the facilitator, or another designated person such as an educator, reviews the components of effective meetings. This helps the team establish standards for its meetings. The following are elements of effective meetings (the first three are reviewed elsewhere in this chapter in more detail):

- Group roles
- Meeting agenda
- Meeting minutes
- Ground rules

Table 8-1. Role Clarification

The Group's Role	The Facilitator's Role	Management's Role
The group's primary role is to accomplish its purpose. Secondary roles for the group may include ▪ Communicating its progress ▪ Writing a report ▪ Investigating a problem ▪ Gathering data	The facilitator's primary role is to help the group accomplish its purpose. Secondary roles for the facilitator may include ▪ Facilitating each group meeting ▪ Coaching the meeting leader ▪ Coaching individual group members ▪ Helping the group obtain resources ▪ Helping the group learn effective group process skills	Management's primary role is to help the team understand its framework. To do this management communicates ▪ The big picture and how the team fits in ▪ An outline of performance expectations ▪ Boundaries and resources for the team A secondary role for management is to ▪ Give feedback to the team

Establishment of Ground Rules

A ground rule is a behavioral expectation. For instance, if the team expects everyone to be present on time for the start of the meeting, that is a statement of a desired behavior. The following are examples of ground rules that teams might set:

- Attendance expectations: who should be notified if a group member can't attend
- Start and end on time
- Don't criticize people, criticize ideas
- If you disagree, always state why
- Decision method: majority or consensus?
- Interruptions: avoid interrupting each other, beepers, phone calls
- Respect for each other's ideas
- Participation
- Meeting evaluation at each meeting
- Confidentiality
- Repeated ground rule violations: how should they be handled?

Establishment of Schedule

To establish the meeting schedule, the team needs to decide how often it will meet, which day of the week, what time the meetings will start, and how long they will last. In addition, the team needs to select a meeting location that is convenient and available on a continuing basis.

Once the group has clarified its purpose and role, reviewed its standards, and set its ground rules and schedule, the first meeting is basically over. At the close of the first meeting, the team leader can ask the group how they feel about the meeting, the amount accomplished, and the pace of discussion and decision making. The team then decides the agenda for the next meeting and then adjourns.

Meeting Facilitation

"The key is to create an environment that shifts attention away from the individual participant and toward community expression."

—Michael Schrage

Whether the team depends on a coach, an outside facilitator, or the team leader and team members to facilitate the meeting, certain techniques help make meetings more productive. Good meeting facilitators are interested in the topics being discussed, but they are also interested in the quality of the participation that the group exhibits. Team members who do not see the benefits of meeting facilitation are usually only interested in expressing their own viewpoints and persuading others that they are correct; this does not work to the advantage of the team or the attainment of its goals. The team profits from balanced participation by all team members. Team members should work to develop a meeting environment that is friendly, supportive, and nonjudgmental.

Meeting facilitators work to improve the quality of the meeting by bringing out areas of agreement, opposing views, facts as well as opinions, and feelings the group has about the issues and problems being discussed. They work to maintain a feeling of respect for all. Facilitators use particular techniques to gain participation, to clarify what has been said, to keep the team on track, and to handle agreement and disagreement.

Eliciting Participation

A primary benefit of teams is that they bring the diversity of their members' ideas, experiences, knowledge, and creativity to a problem. When some people are hogging the floor and others are not participating, diversity of opinion is diminished. Failure to achieve balanced participation may mean that the team will attempt to solve a problem in a way that is less effective than the solution that might have been reached had full participation been achieved. It may also mean that a new program will stumble because it addresses the concerns of only a few team members. Facilitators can use the techniques outlined in table 8-2 to gain balanced participation.

Clarifying Ideas

When the facilitator reads confusion on the faces of team member, and no one has asked for an explanation, the facilitator acts like a mirror and states that he or she has observed confusion. This mirroring technique is one method for stepping in and helping clarify what has been said or what has been observed. If clarification is not sought, the team may miss a vital point or may move in an unwise direction because it did not perceive the meaning or body language expressed by some members. There are several techniques that can be used to clarify, which are outlined in table 8-3.

Keeping the Team on Track

Team members have many subjects on their minds and are tempted to use to team meetings to address issues that are not on the agenda. When a meeting is allowed to wander from the agenda, team members feel frustrated, distracted, or bored while they wait to return to the topic originally under discussion. Straying from scheduled topics threatens the team's efficiency and keeps it from accomplishing desired results within established time frames. The facilitator can use the techniques outlined in table 8-4 to keep discussions focused.

Table 8-2. Specific Techniques for Eliciting Group Participation

Objective	Technique	What to Say
Include quiet members: Bring silent or hesitant team members into the discussion; seek out opinions and ideas	Call on someone by name Encourage someone to continue with a thought or idea Relate the topic to a previous discussion	"Mary, how would this work in your area?" "How would this affect the process as you described it?" "Earlier you described the staff's reaction to the proposal. How do you think they will react to this new information?"
Initiate discussion: Start the discussion, propose ideas and solutions, present opposing opinions to help the discussion	Ask for an opinion Offer an opinion Seek an additional or opposing point of view	"What would you like to do?" or "What do you think about . . .?" "I'd like to suggest . . ." "Can anyone think of an alternative?"
Get people thinking: Ask questions that seek elaboration and information rather than "yes" or "no" answers.	Such questions start with How What How much Who Describe	"How should we handle this?" "How can we improve our results?" "What should we do next?" "What seems to be causing the problem?" "How much information will they need?" "Who else needs to be involved?" "Describe how that would work."
Encourage: Show interest and friendliness, be supportive, give approval	Body language Words and sounds	Smiles, eye contact, nodding Yes, uh-huh
Share feelings: Express emotions, demonstrate sensitivity, bring feelings into the open	Express concerns Express positive feelings Label the feelings of the group	"I feel worried, scared, unsure, anxious, overwhelmed . . ." "I feel happy, enthusiastic, relieved, glad . . ." "It seems like we are all feeling a lot of stress . . ."

Table 8-3. Specific Techniques for Clarifying

Objective	Technique	What to Say
Rephrase: Express the gist of what the speaker has said, while adding your own perception of the meaning	Repeat the basic thoughts and ideas of the speaker	"What I hear you saying is . . ." or "It sounds like . . ." or "In other words . . ."
Repeat: Make sure that the speaker has not misspoken, and make sure the group heard what was said	State word-for-word what the speaker just said	"You said . . ."
Question: Help the group understand what was said by asking the speaker to elaborate or define	Ask for more information	"Tell us what caused you to come to that conclusion" or "Who else was involved?" or "Describe the circumstances surrounding that event."
	Ask for a definition	"That is a pretty powerful word. When you use it, what are you thinking about specifically?"
Mirror: Help the group become aware of a behavior it is exhibiting	State what was observed without making any judgment	"I am noticing that Tom and Mary talk to each other when Betty is speaking. Has anyone else noticed this?"
Summarize: Use a few brief sentences to describe an entire discussion	Try to capture the main points of the discussion in a few words	"And so, in summary, we understand that the presentation was successful, even though the audiovisual equipment wasn't working."

(Continued on next page)

Table 8-4. Specific Techniques for Keeping the Team on Track

Objective	Technique	What to Say
One issue at a time: Get the team back on the subject that was originally being discussed	Ask the group to return to the topic under discussion originally	"Let's finish our discussion of the upcoming survey, before we discuss the location of our retreat."
Parking lot: Keep track of related issues, while focusing on the issue under discussion	Use a flip chart to write down related topics so they can be addressed at another time	"Let's put that item in the parking lot and if we don't get to it today, we can put it on our next agenda."
Summarize: Pull the attention of the team back to the topic	Repeat the progress that has been made on the topic to this point	"Could someone summarize and tell us where we are on this topic?"

Handling Agreement and Disagreement

Whether a team member is agreeing or disagreeing with an idea, it is most helpful to focus on the topic rather than the person. To facilitate participation, team members speak to the center of the table when agreeing and disagreeing, rather than to the person who expressed the idea. Agreements are expressed in short and simple statements. Disagreements generally include more information to explain the other point of view. The facilitator can use the techniques outlined in table 8-5 to handle both agreement and disagreement.

Using a Facilitator

The role of the facilitator or coach is important to the effectiveness of the group process. The facilitator can identify what is happening in the group more easily than those who are actually participating in the discussion. Facilitators can help involve those who are not fully participating; they can help clarify what is being said in a team discussion; they can keep the team on track; and they can help identify points of agreement and disagreement. Meetings move faster and are better able to achieve positive results with the help of a facilitator. Facilitators are especially helpful when disagreement is so fierce that the meeting becomes a shouting match, or when people become so angry that they want to leave before the meeting is adjourned.

Table 8-5. Specific Techniques for Handling Agreements and Disagreements

Agreement and Disagreement	Technique	What to Say
Agreement: The facilitator notices an agreement but it has not been expressed	Ask about the agreement in a positive way	"John, do you support the idea of . . ." or "Mary, are you agreeing that we should . . ."
	State the mood of the group even though they have not expressed it	"I don't hear any disagreements. Do we all agree with Dan's idea?"
Premature agreement: The facilitator believes the team has not fully explored the issue—agreement seems more important to the group than making the right decision	Ask the team to brainstorm alternatives	Before we finish this discussion, let's brainstorm alternatives."
	Ask the team what could go wrong if the decision is implemented	"If we implement this decision, what might go wrong?"
	Ask the team what the opposite point of view is	"If someone disagreed with us, what might they say?"
Disagreement: The facilitator senses anger, hesitancy, or disagreement, but it has not been expressed or it has been discounted	Help individuals express their disagreement in a positive way	"Mary this is a new way to look at the information. Many members of this group may not have thought of it that way before. John, tell the group how you see it."
	Ask for alternatives to diffuse the focus on the disagreement	"We have heard one idea. What are some alternative ways of addressing the problem?"
	Bring the group back to a disagreement that was ignored	"Earlier in our discussion you expressed an idea that is somewhat different. Share it with us again."
	Help the group see the benefits in a disagreement	"Let's try to look at it from our detractors' point of view, and we might learn more about the barriers that they see."

Conflict Management

"Where there is much desire to learn, there of necessity will be much arguing, much writing, many opinions: for opinion in good men is but knowledge in the making."

—*John Milton,* Areopagitica

The price of open and lively discussion among team members is the possibility of conflicts and disruptive behaviors. Conflicts among team members can have a negative or a positive impact on the team. Conflicts have a negative impact when they inhibit constructive communication and cause team members to stop talking and listening to each other. Conflicts have a positive impact when they cause team members to consider different viewpoints and look at alternatives. Such conflicts promote learning and encourage creativity. When conflicts increase the flow of creative ideas they are positive.

Disruptive behaviors are never positive. They destroy the structure that the team has built for itself and weaken the bonds that hold the team together. When a team member or facilitator notices disruptive or nonproductive behaviors, he or she needs to take immediate action. Without intervention to stop the disruption, the team will turn away from the meeting and be distracted from its goals. Methods for dealing with disruptive behaviors are outlined in table 8.6.

Chapter Wrap-Up

Teams function primarily through face-to-face communication in team meetings. Whether the meeting is a five-minute huddle at the end or beginning of the shift or a formal hour-long session, teams can learn techniques to make their time together more productive. In particular, team meetings need structure. They should have clearly defined agendas, roles, minutes, and ground rules.

The first meeting of any group is a trend-setting event. To start the team off right, first meetings need to include time for team building, clarifying the purpose of the team, defining meeting structure and ground rules, and scheduling future meetings.

All meetings benefit from the presence of a facilitator. Meeting facilitators observe the group process and help ensure that it is positive and constructive. Facilitators use a number of techniques to encourage participation by the entire group, open sharing of ideas, learning from each other, and the development of camaraderie. In keeping with the goal of self-management, any team member can use these techniques to help ensure positive meeting outcomes. Meetings are the workplace for teams.

Table 8-6. Specific Techniques for Dealing with Disruptive Behaviors

Disruptive Behavior	Technique	What to Say
Hogging: One or more people are talking too much. Their stories take too long; they comment on everything. Other people are not given time to participate.	Use a round-the-table discussion method	"On this item, let's go around the table and hear what each member has to say."
	Add "balanced participation" as a ground rule	"To avoid problems of not hearing from everyone, or hearing from one or two people too much, let's add balanced participation as a ground rule."
	Ask the dominant speaker to let others have a turn	"John, let's hear from the others on this topic."
Interrupting: A member of the team starts talking before another member has finished what he or she is saying	Point out the behavior to the interrupter	"Mary, let's let John finish his thought, and then we will hear from you."
	Add "no interrupting of others" as a ground rule	"Let's add 'no interruptions' to our list of ground rules."
Ignoring others' input: Someone on the team speaks, and no one gives any comment, idea, or feedback	Encourage team members to build on each others statements or comments	"As we discuss this item, try to build on or elaborate on the comments of the previous speakers."
	Call attention to the failure of the team to comment on someone's input	"Before we move on, does anyone have any feedback on John's last statement?"
Diminishing others' ideas: A team member finds fault with someone else's ideas without explaining why	Ask fault finders to explain their reasoning	"John, you have stated that Mary's idea won't work. Will you explain why you think it won't work?"
	Ask the speaker to elaborate on his or her reasoning	"Mary, we haven't spent much time discussing your idea. Why don't you give us more information on what you are thinking."

(Continued on next page)

Table 8-6. (Continued)

Disruptive Behavior	Technique	What to Say
Shouting, swearing, or other abusive behaviors: A team member begins acting very disruptively, becoming verbally or nonverbally abusive	Call the team member(s) to account	"Mary, we do not (swear, shout, pound the table) in our team meetings."
	Remove arguing team members from the meeting	"John and Mary, if you will come with me, we can continue this discussion next door, so we don't further disrupt the meeting."
	Ask the arguers to delay their confrontation	"John and Mary, will you continue your discussion after the meeting?"
	Bring the behavior to the attention of the team member	"Mary, you are raising your voice."
	Stop the meeting and give the group time to calm down	"Let's all sit quietly for five minutes, and think back over the issues we were discussing. Then, we can calmly review the areas of agreement, and the areas of disagreement."

Suggested Readings

Goal/QPC and Joiner Associates, Inc., editor. *The Team Memory Jogger.* Methuen, MA: Goal/QPC and Joiner Associates, Inc., 1995, chap. 5.

Huszczo, G. E. *Tools for Team Excellence.* Palo Alto, CA: Davies-Black, 1996.

Schrage, M. *No More Teams.* New York: Doubleday, 1995.

Schwarz, R. M. *The Skilled Facilitator.* San Francisco: Jossey-Bass, 1995.

Sholtes, P. R. *The Team Handbook: How to Use Teams to Improve Quality.* Madison, WI: Joiner Associates, Inc., 1993, chap. 6.

Team Activity

Team Building at a First Meeting

Purpose: To develop and expand the comfort level that group members have with each other.

Directions: Have all members of the group tell a little about themselves. They can give their names, their jobs, their departments, lengths of service, how long they have lived in the community, where they were born, where they went to school, whether they are married, whether they have children or pets, and what their favorite leisure activities are.

Sharing personal information is important. It helps people of different backgrounds identify things they have in common.

Chapter 9

Technical System Development

Chapter Preview

"The application of knowledge to work explosively increased productivity. For hundreds of years there had been no increase in the ability of workers to turn out goods or move goods. Machines created greater capacity. But workers themselves were no more productive than they had been in the workshops of ancient Greece, in building the roads of Imperial Rome, or in producing the highly prized woollen cloth which gave Renaissance Florence its wealth. But within a few years after Taylor began to apply knowledge to work, productivity began to rise at a rate of 3.5 to 4 percent compound a year—which means doubling every eighteen years or so. Since Taylor began, productivity has increased some fiftyfold in all advance countries."

—Peter Drucker

Self-managed work teams provide the opportunity for people to create technical breakthroughs. Technical system design was introduced in chapter 5 and is explained in detail in this chapter. The relationship of reengineering, process improvements, and reorganization of individual work into group work is explained. This chapter discusses the importance of "talking to the customer" and describes ways to use customer input in technical system design. Roles will change when new work designs are implemented and the role changes described in chapter 4 are discussed in the light of technical system changes. Communication and education on the new work design are essential, and tips are given to ensure that communications are understood. Problems will inevitably arise during the technical system design process; this chapter gives examples of how teams can overcome these obstacles.

Chapter at a Glance

In this chapter, you will find

- A description of the elements of technical system design
- A summary of changes in stakeholders' roles
- An explanation of the importance of communication
- A discussion of obstacles to technical system design
- Two team activities to encourage dialogue among design team members and communication with stakeholders

Technical System Design

"There is nothing more difficult to take in hand, more perilous to conduct and more uncertain in its success, than to take the lead in the introduction of a new order of things."

—*Niccolò Machiavelli*

Humans have done work since the beginning of civilization; nomads built fires, peasants farmed crops, assembly workers built cars, and programmers wrote software. Work has been done in every age, but the analysis of work did not begin in earnest until 1881. Frederick Taylor was the first person to study the design of work and to suggest new ways to make it more productive. Taylor's "scientific principles" for work laid a foundation for the next hundred years; his philosophy has culminated in the understanding that it is most often the system, and not the people, that fails. W. Edwards Deming took his knowledge of work design to Japan and helped the Japanese earn the respect of the rest of the world for the quality of the products they deliver to their customers. Self-managed work teams are intended to do work. The technical aspect of work is therefore the starting point for the design of teams.

Flow of the Work System

Technology refers to the application of knowledge to tools, processes, and products. This is what is taught in engineering schools. The basic flow of any technical work system is illustrated in figure 9-1.

Technical systems are based on knowledge of the expectations of customers, who receive value from the output of products they use. Information in the form of feedback is used to organize work for workers in an efficient and effective process. The requirements for tools, inputs, and suppliers are determined by data identified in the design of the technical system.

☞ **Team Tip:** It is easy to get bogged down in the minutia of current work processes. The key to drawing a macroflow diagram is to think big!

The first job of the design team is to map the basic flow of its technical work system. The team creates a macroflow diagram—a visual explanation of the major work steps done to meet customer expectations. Communication and openness are especially important at this stage, so it is helpful if a facilitator participates in the drawing process. Exchange of ideas and perceptions helps all team members gain clarity and develop a shared mental model of the technical work system. The first pass at listing customer expectations,

Figure 9-1. Basic Flow of a Technical Work System

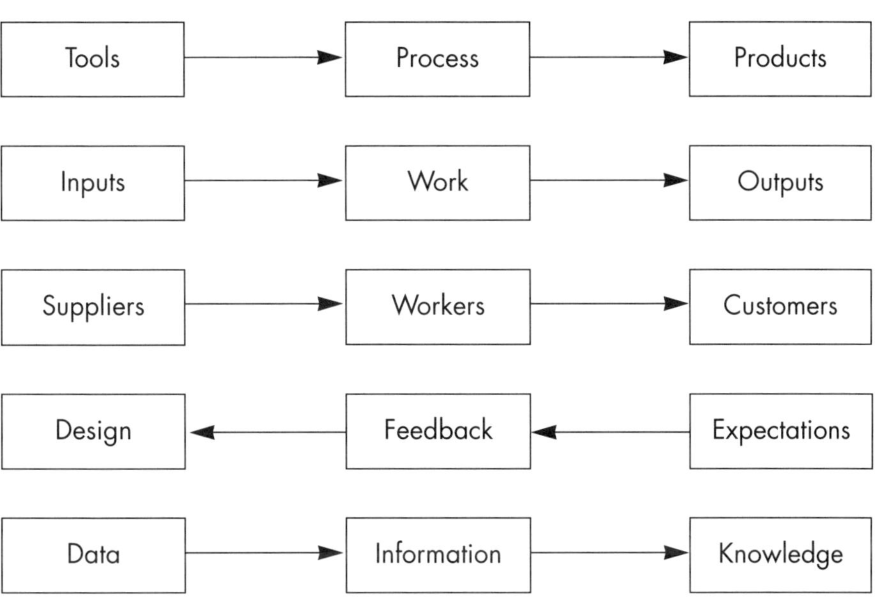

drawing the flow of work processes, and identifying inputs for work will not be totally accurate or complete. The intention is to get the design team thinking about work as a technical system that is focused on meeting customer needs. See team activity 1 at the end of this chapter for the steps in drawing a macroflow diagram. Figure 9-2 shows an example of a macroflow diagram for a hospital medication system.

Data collection begins when the design team agrees on a list of significant customer expectations, on the macroflow diagram, and on a list of major inputs. A structure for data collection is suggested in table 9-1. This table is a summary of ideas from *Design for Total Quality: A Workbook for Socio-Technical Design* by Lawrence M. Miller.[1] This workbook provides a detailed explanation of technical design.

Members of the design team take the macroflow diagram and ask their customers, suppliers, and coworkers the data collection questions listed in table 9-1. The feedback that design team members receive then helps them to revise the macroflow diagram to improve the system.

The feedback process will also lead the design team to major subsystems in the technical work system. Subsystems are work processes used to produce intermediate products required to transform original inputs into outputs needed to meet customer needs. Flowcharts must be developed for the major subsystems. (See figure 9-3.) The interrelationship of the subsystems and the macrowork system will be a major consideration in organizing staff members into self-managed teams.

Figure 9-2. Macroflow Diagram for Medication System of a Hospital

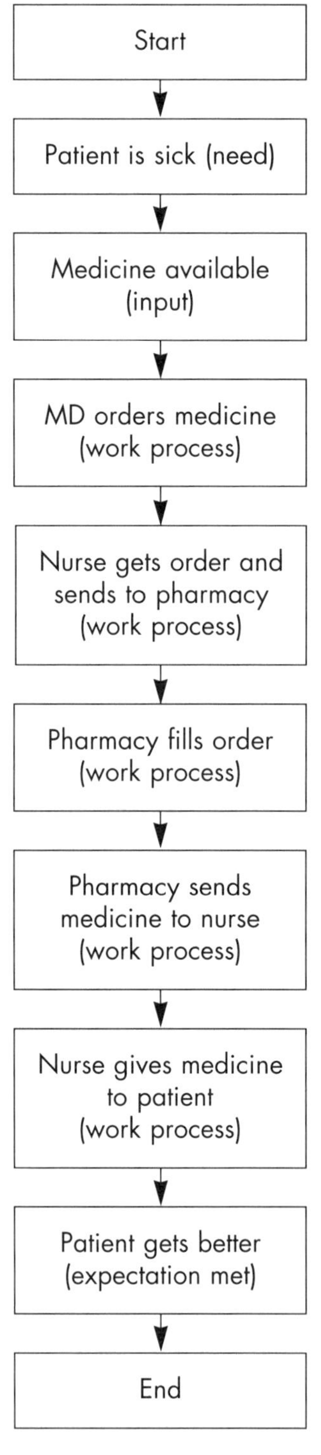

Figure 9-3. Subsystem of Medication System of a Hospital: Pharmacy Fills Order

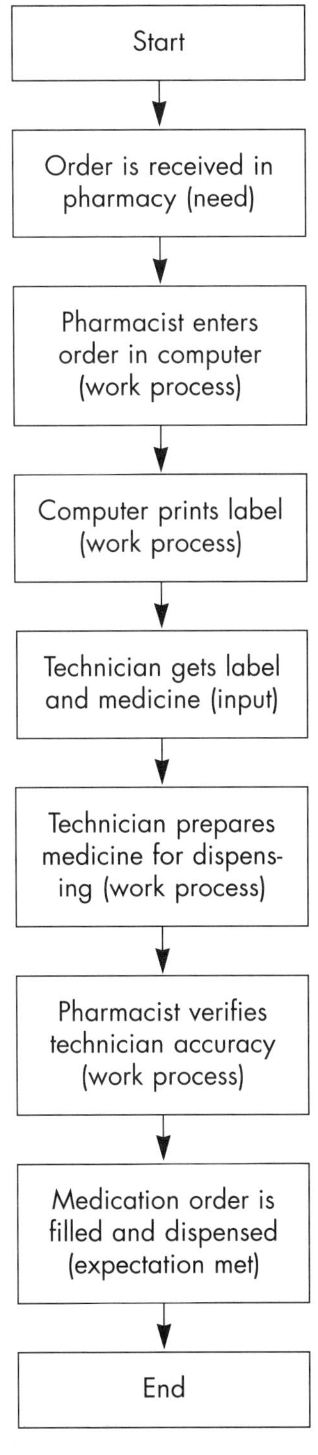

Table 9-1. Structure for Data Collection on a Technical Work System

What Can Be Eliminated?	What Can Be Increased?
Waste: What materials, time, money, and employee energy are lost in the current work processes?	Learning: What data-based feedback is available, and how can this be shared with those responsible for performance?
Quality variances: What are the common defects, breakdowns, complaints, and inspection points in the system?	Employee control: What steps should employees control, and how can authority to make decisions be shifted to employees?
Non-value-adding activity: What are the redundant steps and handoffs that don't add anything to the product or to customer satisfaction?	Speed: What can be done to decrease delays in work flow and decision making, and how can interruptions be eliminated?

Technical system design is a repetitive process. Be prepared to revise the macroflow diagram many times as more data and more feedback are received. The design team will be tempted to ignore the technical work flow and jump directly into the design of self-managed work teams. It is the responsibility of the facilitator to help the design team resist the urge to skip the sometimes tedious task of drawing flowcharts and collecting data on work processes.

Another temptation for the design team will be to focus on the details of the work processes and not take the time to identify customer needs and expectations. The customer is the key. Using technical design to apply knowledge of expectations to work processes ensures that self-managed work teams will make a difference *for their customers.*

Design and Customer Expectations

The industrial age and the application of knowledge to work created a new concept, *productivity*. The term *productivity* was first used in the United States during World War II and the present meaning appeared in dictionaries in the 1950s.[2] The primary goal of the past hundred years of the industrial age has been increasing productivity, but the playing field for productivity has leveled. The fast-food industry is one example: many companies prepare hamburgers as efficiently as McDonald's. Something more than burger flipping is now required to maintain market share.

The information age and the application of knowledge to work has introduced the concept of *customer service*. It is no longer enough to make things bigger and move them faster. Customers want their needs filled. The application of knowledge to meet customer expectations is the critical factor in defining organizational success in an information-based society. Burger wars in the fast-food business are won by those who understand their customers' preferences and know how to fulfill their unique appetites.

Figure 9-3. Subsystem of Medication System of a Hospital: Pharmacy Fills Order

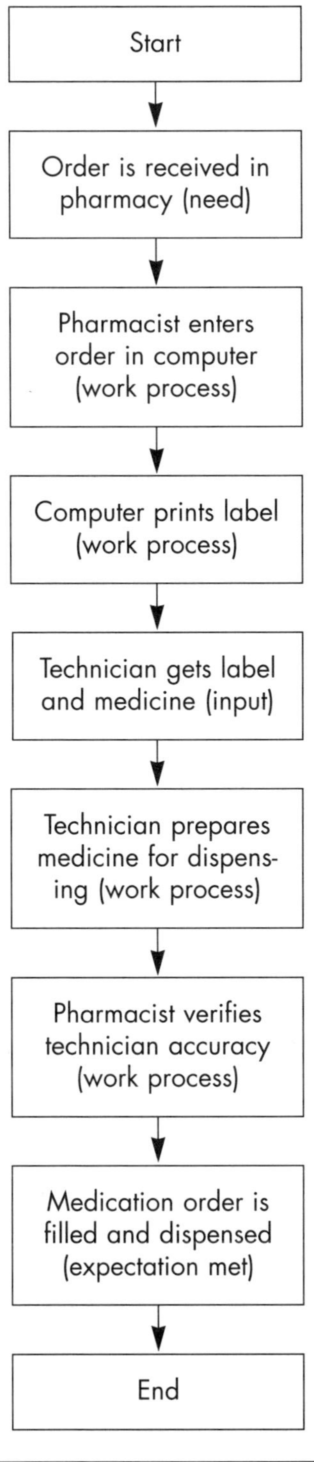

The requirements for meeting customer demands have also changed in health care. Several strategies have emerged to meet changing patient requirements:

- Patient-focused care has resulted in reengineering.
- Total quality management has led to process improvements.
- Integration of services has caused the reorganization of individual work into group work.

Each of these strategies has benefits and drawbacks. The work design process for self-managed teams should consider all of these options. Ultimately, the design team will develop a technical system that uses parts from each to create the self-managed team that best fits customer needs. The medication system of a hospital is used to illustrate the different perspectives of reengineering, processing improvements, and reorganizing.

Reengineering Model Outputs received by the customer are the focus of reengineering. (See table 9-2.) When viewed from the patient's point of view, the first thing that happens is that pills are delivered to the patient. The patient next finds out why the pills were ordered. Then the patient takes the pills and feels better. The processes for ordering medications, providing information, and teaching patients deliver the outputs. Inputs are determined last in reengineering and are chosen to optimally support the processes needed for outputs.

Process Improvement Model Process improvement involves looking at each step in the technical system to see where efficiency can be gained and time can be saved. (See table 9-3.) Obviously, much of the work is centered on work processes, and inputs are evaluated according to their ability to support the processes that are designed to produce outputs needed by the customer.

Table 9-2. Reengineering View of the Medication Process

Inputs	Processes	Outputs
Pharmacy provides medicine	MD orders medicine, and medicine is sent to nurse	Patient receives pills
MD diagnoses patient and orders therapy	Pharmacist provides drug information to nurse	Nurse tells patient what the pills are and why the patient should take them
Patient feels bad	Patient learns what to do to feel better	Patient takes the pills and feels better

Benchmarking is commonly used in the review of processes; technical system designers try to emulate others who have set industry standards for the kinds of systems they are developing.

Reorganization Model Combining individual work processes into group work is the goal of reorganization. (See table 9-4.) Reorganization takes an organic rather than mechanistic view of the technical work system. The primary concern is to make sure that there is an optimal mix of people with the information and skills needed to produce the outputs customers expect. Inputs required for the system are determined by the work groups. Reorganization is centered on the building of relationships and networking knowledge and service workers to effectively produce the outputs of the technical system.

Table 9-3. Process Improvement View of the Medication Process

Inputs	Processes	Outputs
Patient needs medicine	MD orders medicine	Nurse sends order to pharmacy
Pharmacy receives order	Pharmacy fills order	Pharmacy sends medicine to nurse
Nurse receives medicine from pharmacy	Nurse administers medicine	Patient receives medicine

Table 9-4. Reorganizing View of the Medication Process

Inputs	Processes	Outputs
Patient is sick	MDs, RNs, and pharmacists collaborate on therapy selection	Medicine is ordered
Medicine is available	Pharmacists, RNs, technicians, and unit secretaries collaborate for dispensing and administering medicine	Medicine is given to patient
Patient receives medicine	MDs, RNs, pharmacists, and patient interact to make sure patient understands therapy	Patient feels better

Pros and Cons of the Approaches

There are advantages and disadvantages to reengineering, process improvements, and reorganization. Reengineering assumes "that you have blown up the lab" and are starting over because you didn't have a clue about what was being done to start with. Process improvements are sometimes viewed as "rearranging the deck chairs on the *Titanic*," and you lose focus on the endpoint. Reorganization can lead to a "group hug," where everyone feels good but has forgotten why they are there. Table 9-5 illustrates the "perils and pearls" from each strategy.

The design team uses technical work analysis as the basis for applying knowledge to work. Is the goal of the design team to

- Meet customer needs?
- Improve productivity?
- Enhance relationships?

The answer is yes! All three goals are critical to the design's success. The purpose of the design team is to satisfy customers by implementing process

Table 9-5. Design Strategy Perils and Pearls

Design Strategy	Perils	Pearls
Reengineering	Discards processes that work and that people are familiar with; you can throw out the baby with the bathwater	Focuses on patient outcomes and customer expectations; renews staff commitment and develops a strong sense of purpose
Process improvement	Energy is spent on doing what you've always done and perpetuates some processes that don't add value for the customer; you can end up going nowhere faster	Rapid replication of other ideas, which can lead to quick wins and improved customer satisfaction
Reorganization	Building social relationships is time-consuming; you can end up worrying about pleasing each other, rather than the customer	Effective networking of knowledge workers leads to teamwork, sharing of ideas, innovation, and creation of new systems to anticipate customer needs

changes that are managed by new relationships. Balancing the strengths of reengineering, process improvements, and reorganization leads to new possibilities for customer satisfaction.

Identification of Customers and Their Expectations

The survival of any firm, organization, or activity depends on income's exceeding expenses. Bankruptcy is the result when expenses are persistently greater than income. Who provides the income? The customer. This simple economic fact means that the flowchart must end and begin with the customer. Customers will tell you what they need and how much they will pay for it—all you have to do is ask them. It is that simple.

Identifying customers in the health care system is not always straightforward. Look at the example of the medication process presented earlier in this chapter. Who is the customer from the pharmacy's perspective? Is it the nurse, the doctor, or the patient? The puzzle has more pieces if you consider who is paying for the pills. Fast-food businesses face the customers who pay for their products every day at the order counter, and they only accept cash. The pharmacy in a hospital fills prescriptions written by doctors, for pills administered by nurses, to patients, whose bills are paid by "third parties." There are multiple customers in health care systems; it's far different from flipping burgers for pocket change.

One of the strengths of self-managed work teams is that team members themselves are ideally positioned to understand who their customers are. Review of the basic flow of a technical work system, presented in figure 9-1 at the beginning of this chapter, reveals that workers receive feedback from customers. Technical design therefore begins with workers identifying their customers; these customers then tell the workers what their expectations are. This customer feedback can be obtained through the process outlined in figure 9-4.

Often feedback from customers is very positive and confirms that their needs are being met. Usually the survey process uncovers a few simple truths of customer expectations. The design team uses this information to focus the technical design of work systems on these critical success factors. In the pharmacy example, the results of the survey might demonstrate that

- Doctors want to know what medications work best.
- Nurses want the medications ready when the nurses need to administer them.
- Patients want to know what the medications are for.
- Payers want to be billed correctly.

Knowing these facts enables the design team to structure processes to meet specific customer expectations.

Successful designs involve double-loop learning. In the first loop, workers and internal resources are used to review systems and make improvements. The second loop goes outside the circle of internal processes and adds

Figure 9-4. Identifying Customers and Their Expectations

1. The design team presents the list of customers and expectations identified by the macroflow diagram to the workers and asks for their input to confirm or add to the lists.
2. After dialogue with workers and revision of the design team's perceptions of customers and expectations, a simple survey of customers is constructed. The following are sample survey questions to ask:
   a. What is the product or service that we provide you as our customer?
   b. What are your expectations of our product or service?
   c. What do we do well in meeting your needs?
   d. What could we do to improve your satisfaction with our product or service?
   e. What would we have to do in order for you to consider us providers of outstanding service?
3. An alternative to a survey of your individual customers is a focus group of representative customers at which you ask these same questions. Focus groups are best conducted by outside facilitators, without the presence of those who provide the service. This will ensure that you get honest and open feedback.
4. Feedback from the survey or focus group is then used to clarify the outputs, products, and services expected by the customers on the flowchart.

customers to the set of learning resources. Adding the loop of customer feedback to technical work design is essential; it is what separates firms and organizations that enjoy increasing demand from those that struggle with a shrinking customer base. *Talking to customers is where the flowchart ends and begins.*

Changes in Stakeholders' Roles

"The way to tap into energy is not by being autocratic, but by working *with* the players and giving them increasing responsibility to shape their roles."

—Phil Jackson, coach of the Chicago Bulls

The moment the decision is made to look at the work design process, people begin to wonder how their roles will change. If a flowchart is a picture, and a picture is worth a thousand words, then people in action are worth a thousand flowcharts. In a complex system, it is impossible to chart every step in a work process for even one person. People must be trusted to identify their roles in the new technical system and change their actions to make the system succeed. A work system has many stakeholders: they begin with suppliers and end with customers. The design team needs to involve stakeholders at every step of the technical work system flowchart. The earlier in the design process stakeholders are included, the sooner they will begin to see the possibilities for role changes and the sooner their transitions will start.

Technical design of self-managed work teams is an inclusive process, and its endpoint is to be determined by design team members, their customers, and the organization. This is different from a hierarchical/bureaucratic model, where design is the exclusive domain of management and the endpoint is chosen by those at the top, conferring in isolation. Table 9-6 builds on the discussion of role transitions in chapter 4; it describes how particular self-management roles relate to technical work design.

Role changes cannot be made with the flip of a switch. Technical design for self-managed processes requires old roles to fade and new roles to appear, like simultaneous rheostats. The flowchart that the design team develops will provide common ground for people to talk about how their jobs will change and will help them identify their new roles. Involving stakeholders in drawing the flowchart initiates role changes, bringing the flowchart to life.

The Importance of Effective Communication

"Being in leads to buy-in."

Technical design of new work processes will be the basis for self-managed work teams. It is therefore essential that in the design process you share everything with everyone. Suppliers need to know what the customers expect. Customers need to know how their products or services will be delivered. Workers need to know the details of the processes they will use to convert inputs from suppliers into outputs for customers. Management must understand that face-to-face communication among suppliers, workers, and customers is the key factor in designing robust systems that will meet everyone's needs. Team activity 2 at the end of this chapter outlines one way to get everyone involved.

The more people who see and have input into the flowchart, the greater the creativity harnessed in the work process design. Drawing outside the lines is encouraged during the technical design process, and having the flowchart as a shared canvas will insure that more colors and textures will be added. Access to the flowchart also encourages cohesiveness because the flowchart represents a shared mental model for stakeholders. In addition, focusing technical design on an inanimate object rather than on people draws attention to work process details and away from personal issues. It will take time to include everyone in the communication process. There will be many hallway conversations in addition to the design team meetings. Developing a new shared model for the technical aspect of work is an example of a situation where you need to start slow so you can finish fast. The key to communication is getting everyone in the loop.

Table 9-6. Stakeholder Roles in Technical Work Design

Role before Teams	Role after Teams	Role in Technical Design
Vice president	Mentor	To establish general expectations and provide resources for the design team effort
Director	Coach	To free up staff time, provide data, and encourage the design team
Supervisor	Team member	Share experience on dealing with suppliers and customers
Staff member	Team member	Share knowledge of previous work systems and think creatively to design new processes to better meet customer needs
Human resources support	Facilitator	Help design team members work in new roles and follow design process steps
Department educator	Specialist	Share knowledge of technical processes and innovative practices to create state-of-the-art systems
Customer or supplier	Partner	Work with self-managed work teams to establish expectations for outcomes and develop inputs designed to meet system endpoints

Obstacles and Answers

"It's the system that is the problem—and people design the system."

The primary obstacles to technical design will be people. Most failures are system failures, and most system flaws are created by people. Implementing a new work process depends on replacing an old work process. Table 9-7 lists the reasons given most often for maintaining the current system—that is, the "technical difficulties" that make change "impossible"—and gives some tips for dealing with people who hold these attitudes.

Technical difficulties start with poor design. The key to good design is having people work together with customers and suppliers. Providing people with the information, the tools, and the opportunity to properly develop the technical design will enable them to overcome design obstacles and deal with technical difficulties.

Chapter Wrap-Up

Through well-considered technical design, self-managed work teams improve customer satisfaction, develop efficient work systems, and enhance the competitive position of the organization. Flowcharting provides the basis for three ways of dealing with changing customer demands: reengineering, process improvements, and reorganization of individual work into group work. Dialogue with customers and suppliers refines the flowcharts and ensures that the products and services provided will meet the needs of the marketplace. People bring the flowcharts to life: role changes are required to implement new technical designs. Open communication with all stakeholders is essential during the technical design process to get the design changes started. Work design allows self-managed work teams to partner with customers and suppliers to achieve technical breakthroughs.

References

1. Lawrence M. Miller, *Design for Total Quality: A Workbook for Socio-Technical Design* (Atlanta: The Miller Consulting Group, 1991), pp. 105–106.

2. Peter F. Drucker, *Post-Capitalist Society* (New York: Harper Business, 1994), p. 37.

Suggested Reading

Jackson, Phil. *Sacred Hoops.* New York: Hyperion, 1995.

Table 9-7. Dealing with "Technical Difficulties"

Why That Won't Work!	Tips for Overcoming the "Technical Difficulty"	Why This Will Work!
It's always been done this way.	Allow people the opportunity to express their anticipated losses.	Now it will be done our way.
This can't be stopped.	Phase out unnecessary steps one at time, not all at once.	We will only do things that add value.
That's against the rules.	Once boundaries are set, let the team make the rules.	We will make the rules.
Permission won't be given for that.	Give the design team blank permission to make decisions within guidelines and constraints.	We will have authority to decide what's best.
Resources aren't available for that.	Transfer the responsibility for the budget to the self-managed teams and reward them for meeting budget goals.	The budget will be based on customer needs.
No one has cooperated on that before.	Involve everyone from suppliers to customers in the technical design.	We are all part of one system.
There is no time to do that.	Be patient, the dialogue required for design takes time, and provide food at meetings for the designers.	We will spend our time doing the right things, the right way.

Team Activity 1

Drawing a Macroflow Diagram

Purpose: To initiate discussion and dialogue among design team members.

Directions:

1. Have design team members list their perceptions of customer needs and expectations. Rank these, list the top three on a piece of flip-chart paper, and tape the paper at the right end of a wall.
2. List current key work processes on another piece of paper:
   a. Processes that produce your core service(s)
   b. Processes that generate the most customer complaints
   c. Processes that consume the most time or dollars
   d. Processes that frustrate employees the most
3. Now draw these processes in a flow diagram. This can be facilitated by writing major work steps on sticky notes and then arranging the sticky notes on chart paper. Place the macrodiagram of the sticky notes to left of the list of customer needs and expectations.
4. Have the design team list the major inputs, tools, and suppliers of material, information, and resources used in the work processes. Write these on a piece of flip-chart paper and tape this on the wall to the left of the flowchart of sticky notes.
5. The final step is to have the design team complete the loop. This is done by defining the original customer need and placing this at the beginning of the flowchart.

Team Activity 2

Fishbowl Focus Group

Purpose: To inform and communicate with stakeholders about the design process; to promote empathy for stakeholder communication needs and concerns among design team members; to lay groundwork for future face-to-face discussions between stakeholders and design team members.

Directions: After the customer surveys are completed and the initial draft of the flowchart is developed, complete the following steps:

1. Share the flowchart with two representatives each from the supplier, worker, customer, and management stakeholder groups.
2. Ask these representatives to come to a focus group prepared to name two key items that they need to know from each of the other stakeholders to be represented in the group.
3. At the meeting set up the room so that the stakeholders sit around a table with a facilitator who has a flip chart; this is the "fishbowl." The members of the design team are then seated outside of the fishbowl. Each team member is assigned an individual stakeholder to observe.
4. The facilitator is responsible for conducting the discussion of "need to know" items and recording them.
5. The observers from the design team are responsible for identifying communication issues and reactions of the stakeholders present in the fishbowl. They should watch for nonverbal signs of agreement or disagreement about specific items on the flowchart.
6. At the end of the fishbowl discussion, the facilitator leads a group discussion to verify the key issues and to allow the observers to confirm hot topics or sensitive areas with the stakeholders. The group discussion emphasizes positive statements about communication obstacles that the design team will need to overcome.

Chapter 10

Social Systems Design

Chapter Preview

"For many years, the prevailing maxim of management stated: 'Management is getting work done through others.' The important thing was the work; the 'others' were nuisances that needed to be managed into conformity and predictability. Managers have recently been urged to notice that they have *people* working for them. . . . This, of course, brings with it a host of new, relationship-based problems that are receiving much notice. How do we get people to work well together? How do we honor and benefit from diversity? How do we get teams working together quickly and efficiently? How do we resolve conflicts? These relationships are confusing and hard to manage."

—*Margaret Wheatley*

People are social creatures. The implementation of self-managed work teams requires not only the design of technical systems but also of social systems—new ways for people to relate to each other in their work environment. This chapter serves as a blueprint for designing social systems for self-managed work teams, as introduced in chapter 5. The connection between work and social systems is explained. Social systems design is contingent upon changes caused by the transition to an information-based society, and this chapter introduces the implications of the information explosion on work relationships. A method is provided for involving people at all levels to understand the profound changes in relationships they will experience. Self-managed work teams are dependent on a delicate balance of technical and social systems, and this chapter provides tips on how to create synergy between work and human relation systems. Chapter 4 identified the role changes required for the implementation of self-managed work teams, and this chapter links these new roles to the system changes for planning, measurement, personnel, communications, and operations that are described in chapters 12 through 16. New social systems bring about new and complex problems; this chapter concludes with lessons learned in dealing with these issues.

Chapter at a Glance

In this chapter, you will find

- A discussion of social systems design in the information age
- An explanation of the importance of communication in the design process
- A discussion of balance between technical systems and social systems
- A description of the connections between individual roles and systems thinking
- Tips for turning problems behaviors around through trust and accountability
- A team activity that uncovers agreements among design team members and between the design team and process owners

Social Systems Design

"Most people are basically trustworthy. Only workplaces that give their members the chance to learn and add value through their work will succeed in the long run."

—*Art Kleiner*

Kim is a recent graduate of a highly competitive bachelor's degree nursing program. In her course work she learned computer skills and how to access vast stores of medical information to help care for patients. Kim's nursing internship focused on how to listen to patients effectively and teach them to care for their specific disease states. What is the internal motivation for this new nursing professional? Is it simply to cover three 12-hour shifts per week and earn wages to cover payments on a new car, or is Kim excited about applying her knowledge and experience to make a difference in her patient's lives? Will Kim want to be viewed as just another one of 700 nurses on staff at the medical center or as a respected member of the health care team?

Every organization wants to succeed. What this statement really means is that every organization is made up of people and every person wants to succeed. Connecting the personal desire for accomplishment to organizational goals is the challenge of social system design.

The Changing Work Environment

In the hierarchical/bureaucratic command-and-control models of the industrial age, it was assumed that only a few people at the top had the knowledge necessary to understand the organizational view—the "big picture." In order to make life predictable for management and orderly for workers, it made sense to focus workers on the repetitive tasks associated with the technical aspects of production. Social systems were designed to fit this highly structured and seemingly stable environment, in which people were viewed as interchangeable hands that made and moved objects. The inevitable result of this restricted view of work was that any worker interest in the big picture atrophied and workers developed only those social skills necessary to survive in the "system."

Success in the information age depends on interaction among knowledge workers as they coordinate their efforts to anticipate and meet the needs of customers. The health care system is based on a complex set of relationships between a vast array of professional disciplines, technical support personnel, and service workers. Many health care organizations have identified efficient work processes, but only a few have begun to address the social structures that need to be in place for health care workers to serve patients effectively as a team. The key is to connect each worker's internal desire to care to the overall health system goal of improving health.

New health professionals like Kim have access to much the same information as top management—a situation very different from that prevalent during the industrial age. More important, organizational success now depends on Kim's ability to apply her knowledge to achieve organizational goals. Social systems in the information age depend on sophisticated communication systems that allow people instantaneous access to technical and organizational knowledge. It is now assumed that Kim knows the big picture and can work with others to connect her actions with organization goals as an equal contributor. Social systems need to be designed which build responsibility from within.

The History of Relationship Management

The transfer of responsibility to nurses like Kim demonstrates that social systems in the workplace have come a long way from the mechanistic views of Fayol and Taylor. Skinner, Maslow, and McGregor are among the theorists who have undertaken psychological analysis of the workforce. Table 10-1 illustrates the applications of their theories to social systems in the workplace.

Managers have learned much from these theories. They have applied the theories to create participative practices designed to involve workers. But

Table 10-1. Major Theories of Psychological Analysis of the Workforce

Theorist	Premise	Social System Applications
Skinner	Behavior is shaped by control of the system.	Praise and recognize positive behavior; punish negative behavior.
Maslow	People have a hierarchy of needs: physiological, safety, social, egotistical, and self-actualization.	Provide an environment that meets progressively higher needs, ultimately leading to altruistic behaviors.
McGregor	Management has two alternatives: theory X assumes that people work out of fear; theory Y assumes that people want to work	Theory X managers threaten or punish workers who don't perform up to standards; theory Y managers help people develop their own roles, leading to buy-in.

even with worker participation, management is still in control. These theories do not take the ultimate step in social systems design: placing the worker in control.

In the self-managed environment, workers are in control. They are the ones who design and are responsible for the social systems. Understandably, the transition from management control to worker control is an anxious time for managers; but it is equally anxious for workers. While managers feel they are giving way to chaos, workers feel that chaos will overwhelm them. These feelings are natural as the organization makes this difficult but necessary transition. Much of the anxiety felt can be assuaged if the design team recognizes and acts upon the need for open communication.

The Importance of Communication

"The most difficult part of the design process was developing the procedures for discipline and overcoming the fears that staff members had about confronting their 'friends.' We spent a lot of time discussing ideas for discipline with staff members and at the design team meetings."

—*Victor DeLapp, pharmacy design team leader,*
Mission+St. Joseph's Health System

Management Anxiety

The design of social systems in the information age is a series of experiments in personal responsibility and workplace relationships. Good experiments raise questions more often than they provide answers. Management and workers can help one another discover how to manage new relationships by encouraging chaos.

In the team activity at the end of this chapter, the design team starts from scratch, identifying resources and expectations for social processes. This activity produces a grid of social system inputs and outputs. The design team then compares its ideas about social systems with those of the current process owners. The likely outcome is that design team members and process owners will find they have many ideas in common. In this way, fears about the transition from management to worker control can be put to rest.

In fact, experience with self-managed work teams confirms the fact that people do not like uncertainty. Teams will often insist on more structure for social systems than management has required in the past. The difference is that when teams make the rules, they own the rules.

Worker Anxiety

Next, the design team shares the completed grid of social system inputs and outputs with the staff members who will be ultimately responsible for these systems. People like the new nurse, Kim, will have many questions, concerns, and ideas about how changes in the social systems will affect her on a personal level. Do the proposed changes mean that she will be responsible for hiring, discipline, evaluations, and planning for the future? What skills and experience can Kim bring to these critical functions? Which roles does she feel comfortable with, and which roles make her anxious? Does Kim have ideas about how to make these systems work? Which areas interest her most? There is only one way to find out what Kim thinks. Ask her.

Design team members should be encouraged to discuss openly the potential changes in social systems with the staff members they work with and represent. These conversations will elicit the feedback needed to help the design team decide which social systems should be addressed first and which should remain the responsibility of management for the time being. Different people will accept different changes at different rates. Some folks will want to jump right in and be responsible for filling the next vacancy; others will never want the responsibility of confronting a team member about a negative behavior. The main thing for design team members to remember at this point is that the more feedback they receive, the better the decisions they will make.

Because the design team is making "new rules," people will have to live with them when they are put in place. When the founding fathers of the United States met in Philadelphia to write a constitution for a new country they did not come to quick agreement. There were many debates between the members of the Constitutional Congress, and a series of difficult compromises were made as the Constitution evolved through many drafts. The time, effort, and passion that went into the writing of the Constitution produced a document that defines a social system for preserving freedom balanced with responsibility. If they hope to achieve similar success, design team members must also openly debate and share drafts of the workplace "constitution" they are writing.

Design team members need to take the time to listen to people like Kim and to give Kim the opportunity to think about the changes they are proposing. This is one spot on the timeline where it is acceptable—and can be crucial—to take longer than was thought necessary. Self-managed work teams will be the responsibility of people like Kim. Talking to these people is where human systems end and begin.

Balance between Technical Systems and Social Systems

"Today we have to go beyond the information-based organization to the responsibility-based organization. . . . The old-type organization assumed that the superior knew what the subordinate was doing—for the superior, only a few years earlier, had occupied the subordinate's position. The knowledge-based organization, by contrast, has to assume that the superiors do not know the job of their subordinates. They have never held it."

—*Peter Drucker*

As chapter 5 pointed out, the design of self-managed work teams must balance reliance on social systems and reliance on technical systems. Technical systems and social systems should be viewed as complementary rather than competitive. One is not to be preferred to the other. Instead, the design team's task is to create systems in which work and relationships have synergistic effects on each other.

Technical systems controlled by management dominated the industrial age and have survived into the information age. Getting managers to give up control of human relations issues is the greatest challenge in the design of social systems. The second greatest challenge is getting self-managed work teams to take responsibility for managing human relations issues. Meeting these challenges is a matter of instilling confidence in both management and work teams—confidence that will lead to trust. Self-managed work teams must have confidence that management will let them solve their own problems. Management must have confidence that teams are able to deal with personnel issues. Control in the information age is based on trust between workers and management. Both work and relationships are critical to the success of the organization and the individual.

Balance is achieved through a combination of position, timing, and leverage. Balance is also a dynamic state, in which the forces creating balance are in constant motion. Remember, as a child, the joy and frustration that could be experienced on a teeter-totter? When two people on a teeter-totter work in harmony, both are in fluid, almost effortless motion, going up and down. When one person on the teeter-totter changes her position or takes advantage of her size, she can suspend the other in the up position. When one person jumps off, the other drops to the ground with a painful thud. The position of each person on the teeter-totter determines the force needed to achieve balance. Timing plays a crucial role in starting the teeter-totter in motion because the force exerted by one person must be coordinated with the force exerted by the other. Leverage makes it possible for people of different weights to work together on the teeter-totter.

The lessons learned on the teeter-totter can be applied to the design process so that social systems will be in balance with previously dominant technical systems. Design for self-managed work teams starts with talking to customers and developing work processes to meet customer needs. Social systems design then follows. It is absolutely essential to have management stay out of the way during the design of human relation systems. Management was previously "the heavy" in control of social systems. In order for self-managed work teams to "gain weight," they need to be responsible for people issues: they must be allowed to develop social systems on their own. Starting on operational social systems, such as scheduling, allows self-managed work teams to get a feel for being in control. Self-managed work teams should only move on to more difficult social processes, such as conflict resolution, as they gain confidence in their ability to maintain balance and avoid being suspended in air or landing with a thud.

There is no magic formula for achieving balance between work and people. People need to be given the chance to design the social systems they will use to facilitate work processes required to meet customer needs. Allowing the design team the freedom to design new human relations systems is difficult for management, but it is essential that self-managed work teams be given their turn to be in control. There will be some periods of imbalance, and the teeter-totter will not always move smoothly. Do we match work to people or people to work? With practice, we can do both!

Connections between Individual Roles and Systems Thinking

"In quantum physics, *relational holism* describes how whole systems are created among the subatomic particles. In this process, the parts are forever changed, drawn together by a process of internal connectedness."

—*Margaret Wheatley*

Kim is just one of 700 nurses in a large health system of over 3,000 employees. The design of self-managed work teams needs to put in place ways to connect Kim's role with the role of the health system. Kim must understand the system, and the system must understand Kim.

In the hierarchical/bureaucratic management model, Kim would go through an orientation period and be instructed in a rigid set of policies and procedures to follow. In the self-managed work team model, Kim will be acclimated to the workplace by her team and will be responsible for helping make team decisions. This is a whole new world for the organization and for Kim. Social systems provide the connection between Kim and the health system.

Table 10-2 links the management and human relations systems described in chapter 4, to the social systems introduced in chapter 5, and to the self-managed work team systems presented in chapters 12 through 16. This table is a framework that allows people like Kim to understand how their roles as a team members are connected to the organization. The design team should use this table as a reference point in developing its strategy for social systems design. Chapters 12 through 16 describe *systems* for self-managed work teams. There is no division into "work" systems and "social" systems. Self-managed work team systems are inclusive and consider technical and human relations systems jointly.

The design team is responsible for developing systems that link the individual with the self-managed work team and the self-managed work team with the organization. Classic management systems were the responsibility of leaders at the top of the hierarchy. Self-managed work team systems are the responsibility of the people who do the work. The final step in the social systems design process is the development of a clear list of responsibilities for individual team members. Giving this list to everyone will be the starting point for establishing personal responsibility. Figure 10-1 is a checklist of items about which the design team should develop specific statements of individual responsibility.

Table 10-2. Connection of Classic Management and Human Relation Systems to Social Systems to Self-Managed Work Team Systems

Management System (chapter 4)	Human Relation System (chapter 4)	Social System (chapter 5)	Self-Managed Work Team System (chapters 12–16)
Planning	Change implementation	Planning	Planning (chapter 12)
Controlling	Performance review	Performance feedback for teams and individuals	Measurement (chapter 13)
Commanding	Expectation setting	Compensation and celebration; hiring, training, and development	Human resource management (chapter 14)
Coordinating	Formal and informal communications	Communications	Communications; record keeping (chapter 15)
Organizing	Conflict resolution	Decision making; conflict resolution	Daily operations (chapter 16)

☞ **Team Tip:** People want to know three things: (1) what is expected of them, (2) how they are doing, and (3) what they can do to improve. Responsibility starts with knowing what is expected.

Health care workers realize they are part of a complex system. When people understand how the system works and are allowed to help design and improve the system, they can develop personal ways to contribute. Defining individual roles in the context of the overall system builds a holistic organization.

Importance of Trust and Accountability

"Many modern organizations are in pain. Many people sit through meetings listening to their boss and saying to themselves every minute, 'I can't trust you; I know you are out to get me and there is nothing I can do about it.' That's as bad a pain as a toothache. If you expect these employees to do something constructive to make the world better, you are not going to get anything from them until you do something about the toothache."

—*Art Kleiner*

Most of the health care workers with whom Kim will work started out with an internal desire to succeed and make a difference for their patients and the health system. Over time, the stifling social systems of hierarchy and bureaucracy have frustrated these workers. Many times they have asked

Figure 10-1. Personal Responsibilities Checklist

Planning Systems
- Envisioning the future
- Developing the strategic plan
- Identifying goals and tactics
- Specifying and obtaining resources
- Structuring the teams

Measurement Systems
- Monitoring
- Following up
- Evaluating and correcting
- Appraising team and individual performance
- Evaluating team effectiveness

Human Resource Management Systems
- Fulfilling individual role model behavior expectations
- Hiring
- Coaching, counseling, praising, and disciplining
- Training and orienting
- Celebrating and giving recognition

Communications, Record Keeping, and Reporting Systems
- Communicating with the organization, other teams, and team members
- Record keeping
- Reporting
- Communicating with customers and suppliers

Daily Operations Systems
- Allocating and disposing of resources
- Scheduling and making assignments
- Managing time and attendance, and time off
- Decision making
- Holding team, department, and organization meetings
- Resolving intrateam and interteam conflict

why things are done the way they are. And what they have heard from the boss is, "This is they way we do it, like it or lump it." Staff members often have new ideas, but rarely are they heard, and it is almost impossible for them to implement change. The result is a workforce that has little faith in management's desire to listen to them.

The design of new social systems for self-managed work teams will meet great skepticism. People who have been conditioned over many years by rigid policies and procedures and a controlling management style will have difficulty trusting that something different is really going to happen. Over time, workers learn defense mechanisms and tactics for survival in bureaucratic organizations. One challenge in the self-managed team design process is to respond to these people's concerns and turn their defensive behaviors into positive contributions to their teams. Table 10-3 identifies six types of people found in bureaucracies, their organizational survival tactics, and positive roles they can play in the self-managed work team environment.

The key to turning the negative behaviors listed in table 10-3 into positive contributions is trust. People who are trusted to do their jobs seldom let others down. If it is clear from the beginning that management trusts design team members to come up with a new system, they will be accountable. People take care of people problems when everyone is accountable.

Chapter Wrap-Up

Because the implementation of self-managed work teams puts workers in control, relationships in the workplace must change accordingly. Social systems must be designed that assign responsibility. The information age demands a new set of rules that enables people to balance their technical work requirements with human relations needs. Only by talking to the people who do the work and letting those people design their own social systems, can we develop methods to keep both customers and workers satisfied. Social systems and work systems must be linked so that everybody contributes.

Suggested References

Drucker, Peter F. *Post-Capitalist Society*. New York: Harper Business, 1993.

Kleiner, Art, "The Age of the Heretics," *Healthcare Forum Journal* (March/April 1997): 37–38.

Wheatley, Margaret. *Leadership and the New Science*. San Francisco: Berrett-Koehler, 1994.

Table 10-3. Bureaucratic Survival Tactics and Positive Self-Managed Work Team Roles

Behavior Type	Bureaucratic Survival Tactic	Self-Managed Work Team Role
Trooper	Works around the system to provide patient care in spite of system problems	Prime contributor: dedicated worker who focuses on patient care and system improvements
Cynic	Openly criticizes the system and irritates management to make a point	Troubleshooter: worker who identifies flaws and makes on-the-spot fixes
Apathetic	Punches the clock and does the minimum required by the system	Supporter: employee who plays his or her role and stabilizes the system
Moles	Is passively aggressive, appearing to be a supporter, but undermines the system	Test driver: worker who tries out new ideas to make sure they are sensible and workable
Rebel	Tries to change the system; sometimes perceived as a troublemaker; occasionally makes a change	Innovator: creator who is constantly searching for new ideas and taking risks
Politician	Understands the system and manipulates it for personal gain	Diplomat: facilitator who works within a team and with other teams to keep everyone in the loop

Team Activity

Communicating about Social Systems Design

Purpose: To help the design team come to agreement on overall expectations for social system design; to discover ideas about social system parameters that design team members have in common with process owners.

Directions: Each design team member fills out the grid below, listing inputs and outputs for each of the social systems. The design team members then compare their perceptions and with the help of a facilitator come to agreement on the resources and expectations for social systems.

The design team then invites process owners for the various social systems to present to them the current processes used in the organization. For example, personnel interviewers are asked to explain hiring procedures, and strategic planners are asked to describe the planning process.

Social System	Inputs (Resources)	Outputs (Expectations)
Hiring, training, and development		
Communication		
Decision making and conflict resolution		
Planning		
Performance feedback for teams and individuals		
Compensation and celebration		

Chapter 11

Team Roles

Chapter Preview

"I believe we [the 49ers] were able to accomplish what we did because the players believed in each other. Each man was an extension of each other, like a chain-link fence. Our players learned to make sacrifices, to put it on the line for the guys 15 yards away [on the sideline]."

—Bill Walsh, coach

Team roles are a basic building block for teams. They are the mechanism for sharing leadership responsibility and authority and are a critical element of team success. One of the amazing things about a role is that the person who fills the role has an increased interest in the team and an increased commitment to the team. Once roles are established the team is very close to saying good-bye to the hierarchical structure of management. The concept of team roles and shared responsibility helps team members use their own initiative to accomplish the goals, projects, and tasks of the area they are self-managing. Team members are motivated to make things happen for their team and their unit or work area. They want to know their limits and boundaries so they don't create problems or get in trouble. Once team roles are defined, limits and boundaries become clearer, and team members can begin to take action to implement change and accomplish team goals. Members of a self-managed team are expected to participate as equal partners in the direction, operation, monitoring, and improvement of the team's performance. Team roles help reinforce this shared ownership of the team. They are the mechanism that helps bring forth the intelligence and participation of all team members to the benefit of the team, its customers, and the organization.

This chapter helps define the roles teams need and identifies the knowledge and skills that team members will acquire to perform effectively in their new roles. Some team members are hesitant about taking on the responsibility of new roles. They wonder if they will be successful in the roles, if the time they must devote to the roles will keep them from doing their work. Team members can look at roles in two ways. They may look at roles as an opportunity to demonstrate talents that have lain hidden. They may look at roles as a burden that they don't want to accept. This chapter gives examples of team member reactions to roles, how roles are implemented, how often roles rotate, and how team members learn the responsibilities of their roles.

Chapter at a Glance

In this chapter, you will find

- A description of 10 team roles
- A discussion of role rotation
- Four methods of role selection
- Strategies for role education and orientation

Team Roles

"The more participants we engage in this participative universe, the more we can access its potentials, and the wiser we become."

—*Margaret Wheatley*

One of the critical elements of team effectiveness is roles. Roles are the way team members share responsibility and get the work of management done. In the self-managed team environment, the responsibilities that managers have by virtue of their place in the hierarchy are equally distributed among team members through their role assignments. In this way, no single team member has more responsibility or authority than any other team member. Leadership of the team is shared by all team members, just as the work of the team is shared.

Major Roles and Competencies

The primary roles that exist on all teams are the role of team leader and the role of record keeper. Teams can have many other roles as well. They usually also have the roles of educator, scheduler, quality improvement coordinator, human resources coordinator, and safety officer. Each role carries the management responsibilities associated with it. Each role requires specific competencies, or knowledge, skills, and behaviors. If possible, everyone on the team will have a specific role. Along with learning how to function as a team, team members also need to learn how to fulfill their individual roles. The major roles that teams have created are described in table 11-1.

Coordination of Roles and Teams

Once the roles are implemented, the team leader serves as the coordinator for the team. He or she makes sure all team members are aware of their assignments and have the training and orientation to perform the assignments effectively. The team leader does not act in a directing or hierarchical manner. Each member of the team is free to develop the assigned role to the best of his or her ability, given the responsibilities that have been defined for the role.

Team members have clear role assignments. They know what their day-to-day responsibilities are, and they are aware of responsibilities that occur only monthly or quarterly. They are accountable to the team to keep track of project due dates and deadlines. They are encouraged to consult with other team members in the performance of their role responsibilities. Indeed, team members with role responsibilities would not be behaving as participating team members if they did not involve others on the team in their role assignments. They need to share information, develop plans and goals for their role with the team, and request input and ideas from other team members.

Table 11-1. Roles and Competencies

Role	Description	Competencies (Knowledge, Skills, Behaviors)
Team leader/coordinator	■ Schedules team meetings at least monthly; notifies team in advance ■ Sets agenda for team meetings and conducts team meetings ■ Follows up on decisions and assignments made at team meetings ■ May make daily work assignments ■ Gives team members positive feedback ■ Communicates with director or vice president ■ Attends management-level meetings ■ Shares information from meetings with team ■ Serves as liaison with other teams, departments, and groups ■ Assures that team coordinates with other teams to benefit of all	■ Meeting leadership ■ Motivation; motivating others ■ Documentation and follow-up ■ Oral communication ■ Organization skills ■ Listening ■ Work flow ■ Enthusiasm; positive outlook ■ Sensitivity
Record keeper	■ Keeps team records; maintains permanent records and team history ■ Documents team decisions and team member assignments ■ Documents roles and role rotation schedule ■ Prepares team reports ■ Maintains minutes of team meetings; presents verbal meeting summary at end of each team meeting; helps with agendas	■ Minute taking and writing ■ Detail and organization ■ Chronological records ■ Report writing ■ Business writing skills ■ Judgment about what to record and what to omit ■ Accuracy and timeliness skills

(Continued on next page)

Table 11-1. (Continued)

Role	Description	Competencies (Knowledge, Skills, Behaviors)
Record keeper *(continued)*	■ Leads the evaluation of meeting effectiveness ■ May maintain team bulletin board of announcements, flyers, and so on	
Scheduler	■ Prepares staff schedule ■ Documents and keeps track of days off, vacation, and holidays taken ■ Documents sick calls, absences, and tardiness ■ Handles staff time sheets and time records ■ Communicates attendance problems to designated person	■ Knows how to create a schedule ■ Knows time off, absence and tardiness, and overtime policies ■ Detail and organization skills ■ Accuracy and timeliness skills ■ Schedules orientation for new employees ■ Conflict resolution skills
Educator	■ Develops annual education calendar for staff based on staff needs ■ Communicates mandatory education programs in advance ■ May develop educational programs and conduct them ■ Documents participation in educational programs and in-services ■ Documents and maintains records on licenses and certifications; maintains competency records ■ Maintains library of journals, books, and educational materials	■ Knowledge of education sources ■ Knowledge of adult education ■ Course design ■ Competencies ■ Record-keeping skills ■ Computer skills ■ Oral communication skills ■ Coaching ■ Enthusiasm; positive outlook

Table 11-1. (Continued)

Role	Description	Competencies (Knowledge, Skills, Behaviors)
Educator *(continued)*	■ Develops and implements new employee orientation ■ Coaches and gives feedback on work skills and team behaviors and skills ■ Coordinates programs with safety officer and team leader	
Human resources coordinator	■ Serves as liaison with personnel ■ Maintains current personnel policies and procedures ■ May maintain current department policy and procedure manual ■ Participates in policy revision within department ■ Communicates policies and policy revisions ■ Coordinates the hiring and performance review process ■ May coordinate the discipline process ■ May mediate staff conflicts ■ May plan and coordinate team celebrations ■ May coordinate staff satisfaction surveys, results reporting, and action planning	■ Knowledge of personnel policies ■ Knowledge of departmental policies ■ Knowledge of policy formal and approval process ■ Ability to write a policy or procedure ■ Ability to understand and respect different viewpoints ■ Listening skills ■ Conflict resolution skills ■ Knowledge of team hiring and performance review policies and procedures
Quality improvement coordinator	■ Encourages the team's focus on quality improvement and meeting the needs of customers	■ Knowledge of quality improvement process and tools

(Continued on next page)

Table 11-1. (Continued)

Role	Description	Competencies (Knowledge, Skills, Behaviors)
Quality improvement coordinator *(continued)*	■ Coordinates gathering customer satisfaction data; may perform audits ■ Participates on quality improvement teams and projects ■ Gathers, maintains, and displays data about team performance, quality indicators, and goals ■ Maintains records of team progress on team goals ■ Reports at least quarterly to the team on team performance, quality indicators, progress on goals, customer needs, and so on ■ Develops and maintains display of team performance measures	■ Knowledge of data collection and data display methods: charts, logs, and graphs ■ Knowledge of customer survey methods and focus groups ■ Ability to develop a visual display of performance measures ■ Detail and organization skills ■ Ability to prepare written reports
Purchasing/budget coordinator	■ Coordinates the team's participation in purchasing decisions ■ May develop or maintain the budget; maintain and process purchasing records and invoices ■ Serves as team liaison to provide team input during department budgeting process ■ Coordinates team evaluation of potential new equipment ■ Communicates financial information to the team at least monthly	■ Knowledge of the purchasing process ■ Ability to maintain financial and budget records ■ Knowledge of the team and department budget ■ Ability to communicate financial information clearly

Table 11-1. (Continued)

Role	Description	Competencies (Knowledge, Skills, Behaviors)
Maintenance coordinator	■ Identifies and reports maintenance problems ■ Maintains preventative maintenance records and system ■ Follows up on repairs ■ Routinely inspects environment for problems and refurbishing needs ■ Oversees team work area cleanliness; develops routine and deep cleaning schedule; entire team participates in work area cleaning	■ Knowledge of who to call for repairs and maintenance problems ■ Knowledge of preventative maintenance system ■ Ability to identify maintenance and refurbishing needs
Safety officer	■ Implements the organization's safety program with the team ■ May provide safety education classes ■ Monitors the work and customer environment for safety problems ■ Follows up on safety incidents and safety problems ■ Keeps safety records ■ Maintains staff emergency notification list (with scheduler)	■ Knowledge of safety program ■ Ability to provide safety education ■ Ability to identify and report safety problems ■ Takes safety seriously ■ Detail, organization, and record-keeping skills
Public relations/ marketing coordinator	■ Prepares monthly and quarterly communication to management ■ May develop or participate in the development of the marketing plan ■ May develop reports or announcements for organization's internal newsletter	■ Written communication skills ■ Oral communication skills ■ Likes to recognize others ■ Conflict resolution skills ■ Cares deeply about meeting the needs of customers and projects this attitude

(Continued on next page)

Table 11-1. (Continued)

Role	Description	Competencies (Knowledge, Skills, Behaviors)
Public relations/ marketing coordinator *(continued)*	■ Publicizes team accomplishments and individual achievements ■ Handles customer complaints and problems of a serious nature	
Recognition and celebrations coordinator	■ Develops and communicates an annual calendar of recognition and celebration events ■ Plans, organizes, and implements the events ■ Plans at least quarterly celebrations to recognize team accomplishments	■ Ability to discover accomplishment worth celebration ■ Ability to plan, organize, and implement "parties" ■ Genuine interest in recognition of others
Team member	■ Performs daily work assignments ■ Attends team meetings; participates in team activities ■ Fulfills role assignment ■ Follows team ground rules ■ Contributes information, experience, knowledge, ideas, and suggestions ■ Volunteers to help other team members; shares the workload ■ Completes assignments between meetings or by deadline ■ Helps team reach consensus decisions ■ Participates in developing and accomplishing goals ■ Works to improve quality and satisfy customers	■ Performs work accurately and in a timely manner ■ Knowledge of meeting effectiveness ■ Knowledge of team role ■ Knowledge of team systems, policies, procedures, goals, performance measures, and performance expectations ■ Treats others with friendliness, respect, and courtesy ■ Maintains confidentiality and protects confidential information ■ Projects a positive and enthusiastic attitude

Table 11-1. (Continued)

Role	Description	Competencies (Knowledge, Skills, Behaviors)
Team member *(continued)*	■ Lives and models the values of the organization and the team ■ Responsible for own performance ■ Completes self–evaluation; participates in peer/360-degree evaluations ■ Actively pursues self-development ■ Helps orient new team members ■ Is accountable to the customer first, team second, department third	
Coach	■ Coaches team and individuals to help improve effectiveness ■ Meets with team leader before and after meetings to coach and provide feedback ■ Facilitates team meetings ■ May handle certain levels of discipline and conflict resolution ■ Helps assure team performance is acceptable; team is using team systems ■ Intervenes to address problems and improve performance ■ Helps team obtain resources	■ Coaching, feedback, and listening skills ■ Knowledge of meeting effectiveness; meeting facilitation ■ Conflict resolution skills ■ Knowledge of self-managed teams ■ Knowledge of team roles and responsibilities ■ Knowledge of the overall organization

Sometimes team members need to be reminded that as *team* members they are expected to consult with the team and involve the team in decisions. Team members feel a surge of positive energy when they take on role assignments. They want to get the tasks of their roles accomplished, and they want to get them done quickly. They often charge off like the Lone Ranger and leave the rest of the team behind, in the dark about what is happening in the role. When this happens, the team and its members feel left out, undervalued, and unneeded. Lone Rangers can build barriers between themselves and the team. If all team members are not involved in the work of a particular role, they may not support and implement plans developed by the person occupying that role.

A key element of all roles is communication. Team members cannot operate as though they live on separate islands. Each member is expected to share information that is related to his or her role with other team members. The team and its individual members should be current and up to date on all activities relating to all roles. This sharing of information is one thing that distinguishes the team model from the hierarchical model. The typical supervisor is not an excellent information sharer. Supervisors tend to see their departments or sections as their individual responsibility and are not always aware that staff members would like more information on the activities their supervisors are involved with.

Team Role Choice

In addition to team member and coach, table 11-1 reviews 11 different team roles. Not every team needs or wants 11 roles, and it is important to select only those roles that are necessary to the functioning of the team. To make this decision, the team first looks at its boundaries and responsibilities, then at goals, performance measures, and performance expectations for the team. The team must also consider the number of members who are available to fill roles. By reviewing all these areas, the team can decide which roles will contribute to its efficient performance.

Boundaries The first place to look for direction is the boundaries that the team operates within. (See chapter 3.) If the self-managed team is expected to hire new employees, orient them, give performance reviews, conduct some level of discipline, understand personnel policies, and be advised when personnel policies change, then the team needs the role of human resources coordinator. However, if most personnel-related tasks will be performed by the department director, or the coach, then the team will not need a human resources coordinator.

After reviewing the boundaries, the team (or the design team) will know whether they need a scheduler, a financial coordinator, a quality improvement coordinator, and a human resources coordinator. All teams will have a team leader (some prefer to call them "team coordinators") and a record keeper. These two roles are universal and must be present on the team. The team cannot function without someone to call team meetings, conduct them, and take notes on what the meeting accomplished.

Goals, Performance Measures, and Performance Expectations The team next looks at its goals, performance measures, and performance expectations. If improving relationships with physicians is an important goal and an ongoing emphasis, then the team may need a physician liaison role. If communicating the story of the team to the organization is important, then the team may need a public relations coordinator. If scheduling staff is a major function of the team, then the team may need a scheduler role. Safety is important in every health care organization. If the team is responsible for its own safety education, then the team may need a safety officer; or the team may combine the safety officer with the role of educator and have a team educator who not only develops the annual education plan but also conducts or arranges safety education for the team.

Number of Team Members The next consideration is the number of team members. Small teams may not be assigned all the responsibilities that large teams are, and therefore won't need as many roles. When they are assigned as many responsibilities, small teams will need to do two things. They will need to devote more hours per team member to fulfilling those roles, and they will need to combine some roles. For instance, the record keeper may also be the scheduler, and the educator may also be responsible for safety, human resources, and quality improvement. Roles that are present in different self-managed teams are outlined in table 11-2.

Balance between Work Duties and Team Roles

It is estimated that a team needs 20 hours per week to accomplish the tasks previously performed by a supervisor. If there are 10 team members, that is two hours per team member per week, on the average. If there are 4 team members, that is five hours per week per team member. It is obvious that the addition of a team role to a regular full-time job will cause that job to expand. Some staff members are able to absorb the requirements of the job into their daily schedule. Others will need extra time during the week, or the month to fulfill the requirements of the team role. No team or team member should be expected to fulfill new responsibilities through overtime work. Initially, when the team is just starting and there is considerable education, overtime may be necessary. However, after the team is fully operational, team members should be able to accomplish their role assignments during their normal work schedule. This may mean that they have relief for an hour or two a week, or that they have three or four hours a month set aside for project work related to their team role.

Role Rotation

"I was the first team leader for the management team. It was a big responsibility, and I moaned about how much time it was taking. But when it came time for the roles to rotate, I didn't want to give it up."

—*Paula Harty, patient care services management team, Memorial Medical Center*

Table 11-2. Roles and Role Rotations

Team	Roles	Role Rotation
Laundry	Team leader; record keeper; scheduler	6 months
Housekeeping	Team leader; record keeper	12 months
Respiratory	Team leader; record keeper; scheduler; educator; human resources and public relations coordinator; quality improvement coordinator	Varies
Pharmacy	Team leader; record keeper; reporter; scheduler; trainer; cost, safety, and quality coordinator	Some at 4 months; some at 12 months
Dietitian	Team leader; JCAHO/policies and procedures coordinator; educator; food service liaison; scheduler and student coordinator; outcome analyst; purchasing/budget coordinator and librarian; quality improvement coordinator; managed care coordinator; screening coordinator	6 months
Physician office staff	Team leader/physician relations coordinator; record keeper; quality improvement coordinator and data keeper; public relations coordinator; scheduler; educator; safety officer; human resources and policy and procedures coordinator; recognition and celebrations coordinator; purchasing and maintenance coordinator	3 months
Retirement community	Team leader; record keeper and reporter; safety officer; educator; human resources coordinator; quality improvement coordinator	6 months

Table 11-2. (Continued)

Team	Roles	Role Rotation
Nursing unit	Team leader; record keeper; scheduler; educator; quality improvement coordinator; human resources coordinator	6 months
Pre-op/Post-op PACU	Team coordinator; record keeper; communicator and reporter; educator; quality improvement coordinator; safety officer; scheduler and recognition and celebrations coordinator; human resources coordinator	12 months

How often to rotate roles is a team decision. The standard role rotations are three months, four months, six months, and twelve months. There are advantages and disadvantages associated with each of the role durations.

☞ **Team Tip:** A good role rotation decision takes into account the complexity of the roles and the attitude of the staff toward responsibility:

- *3 months:* Roles are not complex
- *4 months:* Roles are not complex; staff is hesitant about accepting responsibility
- *6 months:* Roles are complex; staff is willing to accept responsibility
- *12 months:* Roles are complex; staff is eager to accept responsibility

Teams have good and bad reasons for choosing shorter role rotations. One reason for selecting shorter role rotations is to give everyone on the team the opportunity to have time in all the roles before too many years pass. If a team has 10 members and 10 roles, and the roles rotate every four months, it will take over three years before every team member has a chance to fill every role. If the roles rotate once a year, it will take 10 years before everyone has the chance to fill all the roles.

A less good reason that a team would select the shorter role rotation time frame is that team members lack confidence in their abilities to perform the roles. Team members may be thinking, "I can live through anything! If I only have that role for three months, I will survive. Maybe no one will learn that I can't do it."

Teams may select the shorter role rotation time frame if they lack understanding of the complexities of the roles. The human resources and quality improvement coordinator roles are very complex. Team members in those roles need to learn tools, systems, and difficult analytical skills. The human resources role requires understanding of personnel laws, or at least enough knowledge of hiring and performance review procedures, so that the team doesn't violate the laws. The quality improvement coordinator may need to learn flow diagramming, Pareto charts, fish-bone diagrams, and customer survey methods. Learning these new tools and methods may take several months. If roles rotate every three or four months, the team members may never get to put into practice what they have learned.

Generally, role rotations of longer duration are more desirable. The longer time frame gives team members a chance to learn and practice their new roles, and to succeed in them before they are rotated. It also gives the team some continuity while everyone is learning the new team structure and team systems. (See table 11-2 for some examples.) The pharmacy department at the Mission+St. Joseph's Health System in Asheville, North Carolina, solved the problem of role rotation by designing a system in which some roles rotate every four months and other roles rotate every twelve months. The roles of leader, reporter, and recorder rotate every four months. These roles require knowledge of leading effective meetings, note taking, and report writing but do not require as much in-depth knowledge as the roles that appear on the points of the star. (See figure 11-1.) The scheduling, cost,

Figure 11-1. Pharmacy Team Roles

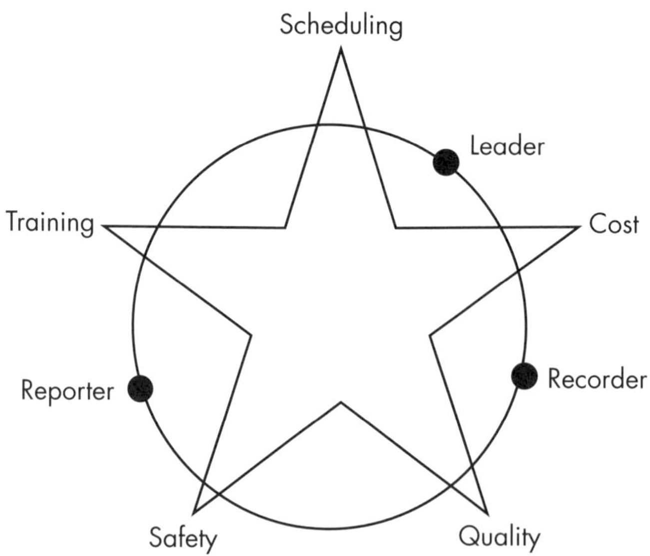

quality, safety, and training roles require knowledge of a specific function, its tools and techniques. These roles rotate every twelve months and benefit from the extended time to permit both learning of the function and time to apply what has been learned.

Role Selection

"I started out as the note taker for the design team and ended up in the role of human resources coordinator for the night shift team. I like having a say in what happens."

—Joy Thomas, respiratory therapist, Mission+St. Joseph's

After the team has determined which roles it needs, the question becomes who should fill what roles. Teams have experimented with many selection methods. The most common methods are application and interview, drawing a name from a hat, volunteering, and listing their top three choices.

Application and Interview

In this method, a team member decides which role he or she would like and completes a formal application for that role, listing knowledge, skills, and experiences that qualify the member for the role. The team interviews the applicants for each role and then, through a discussion of their qualifications, and based on the interview results, the team selects the appropriate person for the role.

This method of selection is the most formal of the methods described. It is complicated and time consuming. However, it is the method most likely to identify the best qualified person for the role. Nevertheless, it is the method used least often for selecting team members for roles. When asked why teams do not choose this method more often, most team members respond in the following manner: "We rotate roles, and so it is not as important to have the best qualified person in the role. Instead, we like volunteers. That way, the person who has the role is looking forward to it, will do a good job, and won't mind the extra work."

Drawing a Name from a Hat

Teams use this method in three ways:

1. *All team members who want a specific role put their names in the hat for that role.* To determine the team leader, everyone who wants that role puts his

or her name in the hat, someone draws a name, and the person whose name is drawn becomes the team leader. The drawing is continued, role by role, until all roles are filled. If there is a role that no one wants, then that role is skipped until all the desirable roles are filled. If no one volunteers for the remaining role(s), all names are placed in a hat, and names are drawn as in method 2 below, until all roles are filled.

2. *All names are put in the hat, and the drawing determines the role each person will fill.* A list of roles is compiled. Starting at the top of the list, one member draws a name for the first role. The person whose name is drawn will fill that role. Then a name is drawn for the second role, and so on, until all the roles are filled. This is a very popular method for filling roles among teams whose members have similar backgrounds or education and experience.
3. *All names are put in the hat, and the person whose name is drawn selects the role he or she wants.* The person whose name is drawn first can select any role, and that role becomes his or hers. The next name is drawn, and that person selects any role from among those that remain, and so on. This is a very popular method for selecting roles. It includes the concept of volunteering, which ensures that the person in the role is interested in that role and presumably willing to do the work required by that role.

Volunteering

In this method, a role is announced, and a member of the team volunteers for that role. If two or more people volunteer, then the person who volunteers first is chosen, or the names are put in a hat and the person whose name is drawn is selected to fill the role. This is a very popular method.

Listing Top Three Choices

This method is complex and time consuming. Each team member lists three roles in priority order: first, the role he or she wants the most; second, the role he or she wants next; and third, the role he or she wants third. One person, possibly the coach or an outside facilitator, takes all the lists and all the choices and makes a grid like the one illustrated in table 11-3. The facilitator tries to give as many first choices as possible, and then as many second choices as possible. After the facilitator has determined all the role assignments, they are announced to all the team members together.

In table 11-3, two people ranked team leader as their first choice, Mary and Paul. If Paul is selected, then Mary can have her second choice, and everyone else will have their first choices. In this way, four out of five people get their first choices, and one gets her second choice. If, on the other hand, Mary is selected as team leader, and Paul gets his second choice, then Sue would have to take her second choice also. Thus, if Mary is selected, we have three first choices (Mary, Tom, and Sally) and two second choices (Sue and Paul).

Any of the methods outlined above—application and interview, drawing names from a hat, volunteering, and listing top three choices—will eventually

Table 11-3. Example of the Top Three Choices Method of Role Selection

Worker	Team Leader	Record Keeper	Human Resources Coordinator	Quality Improvement Coordinator	Scheduler
Mary	1st		3d	2d	
Tom		3d	2d		1st
Sue		1st		2d	3d
Paul	1st	2d	3d		
Sally			1st	3d	2d

enable the team to fill all of its roles. The simpler methods that allow the team member some choice—volunteering and drawing names from a hat—are used more often by teams. The more time-consuming and complex methods—application and interview and listing top three choices—are not used as often.

Role Education and Orientation

"Superior individual effort is still necessary and desirable, but only as it contributes to the output of the team."

—*from* The Organization of the Future

Staff who have been selected to fill roles have two primary concerns: What will my team members expect from me? Will I perform well in this new role? They are understandably anxious. A team member who is the first to fill a particular role has the added responsibility of establishing and documenting the role so that it is successful, and so that it can be passed on to the next person in a way that will not disrupt the team's performance or the performance of the role.

Each role will require several hours of education. The education needed is determined by the responsibilities assigned to the role and the knowledge and skills needed to fulfill those responsibilities. Education for new roles should be spaced out so it is not a burden to the person doing the education, or the person receiving the education. An in-house expert is the perfect person to teach role responsibilities, knowledge, and skills.

Timing Role Education

Ideally, role orientation and education will occur before the team member must fill the role. The team member needs the opportunity to develop skills and confidence before he or she is expected to display those skills. Some skills are best taught to the entire team, such as meeting leadership. When everyone on the team understands the requirements for meeting effectiveness, everyone can help ensure that meetings are efficient and effective. But other skills, such as the use of quality improvement tools, can be taught to the single person occupying the role instead of to the whole team.

Some roles have skills that can be taught in segments, on an "as needed" basis. For example, table 11-4 presents an education plan for the educator role. The plan is scheduled to take about 12 hours to complete. Ideally, those 12 hours will be spread out, so that the education process is not overwhelming and so that a particular topic is taught immediately before the educator must perform a related task or assignment. The time that must be invested in educating team members for their roles is one of the reasons frequent role rotation is not practical.

Finding an Instructor

The team needs to find a person to conduct role education and time for team members to receive education. When several teams are being formed at once, the education for roles can be coordinated to occur at the same time, so that, for example, all educators learn adult education principles at the same time and the person providing the education does not have to repeat the material as often.

The person providing the education for the educator role could be a member of the organization's human resources staff or a supervisor or director who

Table 11-4. Education Plan for the Educator Role

Topic	Time
Adult education	60 minutes
Annual plan development	60 minutes
Competencies	60 minutes
Computer record keeping	60 minutes
Communication methods	30 minutes
Orientation development	60 minutes
Class facilitation	60 minutes
Documentation	90 minutes
Resource finding, ordering, maintaining, check-out procedures	60 minutes
Coaching	120 minutes
Course design	60 minutes

has performed the education function in the past. This person is the in-house expert on the subject and the perfect person to teach it. The person learning the role for the first time should develop a notebook of educational materials, instructions, forms, formats, procedures, and resources. This notebook will be a guide for the next person filling the role. The notebook can be augmented and revised to include new information and to indicate changes in procedures and systems.

Chapter Wrap-Up

Roles provide the primary mechanism for sharing leadership on a team. They also get team members more deeply involved with their team and more committed to the team's success. The roles that a team needs to fill will be determined by the teams boundaries, goals, and size. Team roles rotate with a frequency appropriate to the complexity of the role. One factor making longer rotations desirable is the necessity of role education. Roles are critically important to the team. They are the way the team reduces the need for the hierarchy.

Suggested Reading

F. Hesselbein, M. Goldsmith, and R. Beckhard, eds., *The Organization of the Future* (San Francisco: Jossey-Bass Publishers, 1997).

P. Senge et al., *The Fifth Discipline Fieldbook* (New York: Doubleday, 1994).

Ellen Williams and Dean Strahm, eds., "Team Structure: Self-Managed Work Teams," in *Department of Pharmacy Handbook* (Asheville, N.C.: Mission+St. Joseph's, 1995).

Chapter 12

Planning Systems

Chapter Preview

"Plans are nothing. Planning is everything."

—*Dwight D. Eisenhower*

Planning systems have typically been the exclusive province of management. This chapter introduces the concept of planning and explains the significant changes required to plan in the fast-paced information age. A step-by-step guide is provided to help the design team develop a planning system for their work environment. New planning roles are described for management, team members, and customers and suppliers. Examples of forms, tools, and processes used by self-managed work teams are given. This chapter offers tips on how to overcome planning obstacles and create successful plans.

Chapter at a Glance

In this chapter, you will find

- A description of the planning process
- A recognition of the orderliness of disorder
- Suggestions for involving stakeholders in the planning process
- Forms, tools, and processes for developing written plans
- Tips for breaking through planning barriers and for cocreating
- Three team activities for developing a planning process, writing a business plan, and developing planning scenarios

Planning

"Focus on the process and the outcome will take care of itself."

—Bennett Sims

Human beings use planning to determine where they want to be and what they need to do to get there. People are involved in planning in their daily personal lives and in organizations where they work. Planning is a skill that is learned but rarely taught.

How do people plan? A typical response to this questions is "I think about what I want to do and then work backward through the steps I need to take." Can planning be this simple? Yes. Then what makes planning so complicated most of the time? The answer is that there are five billion other people in the world planning at the same time and somehow all of these plans eventually become enmeshed. Planning does not occur in a sterile environment, and we never have complete control over the implementation of our plans.

Consider a family's plans for a typical Saturday. Mom wants to start the day relaxing with a cup of coffee and the newspaper and would like to spend some time working in the garden, but she also needs to do laundry, go to the grocery store, and cook dinner. Dad wants to play golf, but he needs to mow the lawn and take the car for an oil change. The two children want to watch cartoons and play with their friends, but they need to go to soccer practice and clean their rooms. Every member of the family has things they want to do and things they need to do. Careful planning is required for everyone to be able to do what they want. How is coordination of all their plans accomplished? The answer is by talking to each other. The key to planning is sharing what everyone wants to accomplish and the steps needed to get there. Figure 12-1 reduces planning to its most basic components.

People seem to know intuitively how to make plans, and some people are very good planners. Few people, however, have considered the planning process thoroughly. The result can be conflict and confusion at home and in

Figure 12-1. An Oversimplified, Basic, and Generic Process for Planning

- Identify what you want to happen. Have a personal vision.
- Share this vision with others who will be affected or involved. Develop a shared vision.
- Determine what actions are needed to be taken to accomplish the shared vision. Identify actions to accomplish the shared vision.
- Anticipate obstacles to these actions. Get help to adjust to and overcome the obstacles. Work with others to overcome obstacles.
- Understand that the world never quite turns out as expected. Be flexible.

the workplace. The family described above will have a satisfying Saturday if each of the family members can accomplish his or her their individual goals. One key to the family's success will be the ability of each members to share his or her individual visions for the day. When each member of the family understands the others' goals, the family can work together to overcome scheduling conflicts and achieve enough flexibility to meet everyone's needs.

A self-managed work team can be like a family whose members have different individual plans. The design team can help set the stage for successful team planning by taking time to think about the process of planning itself. Planning how to plan may sound silly, but it is essential. Planning is working backward from vision to action.

The Orderliness of Disorder

"This search for stable, well-defined targets has been, if we can admit, a great cosmic joke. We thought we could pin down reality, get it in our sights, or maybe even line up our ducks; but how to you do that in this elusive world of potentials? We've been playing with 'vast networks of interference patterns,' with 'the continuous dance of energy.' The world is not a thing. It's a complex, never ending, always changing tapestry."

—*Margaret Wheatley*

The first lesson about planning for the design team is the following: *Regardless of what is planned, what is going to happen will happen.* Work principles of the industrial age were developed in analogy with the mechanical principles of Newtonian physics. Closed systems, order, and structure were the hallmarks of work design. Quantum mechanics and chaos theory provide new metaphors for the organization of the world. Certain aspects of life now appear to be based on complex ever-changing relationships. This can be frightening for the design team. How can plans be made if they can't be counted upon? Why should the design team members even think about planning or developing a planning process if they know that the outcome will always be different from what they planned? Let's look at what happened to the family on Saturday.

Mom's day did indeed start with coffee and the paper, but the washing machine was broken so she couldn't do the laundry. She decided to use the extra time to stop by the garden shop on the way home from the grocery store. The grocery store was having a sale on tuna steaks that Mom thought would be great on the grill. Dad's day was immediately blown off course by an early morning storm that wiped out his round of golf. Then he took the car for an oil change and found he needed new brakes pads as well. The children watched their cartoons in the morning while Mom read the paper; the storm meant that their soccer practice was canceled. Their day was brightened when friends invited them to go to a movie. Mom said this would be all right if they cleaned their rooms first. Dad returned home from the auto repair shop just as Mom was returning from the garden shop and the kids were leaving for the movie with their friends. The early morning rain had softened the soil in the garden, and Mom asked Dad whether he would help her plant the roses she had bought. That afternoon the sun came out and Mom and Dad enjoyed working in the yard together and even had time to take a nap together in the hammock while the children were at the movie. The day ended with a family meal on the deck with the tuna that Dad grilled while Mom prepared the rest of the dinner.

Was this day a success or a failure for the members of the family? Things didn't go exactly as planned for any member of the family. Every family member had some disappointments and some unexpected opportunities for happiness. In total, most would agree that the day turned out fine and the family had a good Saturday.

So why plan? Planning is not about structure or predetermined outcomes. Planning is a process through which people communicate their individual needs and desires in relation to the needs and desires of others. Each family member knew what the other family members wanted to do on Saturday, and as circumstances changed, everyone adapted to make the day pleasant for everyone else. Planning is worthwhile because it nurtures and strengthens the relationships needed to connect the individual plans of everyone on the team and in the world. Planning helps people understand the orderliness of disorder and to learn how to just let it happen.

Planning is conversation. Many conversations with many people are needed to create a plan. Then the plan is put into action and encounters unexpected events. These surprises lead to more conversations so that the plan can be adjusted. And this process goes on and on until people being having conversations about the next plan. The task of the design team is to plan for conversations. The more conversations the better, for conversation builds the relationships needed for effective planning.

Team activity 1, at the end of this chapter, guides the design team through the development of a planning process. Several of the steps involve brainstorming or soliciting input from various stakeholders. What will evolve is unpredictable. What is predictable is that, in planning to plan, the design team will learn to talk about chaos.

Stakeholders Who Should Participate in Planning

"I think it's the normal desire of human beings to contribute to a sense of greater holism. . . . It's about finding a level of connection to another person. That then allows 2 or 40 or 2,000 of you to actually envision something that's desirable to all of you. And that's always different from what you thought it was as an individual. Once you discover common ground—it's not usually a very big area, by the way—but once it's there you begin to work together for a desired future."

—Margaret Wheatley

Everyone has a personal plan. Customers, team members, suppliers, and managers are all individuals first and members of a larger organization second. The key to planning is connecting each person's interests in a way that benefits first the individual and then the organization.

"Personal visioning" is a hallmark of the aging generation of baby boomers. Myriad self-help books, videos, and seminars promise to help people "discover the meaning of life." "Personal visioning" usually fails when people aren't given the opportunity to share their meanings of life with others. People want to connect with others. When they don't have a chance to do this, they get frustrated, and the personal vision is repressed or replaced by the artificial values of society.

The information age brings new ways for people to connect to each other and to relate their personal visions. Electronic communication systems give people unprecedented ability to seek out and keep in touch with people who have similar interests. But this increased access to information and communications is just the start of sharing interests. If people are to connect their personal visions in the workplace, they must develop intimate relationships. Intimacy exists when people have the sense of understanding and respecting each other's values. The power of self-managed teams derives from the intimate environments they create—environments that encourage people to share their personal visions and work toward a common purpose.

Individual Team Members

Planning in self-managed teams starts with the individual team members. It does not start with top management, or with customers, or with suppliers. Planning starts within the soul of each member of the team. This is a radical premise and a hard one for management to swallow. Management is accustomed to the hierarchical/bureaucratic model, in which management decides on the plan and puts controls in place to ensure that the plan is followed by the workforce. In the self-managed team model, by contrast, management's role is limited to facilitating the alignment of personal plans. People take actions based on their personal motivations, and a plan is executed only when each individual decides to act.

Discovering Personal Visions The first step in the planning process is discovering how individual team members want to contribute to the meaning of their lives through their work. Team members answer three questions:

1. What is your job?
2. What do you personally contribute to patient care outcome as a result of your job?
3. What is the underlying meaning of your work as it relates to your sense of purpose in life?

Questions 1 and 2 are easily answered. Question 3 is a tough one; few people have thought about their sense of purpose at work. It is important that team members struggle to answer question 3 and then discuss their answers with fellow team members. It is surprising how similar people's responses to this question are. These responses are the basis for shared team values.

Aligning Personal Visions The second step in the planning process is aligning the personal visions of the individual team members. This is where customers come in to play. Customers provide focus. Focus enables alignment.

A health care organization's focus on should be on the patient. Most health care organizations have developed statements of "mission" and "vision" as they relate to their patients. This organizational statement serves as the self-managed team's first focal point. Work teams, however, serve specific groups of patients or provide specific services that support patient care. Therefore, each work team must have its own specific mission and vision. A work team develops these by first finding out what its customers' needs are and what it must do to meet these needs. The work team asks its customers three questions:

1. What are we currently doing for you?
2. What could we be doing to provide better service?
3. What would it take for you to be delighted as our customer?

The answers to these three question, in concert with the organizational mission statement, will be the foundation on which each self-managed team—through discussion among its members—builds its mission and vision.

The self-managed team follows up on this discussion by reviewing its mission and vision in the context of any stated organizational values. The team can then develop its own list of shared values. These will be the values the team uses to accomplish its mission and vision. This is hard work and is best done with the help of a facilitator.

Suppliers, Other Teams, and Management

Self-managed teams do not operate in a vacuum. A team's success depends on complex relationships and interactions with suppliers, other teams or areas of the organization, and management. These are all people with whom teams must work to meet customer needs and overcome obstacles. How do you get these people to cooperate and help? You ask them. A common mistake made by work teams is failing to share their mission, vision, and values with others.

The third step in the planning process for a self-managed team, then, is sharing its plan with suppliers, other teams, and management. When they too understand the team's plan, those who support the work team can align their input to meet the team's needs. Remember, everyone wants to do a good job. But no one can do a good job without knowing what's expected. Work teams will be amazed at the support they receive when they let others know what they need and expect.

What is management's role in the planning process? Management's role is to ensure connection in the system. This is accomplished in two ways:

1. By providing information
2. By facilitating networking

The more information that management shares with self-managed teams, the richer the planning process will be. People who are given the facts will respond with fact-based plans. Without facts, people are forced to make guesses, and everyone knows what happens when people make assumptions. Networking people across the health care system is critical to developing patient care systems that work. Management knows who can do what in the system, and leaders who connect a work team with people and groups who can help the team will see dramatic improvements in patient care. Management needs to provide work teams with information, encourage organizational networking, and then stay out of the way.

Planning starts within each individual. Self-managed teams provide forums for people to share personal interests and plans. The process of connecting personal plans to patient care may seem tedious and time consuming. It is! Is it worth it? The proof is in the pudding. Work teams that take the time to identify and communicate their purpose on an intimate level to other people in the organization will act in uncanny alignment with their customers, suppliers, and managers. These teams will know what to do and when to do it, without being told. In fact, without being told what to do, these work teams will do more than was expected under the top-down planning systems of the past. The key to a planning system "that just happens" is involving stakeholders in the planning by connecting everyone's interests.

Forms, Tools, and Processes

"I skate to where the puck is going to be, not to where it has been."

—*Wayne Gretzky*

There are many books with charts and diagrams for planning. The purpose of all these techniques is to provide a common reference point for the plan so that everyone involved can understand the plan. This section will present some basic forms, provide a simple tool, and describe a process for developing written plans.

Forms for Planning

There are four forms that can aid you in creating your written plans:

1. Mission, vision, and values form
2. Gap analysis worksheet
3. Goals worksheet
4. Role clarification grid

Mission, Vision, and Values Form The form for creating mission, vision, and values statements is the most important any team will use for planning. (See table 12-1.) The team's mission statement expresses its purpose—its reason for existing; it defines the team's customers, services, and scope. Mission statements start with phrases like "We exist to . . ." or "We provide . . ." The team's vision statement describes its picture of an ideal future—where the team wants to be, what the team wants to be recognized for. Vision statements start with phrases like "We will be . . ." or "We will be recognized for . . ." The team's values statement affirms its beliefs and guiding principles—what the team stands for.

The team will invest much time, effort, and energy in writing these basic statements. The statements must be displayed prominently to remind team members of their basic purpose, and they must be shared frequently with customers and suppliers to remind everyone of the team's goals and expectations. Word processing software can be used to display the mission, vision, and values very professionally; in a simple frame, these statements can be presented with pride.

Table 12-1. Example of the Mission, Vision, and Value Statement of the Mission+ St. Joseph's Health System Metabolic Support Team

Mission	Vision	Values
We exist to promote positive patient nutritional outcomes through cost-effective therapies. We offer a multidisciplinary approach and expertise for the patients of the health system and the region.	We will be recognized nationally as clinical leaders in the provision of leading-edge nutrition therapies. Our patients will receive early and aggressive nutrition support.	Mercy, Trust, Dignity of the Individual, Integrity, Excellence, Communication, Expertise, Teamwork

Gap Analysis Worksheet The gap analysis worksheet helps people identify strategies. Strategies are action statements about the major initiatives needed to change the current situation into the desired future. (See figure 12-2.)

☞ **Team Tip:** Goal statements should be **SMART: S**pecific, **M**easurable, **A**chievable, **R**ealistic, and **T**ime based.

Goals Worksheet Strategies depend on goals. Goals are actions to be accomplished. Every goal statement should be accompanied by information on how the team plans to accomplish the goal: who from the team will be the goal leader, what steps are needed, what people or groups need to be involved in each step, when each step is to be completed, and what resources are required for each step. Sharing goal worksheets with everyone on the

Figure 12-2. Gap Analysis Worksheet

Future: What do you foresee as the future for your team?

Situation:

Requirements:

Needs:

Present Situation: Describe your team's current situation.

Situation:

Requirements:

Needs:

Gap Analysis: Identify strategies—What actions do you need to take to prepare your team to meet the future situation, requirements, and needs listed above?

team helps each team member understand what his or her role will be in achieving the team's goals. (See figure 12-3.)

Role Clarification Grid Part of teamwork is having each team member understand his or her role. The role clarification grid is used to clarify roles and levels of involvement for team members and individuals outside the team. It is best completed at a team meeting so that team members agree on their roles and understand their individual responsibilities in achieving each team goal. Actions toward the goal are listed vertically in the left-hand column. Names of people involved in achieving the goal are listed horizontally across the top. The team then fills in the grid with the appropriate symbol for each team member for each step. The result is a visual display of each team member's role. (See figure 12-4.)

Tool for Planning: The Business Plan

The prospect of completing a business plan scares many people. It shouldn't. A business plan is no more than a comprehensive statement of what you want to achieve and what you need in order to make it happen. Moreover, not every task requires the completion of a business plan. The business plan is a tool that the team may need every one or two years (or when requested by top management), primarily in the budgeting process. The purpose of the business plan is to provide a summary of how the work team intends to conduct business.

Figure 12-3. Goal Worksheet

Goal Statement:

Goal Leader:

What steps are needed to achieve the goal?	Who needs to be involved in each step?	What is the target date to complete each step?	What resources are required for each step?
1.			
2.			
3.			
4.			
5.			

Figure 12-4. Role Clarification for Goal

Goal:

Action Steps/Process	Names of Those Affected by Goal on and off the Team

Key:
X: Do the work
F: Be informed
I: Be involved
OK: Approve

When a business plan is needed, teams will find that they have already done most of the work in the process of establishing reasons for teams, setting team boundaries, developing team design, talking to customers, and establishing team mission, vision, values, and goals. Team activity 2, at the end of this chapter, walks a work team through the basic components of a business plan; completion of the activity will result in a business plan. The team will find that the process is more important than the actual document produced. The team should use the business plan as a tool to get everyone on the team involved in planning and to develop a shared understanding of the plan.

Process for Planning: Scenario Planning

The book *Art of the Long View* describes the process of scenario planning using the metaphor of ballistics.[1] Ballistics is the system that allows a quarterback to look down the playing field and throw a pass to a spot where the receiver will be when the ball arrives. The quarterback factors in many variables to determine where to throw the ball. These variables include the route of the receiver, the receiver's speed, where the quarterback will be when the ball is thrown, where the defenders will be, and what effect wind will have on the flight of the ball. A quarterback must have good vision, keen awareness of the players on the field, certain knowledge of the route run by the receiver, experience with the type of defense being played, and the skill to throw the ball where he wants it to go. Planning requires similar skills in order to determine what actions need to be taken in the present to prepare for an uncertain future. One approach to this challenge is scenario planning.

Scenario planning is the process of anticipating several versions of the future and developing plans that are flexible enough to fit these different situations. The power of scenario planning is that it gives people a glimpse of the future—in fact, many possible futures—before it arrives. The development of scenarios helps team members share mental models and gain knowledge of the tactics needed to achieve success. Figure 12-5 is an example of a scenario developed under optimistic assumptions about the future of the health system.

Assumptions need not be optimistic, however. Understanding what will happen if the environment for the health system is hostile is equally helpful. When people face the possibility that the future will be tough, they

Figure 12-5. Optimistic Scenario Report for Pharmacy Services

Scenario

The health system will move to a community health focus while retaining a high occupancy in the hospitals for high-acuity patients. The health system will continue to receive adequate funding from government and third-party payers, which will support building of new facilities for critical care and community health centers. There will be significant investment in automation and information systems for pharmacy support. Pharmacists will be recognized and paid for providing cognitive services, and technicians will manage the drug distribution process.

Critical Success Factors

- Pharmacists need to be educated in clinical skills to meet the needs of critical care and wellness patients.
- Pharmacy leaders need to be involved in planning of new facilities to include pharmacy space.
- Planning for automation and information systems must be done in a multidisciplinary manner to assure acceptance.
- Reimbursement mechanisms for pharmacist cognitive services and systems must be established to allow technicians to manage drug distribution.

Creative Tactics

- Develop shared positions with the school of pharmacy for pharmacist educational development.
- Get a pharmacy coach appointed to each service line leadership team for input on facilities design.
- Establish a planning task with nursing and medical staff for pharmacy automation systems.
- Work with statewide initiatives to develop pilot programs for pharmacist clinical reimbursement and expansion of technician roles.

can honestly assess their individual options and prepare for hard times. Team activity 3, at the end of this chapter, helps a group of planners produce three one-page scenarios—based on optimistic, pessimistic, and realistic assumptions about the future. These one-page summaries represent the options facing the work team and let people know what choice they can make about the future. The most significant product of scenario planning, though, is the creative process it generates. There is nothing more powerful than a group of human beings who are engaged in creating a future for a collectively beneficial purpose.

Many forms, tools, and processes for planning have appeared with the advent of modern management. This section has provided a few simple techniques and suggested some approaches and structures for the planning process. There is no best way or worst way to plan. Planning is a dynamic system and like any system will take on a life of its own. Whatever planning technique a team chooses, it should produce a written plan. Work teams can use these written plans to establish shared models.

Frustration and Elation

"It's an important day in everyone's life when they begin to work for what they want to build rather than to please a boss."

—*Bill O'Brien*

Planning requires change. Resistance to change is the greatest barrier to planning. The following comments are typical of the response self-managed teams will encounter when they propose their plans:

- "A good idea, but . . ."
- "All right in theory."
- "The boss won't go for it."
- "Let's form a committee."
- "We've never done it that way."
- "Yes, but . . ."

Statements like these are based on people's experiences with bureaucratic organizations. Self-managed teams require a new mind-set for change. In the past, people said, "I'll try." As team members people must say, "I can!"

Table 12-2 identifies planning barriers work teams will face, as well as breakthrough responses to help teams deal with the frustration caused by naysayers left over from the bureaucracy. These are just a few of the many barriers that anyone who is planning anything will face. Understanding that people will resist change is a starting point. The teams that make a difference are those that see past the barriers and understand the breakthroughs.

Table 12-2. Planning Barriers and Breakthroughs

Barrier Type	Planning Barrier	Breakthrough Response
General	Lack of time	Time for planning is an investment to make sure that we will be doing the right things and doing them the right way.
General	Desire to conform to adopted patterns	We must unlearn the old behaviors and methods so we can replace them with systems designed for the future.
General	Statistics and past experience	New methods require new measurements; learning is based on understanding previous experience and improving upon it.
General	Too much or too little knowledge of work involved	Doing something new engages the process of discovery and we can invent new ways of doing things as we move forward.
Emotional	Fear of making mistakes	Mistakes are a necessary part of learning; we must celebrate our mistakes as they will be the basis for our success.
Emotional	Desire for security, risk averse	Taking on risks we plan for is better than the risk taken when we accept the risks that others plan for us.
Emotional	Inability to reject one workable solution and search for a better one	New paths are found only when we leave the old ones.
Emotional	Unwillingness to view and accept alternatives	The more choices we have, the more likely we will find ways to improve.

Table 12-2. (Continued)

Barrier Type	Planning Barrier	Breakthrough Response
Thinking	Failure to investigate the obvious	Usually the greatest opportunity for improvement is in what we think currently works best.
Thinking	Failure to ask the right questions	The more questions we ask, the more questions we have, the better answers we get.
Thinking	Failure to understand that creativity is not dependent on work background	Creativity is dependent on diversity and insight, and every person brings experience much deeper than their work background.
Thinking	Difficulty seeing remote relationships	More interaction and networking between team members and others will lead to broader opportunities for new solutions.

Planning in self-managed teams is an exercise in "cocreation." Cocreation is a natural result in human systems that involve more than one person. It is spontaneous and complex. Cocreation occurs whether we want it to or not. Planning is simply a method to help people make choices during the ongoing process of cocreation. Figure 12-6 lists tips for mastering the cocreation mode.

Chapter Wrap-Up

Planning is an active process. Human beings live in a complex world vibrant with intertwining goals and relationships. Planning provides people with a system for working together toward common goals. It provides work teams with a system for aligning the personal visions of individual team members into a team goal and for connecting team goals to the interests of many stakeholders. Learning to plan is difficult but rewarding work. When everyone on the team contributes to planning, everyone wins.

Reference

1. Peter Schwartz, *Art of the Long View* (New York: Doubleday, 1991), p. 30.

Figure 12-6. Tips for Cocreating

- *Start with personal vision.* Every human system is made up of individuals with personal values and aspirations. Personal vision is the starting point for each and every plan.
- *Treat everyone as equal.* When everyone is viewed as equal everyone feels valued. People who are valued will have strong commitment and make contributions.
- *Seek alignment, not agreement.* Expression of differences should be encouraged. Do not try for consensus. Establish dialogue which leads to team and individual learning.
- *Among teams, encourage interdependence and diversity.* Teams need to be different and discuss openly with other teams what they need and what they can do to work together.
- *Avoid sampling, and have people speak only for themselves.* Planning is very personal and everyone must have the opportunity to share his or her individual perspectives and plans. This is time consuming on the front end but time saving when everyone understands and contributes to implementing the plan.
- *Expect and nurture reverence for each other.* Every person's vision and purpose for his or her life is sacred to that person. Respecting and listening to others is the basis for finding the common purpose for everyone on the team.
- *Use an "interim vision" to build momentum.* Don't over promise. Start with a few small steps to demonstrate to the team and top management that you can succeed. Remember that success breeds success.
- *Focus on the dialogue, not just the plan.* The process of planning is more important than the plan. Participation in the creation of the plan is what will carry people through implementation of the plan. The test of the plan is not the written document but the directional force it gives the team.

Suggested Readings

Senge, P. M., A. Kleiner, C. Roberts, and R. B. Ross. *The Fifth Discipline Fieldbook.* New York: Doubleday, 1994.

Sims, B. Workshop for the Institute for Servant Leadership, Flat Rock, NC, April 19, 1997.

Wheatley, M. Interview in *Trinity News* (January 1997).

Wheatley, M. *Leadership and the New Science.* San Francisco: Berrett-Koehler, 1994.

Wheatley, M. Workshop for the Institute for Servant Leadership, Flat Rock, NC, April 19, 1997.

Team Activity 1

Developing a Planning Process

Purpose: To get the design team started on developing a planning system.

Directions:

1. Brainstorm for each of the following four stakeholder groups a list of key people or groups of people: customers, suppliers, team members, and management. These are the people who must be involved in any planning activity by self-managed teams.
2. Identify for each of the key groups of people identified in step 1 methods that self-managed teams can use to get input. Methods might include surveys, E-mail, monthly reports, hallway conversations, and so on.
3. Determine which members of self-managed teams should be responsible for communicating with each of the external stakeholder groups—customers, suppliers, and management—on an ongoing basis. These will be the key contact people.
4. Brainstorm material and information that self-managed teams can scan for trends, new ideas, technology breakthroughs, and future scenarios. Then identify the work team members who will be responsible for reviewing and sharing this information with the rest of the team.
5. Develop a systematic approach by which self-managed teams can talk to customers, suppliers, management, and each other. It is best to schedule this communication as an ongoing activity coordinated with the organization's budget and planning cycle. In fact, the work team planning cycle should be set to run a few months ahead of the organization's planning cycle. It's always fun to turn in "the plan" ahead of the request for the plan.
6. Think of the most off-the-wall people on the self-managed teams, the most cynical people, and the most practical people. Ask two or three of each of these people who represent different areas to get together periodically to look at the planning information the work teams have accumulated. Then ask them to think outside the box and come up with some crazy ideas that just might work and then try them.
7. Develop a communication method(s) for sharing everything with everybody. This is the most important step. Planning is conversation, and conversation is based on communication.

Team Activity 2

Writing a Business Plan for a Self-Managed Team

Purpose: To provide work teams with an outline for writing a business plan.

Directions: Team members should meet and work through the following outline, inserting the information described at each position.

Team name, who prepared the plan, and time frame covered by the plan
Team mission, vision, and values
Team services or products:

Major Services or Products	Key Customers	Critical Success Factors
1.		
2.		
3.		
4.		

SWOT (Strengths, Weaknesses, Opportunities, and Threats) environmental analysis:

Business Issue	Strengths	Weaknesses	Opportunities	Threats
Customers				
Competitors				
Delivery system				
Technology				
Facilities				
Finance/cost				
Information				
Workforce				
Market share				

Service goals: List major services from above and state SMART goals that will improve performance in the critical success areas of quality, cost, and access:

1.

2.

3.

Resource needs: Based on the stated service goals, what resources will be required in the following areas:
- Equipment/technology
- Facilities
- Financial
- Information
- Human resources

Milestones and goal statements: List a summary of goal statements with estimated completion dates. Attach to this a completed goal worksheet (as described earlier in this chapter).

Graphs, charts, and pictures: Include any displays of team accomplishments and quality improvements using data and charts.

Team Activity 3

Scenario Planning for Self-Managed Teams

Purpose: To develop one-page summaries of optimistic, pessimistic, and realistic scenarios along with critical success factors and creative tactics for each scenario.

Directions:

1. Ask the group of planners assembled in step 6 of team activity 1 to brainstorm three views of the future: optimistic, pessimistic, and realistic. Remember that this group of people should include those in the department who scan the literature, talk frequently to customers, think outside the box and should include some cynics as well as some positive thinkers. The purpose of this step is to describe the future environment for the team. It is best to use a facilitator to prevent the planning group from thinking about what the team will do in any of these situations. The outcome of this step should be three paragraphs that describe optimistic, pessimistic, and realistic views of the world that the team face in the future. A tip is to divide the planning group into three separate groups and have them work independently to create three versions. Then have them come back together and present and amend each scenario with input from members of the entire group.
2. Write the three paragraphs on a single sheet of paper and have the group of planners get feedback from individual team members, customers, suppliers, and management. Reconvene the planners and adjust the three scenarios based on the input received.
3. Divide the planners into three groups, and have each group compare one of the scenarios to the current organizational business plan. Each group should answer the following questions:
   - What aspects of the current business plan will be successful in this scenario?
   - What strategies in the current business plan will fail in this scenario?
   - What adjustments should we make to the business plan in the event this scenario unfolds?
   - What creative strategies can we take to thrive with this scenario?
4. Bring the three groups back together and have a dialogue to identify common themes for success, failure, adjustments, and creative strategies. The common issues that arise will be the critical success factors. The issues that are different can be developed into contingency strategies. Most valuable in this process are the creative tactics that are identified.
5. Document and share the findings of the scenario planning process with the work team, the department, and the organization.

Chapter 13

Measurement Systems

Chapter Preview

"One of the main purposes of diagnostic measurement systems is to eliminate the manager's burden of constant monitoring."

—*R. Simons*

Management-level people in an organization usually resist the concept of self-managed teams when they perceive self-management as "out-of-control" and, even worse, "out-of-MY-control." When a self-managed team is implemented, the first-level supervisor position is eliminated or redirected. Sometimes midlevel management positions are eliminated as well. This means that management for a self-managed team is far removed from the day-to-day activities of the employees. The farther management is from its workforce, the less control it has over what that workforce is doing, and the more uncomfortable management becomes.

Self-managed teams exist to accomplish work and produce results. The teams expect to have the freedom to make decisions and the authority to implement change. When staff operate in an empowered work environment, they will make mistakes. Middle and top management worry that those mistakes will jeopardize the organization and cause both the employees and their manager to fail. The failure will reflect poorly on the managers who see themselves taking risks by implementing self-managed teams in the first place. One way to allay management's worries about control and reduce the number and severity of mistakes is to develop a measurement system that will let both the manager and the team know when work and performance are achieving expectations and when they are drifting off target. This chapter can be used by a self-managed team to develop a measurement system that will meet management's need for control of key performance areas and provide feedback to team members so that they can adjust the team's direction if problems begin to occur.

Chapter at a Glance

In this chapter, you will find

- A discussion of the value of measurement systems
- A description of four team measurement systems
- A discussion of considerations in measurement system selection
- Suggestions for measurement system data gathering
- A discussion of the data reporting process

Measurement Systems

"A team typically tracks only a handful of measurements, enough to help its members learn but not overwhelm them. We don't specify which they should follow. We teach the general techniques. Then we leave it to the local people to use their brains, expertise, and theory—and figure out what's right for their processes."

—Edward M. Baker, quality director, Ford Motor Co.

Measurement has performed useful functions in organizations for many years. Measures help define how successful the organization is, whether investors should consider the organization a good risk, and whether the president of the organization should be retained or be fired. For staff members, measures are familiar when they occur in the framework of a performance review or guidelines on the quantity or quality of work expected. Most staff in health care organizations recognize measurements of vital signs, numbers of patients, and numbers of treatments expected. In addition, managers and quality improvement personnel, along with interested staff, spend time contemplating measures such as patient satisfaction, staff satisfaction, waiting times, and productivity. The most common measurement system that organizations use is the budget, a measure of financial performance against the financial plan.

Measures are useful because they help define what is actually happening in the work environment. They present factual information rather than guesses and assumptions. They help by telling what is happening now and providing a comparison with what has happened in the past, as well as with what is expected to happen in the future. They help people assess and evaluate what is being accomplished or achieved. Many organizations use benchmarks, or external measures or performance standards, to assess the performance of the organization, a department, a work process, or a clinical procedure.

Measurement provides data that can be used to guide decisions and to generate motivation to change. For instance, if a team started receiving complaints about its response to telephone calls, and the complaint was "No one ever answers the phone in your area." They could measure how often phone calls occur and how often they are answered before the caller hangs up, or before the call goes to voice mail. They could brainstorm and come up with a plan to improve their telephone answering performance. They might want to establish a goal or a benchmark, such as "95 percent of phone calls between 8 A.M. and 5 P.M. will be answered by a staff member by the third ring."

Once the goal is established and the new system is implemented, the team can measure its success in achieving improvement in telephone answering. Measuring a team system or process can lead to changes to improve performance. Measures help staff identify where changes are needed, and they help staff decide what to do when they make a change.

Measures provide a control mechanism. They help management know how the organization is performing against a plan for organizational performance. They help doctors and nurses assess the health of their patients. They help teachers judge progress in learning. They help the supervisor look at the performance of a segment of the organization. And they can help a team analyze its own performance.

Self-managed teams use measurement systems in a number of ways. The three uses for measures that are of primary importance are to allow management to influence and control performance, to provide data that can be analyzed, and to give performance feedback to the team. Self-managed teams must develop a measurement system that achieves all three results.

A Method for Management Influence and Control

When the team is first starting, it needs to clarify with management what management's performance expectations are. Managers in health care are usually concerned with patient satisfaction, the quality of care patients receive, outcomes, and the cost of patient care. They are also concerned with daily operations performance, such as the volume of patients treated, the volume of treatments, the quantity of supplies used, the amount of overtime incurred, and the number of staff hours it takes to provide a service.

When a team incorporates measures that are important to managers in their team measurement system, they permit management to influence what the team focuses on and tries to address in its goals and improvement efforts. If overtime is an important area of concern and the vice president sees it regularly reported, monitored, and improved, his or her need for direct control is diminished. The team is accomplishing what is important to management, without the presence of a direct supervisor.

Data That Can Be Analyzed

Team members need to select measures that are meaningful to the team. They need to measure something that they are knowledgeable about and that they care about. Respiratory therapists can measure respirations and the percentage of oxygen in the blood. They are educated in the field of respiratory therapy and know what respiration data mean when they are reported. They can also measure the number of treatments performed by each respiratory therapist each hour.

Respiratory therapists and other health care personnel can measure how satisfied other departments are with their services, and they can measure how satisfied patients are. They can measure staff satisfaction and budget performance. All of these measurement areas are familiar to health care staff. Staff are comfortable with their ability to analyze the data that they receive through these measures. They can identify benchmarks and opportunities for improvement. These are data about aspects of their work that they understand and can analyze.

Self-managed teams need to be comfortable with the measures that they select. They also need select only a few measures. If they select too many, they will lose the focus that measurement can provide, and they will end up spending too much time gathering data for their performance measures.

Performance Feedback to the Team

The self-managed team is responsible for its performance. To fulfill this responsibility, the team needs data and information on how it is progressing. Measurement systems provide the data that give feedback to the team on its performance. When the team finds out that its customers are satisfied with its performance, it has received positive feedback. This feedback helps the team tell that all the work and effort it has expended has been warranted. If the team receives feedback that patient charges are rising, it has a focus for its cost reduction efforts. Measurement systems give team members factual data that they can use to assess the quality of their performance. It also gives them factual data that they can report to others on how the team is progressing.

Teams have used a number of different measures, but the measures tend to fall into similar categories. Teams measure their internal performance, and they also measure their performance in external areas, such as with customer satisfaction. The categories used most frequently are:

- Progress on team goals
- Customer satisfaction and service quality (satisfaction of patients, physicians, families, and staff; market share, access)
- Cost (supplies per procedure, cost per procedure, overtime rate, days in accounts receivable)
- Clinical quality (utilization of clinical paths, patient outcomes, vital sign performance)
- Team performance (meeting effectiveness, education of team, participation)

The number of measures that a team selects is important. If possible, the team should select a very small number—three to five measures. If team members must gather and display data on a large number of measures, they will find that they are spending a disproportionate amount of time on measures. A few key measures will help the team focus on the items that are the most important to the team, its customers, its manager, and the organization.

Common Team Measurement Systems

"The team decided to measure patient waiting times. They knew this was important to patients as well as the physicians. It was also embarrassing to them to have a patient wait an hour or two."

—*Shirley Nesbitt, team coach, Regional Surgical Specialists*

When the team selects its measurement system, it will consider several criteria. It wants to measure those few areas that will truly indicate how well the team is performing. It will also want to measure those areas that are important to management and important to customers. Ideally, those areas of importance will overlap because a team does not want too many measures. The list below provides criteria that the team measurement system should meet:

- Measures track critical team objectives
- Measures let the team know whether it is meeting customer requirements
- Measures help the team focus on its mission, vision, values, and goals
- Measures cover the important dimensions of team performance
- Measures are limited to a few key areas of performance
- Data are available
- Measures relate to areas within the team's control
- Measures meet management's need for control
- The team agrees on the measures

There are four measurement systems that are commonly used by teams. Each system allows the team to display its measures visually, so that the team and other interested parties can view the team's performance at a given point in time. Each of the systems meets the criteria for a measurement system described above. Each will accommodate as many measures as the team deems important. The four systems are called dashboard, report card, spiderweb, and scoreboard. The systems will be reviewed in detail below.

Dashboard

The dashboard was introduced by Christopher Meyer as a measurement system for a cross-functional team—a team that comprises members from different parts or functions of the organization.[1] Regardless of whether the team represents a single function, like a nursing unit, or is cross-functional, like the office staff in a physician's practice, the dashboard will be an effective measurement system.

To envision a dashboard measurement system, think of the dashboard of an automobile or an airplane. The dashboard may have gauges like a speedometer or an odometer. It may have a measurement gauge that looks like a thermometer. Figure 13-1 presents one concept of this measurement system.

The dashboard is a relatively simple measurement tool. It can easily be developed once the team identifies what it wants to measure. For instance, if the team decides it wants to measure customer satisfaction, then it must decide what it will display relating to customer satisfaction and how often it will assess satisfaction and update the display.

Once these questions about customer satisfaction are answered, the survey tool can be developed and administered. There will be a result, rating, or score that the team will display. The team may want to work together to

Figure 13-1. The Dashboard

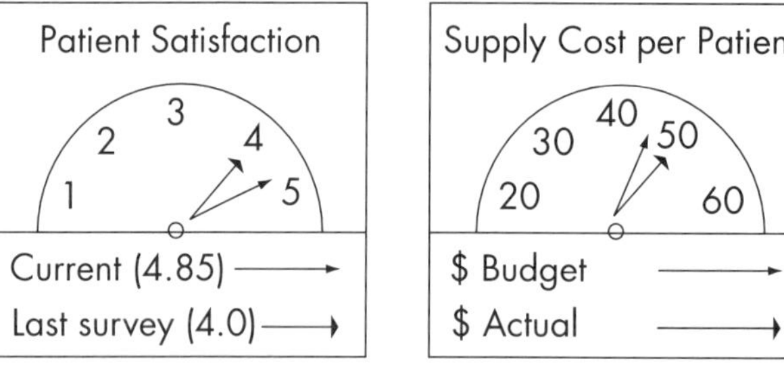

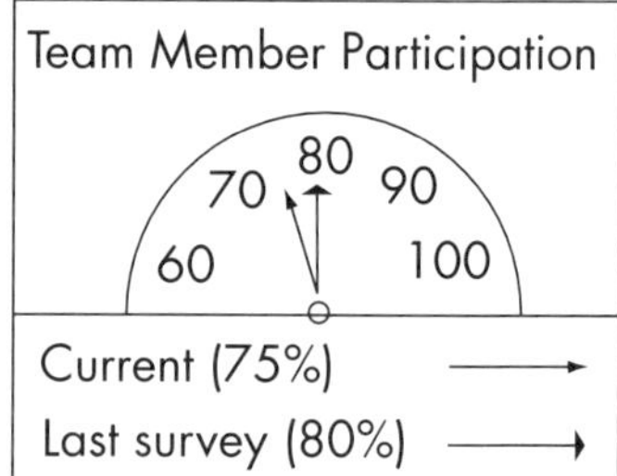

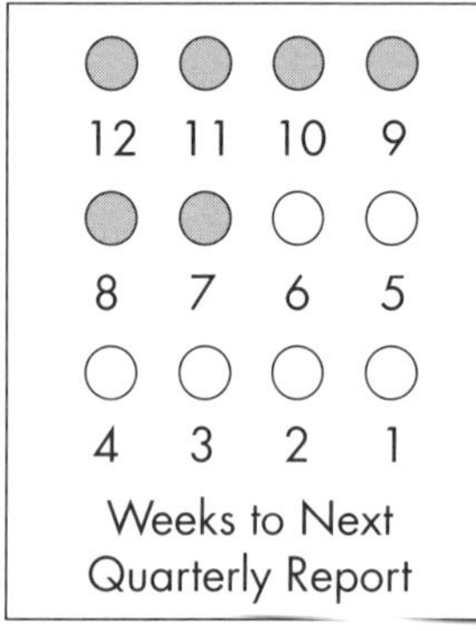

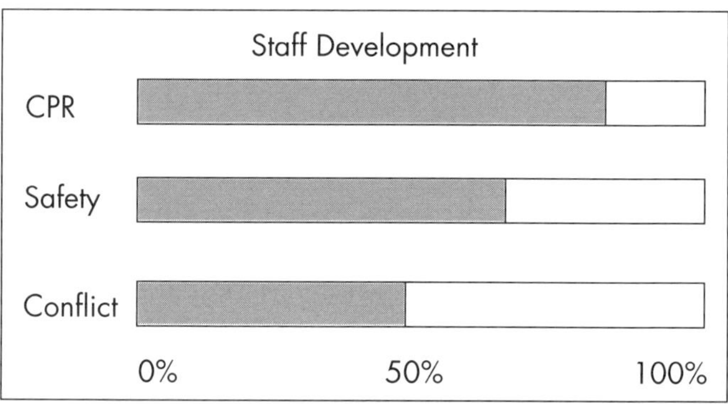

decide how to display the data, and they may assign the data display to one of the team roles, such as the quality improvement coordinator.

If the dashboard is used, then one person should be assigned the responsibility of keeping it up to date. Anyone on the team can contribute data to the dashboard. It is expected that the dashboard will be updated at least quarterly. As can be seen in figure 13-1, there are some items, such as weeks to next quarterly report, that are updated weekly. Other items, such as supply cost per patient, may be updated monthly. The person on the team who is responsible for cost and budget may provide the updated information for the supply cost measure, the educator may provide the information for the staff development measure.

Report Card

The report card is another relatively simple measurement system. Like the dashboard, the first thing the team must decide is what it will measure. After that decision is made, the team will next determine a rating system for the report card. Teams frequently use the classroom system of giving an A for Excellent, B for Good, C for Satisfactory, D for Poor, and F for Failure. Health maintenance and managed care organizations are known for using report cards, and report cards are becoming more common in other areas of the health care industry. Using the same measures that were displayed in the dashboard, a report card would look like the one in table 13-1.

Spiderweb

The spiderweb is more complex than the report card. As with the other measurement display systems, the first thing the team must decide is what will it measure? With the spiderweb, the question is more detailed than with the other measurement systems.[2] The spiderweb is divided into quadrants, or four sections. Each section represents a measurement category. On the spiderweb in figure 13-2, the four sections are

- Quality
- Customer satisfaction
- Team development
- Cost

Within those categories, there are two or three measures that are tracked and reported. If the team decides that it wants to measure quality, then it must identify two or three representative measures for quality that can be included and displayed on the spiderweb. In figure 13-2, the team picked the following two measures of quality:

- Clinical path performance
- Timeliness of quarterly report

Table 13-1. The Report Card

The Surgery Team 1998 Report Card				
Performance Measures	**1st Quarter**	**2nd Quarter**	**3rd Quarter**	**4th Quarter**
Patient satisfaction	A	B	A	
Supply cost per patient	B	B	A	
Team member participation	A	B	B	
Timeliness of quarterly report	A	B	B	
Staff development	C	B	A	

Figure 13-2. The Spiderweb

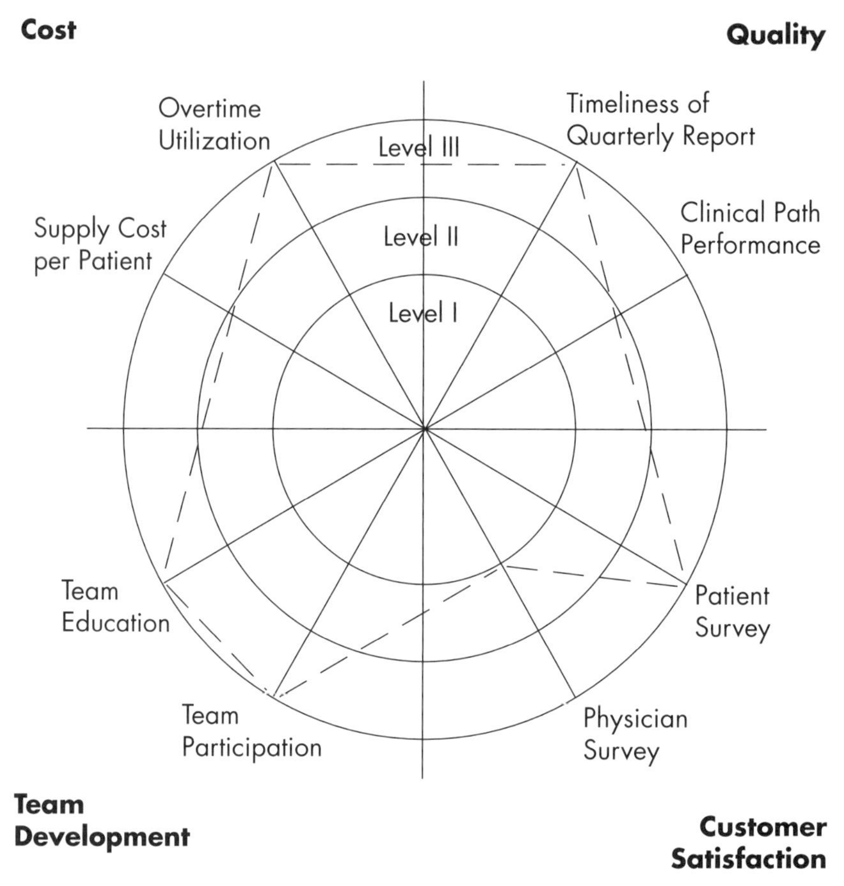

Once the measures in all four categories are decided, then the team must decide how to rate or rank performance. The lowest level of satisfactory performance is the innermost circle, the next and higher level of satisfactory performance is the middle circle, and superior performance is represented by the outermost circle. Each quarter, the team can measure itself and create a new spiderweb to demonstrate its progress and performance level for that quarter. The team also has the option of using lines of different colors to document performance each quarter. If they do this they can show performance changes all on one spiderweb. However, the spiderweb begins to look very cluttered.

Scoreboard

The scoreboard is a complex tool to develop. It includes both team and department measures, targets, and performance. It is an excellent tool to link team performance and overall department performance, which tends to keep teams working together to help the department achieve its performance objectives.

The scoreboard is modeled after the scorecard developed by Robert S. Kaplan and David P. Norton.[3] The scoreboard incorporates predetermined measures, displayed in the center of the board, and then both department and team performance targets. Each team keeps its own scoreboard. A team may have different targets than the department. For instance in figure 13-3 the customer satisfaction target for the team is different from the target for the department. The team is attempting to achieve a customer satisfaction rating that is higher than the rating the department is seeking.

It is expected that each team will have performance targets related to the measures and supportive of the department targets. However, team targets can differ from department targets. In the instance of staff development, the department measure does not specify the skills or knowledge that need to be developed. Each team can determine its own development needs and measure its success in achieving them. This is a flexible measurement display tool and one that most teams can create and maintain without difficulty.

Figure 13-3. The Scoreboard

Team Scoreboard ■ 2nd Quarter 1998

Department Performance Objectives

- Reduce overtime by 20%
- Implement self-managed teams
- Improve customer satisfaction
- Implement staff development plan

Team Performance Measures

- Reduce overtime by 20%
- Implement self-managed teams
- Improve customer satisfaction
- All team members will complete CPR, safety education, and conflict workshops

Department Targets		Measures	Team Targets	
Target 2% of payroll	Performance 3.5%	Overtime (%)	Target 2% of payroll	Performance 2.5%
Fully implemented 10/01/99	Roles implemented 07/01/98	Self-Managed Team Implementation	Fully implemented 10/01/99	Roles implemented 07/01/98
4.90 on 5.0 Scale	4.85	Customer Satisfaction Rating	4.95 on 5.0 Scale	4.9%
100% Complete	60% Complete	Staff Development	100% Complete	CPR = 100%; Safety = 80%; Conflict = 60%

Measurement System Selection

"It was an easy decision for us. We selected the dashboard. It is simple and meaningful. We didn't want to spend a lot of time developing and interpreting the display."

—Joy Thomas, design team member, Mission+St. Joseph's

In order to determine which measurement and display system the team will use, the team should consider the culture and the current practice of the organization. Is there a measurement system that is in common use within the organization? If the organization uses a report card, the team may want to use a report card as well. Within the Mission+St. Joseph's Health System, teams developed measurement systems before the health system adopted one. Some of the teams use the dashboard because it is the easiest to develop and maintain. Other teams use the spiderweb because they like the concept and are familiar with it from quality improvement readings they have studied.

If the team is one of several teams that all exist within one functional department, the scoreboard may be the preferred model because it helps link all teams' measures to department performance measures. Although the measurement system is primarily for the team's use, it is also available for anyone to view. It is important to meet the organization's needs for the measurement display device, just as it is important to meet the team's needs.

To select a measurement system, the entire team should review the options presented in this chapter. Team members should consider the difficulties they will face in developing and maintaining the system. The member of the team who is actually going to maintain the display should practice developing the one that most team members like. If it is too difficult to develop and maintain, it might not last beyond the first or second quarter. Although the dashboard and the report card are the simplest of the measurement systems, the spiderweb and the scoreboard are not too difficult. The most important consideration is: Is the team able to maintain the measurement system by itself? If the answer is yes, and there are no organizational reasons to select one system rather than another, then the team can select whichever system members like best.

Measurement System Data Collection

"It took us several tries, but we finally figured out how to gather the data. What we wanted to know was simple, but gathering the data was a bit more complex."

—Debbie Davidson, team member, Regional Surgical Specialists

Once the team has decided on its measures and on the display system it will use, it begins to develop the data-gathering system. Different members of the team may be involved in gathering data, depending on the measurement. For instance, cost data, such as overtime rates, may be the responsibility of the team budget coordinator or the team scheduler. Data on patient satisfaction may be the responsibility of the team quality improvement coordinator or the public relations coordinator. Staff development information may come from the team educator.

The first rule for the team in gathering data is to determine whether the data are already available from its own records, or records being maintained by another department or team. The team will not want to devise a new system for gathering data if a system already exists.

Table 13-2 is based on data-gathering needs for the dashboard. It identifies the performance indicator, the frequency with which data is gathered, the definition of the measure, the person responsible for gathering the information, and the method for gathering the information.

Many health care organizations retain external consultants to measure their customer satisfaction ratings. Some health care organizations collect satisfaction data internally, within the marketing or public relations departments. In these cases, since a centralized data-gathering system exists, the organization prohibits departments and teams from gathering their own data. This may mean that satisfaction data are not gathered on the specific customers of the self-managed team. The team may need special permission to gather its own data or may not be able to gather data as often as it would like. As the organization tries to protect its customers from receiving too many surveys, it may inhibit the ability of teams to measure customer satisfaction. If a team has permission to develop its own customer survey, it should take the following survey guidelines into consideration:

- Decide which customers to measure.
- Decide how many of them to measure (100 percent or a sample).
- Decide how often to measure their satisfaction.
- Decide on a rating scale.
- Identify what questions to ask the customers—only one topic per question.
- Develop a format for the survey. Will it be a face-to-face interview, a questionnaire, or a telephone survey?
- Decide who will conduct the survey.
- Decide how much time each survey should take.
- Decide how to compile and display the data.

Gathering data is a time-consuming process. Distributing data gathering among team roles such as budget coordinator, quality improvement coordinator, and educator helps reduce the workload that any individual carries and reduces the burden that data gathering can bring. Once the team members see the results of the data gathering and take action to make changes to improve results, they will begin to be more interested in measuring and displaying their performance.

Table 13-2. Data Gathering for the Dashboard

Performance Indicator/ Frequency	Definition of the Measure	Method for Gathering Data
Patient satisfaction (maintained by quality improvement coordinator): Gathered daily during the month, computed quarterly	The average rating of 60 postcard surveys distributed randomly to patients, 20 per month, during the specified quarter	■ The RN distributes a survey postcard to each patient with their discharge instructions. ■ As they are returned, the unit secretary gathers the cards in three envelopes, one for each month of the quarter. ■ Once 20 arrive for the month, the unit secretary seals the envelope and forwards it to the quality improvement coordinator. ■ The quality improvement coordinator computes an average rating for each of the four questions on the postcards based on all 60 responses. ■ The quality improvement coordinator computes an average overall rating, by adding the four ratings together and dividing by 4.
Supply cost per patient (maintained by budget coordinator): Gathered daily, computed monthly	Total charges for supplies for the month divided by total number of patients for the month	■ The unit secretary keeps a log of the total number of admissions and transfers to the unit, month by month. ■ The budget coordinator receives the supply charges for the unit on the monthly budget report. ■ The budget coordinator divides the monthly supply charge total by the total number of patients that month. The result is the supply cost per patient.
Team member participation (maintained by note taker): Gathered monthly, computed quarterly	Total team members in attendance at standing monthly team meetings, divided by total team members	■ The note taker takes attendance at each standing monthly meeting. She documents how many people attended, and the total possible attendance. ■ At the end of three months, she adds each total number attended, and each total possible attendance. ■ The team leader divides total attendance by total team members. The result is changed from hundredths to a percentage and is team member participation.

Table 13-2. (Continued)

Performance Indicator/ Frequency	Definition of the Measure	Method for Gathering Data
Weeks to next quarterly report (maintained by note taker): Gathered once per quarter, maintained weekly	Total full weeks (at least 4 days in the week to be a full week) between the date of the last quarterly report and the date of the next quarterly report	■ The note taker looks through an annual calendar and counts off the number of full weeks between the current report due date and the next due date. ■ The note taker places an identical number of circles on the display board. ■ As each week passes, the note taker updates the circles by coloring them in, to note the passage for the week, starting at the highest number of weeks and working back.
Staff development (maintained by educator): Gathered after each educational offering, computed quarterly	Total course boxes checked divided by total course boxes, multiplied by 100 equals the percentage	■ The educator maintains records by course and by staff member. ■ As each staff member successfully completes a course, the box for that course is checked. ■ At the end of the quarter, for staff members currently employed, the educator counts total boxes and total boxes checked. ■ The educator divides the total boxes checked by total boxes, multiplies by 100, and thus obtains the staff development percentage.

The Reporting Process

"We were anxious about reporting the data. We didn't want to hurt anyone's feelings, but we knew change would be easier once the data were presented."

—Sandra Crouch, team member, Regional Surgical Specialists

As the team develops its performance measures and data collection process and considers a display method, it recognizes that the information it gathers will need to be shared with others outside the team. The vice president or department director who enabled the team to get started established performance expectations for the team. He or she will be wondering how the team is progressing. He or she will be looking for a report. Once the team realizes that others will want to see its performance measures and results, it will need to decide who to share them with, in what format they should be presented, and how often to report its performance. When a team reports data, even to itself, there is the possibility that it will be resisted. Team members will need to consider how to respond to people who resist their data.

Who Receives the Report?

The first decision the team needs to make about reporting the data is *who* would like to see it. Naturally, the team itself is a customer for its data. The person or people who have management responsibility for the team will want to see the data, and the quality improvement department may want to see the data as well. It is possible that the team will want to display the data publicly so that customers will see it. In some organizations, teams have formed customer-supplier partnerships, and the customers believe they too have ownership of the data.

How Is the Data Report Formatted?

The team may want to report its data on a large display board of some type. That way, everyone on the team can see the current results. Moreover, this kind of display focuses attention on the areas of performance that are most important to the team. However, not everyone who wants to see the team performance data will want to see it on a large display board. The team may want to develop a format using word processing software for a quarterly report of performance measures. Each quarter, when the display board is updated, the team can prepare a brief report on paper that can be copied and distributed to whomever is interested. A sample report is displayed in table 13-3.

How Often Should Data Be Reported?

Team performance can be reviewed weekly, monthly, quarterly, annually, or with any other frequency that makes sense to the team. The measures that the team selects help determine how often performance should be reviewed. If data are available only monthly, then it is not logical to review performance weekly. The data would be the same, week to week, until the monthly data are available. It is difficult to demonstrate a change or improvement in a short period of time. Many teams gather data monthly or weekly and only report it quarterly. That way team members are able to see whether an improvement trend has developed because they have multiple data points.

Table 13-3. Sample Team Performance Report

Team: The Rockets
Date: July 1998
Third Quarter Report

Measurement Category	Target	Fourth Quarter	Third Quarter	Second Quarter	First Quarter
Patient satisfaction	4.85 out of 5		4.8	4.9	4.7
Supply cost per patient	$45		$45	$50	$55
Team member participation	100%		85%	80%	75%
Timeliness of quarterly report	On time		On time	On time	On time
Staff development	100% Complete		80%	60%	40%

It generally takes several months or longer to improve a system in a noticeable or measurable way.

Why Will People Resist the Data?

On occasion, when information is reported, team members and others resist the data. They may be dismayed with the results and trying to find a rationalization for why the results are bad. Or they may think the results are too good and that it is not possible for the team to perform so well. How does the team know when someone is resisting its report and its data?

The first sign is when the resistor asks the team to gather more data. Resistors frequently want to know how the data was collected, and whether there is something wrong with the method that the team used. They may criticize the reliability or validity of the data. They may just silently reject the whole report and not discuss it with the team at all. Or, if the results are amazingly good or bad, they may express no surprise, even if the team itself is surprised by the data.

The reasons that people resist data are many. However, the most common reason is that they do not like the results that the data prove. There is little that the team can do when someone resists its data. If the resistor is genuinely interested, the team can share its methods and possibly pick up a tip for improving its data collection system. Finding people who doubt the data is one of the risks of reporting it.

What Do the Data Mean?

Once the information is reported, the team will want to take time to analyze the data. Are this quarter's results positive or not? If they are positive, the team should celebrate! If the results are not positive, the team may want to do some investigation to discover what is happening to its performance.

If patient satisfaction is lower this quarter than last, can anyone think of a reason why? If supply costs have gone up, does anyone know what caused that? If overtime is up, is it because the team has built overtime into the schedule, or is it due to vacancies that occurred on the team last quarter? The quality improvement coordinator on the team may decide to form a quality improvement project subteam to investigate the problem.

It is never enough to just report the data. A high-performance team, striving to improve, will always be interested in investigating performance problems and trying to find ways to improve. The real purpose of performance measurement and measurement display is to focus the entire team on improving its performance in areas that are important to the organization, the customer, and the team.

Chapter Wrap-Up

Although staff who work in health care organizations are familiar with measures, such as blood pressure and temperature, they are not as familiar with the type of measures that are commonly used to assess team performance. Developing a team measurement system and actually spending the time maintaining it may seem a daunting task to most teams, but measurement is necessary to give management a sense of control over the team and to enable a team to document what is actually occurring in areas that are critical to the team's successful performance.

A measurement system is helpful to the team because it provides information on team performance. But it can't end there. The measurements must be reported and analyzed. And then the team must take action to maintain its successes and to make improvements in its performance. Teams will want to report the measures to themselves and their management. They may also want to report their measurement results to their customers. Through a well-developed measurement system, a team can focus on performance and improvement in areas that benefit them, their customers, and their organization.

References

1. C. Meyer, "How the Right Measures Help Teams Excel," *Harvard Business Review* 72 (3, May–June 1994): 95–103.

2. For examples, see M. Kennedy, "Strategic Performance Measurement Systems," *The Quality Letter* (Dec. 1995–Jan. 1996): 2–21.

3. R. S. Kaplan and D. P. Norton, "Using the Balanced Scorecard as a Strategic Management System," *Harvard Business Review* 74 (1, Jan.–Feb. 1996): 75–84.

Suggested Readings

Senge, P., et al. *The Fifth Discipline Fieldbook.* New York: Doubleday, 1994.

Simons, R. "Control in an Age of Environment." *Harvard Business Review* (March–April 1995): 80–88.

Chapter 14

Human Resources Management Systems

Chapter Preview

"It's all about relationships!"

—*Tom Cruise in* Jerry McGuire

This chapter is about trust. The underlying principle of human resources systems for self-managed teams is that people can be trusted to manage themselves and their relationships with others. In this chapter, specific suggestions are given to help work teams design and implement systems to hire, orient, evaluate, discipline, and recognize team members. Human resources management is never easy. Human relations issues are among the most difficult that work teams face. Tips are given to deal with people problems. Freedom is the greatest strength of the self-managed environment and produces its greatest challenges. Human relations is the arena in which work team members learn most about balancing freedom with responsibility.

Chapter at a Glance

In this chapter, you will find

- A description of the human resources environment for teams
- Lessons for designing human resources systems that teams own
- A description of role changes associated with human resources management by teams
- Tips for dealing with people problems

The Human Resources Environment for Teams

"Culture may be defined as the interlocking system of norms and values, implicit or explicit, within an organization."

—*M. Scott Peck*

The Culture of Trust

At a recent conference Margaret Wheatley was asked, "Can we really trust people in self-organizing systems to act responsibly?" She responded with the following story about a middle school principal who has dramatically changed the rules:

> There is a middle school principal who has established a progressive environment for learning and discipline. At a time when our society seems to be out of control and nobody follows the rules this principal has just three rules for the students. They are: take care of yourself, take care of others, and take care of this place. An example of how students behave under this system occurred during a recent bomb threat at the school. It was pouring rain and 600 students were required to wait outside in the water and the mud while the school was searched. When the search was over the students were allowed to return to the school and the principal waited outside to make sure all the students got back in safely. Upon entering the school the principal found 600 pairs of wet and muddy shoes sitting neatly by the entrance.

This story is about establishing a culture of trust. The principal trusts the students, and, as a result, the students behave in a trustworthy—and even exemplary—manner. The hierarchical/bureaucratic systems of the past were based on the belief that workers could not be trusted. Company personnel manuals are filled with rules and policies intended to keep people under control. Self-managed teams require trust, not rules. This chapter is about establishing trust. Trust starts with culture.

The culture of self-managed teams is one of shared leadership. But leadership comes at a price: responsibility. Organizations of the past were run by a few leaders at the top, who bore all the responsibility and thus made all the rules. Ordinary workers did not have any responsibility, and this made their lives easier. Workers simply had to obey the rules. This culture seems to be very efficient. Work should proceed smoothly if everyone follows the rules. But this ideal situation is never realized. Inevitably, people break rules, and then rules are made about what happens when the rules are broken. This process is the vicious circle of bureaucracy: rules about rules. Self-managed teams break that circle. People on teams work together by agreeing to stick to a few simple rules. This team consensus creates a culture of civility.

As Scott Peck observes, "Civility does not come naturally. It takes consciousness and action to achieve. Incivility comes more naturally to us human beings, and because of laziness it is simply easier to be uncivil." Teams must face the fact that managing human relationships is hard work. People on teams cannot be lazy and simply follow some rules laid down by a bureaucracy. Individuals on work teams are each going to be responsible for their own actions and behaviors. Why bother with all this effort? Scott Peck gives the following answer: "While incivility is easier, the creation of a relatively civil organization or culture is in the long run more cost effective. It is also the route to creating something that is more healing and alive."[1]

The middle school students who took off their muddy shoes set an example for everyone who is taking on the difficult task of being a member of a self-managed team. Teams challenge each member to trust the other members and to be civil. This is not easy. Establishing the culture of a self-managed team means cultivating trust and civil relationships—learn the lessons from a middle school.

The Transition to Personal Responsibility and Accountability

People like to do what they do best, and they want to succeed. Recognizing these universal desires and nurturing them lay the groundwork for personal responsibility and accountability among team members. Every new employee and team member comes to work the first day full of hopes and expectations for success. Unfortunately, the workplace throws many obstacles in their paths to success. Some of the barriers can be found in poorly designed work systems. More commonly, however, the barriers arise from human relations issues. Work teams must develop human resources management systems that clear these barriers away.

Performance In the hierarchical model, the new employee must conform to the existing culture to be accepted by coworkers and to abide by personnel policies designed to control behavior. The new employee's ambitions are not focused on job performance but rather on "fitting in." The passive need to fit in becomes a barrier to the employee's success. Self-managed teams that have established a culture based on team and individual responsibility break down this barrier. People need to know that the team is counting on them to contribute and that their contribution to the work effort is the most important aspect of their job performance. Human resources systems designed by work teams must promote rather than hinder success.

Cooperation "People who need people, are the luckiest people in the world." This line from a familiar song celebrates the human desire to have relationships with others. In fact, human survival depends on relationships. Although celebrated by American culture, the spirit of competition is a myth. The spirit of cooperation is the reality. Self-managed teams change the perception that competition is desired and promote cooperation instead. Human resources systems designed by teams need to be different from the hierarchical/bureaucratic systems of the past: they must discourage competition and reward cooperation.

Accountability Every act by every individual is a choice made by that individual. Human resources management systems have historically been designed to limit and control the choices that people can make. These systems have failed and will continue to fail because it is the individual who chooses; no system can choose for anyone. Recognizing that personal choice is a fact is the key to personal accountability. The self-managed environment encourages teams and their members to make responsible choices. The relationship management systems designed by teams place accountability squarely where it needs to be, on the individual. These systems reflect the belief that each person is responsible for the results of his or her choices and actions—for good or ill.

☞ **Team Tip:** Remember the principles of personal responsibility and accountability:

- People like to do what they do best, and they want to succeed.
- People want to cooperate, not compete.
- People make their own choices.

The most profound transition achieved by self-managed teams is the shift of responsibility and accountability from top management to individual team members. The principles of human resources management for teams that follow in this chapter will help teams make this transition. Because in the final analysis, people manage themselves.

Characteristics of Systems That Teams Own

"All I really need to know I learned in kindergarten."

—Robert Fulghum

"Do you think we can manage ourselves?" This is the question most often asked by workers who are no longer going to have supervisors. People ask this question because they find the prospect of managing themselves daunting. But they already manage themselves most of the time. Answering the following set of questions will convince any worker that he or she has the many of the skills needed to successfully manage human resources issues:

- Are you a member of a family?
- Do you have obligations and responsibilities to your family members?
- Are you a member of any church, civic organization, or club?
- Do you have obligations and responsibilities as a member of these organizations?
- What do you do to help members of your family or of the organizations you belong to become familiar with the expectations and standards of these groups?
- How do you address behavior or performance problems with members of your family or organizations?
- Do you have to balance your schedule to meet family, organization, and work obligations?
- What do you do to recognize positive contributions by family and organization members?
- Are you ever involved in conflicts with family or organization members, and how do you resolve these conflicts?

Pondering the questions will quickly lead people to the truth that they are involved in the management of complex human relationships every day. In fact, managing life outside of work is often more complicated than managing life at work. Nevertheless, few people contemplate the systems—or recognize the skills—they use on a daily basis to manage the relationships in their personal lives. Self-managed teams allow individuals to bring these systems and skills to their work.

Different people have different skills and strengths for managing human resources. Work team members must develop a common understanding of relationship management principles. Team members are then given the opportunity to learn and practice these principles by managing the tasks of hiring, orienting, evaluating, disciplining, and recognizing each other. The following are lessons that teams have learned through their experience with self-management. New self-managed teams should contemplate these lessons and adapt them to their own work situations.

Lessons for Hiring

Hiring a new team member is the most critical decision a team makes. Hiring the right people requires patience. Teams must fight the urge to quickly find "a warm body" to fill a slot on the schedule. It is better to work short until the right person is found than hire the wrong person and live with this decision for a long time.

Teams must establish the baseline skills and attributes they are looking for in a new team member. The first step in the hiring process is deciding what kind of person the team needs. Do this before any applications are reviewed or interviews are scheduled.

A positive attitude is more important than an impressive résumé. Teams should only interview applicants who have the minimum skills required for the job. Self-managed teams depend on members who are willing to work as a team and have a positive attitude toward cooperation and the values the team has established.

The best predictor of future behavior is past behavior. Questions asked during the interview need to elicit responses from the applicant that describe how the applicant has handled situations similar to those faced by the work team. It is more important to know how a new team member has handled a customer complaint than his or her vision of world peace. Before interviewing, develop a list of common situations or problems that you would like to have applicants discuss with you.

The first time you meet someone is the most important meeting you'll ever have with them. The tone set during the interview will establish your relationship with the applicant if he or she is hired. Take the interview very seriously and model the values espoused by the team. Expectations for team membership and contributions should be discussed during the interview.

Have a conversation with the applicant, not an interrogation. The applicant will be nervous. Many of the best applicants do not get hired because they do not "interview well." The goal is to hire the person who will work best with your customers and your team, not the person who is best at 20 questions.

Use the personnel department as an asset and have them help you ensure that your job selection process is legal. Personnel can screen applicants and make sure you talk only to people who are qualified and have good references. They know the legal responsibilities to hire someone and can give you a list of questions you cannot ask, as well as suggestions on things to ask.

The more perspectives you get, the more complete the view you have will be. Applicants should be interviewed by several team members and, if possible, by some of your customers. Different personalities will identify different traits. Group interviews are all right if they are limited to three interviewers and there is a balance in the conversation.

Hire the person who best matches the job and fits the team. The most common hiring mistakes are hiring the first qualified person and hiring the most qualified person. Be patient and wait for the person who best matches the needs of the job and the team. Hire someone who will be happy with the job and the team. Avoid hiring someone who is overqualified or who has expectations that your team cannot meet.

Put the offer in writing and send thank-you notes. The team needs two standard letters that can be edited to follow up interviews with all applicants. One letter congratulates the new team member; it includes dates for orientation and information that the personnel department needs to include. The other thanks applicants who took the time to interview with the team. Sending thank-you notes may seem trivial, but it enhances the reputation of the team for professionalism.

Lessons for Orientation and Teamliness Training

Encourage creative individualism. The goal of the orientation period is to enable the new team member to learn the job and determine how to bring unique talents to the team. Teams gain strength by melding the diversity of skills that different team members possess into team skills. Encourage new employees to be creative.

Coach for contribution. The coach needs to meet with new employees to discuss what help the coach can provide. The coach needs to establish rapport with the new team member so the new person feels comfortable discussing concerns and ideas with the coach. The coach's role is to help each new employee develop the skills he or she can contribute to the team's success.

Team trainers teach specific performance standards, techniques, and teamwork expectations. Learning a new job can be a formidable task. Team trainers need to remember how it felt when they started. Trainers communicate clear performance standards and demonstrate the work techniques of the job. Then the new team member performs the job under the observation of the trainer and receives immediate feedback to make sure the job is done correctly. Finally, the trainer acts as a mentor to help the new employee learn the expectations for a team player.

Feedback on baby steps is the key to walking on your own. A key to learning something new is feedback on performance as new skills are developed. Everyone on the team has an obligation to let the new person know how he or she is doing. Establishing an atmosphere of open and honest feedback during the orientation period will educate a team member who will eventually provide feedback to others on the team.

It's best to ask if the new team member is comfortable. Silence does not mean that someone understands. New team members must be asked repeatedly whether they have any questions or frustrations. Identifying problems at an early stage allows the new person to learn the correct way to do the job and interact with the team. Good habits learned at the beginning will provide a solid base for more complex skills.

The probation period is a two-way street. At any time during the probation period either the team or the new team member can decide that the job is not a good match. It is a "no fault" arrangement and can be invoked on friendly terms. The purpose of the probation period is to allow the team and the new team member to decide whether they want to continue the relationship for the long term.

We're glad you're here; let's celebrate! When the orientation has been successfully completed, the new team member should be officially welcomed to the team. Current team members document three positive things they have noticed about the new person and one area for improvement. These items are then summarized and shared with the new person at a team meeting. You may want to take the new team member to lunch to celebrate the completion of orientation.

Lessons for Using Evaluations to Improve Performance

Everyone wants to do better. Human nature includes the desire to improve. In traditional work environments, evaluations are dreaded by both the person being evaluated and the person doing the evaluating. Self-managed teams change the evaluation process into a system to help people improve their performance. Evaluations are not intended to handle discipline or serious performance issues. Evaluations are used to provide feedback on what people do best and to encourage them to do even better.

Seek feedback from inside, outside, and beside. People are hardest on themselves, and assessment of performance needs to start with self-evaluation. The best source of evaluation is a person's customers. Team members identify two or three customers they serve and ask them to complete an evaluation form. Fellow team members also give feedback in the evaluation process. This method of evaluation is called a "360-degree review" because it includes the full-circle view.

Develop panoramic pictures. The evaluation process is best done confidentially using performance criteria established by the team. Each team member identifies up to eight people who will evaluate him or her and have this list approved by the team. These people are sent the evaluation form and asked to return the form to a neutral third party, who will compile the results. The results are given to the person being evaluated, who compares the compiled evaluation with his or her personal performance assessment. In the final step, the evaluatee presents the findings at a team meeting and develops goals to improve his or her performance.

Encourage people to do what they do best. This point cannot be emphasized too often. The most powerful part of the evaluation is the written comments received by the person being evaluated. Those who contribute to the evaluation should be trained in the principles of providing encouragement. You get what you measure. Measuring success leads to greater success.

Constructive feedback is the art of diplomacy. The most dangerous part of the 360-degree evaluation process is the possibility of hurt feelings from inappropriate negative comments. Those participating in the evaluation should focus their comments on job performance and not on personal agendas or attacks. Encourage constructive criticism. Those who are going to evaluate others need to be taught how to write suggestions for improvement in a positive manner.

Personal development plans start and end with the person. The only person who can change anyone's behavior is that person. People need to be given the opportunity to reflect on the feedback they receive and to develop their own plans for improving performance. Personal goals are written and then shared with the team. Having goals in writing enables the team to keep track of what each member is working on and enable team members to help one another achieve their goals.

Connect team performance to organizational standards and compensation systems. The connection between performance and compensation can be a sticky point for many teams. Self-managed teams may not be the norm for the organization. Organizational behavior standards need to be incorporated in the evaluation review, and people should be rated on these standards. Merit pay systems are often associated with the evaluation process. One way to determine the merit increase is to have the team set the criteria for levels of merit increase based on the average score received for the criteria each person is rated on. It is difficult to quantify job performance and give fair merit increases. Most people will be satisfied with the results if the team collectively sets the criteria on the front end. Merit systems based on 360-degree feedback may not be perfect, but they are more accurate than systems based on the opinion of the supervisor.

Lessons to Turn Discipline into Corrective Action

Friends take care of friends. Do we have to discipline our friends? This is the greatest fear of employees who will be working in self-managed teams. The response is that if someone is really your friend you should care enough to help that person. One of the kindest and most civil things that people can do is give candid feedback on negative behaviors. The first step in solving any problem is recognizing that a problem exists. In hierarchical systems, employees tell the supervisor about problems and depend on the supervisor to address the situation. Supervisors don't like being bad guys, and often issues are not addressed. The key to achieving discipline in any situation is that someone has the courage to care.

Discuss the undiscussable. The first time you point out problem with someone new is the hardest time. Remember to stick to the facts and not make a personal attack. Remember it is the behavior of the person that is unacceptable and not the person. Approaching people as a friend to discuss issues is the best way. Also, discuss the behavior as soon as the problem is identified and you have a chance to have a private discussion. Most people avoid such conversations; this is a big mistake. Every time someone does something wrong and gets away with it, the behavior becomes more acceptable to that person and is more likely to be repeated. Be brave, be polite, stick to the facts, approach in private, and take time to listen. People will react negatively at first, but in the long run, they will recognize that you have their best interests in mind. They will appreciate that you cared enough to confront them.

Document and record behavior patterns. Self-managed teams have a responsibility to document team member behaviors. Ideally, the personnel files will contain glowing evaluations of each team member's contributions; but, by necessity, behavior issues and conversations about problems need to be recorded as well. Should teams have access to personnel files? Yes. After all, it is the team that best knows the behaviors of its members. Teams are best positioned to keep track of discussions with team members and to identify and suggest actions to fix problems. Documentation should take the form of simple fact-based statements that describe the issue, make suggestions for improvement, and note the date discussed and who was involved. Follow-up discussions and notations of improvement are equally important and should also be included in the team member's file.

Take steps to make progress. Most organizations have a formal progressive discipline plan that includes the following steps: (1) first discussion, (2) second discussion, (3) probation, and (4) termination. Teams need to be consistent in following these or similar steps. In fact, self-managed teams are generally more stringent in following these steps than are supervisors. At each of these steps there must be documentation containing clearly stated expectations for improving behavior. This system may sound cold, but people need to know the rules. Team members who administer the process will know the process. Teams responsible for discipline generally have few discipline problems.

Involve the individual, the team, the coach, and personnel staff. Corrective action is primarily the responsibility of the individual. The monkey must be placed on the person who needs to change. The team is responsible for making people aware of behaviors that need to be changed and conducting the first and second discussions in the discipline process. Coaches serve as advisers to the team in the initial steps and are directly involved in probation and termination decisions. The coach should be a sounding board for the individual who needs to change, but the coach is not responsible for achieving that change. Personnel staff plays a consultant role for the team and coach to ensure that all discipline steps are well documented and organizational policies are followed.

People make their own behavior choices. Once team members have identified behaviors that an individual needs to correct they must realize that only the person who needs to change can make the change. This is a very difficult lesson to learn. It is hard to stand back and watch a fellow team member struggle. Growth occurs when people recognize that their problems can only be solved when they make the commitment to fix them.

Firing someone can be the best thing for them and for the team. Firing someone is traumatic for a team. It is done after all discipline steps have been followed and it becomes clear that the individual cannot or will not change. The act of firing someone needs to be handled in a way that preserves the dignity of the individual. It should be done confidentially and quickly. The time for discussion is past. The terminated employee needs to leave the workplace, and it should be made clear that they are not to interfere with team members. Being fired is often the best thing for that person, and it is certainly the best thing for the team. Both parties can then move past a difficult time and proceed with their lives and work.

Forgiveness is the path to freedom and responsibility. It strengthens any individual and team to be able to forgive people who recognize their mistakes, apologize for them, and correct them. The goal of the discipline is to change negative behavior, not to punish people. People who have been forgiven, like those who forgave them, end up having a better relationship with the team. Forgiveness is the ultimate act of civility.

Lessons to Grow People through Recognition

Use the five-to-one ratio. Follow the rule of thumb that you should give people five positive comments for every negative comment. Relationships grow through interactions that let people know they are needed. People who receive positive feedback about their contributions will contribute even more.

Say thank you often. Most organizations fail to let people know they are appreciated. Human beings who are thanked for what they do will strive to do more. The simple act of thanking someone for a job well done is more powerful than any monetary reward. People will remember a thank you long after the money is gone.

Give people "Atta Person Awards" in public. Teams can post a grease board with markers in a prominent area and ask team members to write down the names of people who helped them or went the extra mile to get the job done. At the next team meeting, members who wrote down names then state why they want to recognize those people. These recognitions are then documented by the team recorder and shared in the team meeting minutes. This may sound corny, but people really respond to recognition from fellow team members.

Put recognition in writing and share it with those at the top. Top management needs to be informed of significant individual and team accomplishments. The coach can send memos or E-mails to those who need to be recognized and copy these messages to senior management and the team member's personnel file. Positive comments from customers deserve to be shared with the people to whom the team reports to and should also be posted.

Use financial incentives to promote teamwork and outstanding performance. Progressive organizations have implemented team bonuses. The purpose of these bonuses is to get everyone pulling toward the same goals. Criteria for achieving the bonus needs to be stated in terms of meeting customer needs, raising quality, and improving financial performance. Team members should be given the opportunity to help set the goals and to put systems in place to monitor progress toward the goals.

Say thank you and good luck to those who leave the team. There will be a sense of loss whenever a team member leaves. To manage the "grieving" process, teams should have a reception or party to say thank you and good luck. This gathering is therapeutic for the team and will help team members pull together to make up for the loss of a valued member.

Work as a team, celebrate as a team, and grow as a team. The expression "those who play hard, work hard" is true. Teams should be given a budget to celebrate accomplishments and be afforded the time to recognize each other's efforts. People grow the most from positive experiences. Celebrations reinforce the spirit.

☞ **Team Tip:** Remember the principles of adult learning:

- Adults learn what they need to know.
- Adults learn based on their past experiences.
- Adults learn by doing.

Learn the Lessons

If all this seems like common sense, it is. But being common sense doesn't make it easy. These lessons are usually learned the hard way, by being ignored. People don't follow them at first because they require consideration for others and they take time. Human beings like to take shortcuts. The only way to learn some of the lessons above is to fail by taking a shortcut. Work teams will struggle and get frustrated with the processes of hiring, orienting, evaluating, disciplining, and celebrating. Those who persevere and pay attention to these lessons will learn them. Teams that design their human resources management systems carefully and own them are the teams that have learned by doing.

Role Changes for Management, Team Members, and Personnel

"The less control you have, the more influence you have."

Human resources management systems for teams turn the hierarchy upside down and sideways. Management is no longer in control, team members no longer have a supervisor to solve their problems, the personnel department no longer makes the rules, and customers are no longer innocent bystanders. The role changes are significant and uncomfortable. Table 14-1 outlines the new perspectives that come into view when self-managed teams manage relationships.

Chapter 4 reviewed the difficulties and challenges of role changes required for the implementation of self-managed teams. Relationship management with teams is more complex than in a bureaucratic system. Some people will disdain the complexity and call it chaos. But that's the way life is; it is not neat and orderly. People interact with people in a web of interdependent relationships. Organizations work in spite of forced structures. The role changes outlined above will be difficult, but they are necessary for managing relationships in the information age. Making these changes is a step toward creating an environment in which people understand that everybody works for everybody.

People Problems

"Everyone can play nice in the sandbox!"

There is a difficult person inside of everybody. All of us can be a pain in the butt! Otherwise, we wouldn't be human. The title of this section seems to indicate that it is about others. But in fact it is about each of us. Finding fault in others is easy. Recognizing personal weaknesses is painful. The first step on the path to civility is understanding that we are the primary causes of our relationship problems. Others can be a pain in the butt, but it is our responses that either perpetuate the problem or break the downward spiral. Table 14-2 identifies types of problem people and reactions that can either fuel the flames or extinguish the fire.

Members of teams need to realize how their own moods and responses to people who are having "bad days" can cause relationships to deteriorate. Work would be a much nicer place if everyone could recognize his or her

Table 14-1. Role Changes for Managing Human Resources with Self-Managed Teams

Role	What Is Lost	What Is Gained
Management	The illusion of control over employees; having to fix problems that employees bring to them	A new role as mentor and coach; the time to listen, inquire, and *help people* solve their problems
Employees	Having a supervisor to deal with people problems; delays in addressing personnel issues	The responsibility to *manage themselves* and others; the ability to develop and practice relationship skills
Personnel	A firm set of policies and procedures to manage people; having to stick to the rules and be inflexible	Being a consultant to work teams to facilitate use of human resources; the opportunity to *be creative* in helping people
Customers	The ability to demand to see the boss if not satisfied; dealing with workers who cannot solve their own problems	Interaction with service providers who can meet their needs; a chance to *give feedback* to people to improve service.

own negative behaviors and choose to end them. People problems begin and end with everyone.

Chapter Wrap-Up

A participant in a self-managed team workshop asked, "What is the one magic word to make teams successful?" The answer is short yet difficult: Trust! Management must trust teams enough to allow them to manage themselves. Teams members must trust each other enough to cooperate and communicate. Human resources management puts trust to the test. Management, personnel, and customers must accept new roles. Team members must be responsible and accountable for hiring, orienting, evaluating, disciplining, and celebrating each other. They must be willing to encourage each other, discuss the undiscussable, and celebrate the wonderful. They must also learn how to deal with problem people and to recognize that these problems begin with each person on the team. People on self-managed teams will experience much pain as they begin

Table 14-2. Problem People: Fueling the Flames or Extinguishing the Fire

Problem People Who . . .	How to Fuel the Flames	How to Extinguish the Fire
Don't want to plan	Decide you won't play either and take your toys and go home	Let them take a time out and ask them to think about what they would like to do
Want to fight	You fight back, only you hit harder	Find out why they are so angry, listen, then ask what you can do to help
Will stab you in the back	Wait patiently and think of something meaner to do to them	Tell them how they have hurt you and ask them to consider how it would feel if the tables were turned
Gossip	Add a few "facts" to their story and whisper it in someone else's ear	Suggest that they may want to check their facts and talk directly to the person they are talking about
Bring personal problems to work	Tell them about your problems, being sure to point out that you have it worse	Listen politely, let them know of your concern, and ask how you can help them focus on their work
Aren't there when needed	Take advantage of them when they are there by leaving yourself	Point out that they were absent, record this fact, and ask them to think about how much they are missed when they are gone
Want to take over	Look for your chance to be in charge and make sure you give them clear orders	Ask others on the team whether they have any different ideas and suggest ways to share the responsibilities

to manage their relationships. The pain is a precursor to growth. Teams will need to have grace to get them through the initial struggles of relationship management. Don't expect miracles—count on them. People want freedom and can be trusted.

Reference

1. M. S. Peck, *The Road Less Traveled and Beyond* (New York: Simon & Schuster, 1997), p. 196.

Chapter 15

Team Communication Systems

Chapter Preview

"When our team first started, it was like we had opened Pandora's box. All of the problems and concerns that we had buried over the years came tumbling out. I wanted to hide from these problems but knew it was healthy to begin dealing with them one at a time."

—Peggy Carlson, team leader, Mission+St. Joseph's

Communication has particular significance in the success of self-managed teams. Through open and honest team communications, self-managed teams are able to achieve better results and make better decisions. The free exchange of ideas, thoughts, agreements, and conflicts enables all team members to learn and grow, and gives rise to quality communications that are frequently missing in a more hierarchical organization structure. In an hierarchy, the staff are more tentative in their disagreements and are frequently unwilling to challenge a supervisor who has said or is preparing to do something that they cannot support. This unwillingness to engage in conflict leads to poorer decisions. Alternatives are not expressed and potential problems are not uncovered prior to making the decision.

Effective communication is a great challenge for the self-managed team. The information age has not only added to the quantity of information that is available but also to the complexity of communicating. Self-managed teams face a difficult undertaking when it comes to communications. They must communicate vertically because they generally exist in hierarchical organizations. They also must communicate laterally within their team and to other teams and departments in the organization.

In addition, members of self-managed teams must communicate with sensitivity. Developing high quality relationships within the team and between the team and others in the organization is critical to the team's success.

This chapter provides a method for developing the team communication system. It weaves through the complexity of organizational communications and provides a simple formula for communicating with the many public groups that self-managed teams have contact with. It provides insight into the communication responsibilities of the roles that exist on teams, as well as providing examples of team communication plans and report formats that can be adapted for general use. It helps team members develop a plan for one-on-one communication to enable team members to build better relationships with others.

Chapter at a Glance

In this chapter, you will find

- A four-step process for developing a team communication system
- A discussion of the importance of within-team communication
- Suggestions for communication with other teams
- A description of formal and informal communication with the hierarchy
- A discussion of the importance of communication with the rest of the organization
- A description of the ways communication with customers improves service

The Communication System

"If we want to be heard, we must speak in a language the listener can understand and on a level at which the listener is capable of operating."

—*M. Scott Peck*

When communication within an organization is considered, the importance of the individual staff member's role in communication is rarely emphasized. With self-managed teams, the role of individual team members in ensuring the highest quality of communication is paramount. Communication links the team members to each other, the organization, the external environment, and the customer. Individual team members fulfill their communication roles by building, responding to, and managing the communication interactions they encounter.

Since communication is so complex and so integral to the effectiveness of the team, teams spend considerable time developing their communication system and their communication plans. They develop the system and plans so that they know *whom* to communicate with, *what* to communicate about, *how often* to communicate, and *what medium* to use. They design their communication system to meet the needs of their linkages, as well as to meet their own needs for sharing information and telling their story. There are four basic steps that the team will take to develop its communication system:

1. Determine who your team's communication customers are
2. Identify their information needs
3. Determine the best method for communicating with them
4. Specify the frequency of the communication

Because communication is a time-consuming task, the team may want to begin its communication process with a smaller set of customers than is defined in the communication system. As in any endeavor that the team undertakes, starting in a small way, devoting time to learning and developing the system, and then expanding to fully embrace the new role or activity is best. The team can become comfortable with its new task, while working out any problems, before it tackles the entire new responsibility.

Step 1: Determine Who Your Team's Customers Are

The first step in developing the team communication system is to review the communication linkages that the team has and then identify specific customers within those linkage areas. The team can brainstorm together to create a list of "communication customers." (See figure 15-1.) If each of these linkage groups is considered, the team will soon arrive at a list of communication customers. The matrix in table 15-1 can be used as a guide to help the team identify its customers. Once the communication customers of the team have been identified, the team needs to determine what information these customers would like from the team.

Step 2: Identify Their Information Needs

The team can brainstorm to try to identify the information needs of its customers, or it can ask its customers. Team members may want to try to brainstorm first and then present a list of ideas they have to the customer. This method works when there are a limited number of customers in a category. However, the method does not work as well when the customer is the entire organization. For large customer groups, the team may sample the group and obtain information from several customers, instead of all customers.

Step 3: Determine the Best Method for Communicating with Them

There are many communication media available today for staff members and self-managed teams. Although face-to-face communication is widely accepted as the most effective communication method, it is not always the best choice.

Figure 15-1. Communication Linkages

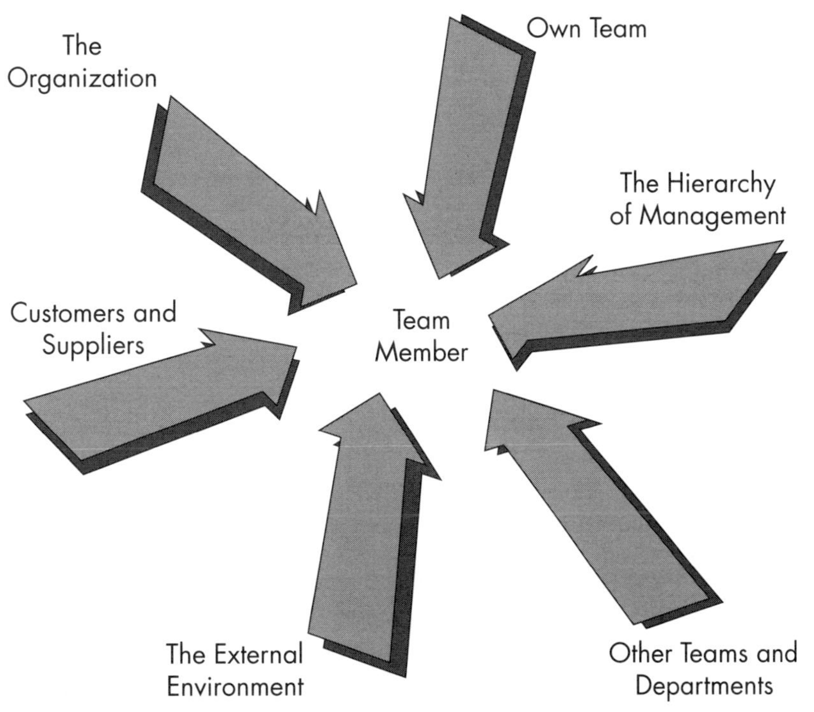

Table 15-1. Communication Customers

Linkages	Customers	Information Needs
The Organization	■ Readers of the organization's employee newsletter ■ All employees ■ All managers	■ How self-managed teams are working ■ What the team is doing that is new or different
The External Environment	■ The community ■ Insurers ■ Employers ■ Managed care organizations ■ Other health care providers ■ Professional organizations that team members are affiliated with	■ What the team's services are ■ What successes the team has had in improving services ■ Credentials of the team members
Customers and Suppliers	■ Patients ■ Families ■ Physicians ■ Suppliers of products ■ Internal customers and suppliers	■ Team services ■ Team member credentials ■ Team goals ■ Team ideas for the future ■ Changes that will occur
Own Team	■ A list of all team members that includes part time, PRN, or occasional workers, contract workers, and so on	■ What the team is planning and doing ■ Who is on the team ■ Personal information about team members ■ Team roles ■ Performance expectations ■ Performance and goal progress ■ Daily activities and events ■ Any anticipated changes at work that might affect the team

Table 15-1. (Continued)

Linkages	Customers	Information Needs
The Hierarchy of Management	▪ The immediate manager for the team ▪ The manager that he or she reports to ▪ Middle management ▪ Senior management ▪ The CEO ▪ The board of directors	▪ Major goals of the team ▪ Team performance measures ▪ Team performance results ▪ Team achievements ▪ Team members ▪ Resource needs
Other Teams and Departments	▪ Other teams within the department ▪ Teams in other departments ▪ Other departments, people, or teams that the team interacts with, provides services to, or depends on for supplies or services	▪ Team membership ▪ Team services ▪ Team goals ▪ Support needs that team has

The best choice depends on the purpose of the communication, the subject that is being communicated, and the audience. Face-to-face is the best choice when the team is trying to convince, persuade, or resolve conflict. In fact, in situations of conflict, face-to-face is the only acceptable method. A written report, letter, or memo is the best method for communicating when the subject needs to be studied and contemplated. See table 15-2 for a summary of media choices.

Step 4: Specify the Frequency of the Communication

A helpful guideline for communicating frequency is to consider the closeness of the relationship with the person or group. While the team and its members will want to communicate among themselves on a daily basis, the team and its manager may only need to communicate monthly. See table 15-3 for examples.

Communication is critical to a team's success. As the team develops its communication system, it can perceive the scope of the communication

Table 15-2. Media Choices for Various Communication Purposes

Media Examples	Daily		Monthly		Quarterly
	Daily Activities; Personal Information Resource Needs; Service and Support Needs	How Teams Are Working; Team Membership, Credentials, Roles, Services, Changes	Team Performance Measures; Team Achievements	Goals; Goal Progress; Ideas for the Future	Quarterly Update
Face-to-face	√	√	√	√	√
Telephone	√				
E-mail	√				
Memo, Letter	√				
Report		√	√	√	√
Bulletin board		√	√	√	
Policy		√			
Newsletter		√	√	√	
Flyer		√			
Meeting/Minutes	√	√	√	√	√

Table 15-3. Communication Frequency

The Closeness of the Relationship	Communication Frequency
The external environment	Annually
The organization	Quarterly
The hierarchy of management	Monthly/weekly
Other related teams or departments	Weekly/daily
Customers and suppliers	Daily
Own team	Daily

responsibility. Communicating takes time and thought. There is a tendency among teams to isolate themselves from the rest of the organization. Team members become close and can form a relationship almost like a clan. Within this clan, people may shield themselves from the outside world, becoming distrustful and distrusted. That is not an environment that will enable a team to succeed. It takes energy and an uncompromising belief in the importance of communication to devote the time and commitment to meeting the communication needs of the organization. The team will find that this commitment is well worth the time and energy devoted to it.

Communications within the Team

"I never knew I would be thankful for E-mail. We could keep everyone up to date at once, no matter what their schedule or shift was. Communication would have been impossible otherwise."

—Jean Van Horn, pharmacy team, Mission+St. Joseph's

When the team works to establish a communication system within the team, or to improve the existing system, it needs to think about all the different types of communication the team has and the purposes of team communication. Communication within the team is truly the glue that binds the team together. It helps the team clarify its purpose, set and accomplish goals, improve performance, do daily work, make decisions, resolve disputes, implement change, and build trust and support. An important element of teams that needs to be reinforced and respected in team communication is the differences that team members bring to the team. This section of the chapter will address building relationships and a sense of team, resolving conflicts, listening effectively, giving feedback, and using gossip and the grapevine.

Building Relationships and a Sense of Team

Teams build or destroy themselves through the ways they use communication. Communication creates lasting relationships among team members, trust between and among team members, and positive energy that helps the team accomplish its purpose. Communication techniques can also destroy relationships, harm the self-esteem of team members, and place barriers in the way of team performance and achievements. Table 15-4 describes the communication techniques that help build relationships within the team and that help build a sense of team. If the team is trying to establish or improve how it works together, this table will provide helpful information. Teams and individual team members can measure how well they are building relationships and a sense of team by assessing the frequency with which they hear or observe the techniques in table 15-4.

Resolving Conflicts

Conflict resolution is a daily communication need of teams but is often left unspoken. Many people believe they will hurt each other's feelings if they even suggest that there is a conflict. They perceive that hurt feelings will lead to an unwillingness to cooperate and work together that will be even more

Table 15-4. Building Relationships and Building a Sense of Team

Communication Technique	What You Might Say or Do
■ Focus on what we have in common	■ We and Our *not* Me, my, I, or You
■ Build a sense of team	■ "Our team is . . ." or "Our team can . . ." or "Our team likes . . ." or "Our team needs . . ." ■ "Our team would never . . ."
■ Build self-esteem	■ "You have a great talent for . . ." or "I like the way you . . ."
■ Give positive feedback	■ "Whenever I am trying to decide how to approach X, I ask myself how you would do it." ■ "Help me understand . . ." or "Help me see this more clearly . . ." ■ "Help me learn how you . . ." ■ "I like, admire, appreciate, value a specific skill, talent, or characteristic you possess."
■ Build on each other's input	■ "I agree with Mary that this is . . ." ■ "I agree with Mary that this is . . . and I have interpreted the data somewhat differently." ■ "Mary brought up a good point that I would like to bring back to the team's attention."
■ Be clear about your feelings, needs, and expectations	■ "I need . . ." or "I expect . . ." ■ "I feel happy, frustrated, used and abused, unappreciated . . ." ■ "I would like . . ."
■ Offer to help	■ "I see that you have a big deadline coming up. How can I help?" ■ "I see that you have a great deal to do today, how can I help?" ■ "I have a few free minutes today. Is there anything I can do to help?"
■ Listen first to understand	■ "Let me make sure I understand . . ." ■ "So, this is how you see the situation . . ." *(Repeat or restate what the person has said before saying what you think and before providing your input.)*
■ Do what you say you are going to do	■ "I'll have that done before I leave tonight." ■ "I can't take a break now because I promised I would get this done today." ■ "I'd like to help, but I know I won't have time, and I don't want to promise something I can't deliver." *(Projects, assignments, phone calls, follow up—anything that you agreed to do as a team member needs to be done, so team members can trust that they can rely on your word.)*

harmful to the team than the failure to bring a conflict to light. Team members believe they are helping the harmony and the smooth functioning of the team when they maintain silence when a conflict or disagreement occurs. A favorite phrase of team members who don't address conflicts is: "Whatever." Some teams develop a rule: "If you don't confront the conflict, you must forgive and forget." Brooding and holding grudges have a negative impact on the entire team. The communication techniques listed below help team members verbalize issues and conflicts while maintaining each other's self-esteem and maintaining harmony. The following techniques are helpful for handling conflict situations that may arise:

- Use statements that begin with "I feel" to let the team member know how his or her behavior is affecting you.
- Express your needs clearly.
- Don't label the behavior . . . just state your feelings. Do say, "I feel frustrated when I see you reading a magazine." Don't say, "I feel frustrated because you are so lazy."
- Ask your coworker to help you understand the situation from his or her point of view.

Table 15-5 gives examples from typical conflicts that occur on teams.

Teams develop formal conflict resolution systems so that conflicts don't create permanent and destructive barriers between team members. The conflict resolution system developed by the office staff team at Regional Surgical Specialists is shown in figure 15-2. (For more information on team conflicts, see chapter 16.)

Listening Effectively

Many educators are now suggesting that communication or speaking skills don't need to be taught as much as listening skills do. People have come to believe that communication is speaking, initiating the conversation, placing the phone call, and making the presentation. Unfortunately, that is only half of the communication process; listening is the other half. Stephen Covey, a nationally recognized management consultant encourages people to "first seek to understand, then to be understood."[1]

Team members can show that they are listening in two ways. First, they can communicate verbally that they are listening. They do this by exploring what has been said and trying to understand what the speaker really means. To do this effectively, team members can repeat what was said, word for word, or summarize and put what was said in their own words. As listeners, they can say, "This is what I heard. Is it what you meant?" They can ask for clarification by saying, "Help me understand how you arrived at that belief or conclusion."

Second, they can demonstrate that they are listening by using nonverbal body language. Maintaining eye contact, facing the speaker, keeping an open posture, and nodding occasionally let others know that listening is occurring. Listening is an art, and one that can be set aside when emotions

Table 15-5. Resolving Conflicts

Conflict Issue	What You Might Say or Do
A team member is not doing his or her share of the work	"I really feel taken advantage of. I work hard from the time I come in and don't have a moment for breaks. I see you reading a magazine. I need to feel like you are working as hard as I am."
A team member is doing work that is below standard	"I feel let down when I see (your documentation). The team agreed that we would all do it like this, and you are not. Help me understand what is happening."
A team member is chronically late	"I feel frustrated. Our shift starts at 7:00 A.M., and yet you arrive anytime between 7:00 and 7:15 A.M. I would like you to be here at 7:00 A.M. Help me understand what is happening."
A team member's communication style is abrasive	"I feel attacked when you stand over me and talk to me in a loud voice."
One team member believes he or she deserves more privileges than others	"I feel belittled when we do the vacation schedule, and you believe you should always get Christmas off. It makes me feel like my needs are not important."

Figure 15-2. Regional Surgical Specialists Conflict Resolution Process

Step 1 One team member believes another team member is behaving in a way that has or will negatively affect them.

Step 2 The two team members meet in a private place and try to resolve the conflict using "I feel" statements and listening to each other's points of view.

If that doesn't resolve the conflict, then take the follow action:

Step 3 The two team members put the conflict in writing together. They describe what the issue is, and their two different points of view. They give the document to the team leader, and ask that their conflict be placed on the agenda of the next team meeting.

Step 4 The team meets, reviews the conflict, and recommends a solution to the conflict, and the team members implement it.

If that does not resolve the conflict, try the following steps:

Step 5 The team leader asks the coach to meet with the two team members involved.

Step 6 The coach reviews the conflict and requires a resolution.

and anger enter a communication situation. It is a necessary skill for building relationships within the team, and throughout the organization.

Giving Feedback

Another technique and skill that team members need to develop is the skill of giving feedback. Feedback helps the team establish norms and accepted ways of behaving. It helps in that it can maintain or enhance the self-esteem of individual team members. Every person wants feedback. Everyone looks in the mirror, watches for nonverbal cues and feedback from others, and asks, "How am I doing?" As children, we come rushing in from school to tell our mothers what happened today and to get feedback in the form of praise, a scolding, advice, or reassurance. Feedback is the way we start to evaluate the effectiveness of our actions and develop our sense of self-worth. Feedback in the work environment comes from customers, staff, and team members. In a hierarchical setting, important feedback also comes from the supervisor or director. Since self-managed teams are removed from daily interaction with management, team members need to absorb the supervisor's role in giving daily feedback and give it to each other themselves.

Feedback has three general characteristics: how often it is given, the degree of judgment or evaluation it displays, and how soon it follows the action. Feedback that is given too often tends to lose its impact. An example from the past serves to illustrate this point. A child has been playing in the living room and has left a clutter of toys. The mother, throughout the day, comments on the untidy living room and asks the child to pick up his or her toys. The child hears the mother, recognizes the mess, promises to clean up the toys, but takes no action. The father comes home at the end of the day and comments once on the state of the living room. The child immediately starts picking up the toys.

In self-managed teams, the team leader and the coach have specific responsibilities for providing feedback. Although all other team members are expected to provide feedback, the team leader and coach, as cheerleaders, are expected to ensure that feedback occurs. If the team leader gives constant positive feedback, the effectiveness of the feedback tends to be limited. Psychologists generally agree that positive feedback is more likely to influence behavior than negative feedback. Nonetheless, if it occurs too often, the receiver of the feedback begins to doubt its sincerity and its value. The receiver may even wonder whether the team leader has the ability to discriminate between excellent and mediocre performance.

Feedback can be judgmental, giving an evaluation such as praise or criticism, or it can be nonjudgmental, merely stating or describing what was observed. Both judgmental and nonjudgmental feedback are appropriate. Team members want to know what their coworkers are thinking and feeling, but they do not want feedback that harms their self-image. Nonjudgmental feedback would be: "I heard the report you gave to management today." Judgmental feedback would be somewhat different, as the team member describes his or her reaction: "I particularly liked the way you outlined the reasons that we want to implement the new procedure. You really got the attention of the entire roomful of people."

In the first situation, with nonjudgmental feedback, the person giving the feedback opens the door for discussion. The person presenting the speech can then make his or her own evaluative comments.

Nonjudgmental Feedback: "I heard the report you gave to management today."

Presenter: "I was worried that I was boring everyone."

Nonjudgmental Response: "I noticed two people in the room were fidgeting in their chairs when you were talking about the implementation plan."

Presenter: "Yes, I think I went into too much detail on the implementation plan."

In a situation like the one described above, the person making the presentation is obviously concerned about how it was received. The person listening, instead of giving evaluative feedback, is merely stating observations. The benefit of nonjudgmental feedback is that it opens the door to a discussion and a sharing of perceptions, while not harming the self-image of the person receiving the feedback.

When giving judgmental feedback, it helps to be specific. Saying, "I really liked your presentation" may make the receiver of the feedback feel good momentarily, but it really tells the person little about the quality of the presentation. By being more specific and saying, "I particularly liked the way you outlined the reasons that we want to implement the new procedure. You really got the attention of the entire roomful of people," the speaker gives information that is helpful and useful to the presenter.

People are more receptive to feedback immediately following an action than after a delay of several days. If one team member wants to give feedback to another, it is best done shortly after the event or action that generated the desire to provide feedback. The event is still on the mind of the individual, and it is likely that the individual is performing a mini-self-evaluation. But be aware that immediate feedback may run the risk of being too emotional or volatile. Feedback given in the heat of emotion may be hurtful, when it is not intended as such. However, it will undoubtedly contain the true and honest feelings of the speaker.

Individuals, as well as the entire team, learn from feedback. It is a simple way of sharing information and communicating in a manner that will help others learn and grow. It helps maintain and enhance the self-esteem of the receiver and points out opportunities for improvement. All people want feedback, even if it does not always flatter. Giving feedback successfully requires that it not be given too often, that it be specific and report what was observed, and that it be given immediately following the action.

Using Gossip and the Grapevine

No discussion of team communication systems would be complete without reference to gossip and the informal communication tool the grapevine. Gossip is one of the most harmful pastimes that team members can engage in. When one team member gossips about another, there is the possibility that a reputation will be harmed and a relationship will be destroyed. So much of what a team can accomplish depends on the ability of team members to trust one another. Gossip, cliques, and subgroups of the team work to destroy team spirit and positive team behaviors.

On the positive side, gossip and the grapevine frequently communicate more rapidly than other more formal communication systems. They also may contain a truth that was not disclosed in the formal communication. For a team that is trying to establish a good communication system, gossip and the grapevine teach two lessons: communicate rapidly after an event occurs and be honest and truthful in communications.

Fulfilling Communication Responsibilities

Each role on the self-managed team has communication responsibilities for formal communication. Those responsibilities need to be clear early in the life of the team. If a team member fails to fulfill his or her communication responsibilities, other people, including the customers, might suffer because of it. When introducing team members to their communication responsibilities, a chart or graphic display of responsibilities, like table 15-6, helps clarify the assignments for everyone.

Communication with Other Teams

"We set up star point teams for all the roles. The disadvantage was that people in the roles had one more meeting to attend. The advantage was that every team was current and could coordinate with every other team."

—June Riddle, director of respiratory care, Mission+St. Joseph's

If the team is one of several teams within the department, or one of several within the organization, it will need to communicate with other teams. Usually, communication among teams is funneled through the team leader. Team leaders from all teams may meet regularly and share updates and information, or they may meet informally. Information that is of interest to other teams includes updates on each team's goals, and also details about how each team functions. Teams are a new structure in most organizations, and all teams are looking for advice and experiences that will help guide them to success.

Many organizations have star point teams that serve as a line of communication among teams. (See figure 15-3.) A star point team is a team composed of all the staff who are filling a specific role on all of the teams in the department or the organization. Within these star point teams, the staff who fulfill the role are able to be oriented to the role expectations and to the knowledge and skills required in the role.

Table 15-6. Communication Responsibilities

Team Role	What Needs to Be Communicated
Team leader	■ Goals ■ Plans ■ Updates ■ Priorities ■ Changes ■ Progress ■ Successes ■ Current news ■ Feedback from the organization ■ Feedback on individual team members ■ Overall team performance
Note taker/record keeper	■ Minutes from meetings ■ Historical events ■ Reports ■ Reminders ■ Invitations ■ Announcements
Educator	■ Goals and annual plan ■ Updates on education ■ Priorities ■ Changes in education plans and programs ■ Progress, successes ■ Workshops, in-services ■ Competency assessments ■ Licensure, certifications, and degrees
Quality improvement coordinator	■ Customer needs ■ Team performance ■ Goals, plans, updates ■ Data and data needs ■ Priorities, changes, progress ■ Customer service standards ■ Successes ■ JCAHO requirements ■ Current news ■ Quality improvement tools, processes, projects
Human resources coordinator	■ Goals and annual plan ■ Applicants, hiring process, date hired ■ Priorities ■ Performance review process and deadlines ■ Progress, successes ■ Discipline process ■ Policies and procedures ■ Celebrations and recognitions
Scheduler	■ Old and new schedules ■ Changes to the schedule in advance ■ Vacation and holiday schedules ■ Overtime rate ■ Absences and tardiness ■ Staffing requirements ■ Scheduling policies

Table 15-6. (Continued)

Team Role	What Needs to Be Communicated
Public relations coordinator	■ Goals and annual plan ■ Physician needs ■ Priorities ■ Physician satisfaction survey ■ Progress, successes ■ Other department/ team needs
Budget coordinator	■ Goals and annual plan ■ Annual budget ■ Monthly budget updates ■ Capital budget ■ Progress, successes ■ Purchases and expected delivery dates
Coach	■ Feedback from the coach, the department, the rest of the organization ■ Information from the rest of the organization

Figure 15-3. A Star Point Team of Educators

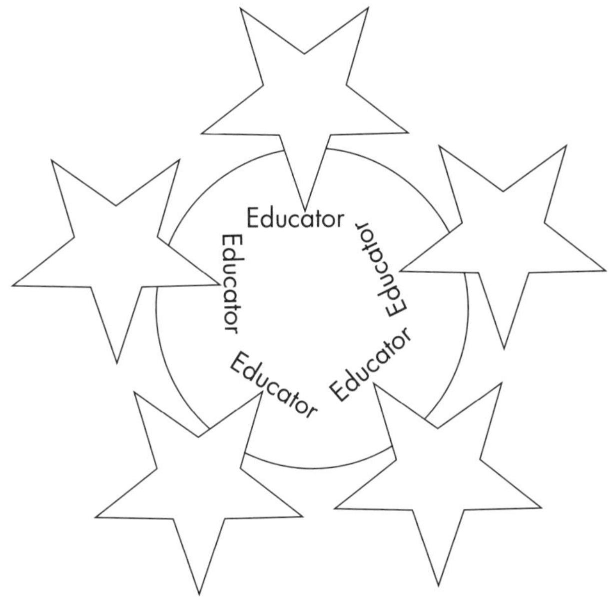

In addition, the star point teams share news about what each team is doing and about the problems and issues the teams are facing. The star point teams set goals together so that there is unity in the actions and methods that teams use in the areas of education, quality improvement, human resources, note taking, team leading, and so on.

Communication with the Hierarchy

"We get team meeting minutes from all the teams. It keeps us informed and gives us an opening for feedback. The quarterly meetings, where every team presents, fill us all with pride."

—Allen Squires, CFO, Givens Estates

Although management has given approval for a team-based organization, that does not mean that managers are entirely comfortable with the freedom from direct control that teams have. In addition, management retains responsibility for the effective performance of the organization, whether it is structured in teams or in a hierarchy. The best method for reassuring management about the effectiveness of teams is to make certain that teams perform well and to communicate regularly to management. Communication with the hierarchy should be both formal and informal.

Formal communication to the hierarchy will occur in a monthly or quarterly report to management from the team. The report will contain information on the team's goals, its measures, issues it has addressed, and actions that will occur in the future. The team report is short and to the point. It includes information that is important to management and information that demonstrates how the team is performing and how the team is handling problems and issues that come its way. A sample team report is displayed in figure 15-4.

The team will also communicate with the hierarchy in an informal manner. Team members will want to establish relationships with members of management who can offer experience and advice to them, and who can help them as they wander through the maze of approvals and influence within the hierarchy. The team and its members will need to learn and practice the skill of "networking." Networking is the art of developing and maintaining relationships with other people even though there is not a direct business or family link with them. Teams network to obtain mentoring. They network to learn how the organization works. They network to obtain feedback and advice from members of management and from their physicians. Networking requires that team members spend time outside the team and outside the department developing relationships and communication links with the larger organization.

Once management can see that the team is making progress on its goals, that its performance measures are positive, and that it has handled problems with common sense and maturity, the team will have gained the respect of management. Most managers will not want to lose all contact or influence with a self-managed team. The team can take the initiative and establish a formal and informal communication system with management that meets both the team's needs and management's needs.

Communication with the Rest of the Organization

"I make it a point to find out what is going on in the whole organization. I talk to the president and people all over. I listen and and I tell them about our teams. We do better when we understand one another."

—*A. J. Ward, housekeeping team, Mission+St. Joseph's*

The team does not operate in isolation. Many of the ideas and projects that a team undertakes will have an impact on others in the organization. The first rule of good team relations with the rest of the organization is *Involve those who will be affected, before a decision is made.*

The team will gain not respect but ill will if it operates like the Lone Ranger when it relates to the rest of the organization. A first step in any goal or project, and before a decision is made, is to consider who needs to be involved. Once that decision is made, the team can involve the members of the organization formally, or keep in touch with them informally, obtaining input

Figure 15-4. Sample Team Report

Team Report
Team Name
Date

Goals Progress
Goal 1: A brief sentence or two about accomplishments since the last report
Goal 2: A brief sentence or two about accomplishments since the last report
Goal 3: A brief sentence or two about accomplishments since the last report

Financial Performance
One or two paragraphs or a graph or chart showing the team's performance in relation to the team's budget. *(Not all teams will have a specific team budget.)*

Team Performance Measures
A brief report on each of the team performance measures showing trends since the beginning of the year.

Quality Improvement
An update on any quality improvement projects the team is involved with.

Team News
A brief report of other activities the team has been engaged in, including education programs, task forces, meetings with or feedback from customers, employee issues or concerns, and celebrations and recognitions.

as needed. Whether the team is doing something as simple as changing a form or sending a different person into a department, it does affect people outside the team, and they need to be involved before the change is made. The team has an obligation to the rest of the organization to integrate its actions and its services in a way that meets the needs of the organization and the team.

The rest of the organization will have some curiosity about the team. They will want to know how it works, who is on it, how it is different from a regular department. The team may want to submit an article to the organization's newsletter at least annually to keep the rest of the staff up to date on what the team is doing and what it is like to be on a self-managed team.

Communication with Customers

"When we started the team, I went to the head nurse and said, 'You are my customer. What would you like cleaned today?' She was really surprised because we had never asked before. It was the beginning of a very positive relationship."

—Martha Ballard, housekeeping team, Mission+St. Joseph's

Teams have both internal customers and external customers. It is the goal of all people who provide services to customers to keep their customers happy and maintain their loyalty. This would be difficult, if not impossible, without regular communication and feedback from the customers.

In hospitals, teams will want to build strong relationships with their internal customers and suppliers. For instance, nursing will want to maintain excellent relations with pharmacy, radiology, and laboratory personnel, as well as with housekeeping, food service, purchasing, and distribution.

It is through these relationships that nursing is able to obtain the services they need to care for their patients. If a patient is admitted late in the day and needs special attention from the lab, pharmacy, and food service, nursing will know people to call who will provide the service without a hassle. If a special service or an exception is needed, nursing is more likely to receive it. If there is a conflict, but good relationships have been established in calmer times, the conflict will be more easily resolved. Strong relationships enable both sides to develop a greater appreciation and respect for each other. Strong relationships make communication easier and less fraught with misunderstandings and hard feelings.

Teams will also want to establish strong positive relations with their external customers. When a nursing unit has a good relationship with a physician, unit staff know when they can and should call him or her about a patient's condition. They know how to interpret the physician's notes. The stronger relationship builds increased understanding. Physicians, on the other hand, will have a greater appreciation for staff who have built relationships. They will understand the strengths and weaknesses and clinical and interpersonal skills of the staff. Patients will receive better, more efficient care as result of the enhanced relationships and ease of communication between physicians and nurses.

Communication between the self-managed team and its most important customers, patients, is what guides and directs the team to achieve excellence in its daily work. Team members who provide services to external customers need to interact with them on a daily basis. It is through effective listening and sharing information that the relationship between team members and customers grows. Teams will use their communication skills to listen to and develop a deeper understanding of customer needs and expectations. Teams will share information with and educate their customers about the services they provide and the benefits customers will obtain from using those services. Changes can be made in a more timely manner when there is strong communication between the self-managed team and its customers. Team members need to have face-to-face contact with their customers to truly understand their needs, build relationships, and overcome barriers.

Chapter Wrap-Up

Each self-managed team has a large communication responsibility. Early in the development of the team and team operating systems, the communication system needs to be created. This investment of time and energy will provide a considerable payback to the team. Internal communication, especially, is critical to the team's performance. Through regular meetings and daily interpersonal contacts, the team establishes who it is and what it stands for. Strong internal communication enables the team to resolve conflicts, listen and give feedback, and build a constructive grapevine.

Teams also have important communication responsibilities outside the team in the larger organization. They communicate with other teams to gain knowledge and skill in team leadership and to integrate their actions with the actions of other teams. Teams have communication responsibilities to management. They communicate with managers to keep them informed of what the team is doing and also to develop comfort within management ranks for empowerment and self-management. Communication will also build trust for the team's capabilities and head off conflicts before they occur. Within the organization, a team is just one small organizational unit. However, that small unit can create havoc if it does not integrate its actions with the rest of the organization. Lone Rangers are not respected in an organization that depends on the smooth blending of services throughout all departments and teams.

Another critical communication linkage is with external customers. Teams are directly and inherently responsible for building strong positive relationships with their customers. They will need to regularly modify and revamp their services to meet changing customer needs. They can only do this if they have regular communication with customers. Taken all together, communication is the superglue that teams need to hold themselves together, integrate with the rest of the organization, and provide excellent services to their customers.

Reference

1. Stephen R. Covey, *The 7 Habits of Highly Effective People* (New York: Simon & Schuster, 1990), p. 238.

Suggested Reading

Peck, M. Scott. *The Different Drum.* New York: Bantam Books, 1997.

Chapter 16

Daily Operations Systems

Chapter Preview

"While fire fighting gets public attention, departments spend only a small part of their time putting out fires. . . . All kinds of organizations can learn from the local fire department. In emergencies, command and control prevail. For routine situations and environments, rules and regulations provide standards. Networks educate innovate, motivate, and provide backup when a hierarchy reaches its limits. Fire departments—among the oldest of America's institutions and found throughout the world—may be role models for the 21st-century organizations."

—Jessica Lipnack and Jeffrey Stamps

Daily tasks—scheduling, conflict resolution, decision making, crisis management, and personality weaving—can seem like never-ending problems to clinicians in health care. By their nature, these tasks crop up day after day after day, yet they appear unrelated to the basic job of treating patients. Traditionally, management has viewed daily operations as a burden and has attempted to get them out of the way of what is considered the real work of the organization. Success in this approach is achieved when daily operations have no effect on patient care.

This chapter discusses daily operations from the viewpoint of self-managed teams, arguing that daily operations should be regarded as opportunities to improve patient care. Each day that staff need to be scheduled, conflicts and crises must be managed and decisions have to be made: this means that every day self-managed teams can adjust schedules that resolve crises and make decisions in ways that benefit patients. By embracing daily operations as part of their real work—not merely a burden—

teams can develop systems that connect these daily activities to the overall goal of responding to customer needs. This chapter makes suggestions for dealing with daily operations. Use it as a springboard to understanding how to make a difference in patient care on a daily basis.

Chapter at a Glance

In this chapter, you will find

- A perspective on the five daily operations systems
- Eight suggestions for scheduling
- Six suggestions for conflict resolution
- Five suggestions for decision making
- Five suggestions for crisis management
- Four suggestions for personality weaving

Operating Systems

"Write all the books you want. Give all the speeches you want. Run all the meetings, workshops, and conferences you want. Bleat out your longing for how the world should work, and you will get only one question back. . . . 'How?' . . . It only takes one diet to lose weight, it only takes one instant to stop smoking, only one gesture to remove the crown from our head. We know how. We only have to choose and have the courage to live with the consequences."

—*Peter Block*

Which is the better fire department: the one that can put out a fire in half the time or the one whose community has half the number of buildings damaged by fire? The answer to this question gives a proper perspective on how to develop daily operations systems. Should self-managed teams spend their time putting out fires or taking actions to prevent problems from occurring? In *The Age of the Network,* Lipnack and Stamps review the great strides that have been made by fire departments in working with local communities and children to prevent fires and teach fire safety.[1] Teams in health care need to learn this lesson and design and implement systems that respond to patient needs and teach patients how to stay healthy.

Health care workers face the daunting task of meeting acute patient needs with limited resources. It is easy to get caught up in daily demands and lose sight of the big picture. Daily operations systems must be developed to connect the daily activities of clinicians with efforts to promote the health of their patients. Five systems that are rarely thought of as clinical processes are the key to patient care:

1. *Scheduling:* Staffing must anticipate patient needs and afford clinicians time for patient education.
2. *Conflict resolution:* Health care workers must know how to collaborate with members of their department and other medical disciplines and how to resolve the turf battles that hinder patient care.
3. *Decision making:* Self-managed teams must make decisions as individuals and as teams that support the short- and long-range plans for improving care processes.
4. *Crisis management:* Stuff happens! People need to realize that unplanned events are opportunities to respond in creative ways to meet unique events.
5. *Personality weaving:* Health care teams must take advantage of the diversity of skills and personalities among their members and in the organization as a whole.

These five systems are often seen as obstacles to patient care. In fact, they can be the glue that helps clinicians work together.

People already know the five systems for daily operations. They use them regularly to manage their personal lives. The most common question that comes up in the workplace when self-managed teams are being considered is

"How?" The answer is "When!" How is an excuse and a defense. People who ask "How?" are being lazy and placing the burden on someone else. Supervisors are used to bearing this burden and are reluctant to give it up. For their part, employees like the idea that someone else is responsible. Self-managed teams change all this because daily operations become the responsibility of each team member. "How" is no longer relevant. When is now.

Now it is up to the team to schedule staff, resolve conflicts, make decisions, manage crises, and weave personalities. Health care workers who accept responsibility for daily operations do a better job of linking patient care to operations systems because they are the ones touching the patients. This resulting integration is much different from operations decisions made by supervisors and managers, and it is a vast improvement for the patient. How do we develop operating systems for teams in health care? By making teams responsible for operating systems, connecting the big picture and daily demands.

Scheduling

"I would play a sport I dropped again if . . . Practices were more fun. . . . I could play more. . . . Coaches understood players better. . . . *There was no conflict with studies.* . . . Coaches were better teachers. . . . *There was no conflict with personal life.*"

—Youth Sports Institute of Michigan State University (emphasis added)

Two of six conditions under which kids would return to a sport they had dropped are related to conflicts with their personal time. These conflicts for kids are with social life and studies. The difficulties of workplace scheduling are related to similar issues. People have family commitments, social commitments, and the desire to do something fun outside of work to maintain balance in their lives. And for many health care workers, there is a potential conflict with personal educational efforts to improve skills or earn advanced degrees.

On the other side of the scheduling equation is the fact that health care is needed 24 hours a day, 365 days a year. Illness does not take time off on evenings, weekends, or holidays. Aligning staffing with patient needs is one of the most challenging aspects of health care. Members of self-managed teams often say that the ability to do their own scheduling is one of the greatest advantages of the team system.

This section offers suggestions based on team successes with scheduling systems. Remember that each team is different. These tips should be a starting point for further scheduling system development. The goal of scheduling is to match as closely as possible the needs of patients with the lives of team members. The match will not always be perfect, but when the effort is made, people will better understand the realities of scheduling and there will be fewer conflicts between work and personal commitments.

Scheduling Suggestion 1: Have a Scheduler and a Scheduling Team

Each team needs to have scheduler. We have yet to find a team on which no one is willing to be the scheduler. The scheduler is usually very organized and has a natural talent for putting together puzzles. He or she is in touch with the demands of daily work flow and appreciates the personal needs of team members. Another common trait in a good scheduler is creativity. In large departments with multiple teams, schedulers should meet on a regular basis; they can learn from each other. This scheduling team can be called upon when individual teams have staffing requirements they can't fill.

Scheduling Suggestion 2: Use a Schedule Shell and Ask Team Members to Fill in the Blanks

Decide how often team members need to take turns working evenings, nights, and weekends. Then have a set rotation for covering these shifts. This becomes a template for the schedule shell, which can be used on a repeating basis determined by the length of the schedule period. The length of the schedule will vary from situation to situation and is often a product of the rotation for weekend coverage. If people work every other weekend, the schedule may last for four, six, or eight weeks. If people work every third weekend, then the schedule may last three, six, or nine weeks.

Once weekend and evening responsibilities are fixed, team members can fill in the blanks to cover day shifts and days off. "Holes" in the shell for evenings and weekends will occur if you have a vacancy. People may need to work extra time to cover the holes. Let people volunteer for this extra work. It's amazing how people will work together informally to cover the schedule. If there aren't enough volunteers to fill all holes, start a list from which people are pulled in order to fill in. The simple existence of this list gives people incentive to volunteer, so that they can choose which shifts they will cover rather than take a random assignment.

Scheduling Suggestion 3: Make Team Members Responsible for Their Own Schedule Swaps

This is a straightforward rule that shifts the responsibility for schedule changes to the individual team members. This rule is especially important for required weekend and evening rotations. People will cooperate with those team members who trade with them. Maintain this rule and the schedule will take care of itself. Allow people to break this rule and the schedule will fall apart, with people becoming angry and upset with each other. Enough said.

Scheduling Suggestion 4: Vacation Requests Must Be Made in Advance and May Not Interfere with Weekend or Evening Rotations

Everyone earns and deserves their time off. Requiring people to turn in their requests in advance makes the scheduling of vacation time fair for everyone.

If someone wants to take a weekend off on short notice, they can if they trade with someone else. Having this guideline in place forces people to think through their plans and promotes cooperation among team members. Post vacation requests on a yearlong calendar so that people can see who has requested what. The team should also make rules specifying the number of people who can be off simultaneously and the length of time people can be off. The informal discussions generated by clear procedures and the display of requests will encourage people to work together.

Scheduling Suggestion 5: Define the Holidays and Have a Set Rotation for Holiday Coverage

Few people like to work on holidays. The idea here is to share the burden equally and let people know in advance what holidays they will be required to work. The team decides which days of each year it will consider holidays and then divides them up into two, three, or four groups depending on how often team members need to work holidays to ensure that these days are covered adequately. For example, if the team defines nine holidays, there are nine team members, and three team members are needed to cover each holiday, then each team member needs to work three holidays. The nine holidays are then divided into three groups, and team members are assigned to each group. If a team member leaves, the replacement simply takes his or her spot in the holiday rotation. This system allows team members to project which holidays they will work each year into the future. Team members who want to swap holidays for special reasons can then do this on their own.

Scheduling Suggestion 6: Set Parameters for Overtime and Make the Team Responsible for Using It Wisely

Clinical coverage will require the occasional use of overtime. A few people like to work overtime. Most people prefer to work their scheduled hours and enjoy their time off. These simple facts set the tone for the use of overtime. The team needs to own the overtime budget and distribute overtime hours to those who want to work them and share the burden when everyone needs to work some overtime to cover unforeseen absences, vacancies, or periods of higher than expected workload. Management can offer self-managed teams incentives for target levels of overtime and reward those teams that come in under budget with bonuses or celebrations.

Scheduling Suggestion 7: Have a Plan for Covering for Personal Emergencies, Leaves of Absence, and Contingencies

Self-managed teams that anticipate these situations, talk about them, and plan for them know how to deal with them. Teams need to discuss the following questions:

- What will we do if two team members cannot make it to work on any given day and there is no one available to cover for them?
- What services can we cut for the day?
- Can we get another team to help us cover?
- How will we notify our customers?
- Can we hire a temporary replacement if someone is going on personal leave?
- Can we use overtime to cover for extended vacancies?
- In case of a weather emergency, how can we get team members to work?
- What is our systematic plan for cutting back on services if we are one, two, or three people short?

Each team will have more questions than this. The key is to openly discuss possible solutions. These situations will arise at some time; when they do the team will be prepared.

Scheduling Suggestion 8: Make Team Members Responsible for Finding Their Own Replacements When They Can't Make It to Work

People calling in sick is an age-old problem. Self-managed teams can solve this problem. One department of 60 people routinely had four or five people in counseling for "unexcused absences" before self-managed teams were implemented. After teams had been in place for 18 months, no one was in counseling. The corner was turned by simply asking team members to find their own replacements when they could not come to work. If they found a replacement 24 hours in advance, it did not count as an absence. People still get sick or have personal emergencies, but these are truly rare occurrences. People go the extra mile to cover for fellow team members whom they know have serious needs. Those who have been helped will return the favor. If no one can be found to cover a shift, the team works short and there are few complaints.

☞ **Team Tips from a Team Scheduler:**

- Publish the rules and guidelines for scheduling.
- Be firm and stick to the rules.
- Be open to suggestions on how to improve the scheduling process.
- Make people responsible for their own swaps.
- Have a specific time for dealing with the schedule and do not let this interfere with work time.
- Have a thick skin and don't take complaints about the schedule personally.

—Jennifer Robertson, ONTAP team scheduler, Mission+St. Joseph's

Will following all eight of these suggestions eliminate scheduling issues and problems? No. The schedule remains a topic of conversation for self-managed teams, and a few individuals will continue to try to take advantage of the system. Putting the schedule in the hands of the team and openly discussing will it eventually lead to a system that everyone knows and understands. Each team member realizes that his or her schedule is a personal responsibility when these suggestions are followed. Self-managed teams allow people to create scheduling systems that balance staff and customer needs.

Conflict Resolution

"This tendency to react to any emotionally meaningful statement by forming an evaluation of it from our own point of view is, I repeat, the major barrier to interpersonal communication. . . . The solution is provided by creating a situation in which each of the different parties comes to understand the other from the *other's* point of view."

—Carl R. Rogers and F. J. Roethlisberger

Conflict is good. Staying in conflict is bad. People and teams are always going to have differences of opinion. Conflict causes problems when people don't understand its source or don't know how to draw from it a solution that benefits both parties. In a hierarchy, conflicts are often handled by having the boss listen to both sides of the story. The boss then decides who is right. This system is efficient, but the boss's decision usually satisfies one person more than the other and rarely meets the needs of both. Conflict resolution is hard work, and as a result many people learn to avoid conflict.

Self-managed teams afford their members the opportunity to learn skills that can turn conflict into collaboration. The following suggestions are intended to give teams a framework for developing a conflict resolution process and for helping people understand that conflict is an essential part of daily operations systems.

Conflict Resolution Suggestion 1: Break the Pattern of Defensive Communication

Eighty percent of time spent listening is spent in boredom. The human brain processes information much faster than people can speak. When someone else is talking, people do one of three things: they don't pay attention, they listen intently trying to understand the other person, or they react by forming their own opinions about what the speaker is saying. During a disagreement the last option is the one usually taken. People naturally fall into defensive communications and try to come up with arguments that further their own viewpoints, countering the other's ideas. This cycle can deteriorate rapidly and often people end up in a full-blown argument.

The first and most important step in conflict resolution is making the effort to really listen to the other person—to make sure that you understand their point of view. The simple act of trying to understand someone's perspective will set the stage for that person's attempts to understand your thoughts on the matter. When people make the effort to listen to each other, they usually find that they have more points of agreement than of disagreement. This is particularly so in health care, especially when people realize that they are both acting as advocates for patients. When people agree that they have common ground, they are ready to move on to collaboration and can work to resolve their conflicts.

Conflict Resolution Suggestion 2: Move from Discussion to Dialogue

Discussion between two people who have different points of view is like a Ping-Pong match. Both sides try to win points and put spin on their shots, waiting for an opportunity to slam a winner past the opponent. Dialogue is a more civil path. To move to dialogue, both parties must agree to suspend their individual perspectives. They do not have to agree with the other person's ideas, but they do have to agree to search for new ideas and options that meet the needs of both of them.

This cease-fire is extremely hard to achieve. Our Western culture and American spirit of competitiveness are hard to overcome. We want to win. Winning does not imply the other person must lose, however. Dialogue is the process used to create solutions where both people win. Health care workers who are embroiled in discussion and want to move to dialogue can be encouraged to pause for a moment and think about what it would take for the patient to win. Once people have chosen to engage in dialogue, they are ready to move past conflict and begin looking for solutions where everyone wins.

Conflict Resolution Suggestion 3: Call a Time-Out

People get angry. To move past anger, it is wise to agree to take some time and walk away from the argument. Both parties should use this time to divert their attention from the disagreement. During this time, people should consider what they really want to accomplish and think about what the other person wants. When the parties get back together, they can begin by stating what they think the other person wants. This will often break the ice and lead to a clarification of the issues in a less emotional manner. People will discover that they usually agree on more points than they disagree on, and dialogue will follow.

Conflict Resolution Suggestion 4: Define the Processes for Resolving Conflicts between Team Members, Teams, and with Those Outside of the Team Structure

Chapter 10 discussed social systems design. Conflict resolution is definitely an issue that the design team needs to address. Flowcharts can be drawn to illustrate the process for conflict resolution. (See figures 16-1 and 16-2.) More important than flowcharts is the training of team members in processes and skills needed for conflict resolution. As with any new skill, people will struggle at first and get better with practice. Setting expectations for how conflicts are to be resolved encourages people to learn to handle conflict on their own.

Conflict Resolution Suggestion 5: Use Third Parties to Help Those Who Are Stuck at an Impasse in a Conflict

Sometimes two people can't work things out on their own. It is OK to ask for help. The first choice is to call on a team member who is neutral on the issue under discussion. If a team member cannot be impartial, seek out a coach. The role of the third person is to help the two people in conflict move from discussion to dialogue, to listen, not making judgments or finding solutions. Part of the training for a self-managed team should be in the area of mediation, a life skill that will help both at work and at home. On rare occasions, there will be an impasse between two team members, between two teams, or between a team member and someone outside the team that requires the use of a professional mediator. Don't be afraid to ask for this assistance. The time and money invested in getting expert help to resolve a critical conflict is well worth it.

Conflict Resolution Suggestion 6: Encourage People Who Have Just Resolved a Conflict to Reflect on the Steps Taken, in Order to Have Them Learn from the Experience

Conflict resolution is hard work. People need to pause after going through this process. They need to recognize the turning points in resolving the issue. They need to consider their feelings at different points in the conflict and begin to recognize what they learned about active listening, dialogue, and discovering alternatives. The third party can ask the people who were in conflict to share what the keys to resolving the conflict were and what the other person did well to move past the impasse. Getting feedback on what was done well encourages people to repeat the actions the next time they find themselves in a conflict. Learning from experience helps people improve their ability to move from conflict to collaboration.

Resolving conflict is an art. Rather than avoid conflict, self-managed teams need to provide team members with the opportunity to confront tough issues and learn how to work through them. Initial efforts to resolve

Figure 16-1. Conflict Resolution

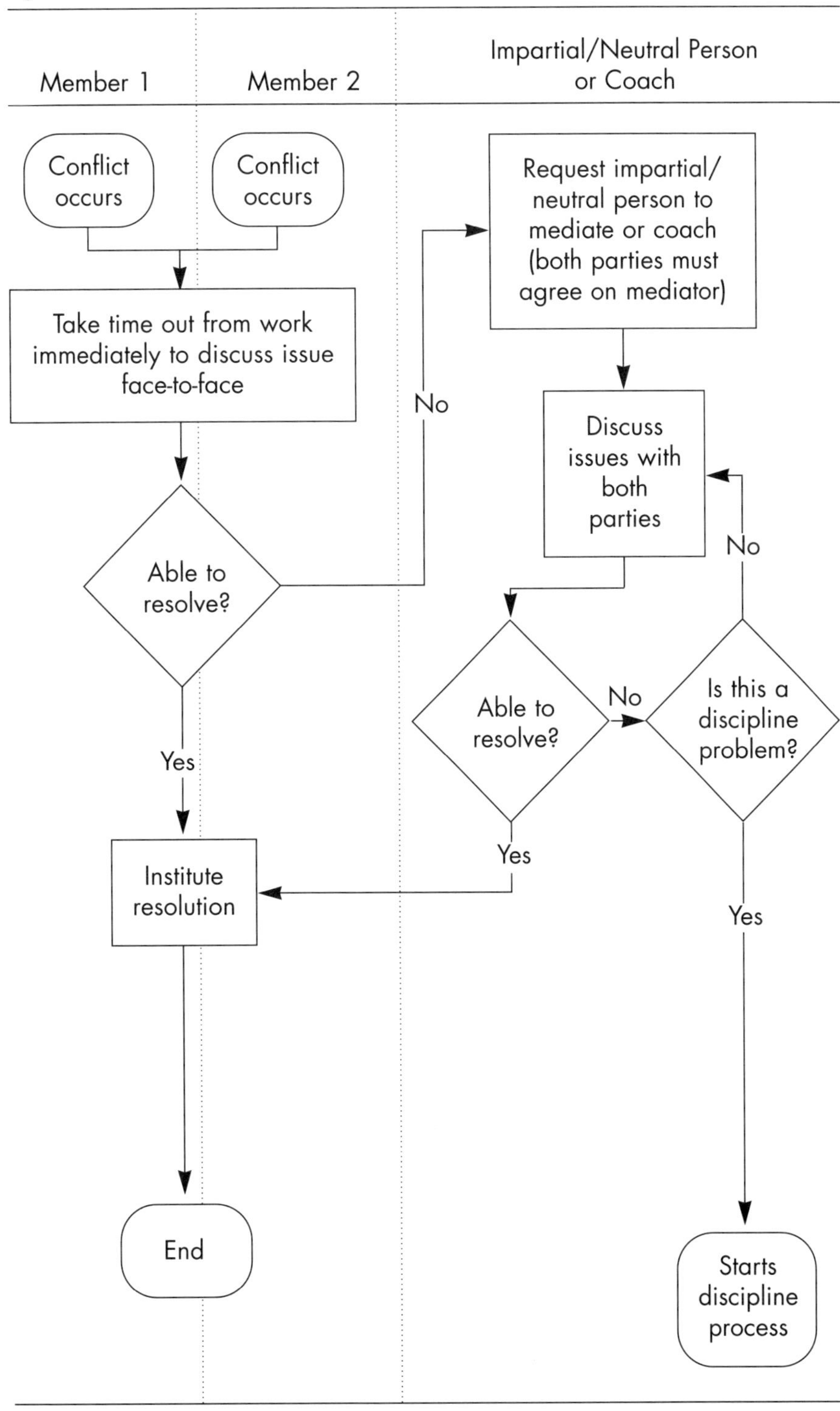

Figure 16-2. Interteam Conflict Resolution

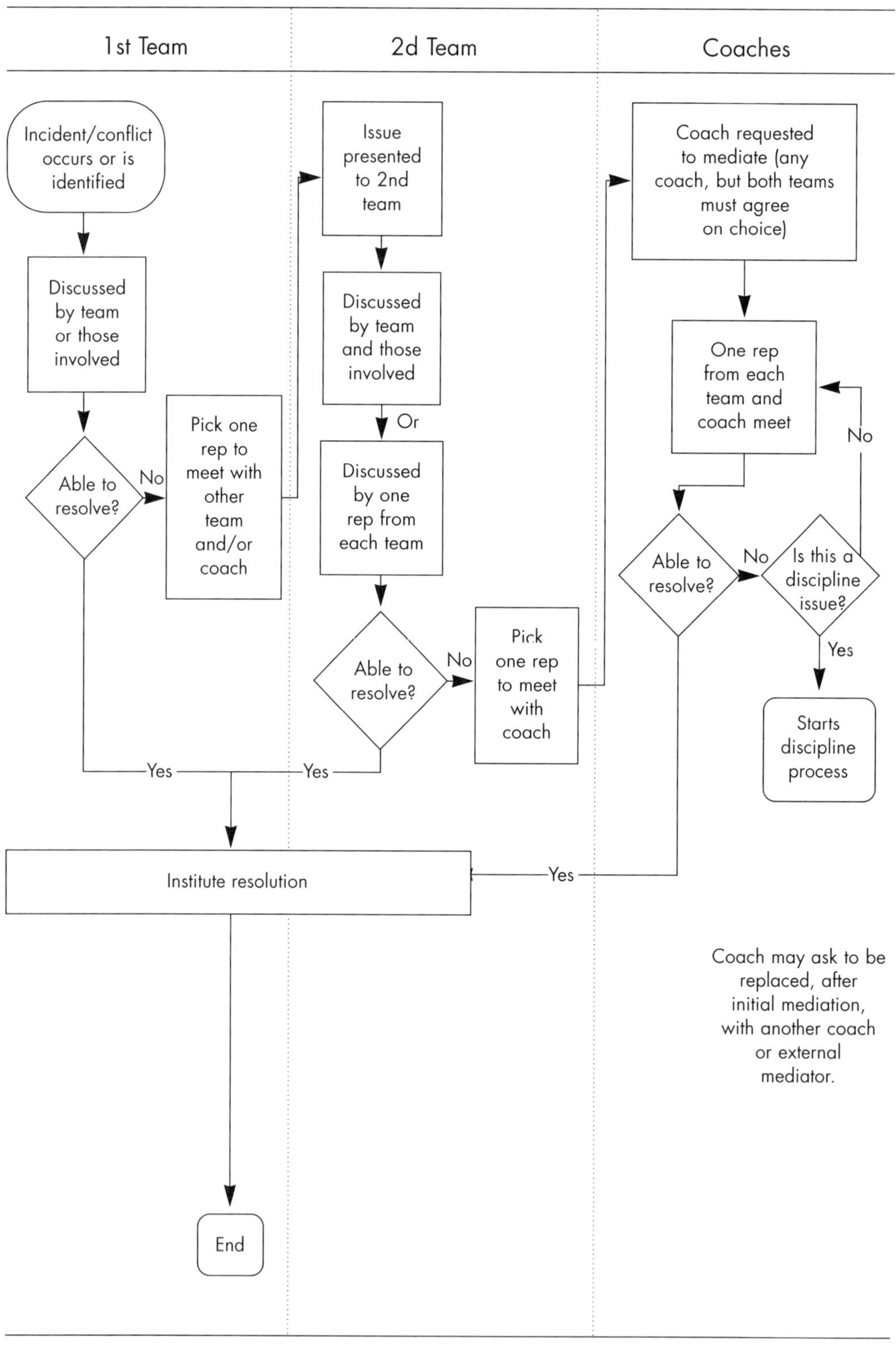

conflict will be difficult, but with practice individuals will learn the skills and discover what works best for them. People who use conflict as a positive force are those who learn to anticipate collaboration and to discover new paths. The key to conflict resolution is fighting the urge to fight on.

Decision Making

"You miss 100 percent of the shots you never take."

—*Wayne Gretzky*

Planning is a learning process. Decision making is an extension of the planning process. Decisions are made by everyone every moment of every day. Most decisions are unconscious acts based on experiences and knowledge that people have stored away in their brains. Occasionally, something triggers the realization that the current situation requires conscious thought and the explicit contemplation of choices. This section offers tips to help self-managed teams make decisions that advance team goals and benefit patients and customers.

Decision-Making Suggestion 1: Realize from the Start That Some Decisions Will Work and Some Will Not

Babe Ruth was one of the greatest home run hitters of all time. Few people realize, however, that the Babe struck out more times in his career than anyone else. Some decisions will be home runs. More often than not, decisions will not work out as expected. Because of this uncertainty, many people are timid when it comes to making a decision. Members of self-managed teams relied in the past on the supervisor to make decisions. Now it is time for the team to step up to the plate. The first step in decision making is realizing that only some decisions get results exactly as planned. The second step is realizing that other chances to make decisions will follow.

Decision-Making Suggestion 2: View Decisions as a Series of Experiments

A choice has been made and an action is taken. Good decision makers don't close their eyes and pray at this point. They keep their eyes open to see what happens. This is how people learn: they consider the alternatives, try something, observe the results, and think about what will work better next time. Decision making is experimenting. The more experiments you do, the more information you gather, and the better choices you make. People considered the best decision makers are people who have done the most experiments. Teams that are given the chance to experiment will learn how to make better choices.

Decision-Making Suggestion 3: When You Gather 90 Percent of the Information, Make a Decision and Act

Bureaucracy is noted for having "analysis paralysis." Self-managed teams cure this disease. Decisions are based information, and teams collect and process information much faster than bureaucracies. It takes 10 percent of the time to collect 90 percent of the information. When you get 90 percent of the information, make a decision. Making decisions quickly will scare people at first. But the more decisions made, the better the decisions. You can always try something else when more information becomes available. The 90 percent rule will seem radical to many people, especially those in the old hierarchy. It is! And it has to be, in order for self-managed teams to make a difference for their patients and customers.

Decision-Making Suggestion 4: Visualize Success, Analyze Risks, Anticipate the Next Decision, and Focus on the Immediate Action to Be Taken.

Decisions result in change. Change brings risk. It is the risk that causes people to flinch when decisions need to be made. Each decision can be viewed as a miniature change action process. Successful change actions have the following steps:

1. Visualize success
2. Analyze the risks
3. Anticipate the next decision
4. Focus on the immediate action to be taken

Think about the process that Tiger Woods uses when he tees off. First, he visualizes where he wants the ball to go. He considers the risks and rewards of using his driver or his two iron. Then, he contemplates how the result of his tee shot will set up his next shot. Finally, he focuses on the ball and his swing for the tee shot, blocking out all his other thoughts. The lesson is to think through the decision and then concentrate on the action you have chosen.

Decision-Making Suggestion 5: Think about the Decision from the Customer/Patient Perspective

Every team faces ethical dilemmas in which there seems to be no right or wrong answer. In these situations ask, "What would the patient want me to do?" Health care is about patient care. Self-managed teams need to consider several criteria when making decisions, but the most important criterion is the interest of the patient.

Decision making is the virtual aspect of planning. There is no such thing as an on-the-spot decision. Everything is related to everything else. Self-managed teams must accept that more of their decisions will fail than will succeed. The decision-making process bears fruit in the lessons it provides, lessons that can be applied to future decisions. Taking action sets the stage for taking more action. A decision has not been fully considered until the decision maker understands how it sets the context for the next decision. Teams that focus on the action at hand and act in the patient's best interest will practice good decision making, seeing around the corner.

Crisis Management

"You think you know everything, but you don't know the difference between an inconvenience and a problem. If you break your neck, if you have nothing to eat, if your house is on fire—then you got a problem. Everything else is inconvenience. Life *is* inconvenient. Life *is* lumpy. Learn to separate the inconveniences from the real problems. You will live much longer. And will not annoy people like me so much."

—Sigmund Wollman

The Chinese sign for crisis is composed of two characters, danger and opportunity. Self-managed teams will face "crisis" on a daily basis. A crisis exists when someone perceives a problem that requires an immediate solution. Teams members need to develop confidence in their ability to handle crisis situations. People who have cool heads during crises are well respected, and others seek them out when there are big problems to solve. What makes these people different from those who panic is primarily their perspective. The tips that follow will help self-managed teams find opportunity in the face of danger.

Crisis Management Suggestion 1: Determine Whether You Are Dealing with a Problem or an Inconvenience

Crisis is in the eye of the beholder. Robert Fulgham tells a story about Sigmund Wollman. Sigmund was a German Jew and a survivor of Auschwitz. Fulghum concludes his story about Wollman with "the Wollman test of reality": "Life is lumpy. And a lump in the oatmeal, a lump in the throat, and a lump in the breast are not the same lump. One should learn the difference." The first step in crisis management is to decide whether you are dealing with a true crisis. When someone comes to the team in a panic, listen first. The "problem"—once fully revealed—may turn out to be just an inconvenience.

Crisis Management Suggestion 2: It's OK to Be Anxious, Don't Be Afraid

Sometimes you do have an immediate problem that requires extraordinary attention. People will get scared. The body's autonomic fight-or-flight reaction is not necessarily a bad thing. Extra hormones are released, the nervous system is placed on alert, and the body is ready for action. The trick is to balance the natural energy of the body with the rational thoughts locked somewhere in the brain. A certain amount of nervous anxiety can be helpful. But don't be afraid. The first crisis that a new team faces will be a test of its ability to face a challenge. Teams should not be scared to take the actions necessary to handle the problem.

Crisis Management Suggestion 3: Respond, Don't React

The key to handling a crisis is the ability to respond and not react. Team members will want to do the first thing that comes to mind. This is reacting. What is needed is planning. Planning requires decision making and decision making requires information. The first thing that a fire fighter does when he or she gets to a fire is ask questions. He or she will ask whether anyone is in the building, where the stairways and exits are, how long the fire has been burning, where it started, and whether there are there any chemicals involved. The fire fighter does not rush into the building or immediately start trying to douse the flames. He or she seeks information and then responds. Self-managed teams need to learn the discipline to pause and ask questions before taking any action in a crisis.

Crisis Management Suggestion 4: Ask for Help

This simple suggestion draws on the primary power of self-managed teams. It is human nature to help people in need. Team members and teams are not alone. There are others who can and will help. Just ask. If a true crisis exists and people simply state their needs, others will help. The assumption here, however, is that the team knows it is not dealing with an inconvenience that it should be able to handle by itself. If others come to help and find they weren't really needed, they will hesitate to help again.

Crisis Management Suggestion 5: Make the Choice to Rise to a Challenge Rather than Complain about a Problem

People are rarely faulted for trying to meet a challenge. Moaning about problems is another matter. The choice of approach is the only difference. Tough situations have to be faced one way or another. Successful teams make the most of the opportunities and give their best efforts. They make a difference for their patients and customers.

This moment only happens once and the time is now. Zen teaches that each instant and each situation is present with itself. Nothing else matters. People will perceive crises where they do not exist and will not recognize crises when they see them. There is no great ruler who decides what is or is not a crisis. No one is the supreme judge of how a crisis was or wasn't handled. What matters is how the individual members of a team respond to situations they face. There really is no such thing as crisis management. However, there are unique opportunities for glory.

Personality Weaving

"Blending personalities is like combining spices to create a unique recipe."

People are similarly different. Self-managed teams expose differences. This is a big change from bureaucratic systems, which seek to suppress diversity. The industrial age valued conformity in the service of its machinelike processes. Success in the information age depends on uniqueness. Team members, however, may not yet be used to an atmosphere of contrasts. Personality clashes are among self-managed teams' biggest stumbling blocks. This section suggests ways to take advantage of the strengths of different personalities.

Personality Weaving Suggestion 1: Recognize That One Strength of a Team Is the Diversity of Its Members

If two heads are better than one, then how about six or ten? It is hard for people to understand that more and different are better. Perhaps the greatest strength of a self-managed team is the release of individuality by each member of the team. This emphasis on individuality may seem at odds with the concept of a team. But teams are built around a common purpose not a common personality. People need to be able to exploit their individual talents and viewpoints to work for the same goals. People who are free to be themselves and use their abilities will thrive, and the team will excel as a result.

Personality Weaving Suggestion 2: Team Members Must Respect Each Other, Not Necessarily Like Each Other

Will Rogers is famous for saying "I never met a man I didn't like." Will Rogers was an unusual man. People will have to work with people they do not like. Self-managed teams depend on respect rather than congeniality.

Respect comes from consistent behaviors that reflect a person's core values. Team members can tolerate differences if people act in a civil manner. This environment of mutual respect differs from a hierarchy, where those at the bottom are stuck with the behaviors and values of those at the top. Self-managed teams require each team member to honor the core values that the team has decided upon. Beyond that, each team member is responsible for developing respect for himself or herself by being civil and respecting the values of others.

Personality Weaving Suggestion 3: Use Tools to Help People Understand, Recognize, and Appreciate Their Differences

The first step in dealing with a problem is recognizing that a problem exists. Similarly, dealing with personalities begins with recognizing that everyone has one. We all know that the world would be a much better place if everyone were just like us, and nothing could be further from the truth. We are all different, and we all have strengths and weaknesses. A new team should complete individual personality profiles as a group. There are many tools for this purpose, and most organizations have resources and trained facilitators available to help teams with this important process. Many other personality profiling tools are also available.

A word of caution is warranted here. Do not label people based on a specific personality profile! Use the profiling process to find out about yourself as an individual and to understand that other personalities have strengths that can support you and your team. Blending personalities is a challenge, and a good beginning is to understand your own.

Personality Weaving Suggestion 4: Balance the Perspectives of Monomaniacs and Dissidents to Help the Team Work for a Common Purpose

Every team has at least one of each—perhaps more if you're lucky. Monomaniacs and dissidents are basic ingredients of team success. Monomaniacs champion causes and ideas. They are like dogs with new bones; they just won't let go. Dissidents will take a contrary point of view simply because they can. They are the devil's advocates. It is difficult when the team gets caught up in a fight between a growling dog and the devil. These people are generally eccentric. Eccentric means being off-center. Progress and growth result from off-centeredness, not from being in the middle of the road. The key to working with monomaniacs and dissidents is to keep them focused on team goals. These people are generally very passionate, and if you can focus their attention and questions on patient interests, your team will discover new ways to improve patient care.

Weaving personalities requires patience and knowledge. It takes time to get used to working with others in a team environment. Self-managed teams allow individuals to express themselves. Team members begin to see fellow team members in a whole new light. Knowledge of your own personality is the starting point for understanding the personalities of others. Personality weaving is the key to taking advantage of the vitality of diversity.

Chapter Wrap-Up

Scheduling, conflict resolution, decision making, crisis management, and personality weaving—these tasks are required every day of every week. Clinical staff have historically abdicated these functions to management. The implementation of self-managed teams has allowed workers to take these functions back. Can self-managed teams handle all these day-to-day issues? Absolutely! Teams who work toward a common purpose with the patient in mind will understand the outcomes needed from daily operations systems. Team members who help design these processes for their particular environment are best positioned to take actions that benefit their patients and customers.

Reference

1. J. Lipnack and J. Stamps, *The Age of the Network* (New York: John Wiley & Sons, 1994): 34.

Suggested Readings

Block, P. *Stewardship.* San Francisco: Berrett-Koehler, 1993.

Fulghum, R. *Uh-Oh.* New York: Villard, 1991.

Rogers, Carl R., and F. J. Roethlisberger. "Barriers and Gateways to Communication." *Harvard Business Review* (November/December 1991): 105–11.

Part III

Teams in Action

Once teams really get started, there is no holding them back. It is humbling for management to see how much their employees are capable of when they are given the opportunity to truly play a responsible role in the organization. Teams have resolved problems with physicians and other departments that have plagued their managers for years. Teams can reduce turnover and change the behavior of poor performers. Teams can accomplish a lot when they have the authority, permission, knowledge, and skills to perform.

In this section the authors provide information on key elements of team performance. Teams cannot just become cohesive because it is asked of them; they need team-building opportunities and education to develop their sense of teamness and knowledge of the expectations that teams have of their members. Once teams are formed, the members are just beginning their journey of learning and growing. Education, in frequent doses, is a prescription that will help teams succeed and continue to maintain strong performance. Team development is not a smooth process. Teams fluctuate from ecstasy to agony and back. This section helps define the bumps in the road and ways to help smooth them out.

There are clear criteria for team excellence. Teams should be aware of these criteria from the start and focus their efforts on performing well in these specific areas. The criteria are outlined in chapter 22. Teams who are making improvements in their performance also need time, resources, and permission to stop and celebrate, reflect on their progress, and renew their commitment to continued high performance.

Finally in this section the authors explore the future of teams. They answer the question "What is next after teams?" They explain why a sound foundation in teamness is essential to anyone who wants to perform well in the future in an environment of networks.

Part Contents: Teams in Action

Chapter 17

The First Team Meeting

"Meetings are not a distraction from work. Thinking is not lost production. People talking and deciding together is the work."

—*Peter Block*

Chapter Preview

The first team meeting is the beginning of a new system of working for many staff members. They may have worked on temporary teams or in groups before, but very few have actually been employed as a member of a self-managed team. The first team meeting is the signal that this exciting adventure into self-management is beginning. It marks the first of many significant changes for the staff and management who are participating. To ensure that this kickoff for the team is successful, considerable thought and planning need to be invested in this first team meeting.

This chapter will help the team, and particularly the new team leader, plan and prepare for that first team meeting. It may seem like a simple task to people who have conducted and participated in meetings frequently. Unfortunately, it is a new experience for most staff. They may attend department staff meetings, but most staff have had few opportunities to plan and lead meetings. This meeting will be the opportunity for the team leader to demonstrate how well he or she can conduct a meeting. It will be the turning point for team members who never really believed self-management would occur. This meeting opens the door for the staff to demonstrate their abilities to manage the work and make decisions.

Chapter at a Glance

In this chapter, you will find

- A detailed description of the planning process for the first team meeting
- A description of the first team meeting that emphasizes the role of the team leader

Planning for the First Team Meeting

"Every moment spent planning saves three or four in execution."

—Crawford Greenwalt, president of DuPont

The first official meeting of the self-managed team is an important meeting. It establishes a format for how team meetings will be conducted. It sets the tone for team member interactions and communications. It develops the understanding that team members have of the roles and responsibilities that they need to fulfill, and it begins the team-building process. It accomplishes many things, but it should be only an hour-long meeting.

The first meeting of a team, and all subsequent meetings, are as short as possible, generally limited to one hour. This time constraint is due to the normal time pressures and resource limits in health care organizations. Because of this time constraint, planning for the meeting reaches a critical level of importance. Much needs to be accomplished, but there is a limited time frame.

In the planning phase, the purpose or objective of the meeting is established, as well as the sequence of the agenda and the roles and methods that will be utilized. The team leader is under pressure to make sure that every minute of the meeting is useful and directed toward the purpose of the meeting. To help in planning for the meeting, the team leader will want to involve the coach and the note taker. In preparation for subsequent meetings, the team leader will want to contact all members of the team for input into the agenda, but there are specific content requirements for the first team meeting, as described in chapter 8.

Administrative Details

One aspect of planning is the coordination of the administrative details for the meeting. (See figure 17-1.) The agenda needs to be prepared and copied for the meeting. The team leader may decide to publish the agenda in advance, post it, circulate it, or send all the team members a copy. If everyone is to receive a copy before the meeting, will the team leader need to take copies to the meeting? Yes! People frequently forget to bring their copies of the agenda to a meeting. Distributing or announcing the agenda in advance gives the participants the opportunity to think about the topics in advance and plan their participation. It does not guarantee that people will bring their agendas to the meeting.

In order to prepare the agenda, the team leader needs to have reserved a meeting place and confirmed its availability on the date and at the time that will work well for the team. The team leader wants to find a location for the team meeting that is close to the physical workplace of most team members, as well as convenient and available for a routine meeting time. The meeting space needs to be large enough to accommodate the entire team, preferably around a boardroom-type table.

Figure 17-1. The Administrative Details

Before the first meeting, the team leader must prepare for it in the following ways:

- Reserve a meeting place
- Notify the team of the date, time, and location for the meeting
- Develop the agenda (send the agenda out in advance?)
- Make copies of the agenda
- Make copies of the other handouts, such as the meeting evaluation form
- Make sure there is a flip chart or white board and markers
- If using a flip chart, obtain masking tape
- Make sure there is a method for taking attendance at the meeting
- Order refreshments if you plan on having them

Other administrative duties include making sure that there is a flip chart, white board, or chalkboard, and markers. These tools are typically necessary when a group meets and are required for the first team meeting. If the team is planning on using flip-chart paper, then masking tape may also be needed to stick the flip-chart pages on the walls. Some organizations use flip-chart paper that has a sticky edge and does not need to be taped. If the team is planning on having refreshments, the team leader will need to order them. In most organizations, since teams meet frequently, they omit refreshments unless the meeting is to recognize a person or a special event.

Whether the team is large or small, it helps to have an attendance roster for team meetings. The roster is a simple way for the team to keep track of who has attended meetings and who has been absent. The team will want to make sure that it follows up with staff members who miss a meeting in order to keep them informed. If some team members are missing meetings chronically, the team leader or coach will want to investigate and identify whether it is the meeting time or place that is the problem, or whether it something else entirely. Once the administrative details are decided, the meeting content and structure can be addressed.

Role Clarification

During the planning for the first team meeting, role clarification begins to occur. When the team leader, note taker, and coach get together to plan this first meeting, they start to see how their roles will play out in the meeting.

The Team Leader The team leader takes charge of the planning to develop this agenda and all future meeting agendas. That is part of the role of the team leader. Working with the coach and the note taker, the team leader reviews the purpose of the meeting, develops the specific meeting objectives, and specifies the agenda items. He or she places the agenda items in a logical order, so that they build one to the next. Then the team leader, note taker, and coach estimate the time requirements for each agenda item and decide who will be the lead person for the agenda item. They discuss the best method for handling the agenda item. Is it an item that requires a decision? How much discussion time will be needed before the decision? Will we want the team to generate ideas, through brainstorming and then select the best idea?

In the first meeting, most of the agenda items are led by the team leader. The coach may play the facilitator role when team involvement is needed, for instance, in brainstorming. The team leader helps manage the group process, making sure that everyone on the team participates and has the opportunity to be heard. At the end of the meeting, the team leader guides the team in a discussion of the effectiveness of the meeting and then adjourns the meeting.

The Note Taker The note taker has four responsibilities during the meeting:

1. Taking notes
2. Documenting attendance
3. Summarizing the meeting
4. Reviewing the minutes

The primary responsibility is to take notes of decisions, agreements, assignments, and items that are to be deferred to another meeting. The note taker completes the attendance roster to document who attended the meeting and who was absent. He or she also provides a summary of the meeting at the end of the meeting and reviews with the team what they would like to see on the next meeting agenda.

By the time the meeting is over, the note taker has a fairly clear idea of what will be needed on the next meeting's agenda. This speeds the process of developing the agenda in the meeting planning session with the team leader. It is difficult for the note taker to participate in the discussion because he or she is occupied with documenting the meeting. If there is an agenda item that is of particular importance to the note taker, he or she may request that someone else take notes during that segment of the meeting.

The note taker is also responsible for writing the minutes, distributing the minutes, and maintaining a minutes notebook. At the beginning of subsequent team meetings, the note taker will ask everyone to read through the minutes and advise if there have been changes to them.

It is during the planning meetings that the true value of the note taker becomes clear to the team leader. With documentation of the past, the note taker is able to clarify information that may be unclear to the team leader from prior meetings. The note taker also has information on what needs to be discussed at future meetings.

The Coach The coach serves as a support person in planning upcoming meetings. During the meeting planning session, the coach may ask questions to help the team leader think through the agenda and the methods that will be used to address the agenda items. The coach may ask, "Would it help to have the get-acquainted exercise already written on a piece of flip-chart paper before the start of the meeting? Have you thought about a way to cut the discussion off if it looks like it will go beyond the time allotted? Do you know of anyone on the team who will be seriously opposed to that aspect of the get-acquainted exercise?"

The coach may volunteer to go to the flip chart or white board and take notes of brainstorming activities or to lead the brainstorming activity. It is through the discussion at the planning session that the meeting content, methods, and roles are developed. It is possible that planning for the meeting can take an hour, just as the actual meeting may take an hour.

The First Meeting

"Leaders must behave the way they wish their followers would behave."

—*S. A. Kirkpatrick and E. A. Locke*

The team will perceive this first meeting as a model for future meetings. For that reason, the tone of this meeting is of particular importance. If it becomes a gripe session or is disorganized and disruptive, it will not create a positive feeling about self-managed teams. It may also lead the team members to the conclusion that the team leader is not an effective meeting leader. The tone that is established in this meeting will set a precedent that will be hard to break in future meetings.

The team leader is responsible for setting the tone. He or she does this through both overt and subtle behaviors. If the team leader *smiles* and communicates energy, enthusiasm, and interest, the interest and enthusiasm of team members will be engaged. If the team leader acts bored, as if the meeting is drudgery or a burden, the team will start to see the meeting that way also.

In setting the tone, the team leader will want to start reinforcing the "teamness" of the group. By using words like "we" and "our," the team leader starts giving the group a team identity. If the team leader starts to link his or her comments with those of someone who spoke previously, the team will do the same. For instance, the team leader could say, "I've been thinking about Mary's concern about the meeting time and I'd like to suggest an alternative." Others will start to use the same phrasing. If the team leader is open to opposite points of view, and even asks for them, the team will begin to see that expressing disagreement is an acceptable part of team membership.

The team leader will want to reinforce the concept of shared leadership. If the team defers in a decision to the team leader, merely because they perceive the leadership role as having power, the team leader or coach will need to quickly address this misconception and reinforce the concept of equality on the team. It is through these types of behaviors that the team leader sets the tone of the meeting.

At the planning session, the agenda was developed. It may look like the sample agenda in figure 17-2. The agenda in figure 17-2 is an aggressive agenda and does not allow much time for the group to discuss the items included prior to making a decision or prior to finalizing them. The team leader may want to put fewer items on the agenda and establish a more relaxed tone for the meeting. Establishing the agenda and setting the tone of the meeting are significant aspects of the team leader's responsibilities.

There are three distinct parts to the agenda: the heading, the objectives, and the agenda itself. The heading lets everyone know what the meeting is, where and when it will be held, and how long it will last. The objectives identify what the people attending the meeting should try to accomplish in the time frame of the meeting. The agenda itself lists the agenda topics in chronological order, giving the name of the person who will lead the agenda topic as well as the amount of time that person should take on the agenda. The agenda displayed in figure 17-2 has notes about the items to help guide the participants and the team leader in what will happen when that item comes up.

Chapter Wrap-Up

The first meeting of the self-managed team can be seen as the maiden voyage for the team. If it goes well, team members will come back for another sail. If it is difficult and cold, and the team leader is seen as floundering, the team may come back, but with less enthusiasm. The sample agenda presents a considerable amount of information to be covered in a very short time. It is the team leader's responsibility to decide what to include on the agenda and what to leave off. If the meeting does not move as rapidly as the team leader anticipated, he or she is perfectly free to postpone an agenda item to the next meeting, with the team's permission.

During the planning session, the team leader identifies the administrative details that must be addressed prior to the team meeting. The team leader develops the agenda, with the assistance of the note taker and the coach. The team leader conducts the meeting and may call on the coach to facilitate different parts of the meeting. The coach supports the team leader and the note taker by offering suggestions, asking questions, and helping before, during, and after the meeting. The note taker documents the meeting, attendance, and items for the next meeting's agenda. The note taker also prepares and distributes the minutes, develops a minutes notebook, and asks for revisions to the minutes at the next team meeting. At the end of the meeting, the note taker summarizes the key points, decision, and assignments.

Each participant in the meeting plays an important role. They are there to help the meeting accomplish its purpose and to achieve a successful launch of the team. They have a considerable amount to accomplish. For something as important as a team meeting, an hour is not a lot of time.

Suggested Readings

Block, Peter. "The End of Leadership." *Leader to Leader* 3 (winter 1997): 13.

Greenwalt, Crawford. Quoted in A. Mackensie, *The Time Trap.* New York: McGraw Hill, 1972.

Kirkpatrick, S. A., and E. A. Locke. "Leadership: Do Traits Matters?" *Academy of Management Executive* (May 1991): 57.

Figure 17-2. Sample Agenda

(Organization name)
(Department) (Team name)
(Time of meeting, date of meeting)
(Location of meeting)

Objectives

1. Set the tone and get organized for future meetings; begin the team-building process
2. Clarify our purpose and establish our mission
3. Learn how to have an effective meeting and set ground rules
4. Establish future meeting times and dates

Agenda

1. Welcome	Team leader
Review of meeting objectives	3 minutes
Clarify roles: team leader, note taker, timekeeper, coach	
2. Get acquainted (group activity) (Coach or team leader may facilitate)	Group
(Name, job, length of service, one positive about self-managed teams)	10 minutes
3. The purpose of our team (discussion) (Coach may facilitate or team leader can) A. Purpose of the team B. What is a self-managed team, how does it work? C. What will be the same, what will be different? D. Our mission statement; team member commitment	Team leader 25 minutes
4. Ground rules and effective meetings (group brainstorming and review) (Coach may facilitate or team leader can)	Team leader 10 minutes
5. Future meetings and meeting times (group decision)	Team leader 5 minutes
6. Summary and next meeting topics (review and discussion)	Note taker 5 minutes
7. Meeting evaluation and adjourn (group feedback)	Team leader 2 minutes

Chapter 18

Team Building

Chapter Preview

"The way a team plays as a whole determines its success. You may have the greatest bunch of individual starts in the world, but if they don't play together, the club won't be worth a dime."

—*Babe Ruth*

The goal of team building is to reduce the social distance between staff members so that communication is clearer and more honest. Social distance can be reduced by creating an environment of trust. On some teams establishing trust is difficult because of the history that team members have with each other. It is possible that team members hold grudges for slights or wrongs done to them years ago by other members of the team. While recognizing that there may be some old animosities or good reasons for distrust, team members must lay those old hurts to rest. They must move on and demonstrate their willingness to forgive and forget. The process of moving from distrust to trust, independence to interdependence, and social distance to closeness is the process of team building.

This chapter discusses the value of team building. It also warns of the necessity to move slowly so that team members remain comfortable as their social distance decreases. The chapter presents activities that will help the team develop closeness and a strong team identity. The activities are arranged in a progression, from "getting acquainted" exercises to exercises that build confrontation skills.

Chapter at a Glance

In this chapter, you will find

- A discussion of team building
- A discussion of the process of getting acquainted
- A discussion of team differences
- A discussion of social masks
- A discussion of the ability to confront with honesty
- Nine team activities for progressive team building

Team Building

"There is virtually no environment in which teams, if done right, can't have a measurable impact on the performance of an organization."

—Jon Katzenbach and Douglas K. Smith

When a self-managed team first forms, its participants have many questions and concerns, most of which focus on themselves. New team members want to know how being on a self-managed team will affect them: "Will I have a positive experience? Will I have opportunities to excel? Will I be held back by poor performers? Will it be too much work? Will I succeed or fail?" Someone asking these questions is thinking as an individual who serves on a team, not as a team member. The path that the individual takes to gain a team focus is a long and bumpy road, with several detours. The inclination is to remain a separate individual who is a member of the group and to avoid getting absorbed, swallowed up, or too enmeshed in the group.

Forming a team is not as simple as telling a group of people that they are now a team. It is a lengthy process during which team members learn about each other, develop trust, and learn to communicate at a deeper level. When a team truly exists, its members will feel and demonstrate interdependence. They will know each other well and communicate more clearly than people who are not part of a team. They will be able to talk with each other openly and honestly, and they will be comfortable confronting and questioning each other. None of this is achieved easily. It takes time and effort on each team member's part.

Team building occurs in many ways. It occurs naturally when people are working together to complete a project or accomplish a goal. In the process, they develop a deeper understanding of each other and respect for each other's talents and idiosyncrasies. Team building also can be accomplished through team-building exercises that have no deeper purpose than to draw the people on the team closer together and to break down barriers that inhibit open and honest communication. Many individuals focus so much on tasks that they see little value in what they call "touchy-feely" team-building exercises. They do not see how team building enables a team to achieve its goals and improve its performance and consider the exercises a waste of time.

The Value of Team Building

The research on effective teams indicates otherwise. Team building creates an environment of trust, respect, fun, and interdependence. It helps individual members of the team appreciate the knowledge, skills, and abilities of others on the team. It brings team members together so that they can act in concert, smoothly and effortlessly, without the barriers and hurdles that distrust and lack of respect bring. A sense of closeness makes it easier for team members to be honest with each other and to take action to confront problems and issues that arise among them.

When teams come together to accomplish work, they spend part of their time on relationship activities and part of their time accomplishing the work. The relationship activities that they engage in enable them to decide who will take the lead on projects, who will gather information, who will write reports, and so on. They make their decisions based on their knowledge of each other's strengths and weaknesses, as well as on their desire to help each other grow and develop. They know who works well together on the team and where friction exists. They know which team members are especially focused on tasks and which ones can help smooth and develop relationships.

Team building helps the members of the team get to know each other, and it helps them develop respect for the different knowledge, abilities, and perspectives each team member brings. It helps build a bond between the individuals on the team that is a source of strength during difficult times. It keeps team members from making false assumptions about the behaviors and actions of team members.

Successful teams are characterized by the trust and mutual regard with which members treat each other. This high level of mutual confidence and mutual understanding usually results only after team members have spent much time working together. Team-building exercises, however, can accelerate the process of developing the closeness, trust, and regard that team members need to have for each other in order to work together smoothly.

"Teamness" Audits

After their team has been in existence for some time, team members may want to know how far they have come in developing their "teamness." In her book *Team Talk,* Anne Donnellon suggests that teams perform a team talk audit.[1] The audit will help team members identify the degree to which they are functioning as a real team rather than as a group of people assigned to work together. Donnellon identifies six areas that are to be analyzed in the team talk audit:

1. Identification with the team
2. Interdependence
3. Power differentiation
4. Social distance
5. Conflict management
6. Negotiation.

Table 18-1 provides examples of phrases and behaviors that would be expected in a cohesive team.

To conduct the audit, team members record or take notes of words and phrases used in team meetings. They then analyze what they have heard and documented. Using this information, the team can evaluate where it is in its development on each of the six dimensions of cohesion.

Table 18-1. Team Characteristics

Characteristic	Phrases and Behaviors
Team Identification	■ We, Our *not* Me, My, I, or You
High interdependence	■ Asking for each other's input ■ Expressing own needs without apology ■ Suggesting ways the team members can work together to accomplish a task ■ Asking for input from other team members
Low power differentiation	■ Respect for all input, regardless of who provides it ■ Treating everyone on the team equally ■ Absence of interruptions and discussions in which one person is not listening to the other ■ Politeness to all team members ■ Apologies to the team
Social closeness	■ Use of informal language ■ Listening with empathy and sensitivity ■ Helping interpret what another person is trying to say ■ Building on each other's comments ■ Expressions of friendship and caring ■ Physical closeness, touching ■ Spontaneous humor and fun
Conflict management style (confronting and collaborating)	■ Exploring what is meant rather than contradicting it ■ Helping clarify each other's needs ■ Surfacing issues on which there is apparent or potential conflict ■ Identifying what is needed to resolve a conflict ■ Summarizing and reviewing areas of agreement ■ Entering a discussion around a conflict or disagreement instead of avoiding the discussion
Negotiation style (win-win)	■ Exploring what is needed for an agreement ■ Helping to incorporate apparently different perspectives into a creative solution that meets the team's needs ■ Expressing willingness to spend the time to resolve an issue so that all members are comfortable ■ Stating the positions and needs of others to achieve understanding and clarity

Most teams need some help in developing their effectiveness and identity as a team. The rest of this chapter contains team-building exercises. The exercises are arranged so that, as the team progresses through them, social closeness will increase. They start with get-acquainted exercises appropriate for teams that have just gotten started or that have not progressed too far in developing team identity.

If teams implement any or all of the team-building activities described in this chapter, they need to be aware that team identity and closeness can erode over time without continued emphasis and ongoing team-building activities. People enter and leave the team and take different roles on the team. The team has engrossing projects and activities, and then it loses steam. Teams react to forces in the environment, and they react to the personal challenges that the individual members are facing. Team building does not ensure a smooth passage through the turbulence and bumps in the road that teams encounter. It does ensure a smoother passage and the possibility of reaching higher peaks in performance than a team will achieve if it does not address and implement team-building activities.

Getting Acquainted

It is amazing that people can work side by side for several years and yet know almost nothing of the backgrounds, histories, current lives, and dreams of their coworkers. But this is the common state of affairs. When team building commences, the members of the team may have encountered each other often in the workplace and yet know very little about each other. This situation must change. A functioning team is more than just a collection of unfamiliar individuals. Team members must become closer emotionally as well as intellectually. They can begin by getting acquainted. Team activities 1 through 4, at the end of this chapter, are four simple team-building exercises to help team members get acquainted.

Team building starts when team members learn more about each other. It is best, however, to avoid delving too deeply at the beginning. Most people in the United States are uncomfortable with too much closeness, particularly closeness to the people they work with. The American workplace is often infused with a sense of distrust. People believe that if others know too much about them, that information may be used to their detriment. In general, a comfortable work environment is thought to be one in which people maintain a certain degree of social distance.

One of the goals of team building is to reduce that social distance, but not so quickly that team members are scared or offended. People feel vulnerable and threatened when they believe others are learning their innermost secrets. It may be because of self-esteem issues, or out of a fear of being manipulated, ridiculed, or harmed, or for other reasons. Most groups of people first forming as teams will want to move slowly in closing social distance. Team building is like stepping into a pool of very cold water. Most people are willing to put just their toes in, and it takes a considerable amount of cajoling and time before they are willing to go deeper. Superficial get-acquainted team building will be tolerated by most people and even enjoyed by some. It is therefore a good place to start. Leave the team building that dives deeper until all team members have become comfortable with a quick dip into the waters of social closeness.

Respecting Differences

Teams get their strength from the differences that individual team members bring to their teams. Team members are different ages, different genders, different races, and different religions; they have different educations, grew up in different places, and have different backgrounds. All of those differences translate into a wealth of perspectives on problems and issues, and these many perspectives help teams make better decisions and work more creatively than if all team members were alike. Those differences can also translate into more conflicts than if all team members were identical.

At times, team members unable to see how their differences are strengths. They can only remember the squabbles that arise out of the different ways they look at things. Team activities 5 and 6 are designed to help team members perceive the positive side of their differences. There are numerous other exercises that perform this function that are not included in this chapter. Teams can find exercises in other sources that will help them find their way out of a desert, or rescue themselves after being stranded in a plane crash, or discover their way while searching for a gold mine. All of these exercises reinforce the advantages of a team and its variety over an individual.

Understanding the Person behind the Face

The first two levels of team building, getting acquainted and learning to respect differences among team members, help team members expand their knowledge about each other. While these exercises open the door to greater social closeness and begin to build trust and understanding, they only move the team part of the way toward the closeness that it will need to perform its best. Many people hide behind masks that only show the world the little they are willing to reveal. These social masks keep others from understanding the real person. There are many reasons for wearing social masks, but they all boil down to one basic reason: shielding one's vulnerability from deliberate or unintentional harm by another person.

Self-managed teams can survive if these masks are never penetrated. However, the members of the team will gain more personally and reach a higher level of performance if the masks come off. It is when team members become vulnerable to each other and trust each other that the strongest teams are built. Team activity 7 helps team members delve below the superficial.

Confronting Others with Honesty

One goal of team building is to enable the team members to confront each other with openness and honesty. When team members lack the ability to confront, the team will be unable to resist the forces pushing it apart. Team members will begin to withdraw from the team, physically, verbally, or both. They may reduce their participation in team meetings, or they may attend fewer team meetings. They may slow down their team work, missing deadlines, or they may not get their team work done at all. They may form cliques and communicate a lot with some members of the team and very little with others. All of these behaviors are divisive and harm the team. Although they can occur in any self-managed team, they are less likely to threaten the team that has the skills to handle them. A signal of the team's effectiveness is how it approaches and confronts these behaviors.

If the team has developed social closeness and one member observes a new set of divisive behaviors in another member, it is normal and natural when he or she shares the observation with the other member. Without judging, the team member might observe, "I notice that you don't interact with team member X as much as you used to" or "I notice that you are spending more time with team member X and less time with team member Y than you used to." The discussion that follows the observation may help identify a problem that is brewing and needs to be addressed. On a healthy team, the problem is identified and addressed immediately. On a team that is not so healthy, the problem may be ignored; if not confronted, it may cause permanent damage to the team's interactions and effectiveness. Team activities 8 and 9 help team members develop the ability to confront each other honestly and constructively.

Chapter Wrap-Up

Successful self-managed teams need clear challenging goals, clear roles, the authority to make change, shared leadership, respect for diversity, a way to achieve feedback from customers and the organization, and systems of operating that support team behaviors. If any of these elements are absent, all the team building in the world will not help the team succeed. However, even if all of these elements are present, the self-managed team will still not perform at its highest level without developing a true team identity and team member closeness.

Team members will be uncomfortable if too much closeness is demanded at the beginning. Team building starts with basic get-acquainted exercises, then progresses through celebrating differences, penetrating masks, and confronting with honesty. In this way, team members gradually close the social distance between them. The team achieves the cohesion that enables it to pursue its goals effectively.

Reference

1. A. Donnellon, *Team Talk* (Boston: Harvard Business School Press, 1996), pp. 259–61.

Suggested Readings

Katzenbach, Jon, and Douglas K. Smith. *The Wisdom of Teams.* Cambridge, Mass.: Harvard Business School Press, 1993.

Lynberg, Michael. *Winning.* New York: Doubleday, 1993.

Silberman, Mel, ed. *The 1998 Team and Organization Development Sourcebook.* New York: McGraw Hill, 1998.

Woodcock, Mike. *50 Activities for Team Building.* Amherst, Mass.: HRD Press, 1989.

Team Activity 1

Paired Introductions

Purpose: To increase the level of comfort people have about speaking in front of strangers; on self-managed teams, to enable everyone on the team to achieve greater knowledge of fellow team members. Time frame: 45–60 minutes.

Directions: At the beginning of a class or workshop

1. Divide the team into pairs.
2. Ask each person in the pair to interview the other and prepare to introduce the other person to the team. Suggest interview information that the team would like to know about each team member.
   - Name, preferred nickname
   - Date of employment
   - Place of birth and birthday (not birth date)
   - Present job: has the person worked elsewhere in the organization, and if so, doing what?
   - What does he or she like most about the job?
   - What is a pet peeve or hot button he or she has at work?
   - What is his or her favorite hobby or pastime outside of work?
   - Does he or she have children, pets, or both?
   - What is something unusual about this person that others on the team may not know?
3. Give each person 10 minutes to interview the other in the pair.
4. Give each team member 3 to 5 minutes to introduce his or her partner.

At the end of the introductions, ask the team to comment. Did they learn things they did not know about each other? Did they find out things they had in common, or differences? Did they discover things that will enable them to work together better in the future?

Team Activity 2

Answering Questions

Purpose: To enable everyone on the team to achieve greater knowledge of fellow team members; to enable team members to achieve greater knowledge of the team as a whole. Time frame: 45–60 minutes.

Directions: Before the meeting, make copies of the following set of questions, one copy for each team member.

- Who is a public figure or a famous person that you admire and why?
- What is a lesson you learned when you were young that you have never forgotten?
- What is your greatest fear?
- What is your greatest accomplishment?
- What is one of your happiest moments?

At the meeting

1. Distribute the questions to each team member.
2. Give the team about 5 minutes to read through the questions and come up with answers.
3. Throw a soft ball or Koosh ball into the middle of the team. Whoever catches the ball answers the questions first; then that person throws it to another team member, who answers the questions next; and so on around the room until all have had a chance to answer the questions.
4. At the end of the exercise ask the team whether they learned something about each other that they did not know before. Ask them what they know about the team as a whole that they didn't know before.

Team Activity 3

Alligator Swamp

Purpose: To get the team to think about the benefits of working together and to achieve comfort in being physically close together. Time frame: 15–30 minutes.

Directions:

1. Get one piece of $8^1/_2$ x 11 inch construction paper for each person on the team.
2. Arrange the papers on the floor in a large circle, allowing approximately 12 inches between each piece of paper.

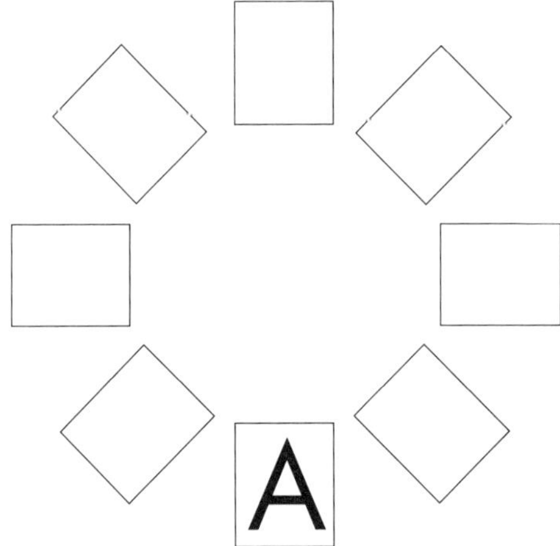

3. Ask each team member to stand with both feet on a piece of paper.
4. Explain that the purpose of the exercise is to have everyone move around the circle, one piece of paper at a time until the person in position A is back into position A.
5. Review these rules:
   a. These pieces of paper represent safe zones in an alligator swamp. If you step one foot off the paper onto the floor, you can be eaten by an alligator.
   b. There can only be two feet on each piece of paper at any one time.
6. At the end of the exercise, ask the group how they were able to get the person from A all the way around the rocks and back to A again. What did they do? Ask them what they learned about team work.

Team Activity 4

My First 10 Years

Purpose: To develop a greater knowledge of individual team members, their backgrounds and experiences. Time frame: 2–3 hours.

Directions: This is an advanced pairs discussion and get-acquainted exercise. It may be uncomfortable for some team members who have had a difficult childhood. If there is a person who is unwilling to discuss his or her first 10 years, ask that person to pick a period in his or her life that was more pleasurable.

1. Divide the group into pairs.
2. Give one person in each pair 10 minutes to discuss their first 10 years of life: where they were born, where they lived, what they did for fun, who their childhood friends were, how they liked to spend time, any memorable events, and so on.
3. Call time at 10 minutes, and ask the other person in the pair to share their first 10 years.
4. Call time at the end of the next 10 minutes.
5. Rotate the people in the pairs so that they are each with someone different. Continue calling time at the end of 10-minute intervals and rotating people until everyone has had 10 minutes with everyone else on the team.

If it is necessary to reduce the time for the total exercise, allow each person less than 10 minutes before calling time. Ask the group as a whole what the benefit of the exercise is. Ask them how it will help them function as a team.

Team Activity 5

Celebrating Differences

Purpose: To bring the differences present on the team to everyone's attention; to get the team to start to see those differences as assets rather than liabilities. Time frame: 30–45 minutes.

Directions:

1. On a piece of flip-chart paper or a white board, draw two columns labeled "differences" and "things in common," as shown below.

Differences	Things in Common

2. Ask the team to brainstorm all the differences they think they have as people.
3. Once that list is complete, ask them to brainstorm all the things they have in common with *everyone* on the team. (Several things they may have in common with everyone on the team are that they all have the same employer, live in the same state, and so on.)
4. Ask them to total the similarities and differences.
5. Ask them which list was easiest to come up with and which was hardest.
6. Ask them how their differences will benefit the team.
7. Ask them how their similarities will benefit the team.
8. Summarize the comments that are made.

Team Activity 6

The Myers-Briggs Type Indicator

Purpose: To help each member of the team see how the others on the team, because of their differences, have helped the team be stronger. Time frame: 60 minutes.

Directions: In order to accomplish this exercise, the team needs a qualified Myers-Briggs facilitator. There are other similar tools that can be obtained from team-building exercise books that allow team members to take a brief test identifying aspects of their personalities. The facilitator leads the group through an understanding of the strengths that the personalities bring to the team, and the areas in which each personality type needs help from others on the team.

Team Activity 7

Influences in My Life

Purpose: To provide team members with more information about themselves and more information about each other. Time frame: 60–90 minutes.

Directions: This exercise should not be attempted as an initial team-building exercise. The team needs a degree of social closeness first; then this exercise will be more successful.

1. Give each team member a large piece of flip-chart paper and several colorful markers.
2. If possible, allow them to work on their drawings at separate tables.
3. Give team members 15 minutes to draw pictures on the flip-chart paper representing the influences in their lives that made them the people they are today.
4. Ask each team member to take turns sharing and describing what he or she has drawn.
5. Encourage team members to ask questions, or to comment on what they are discovering about each other.

At the end of the exercise, summarize. Ask the team to respect the confidentiality of the information that they have heard during this exercise. Ask them if they have a deeper understanding of the people on their team. Ask them how this deeper understanding will help them be successful as a team.

Team Activity 8

What I Admire Most about You, Level I

Purpose: To reinforce the self-esteem of team members; to begin to confront problem behaviors on the team; to establish norms for team behavior. Time frame: 30–60 minutes.

Directions: This brief team-building exercise can be conducted at any time after the team has completed its get-acquainted process. It can be repeated at intervals during the life of the team to provide an opportunity for all team members to share observations that will build and enhance self-esteem and improve the way the team functions.

The entire team gets instruction in providing specific feedback before the exercise begins. Specific feedback is much more useful than general feedback. For instance, in response to "What I admire most about you," a general comment would be "Your friendliness"; a specific comment would be "The way your face lights up with a smile when anyone approaches you." Or, in response to "What I would like you to do more of," a general comment would be "Be timely"; a more specific comment would be, "Come to work before 8:00 A.M."

1. Each team member is given a piece of 8-1/2 x 11 inch paper and asked to put his or her name on the top. The team member then divides the paper into three equal columns, as shown below:

What I admire most about you	What I would like you to do more of	What I would like you to do less of

2. Everyone passes their paper to the person on their right.
3. That person writes specific feedback on the paper in all three columns and passes it on until everyone has the opportunity to write comments on each team member's page.
4. Once the papers are back with the person whose name is on the top, everyone is given several minutes to read the feedback received from coworkers on the team.
5. Each team member is then asked to summarize the feedback received from the team and relate it to the entire group.

The group as a whole is asked whether they received any feedback that is unexpected or a surprise to them. After surprises are discussed, the team is asked whether the information is helpful and how they plan to use it.

Team Activity 9

What I Admire Most about You, Level II

Purpose: To reinforce the self-esteem of team members; to begin to confront problem behaviors on the team; to establish norms for team behavior. Time frame: 3 to 4 hours.

Directions: Have team members gather in a room or outdoor space large enough that pairs of team members will have a private places for discussion. A facilitator will be needed to call time, every 20 or 30 minutes, so that team members can rotate until every member has been paired with every other team member.

1. Distribute a piece of paper with instructions and questions to each team member. **Instructions:** Take turns responding to the statements below. The facilitator will advise you when your time is half used and it is time to switch partners. Answer the following statements:
   - What I admire most about you:
   - What I see as your greatest strengths:
   - How I like to be communicated with (telephone, face-to-face, E-mail):
   - What I would like you to do more of:
   - What I would like you do less of:
2. Ask the team to divide into pairs. If the number of team members is odd, one person can sit out each time, or one group each time can be a threesome. The pairs then separate from each other for private discussion.
3. The pair members take turns responding to the questions on the paper.
4. A time signal is given by the facilitator when the pair should be halfway through the question list.
5. When time for the first round is up, the facilitator notifies the participants and they regroup to form new pairs.
6. The exercise continues until all team members have been in pairs with each member of their team.

At the end, the entire group is brought back together. The team is asked the following questions:

- Did you learn anything new, or uncover any surprises?
- Will the information you received be helpful? How?
- How will you use the information you learned in the exercise?

Chapter 19

Team Education

"The only limit a person ought to have is his [or her] own ability to learn, grow and develop."

—*The Fifth Discipline Fieldbook*

Chapter Preview

There are several reasons for the failure of teams. Some reasons are external to the team, and others are problems that the team creates itself and can correct itself. Although teams cannot always overcome the external obstacles to their effectiveness, they can address one major internal obstacle: lack of training. Without the necessary training, team members will lack team skills. Team work will not occur, and team roles will not be filled effectively. This chapter will introduce teams to the education they need in order to be effective.

In an ideal world, all teams would stop work for four weeks of intensive education and team building. This would enable teams to start down the road toward excellence with a full range of skills and shared experiences as close to them as their backpacks. The reality is that teams need to install training in short segments amid all the other requirements of their jobs. This chapter helps teams identify the education segments, and a likely chronology for incorporating those segments in daily work life. It provides training guides and resources, as well as an overview of adult education principles. It gives teams the basics they need to develop their own education programs, while encouraging teams to obtain external education whenever possible so that all team members can participate in the education process together.

In some organizations, team skills are developed into competencies that are expected of all team members. In other organizations, teams are certified at levels of proficiency based on the amount of education they have obtained and the skills they demonstrate. In a few organizations, there are no resources for team member education, and the team has to educate itself.

Chapter at a Glance

In this chapter, you will find

- A discussion of team education as a five-stage process
- Suggestions for finding coaches
- A do-it-yourself guide to making a lesson plan
- Eight principles of adult education

Team Education

"The biggest mistake we made was not enough training early in the process."

—Ellen Williams, pharmacy team, Mission+St. Joseph's

For most staff members in health care organizations, education has focused on developing technical competencies, the knowledge and skills needed to fulfill the technical requirements of the job. They learn how to mix chemicals to create cleaning solutions, perform treatments, administer medicines, validate insurance, run lab tests, and document, document, document. In addition, health care organizations emphasize safety training, so that staff can respond effectively to fires, disasters, or clinical emergencies. Very few health care organizations teach their staff how to run effective meetings, make decisions, and plan and set goals. Those skill sets are reserved for managers. Being on a self-managed team requires all the knowledge and skills of being a staff member, as well as a whole new set of skills related to team effectiveness.

In spring training for baseball, the players hone the specific skills of pitching, catching, batting, and fielding. They also learn how to cover for each other and coordinate their skills to heighten their effectiveness as a team. Being a member of a team is different from being one member of a department. It requires different skills, attitudes, and knowledge. It is a whole new ball game.

Table 19-1 presents examples of the organization's expectations for team performance and the competencies that team members will develop during their experience on the team. Most organizations will expect self-managed teams to have a basic understanding of what self-managed teams are. They will expect strong performance from self-managed teams, not only in clinical and technical areas, but also in the areas of management that had previously been performed by supervisors and directors. They will expect teams to develop and maintain good relationships with other departments and with their customers. Organizations will not support self-managed teams if the teams isolate themselves from the organization and neglect their responsibilities as members of the organization. Teams will be expected to manage and reduce costs whenever possible, as well as develop excellent safety records. None of these expectations for performance are beyond the capability of any health care self-managed team. However, it is impossible to meet these expectations without a comprehensive education program for team members.

Spring Training: The Basics

When a self-managed team is first formed, the team members have many questions. They want to know what it means to be self-managed, what

Table 19-1. Team Development

Expectations	Team Competencies	Staff Competencies	Performance Measures
Basic understanding of teams	Team effectiveness	■ Self-managed teams ■ Team roles ■ Team systems ■ Effective teams ■ Team development stages ■ Team mission, vision, and values	Staff satisfaction
Effective relationships within the team, with departments and customers	Communication and relationship building	■ Building trust ■ Communication (listening and feedback) ■ Conflict resolution ■ Consensus decision making ■ Meeting effectiveness ■ Report writing	Customer service Staff satisfaction
Strong, responsible team performance	Team management	■ Coaching, orienting, and educating the team	Staff satisfaction
Continuous performance improvement	Team management	■ Conducting performance reviews ■ Role education ■ Discipline ■ JCAHO requirements ■ Quality improvement and work process improvement ■ Data gathering, charts and graphs ■ Planning and setting goals ■ Project management ■ Scheduling ■ Selecting and hiring	Quality improvement Financial performance
Clinical and technical excellence	Clinical and technical competence	■ Computer skills ■ Equipment skills ■ Job competencies	Clinical and other performance outcomes

Table 19-1. (Continued)

Expectations	Team Competencies	Staff Competencies	Performance Measures
Cost management	Integration with the organization	■ Business of health care	Financial performance
Support of the organization	Integration with the organization	■ Financial system and cost management	Compliance with policies
Safe practices	Integration with the organization	■ Mission, vision, and values of the organization ■ Strategic direction ■ Policies: administrative, department, and personnel ■ Safety	Safety record

they control and what management retains responsibility for, how to succeed as a self-managed teams, and how a team functions. These items are standard topics in early team education. Until staff members understand the basics, they cannot begin to function as members of a self-managed team.

Spring Training, Stage I: Team Effectiveness It is helpful to remember that the group of employees that has come together to be a self-managed team, although in a learning stage, is not yet a team. There is a sense of camaraderie, as in "We are all in this together," but the support for each other and thinking as "we" have not developed. Because team members have different expectations of what it will be like to be a team together, another critical part of early team education is providing knowledge of the states of team development. Once team members have information about the states, they can observe what is happening on their team without feelings of betrayal—"I never thought it would be like this!"—or unwarranted optimism: "Oh, this is fun, wonderful, so easy!" They will have the information they need to place their current development state in perspective and to temper their reactions with the knowledge of team development patterns.

Another building block, or basic, for team effectiveness is for the team to create its mission, vision, and values. The team needs to know its purpose (mission), where it hopes to be in the future (vision), and its values (what it stands for and how it will behave as a team). These basic building blocks keep the team centered and focused throughout the life of the team. They need to be in place before the team moves forward to developing more specific skills. Information on the topics in Spring Training, Stage I, are found in various chapters of this book, and table 19-2 summarizes the location of information on these topics.

Table 19-2. Resource Location for Spring Training, Stage I: Team Effectiveness

Training Topic	Resource Location
The ABC's of teams: teams, team roles, team boundaries, and team systems	Teams: chapter 1 Team roles: chapters 4 & 11 Team boundaries: chapter 3 Team systems: chapters 10–16
Team effectiveness: characteristics of effective teams	Chapter 22
Team development states: whoopee, whoa, well, and wow	Chapter 20
Mission, vision, and values	Chapter 12

Spring Training, Stage II: Communication and Relationship Building Effective communication is a characteristic of high-performing teams. Teams depend on internal communication and on the quality of the interaction between team members and among the entire team. Teams also need to communicate to other teams, management, their customers, and the entire organization. It is almost a reflex action for teams to become inwardly focused in their early development states. Since being inwardly focused can cut the team off from needed information, the team needs to take steps to ensure that a "circling of wagons" does not occur and that the team communicates out into the organization from the start. The second stage in spring training is devoted to developing team communication and relationship-building skills. (See table 19-3.)

The Major Leagues

Once the team has left spring training and has a good grasp of the basics, it is ready to play major league ball. The knowledge and skills at the major league level include advanced team management skills, clinical and technical job competencies, and knowledge and skills that help the team integrate with the rest of the organization.

The Major Leagues, Stage III: Team Management Team management skills include human resources and planning skills that generally reside within the hierarchy of supervisors and managers. Self-managed teams need many of these skills because the tasks they are associated with are performed by the team rather than by an outside level of management. Since these team management topics are complex and difficult to learn, the team may decide to train only a few team members initially, so that the skills are present on the team, recognizing that not all team members need to possess these skills at once. (See table 19-4.)

Table 19-3. Resource Location for Spring Training, Stage II: Communication and Relationship Building

Training Topic	Resource Location
Building trust	Chapter 14
Communication: listening and feedback	Chapter 15
Conflict resolution	Chapters 15, 16, 18, & 19
Consensus decision making	Chapter 16
Customer service	Chapter 9; and see the library or education department for resources
Meeting effectiveness	Chapter 8
Report writing	Chapter 15

The Major Leagues, Stage IV: Clinical and Technical Competence Self-managed teams have the responsibility to develop the clinical and technical skills that team members need to perform their jobs. Regardless of other skills, each team member needs to be competent to perform the duties that are outlined in his or her job description. It is assumed that newly hired employees will learn job skills during their orientation periods or will have a development plan to follow after orientation is complete. Regardless, every staff member needs a development plan, revised and updated annually, to continue to grow and develop knowledge and skills. The oft-quoted admonition to teams of "You are only as strong as your weakest link" has proved true. Teams need to invest time and resources in the development of their members so that all are highly capable of performing their jobs. Team members need to be aware of future trends and able to adapt to new ways of doing things. It is hoped that the energy and creativity of a self-managed team will help keep it performing at the forefront of the profession or professions that it represents.

The World Series, Stage V: Integration with the Organization

"When our team got started, we learned so much. It was the first time I had ever seen the hospital's strategic plan and goals."

—*Ann Sweatt, laboratory team, Mission+St. Joseph's*

Table 19-4. Resource Location for the Major Leagues, Stage III: Team Management

Training Topic	Resource Location
Coaching, orienting, and educating the team	Chapter 19; and see education department or resource staff
Conducting performance reviews	See personnel or the personnel resource person in the organization for help in developing a team-based system and for education on the process
Data gathering, charts, and graphs	Chapter 13; and see quality or finance departments
Discipline	Chapter 14; and see personnel for help in developing a team-based system
JCAHO requirements	See quality department or resource person
Planning and setting goals	Chapter 12; and see planning department or resource staff
Project management	Chapter 12; and see planning or computer services department or resource staff
Quality improvement and work process improvement	Chapter 9; and see quality department or resource staff
Rewards and recognition	Chapters 14 & 21
Role education	Chapter 11; and see resources within the organization
Scheduling	Chapter 16; and see resources within the organization
Selecting and hiring	Chapter 14; and see personnel for help in developing a team-based system

The self-managed team will finally feel that it has come into its own when it has achieved integration with the rest of the organization. It will already be performing in a superior manner, both as a team and as a group of individuals who provide specific skills and services to the organization. When the team embarks on integration with the organization, it is ready to develop a deeper understanding of the entire organization. It will know what the strategic plan is, what the goals are, what the organization's mission, vision, and values are. The team can modify its direction to support the direction of the organization. It will strengthen the entire organization to the degree that it is also focused on achieving the organization's goals.

Teams and departments need to develop a deeper understanding of the organization in which they exist. However, it is not often that a team or department makes the time, or has the opportunity, to be educated on what the business of health care is and what the organization is all about. Teams should have copies of organizational policies and procedures in an accessible place. Not every team needs its own set, but all teams need an overview of the contents and the ability to review the policies when specific direction is needed from them. Almost all staff in health care organizations are aware of the safety requirements and their safety responsibilities. Each team should have its own safety officer to help the team stay current on safety policies and rules.

Although all the education topics presented in this chapter are important to team development, they do not need to be implemented in the order that they are outlined. A team may want to begin with an introduction to the business of health care and an orientation to the strategic direction and goals of the organization. What is important is that the team understands the scope of the knowledge and skill that the team must possess in order to function effectively. Educating the team should be seen as a several-year project. It is not something that can happen quickly, and it does not need to.

When the team has achieved World Series status, it is a mature team. Being mature means that the team has learned the basics from spring training and is applying them. It means that the team understands how to communicate and build relationships and is actively using communication techniques. It means there is a plan in place for developing job competencies for all team members and, finally, that the team is ready to take its place as a fully contributing member of the organization. (See table 19-5.)

The Coaching Staff

"It is one of the hardest roles to learn. I wanted to *tell* the team what to do. It is hard to listen, ask questions, and be the support person instead of the supervisor. I can see the value in the role now, and I enjoy being able to help without having to be the boss."

—*Campbell Cauthen, coach, Mission+St. Joseph's*

Table 19-5. Resource Location for the World Series, Stage V: Integration with the Organization

Training Topic	Resource Location
Business of health care	See members of top-level management
Financial system and cost management	See members of the finance, budget, accounting, or management engineering departments
Mission, vision, and values of the organization	See members of department or top-level management
Policies: administrative, department, and personnel	Obtain a policy manual from the originators of the policies
Safety	Safety officer
Strategic direction and goals	Members of department or top-level management

Ideally every team will have a coach who is attuned to the group's interactions and behaviors and can give feedback to the team on its performance. Whether the team has a specific coach or not, the team will need resources to help it grow and learn and an objective outside person to give the team feedback. As described earlier in this chapter, teams need many skills and it is difficult to find a single person who can be a coach in all these skill areas. A team can meet its needs for knowledgeable coaching by talking to its own coach, by seeking resources throughout the organization, and by contacting other organizations or reference services.

Within most large health care organizations, there exist specialists with knowledge of planning, human resources, quality, finance, and so forth. These specialists are ideal resources and coaches for teams that are developing their skills in these disciplines. The specialists will be pleased with the opportunity to share their knowledge and expertise, and the team will learn a great deal from them. In small organizations, the specialists may not have their own designated departments or roles and may not be as visible as they are in large organizations, but by asking around, the team can generally uncover a member of the organization who possesses skills in the area in which the team is seeking development.

The team can also seek coaching outside the organization. One exceptional source for coaching is the vendors who supply equipment and materials to the department. Large vendor organizations frequently offer "value-added" services to their customers. They may have resources within their organizations that can help the team, or they may be able to obtain those services for the team. It doesn't hurt to ask.

The library and the Internet are two additional areas outside the organization where specialized knowledge and coaching may be available. If there is a topic that the team needs to learn about, members can go to the library or look the topic up on the Internet.

Teams can seek help from the professional organizations of which they are members. The team can contact the president of the organization and express the need that it has. The organization may respond by sending literature or by referring the team to a person with the expertise. A final resource for teams that is available in most communities is the Service Corps of Retired Executive Counselors to America's Small Businesses (SCORE). This is a nonprofit volunteer organization of retired and still working executives who provide free services to people in their community who have business needs but do not possess the resources internally to meet those needs.

A Do-It-Yourself Guide

"The team educators were hungry to begin a comprehensive education program. They wanted to provide training in work skills as well as team skills. We have the best education program we have ever had because of the efforts of our team educators."

—June Riddle, director of respiratory care, Mission+St. Joseph's

When a team has few internal and external resources at its disposal, it can still have a comprehensive team education program. It will be more difficult and time consuming for the team to develop all of its education, but not impossible. Remember that lack of team member education is one of the top reasons for team failure. The team will want to develop a plan and schedule for education that will allow time for team members to research topics and develop educational programs. All team members can participate in the education process. If one of the roles on the team is educator, the educator can coordinate the education programs. He or she should not be responsible for the entire education process of developing and conducting each class, however.

The team will want to review the team development chart (table 19-1), or create one of its own, and identify education priorities. Once the priorities are determined, the team should develop a schedule and an assignment roster. Team members can work together in groups of two or three to design the education programs and conduct them. Education materials should be saved by the team record keeper for use with newly hired employees or in case the team decides it needs more education on a topic. A learning resource library can be established for any staff member who would like a refresher.

The Lesson Plan

Once the assignments are made, team members will create a lesson plan for a team miniworkshop. All lesson plans will name a specific topic, set learning objectives, establish time frames, outline content, and specify methods. See table 19-6 for an example of a lesson plan for a miniworkshop on conflict resolution.

Topic The topic is the subject matter for the miniworkshop. It can be any subject in the team development plan, including

- How to set goals
- Conflict resolution
- Conducting performance reviews

Learning Objectives A learning objective relates to the purpose or goal of the education program. The program is being taught so that team members will learn a knowledge or skill set. Frequently, objectives are stated like this: "Participants will be able to . . . at the completion of this program." Learning objectives start with words like the following:

- Describe
- Explain
- Compare
- List
- Display
- Demonstrate
- Define

Time Frames The time frame for each topic should vary, depending on the complexity of the topic and how much the team already knows about the subject. However, every subject can be subdivided, if necessary, so that it will fit into one-hour time frames, if that is the longest block of time the team can allot. The team can develop self-study programs, too. Frequently, more content can be included in a short self-study session because time is not needed for group interaction.

Content The content includes the basic information that will be taught in the education program. If there is a definition, a list, or a body of knowledge, these will all be included in the content section. By including this information in the lesson plan, most members of the team will be able to teach it. The knowledge or information will be explained in the lesson plan, in the content section. If the content is extensive, the person developing the lesson plan can include a reference such as "see pages 24–27 in the book . . . for a full discussion of this topic." When possible, a copy of the reference can be attached to the lesson plan so the person who teaches the class does not have to look it up again.

Table 19-6. Lesson Plan for Team Miniworkshop on Conflict Resolution

Topic and Objectives	Time	Content	Methods
Subject matter and what participants will know and be able to do after the class is completed	Time allotted to cover the topic and accomplish the objectives	Detailed knowledge and skill sets that you need to teach	Application of adult learning: how you plan on imparting the knowledge and skills to staff
Conflict Resolution: Participants will be able to	60 minutes	Conflict resolution	■ Lecture ■ Discussion ■ Skill Practice
1. Define a conflict	5 minutes	Definition of conflict: "A conflict exists when one person believes that another person has done something to harm him or her or is about to do something that will harm him or her."	■ Overhead transparency of definition ■ Review definition ■ Explain what a conflict is and what a conflict isn't
2. Give examples of work conflicts	5 minutes	■ Belief that one team member is doing less than his or her share of the work ■ Belief that a team member has repeated harmful gossip	■ Ask the staff for real work examples ■ Give examples ■ Give feedback
3. Explain why conflicts occur	10 minutes	■ Conflicts occur because of differences that team members have, such as age, gender, race, education, background ■ Conflicts occur because team members see things differently	■ Ask the staff to describe the differences on the team ■ Show the staff a drawing that can be seen in different ways ■ Ask the staff to describe what they see

(Continued on next page)

Table 19-6. (Continued)

Topic and Objectives	Time	Content	Methods
4. Describe the steps to follow in resolving a conflict	5 minutes	■ Review the steps to follow in case of a conflict between two team members: 1. Get control of your emotions 2. Find a convenient time and place to meet together 3. Using "I feel" statements, describe the problem 4. Ask for and listen to the other side 5. Agree on the problem 6. Agree on the resolution	■ Overhead transparency of conflict steps ■ Explain the steps ■ Ask for questions
5. Demonstrate conflict resolution skills	30 minutes	Break the team into groups of three. In those groups, team members will practice resolving typical team conflicts using the conflict resolution steps. The observer will give feedback: things the team members did well and suggestions for improvement.	■ Form teams of three for a skill practice—two will practice, one will give feedback—and rotate if time allows ■ Ask the team members what was easy and what was difficult ■ Ask the team members whether they will be able to use these steps in the future

Table 19-6. (Continued)

Topic and Objectives	Time	Content	Methods
6. Review what they have learned	5 minutes	Review the definition of a conflict, what causes conflict, the differences among the team, the conflict resolution action steps, and their belief that they can use these steps	■ Review the objectives

Method Adults learn in many ways, but the least effective way to teach adults is by lecturing, standing in front of the group and imparting knowledge to the group. Most adults learn best through doing and through sharing stories of past experiences with others in a comfortable learning environment. Adult learners need to engage their minds by solving problems or considering case studies. Asking adults to work together in small groups enables them to express themselves and practice in a comfortable environment. Many adults are too self-conscious to speak up or demonstrate a new skill in front of an entire class. For these reasons, the mini-workshops should all be designed so that participants are actively involved either by themselves or in small groups, solving problems or practicing new skills.

Principles of Adult Education

"We wanted to give up several times. It was discouraging because we couldn't find time to fulfill our roles, work on our goals, and get our work done. We still struggle, but we agree that we never want to go back to having a supervisor."

—Debbie Davidson, Regional Surgical Specialists

Adults are particular about how they want their learning environment and their learning experience. If the team is responsible for developing its own education, it needs to be aware of the principles of adult education. The following characteristics describe adult learners. If each of these is considered when a class is being developed, it will likely meet the needs of the adult learner:

- Adults prefer self-direction. They like to select what they will learn and when they will learn it.
- Adults learn through experience, discussion, and problem solving, rather than through passive listening.
- Adults want to learn knowledge and skills that they can apply in a practical way.
- Adults need to see a reason for what they are learning, a greater meaning or benefit.
- Adult learning needs to be problem-centered.
- Adults will learn for personal growth and gain.
- Adults like to learn in a low-risk environment. They don't like being videotaped or having to perform or do a demonstration for the first time in front of an entire class.
- Adults like to learn in comfortable surroundings. They prefer soft chairs and seating at a table to small, hard-bottomed student desks.

Chapter Wrap-Up

Any organizational unit that is newly created will struggle and falter before it becomes fully effective and competent. Self-managed teams are no different. It is sometimes overwhelming for a group of staff to review all that they need to learn to be effective as a team. Before becoming a team, all that a staff member had to worry about was developing his or her own skills and maybe helping orient a new employee. As a member of a self-managed team, a team member has a much broader set of skills to develop.

Team members need a basic understanding of teams, team roles, boundaries, and systems. Team members also need excellent communication and relationship-building skills because much of a team's work is accomplished through communication and relationships with others. Teams need to learn the management skills that their supervisors possess: how to plan and set goals, perform hiring and performance review functions, and even implement discipline. None of these areas of performance can be achieved without education and skill practice. When a team has accomplished basic skills and team management skills, it cannot neglect the development of its members' own clinical or technical skills. Team members need to maintain competent performance in the areas described in their job description so that they will be dependable and valuable members of the team. A team has achieved the pinnacle of its performance when it is fully integrated with the organization, molding its actions and skills to provide the support that the organization needs to achieve its strategic direction.

A team can accomplish much in the area of education because it has many resources to draw upon. It can look within the team, to its coach, in its department, in the organization, and outside the organization for help with education. Teams can use the library, the Internet, and the expert down the hall to help them gain the skills they need. Regardless of the resources that teams use to continue their growth and development, they need to make sure that they incorporate the principles of adult education in the training they provide for themselves. It would be unfortunate if the education was available but no one participated in it because it was presented in a manner that offended or bored the team members.

In some organizations, teams are certified once they achieve certain levels of knowledge and can demonstrate certain skills. In other organizations, team development is left entirely to the team. Whatever the circumstance, the team can take control of its education to make sure that it is presented at the pace, in the amount, and on the topic that the team needs at the time to function effectively. Team education should be practical.

Chapter 20

Bumps in the Road

Chapter Preview

"I have been to The Land of Happy

What a bore!"

—*Shel Silverstein*

Self-managed teams face common and necessary problems as they develop. Problems are actually opportunities for learning and growth. Teams that face their difficulties openly are strengthened and thrive.

This chapter provides a model to help team members understand the states of team development. The obstacles encountered during each state are discussed, and tips are given on how to overcome them. Self-managed teams are all different, and the chapter explains how teams develop along random and not linear paths. Finally, the chapter explains that each self-managed team will eventually have to change.

Chapter at a Glance

In this chapter, you will find

- A discussion of the problems every team will face
- A description of the four states of team development
- A discussion of the randomness of development
- A discussion of the reasons teams end

Problems Every Team Will Face

"I think the biggest problem for our team was getting used to everyone's individuality."

—Sandi Ducker, inventory control team, Mission+St. Joseph's Health System

Implementing self-managed teams is a journey and, like every journey, is fraught with obstacles and unexpected problems. The bad news is that those who implement teams will have problems. The good news is that those who implement teams overcome these problems.

Self-managed teams are made up of human beings. The problems that teams face are individual human problems and the problems created by human relationships. Every member of the self-managed team will bring "baggage" to the team. Each person will have personality traits and work habits that annoy others on the team. Those who are very organized and detail oriented will drive those who improvise crazy, and vice versa. Sensitive, caring types will not understand the matter-of-fact, no-nonsense types, and vice versa. The rah-rah cheerleaders will unnerve the serious workers, and vice versa. The personalities and behaviors that people bring to their teams are not new to them or their teammates. The difference is that in the team environment, individuality is encouraged and not suppressed.

Self-managed teams require people to work together—to form relationships. Every person on every team will adapt his or her uniqueness to that of other team members. People who have worked alongside one another for years in a bureaucratic environment will discover problems with their coworkers that they knew existed but didn't have to deal with in the past, when there were policies and procedures to follow and a supervisor to enforce the rules. Respect was achieved passively by conformity to the system.

In self-managed teams, respect is active, growing out of shared responsibility and accountability. The trouble is that few people have experience receiving respect from coworkers or according it to them. Team relationships seem unusual at first, with no one "in charge" and everyone in charge. In a new team, without a supervisor to control their behavior, people may be rude, intolerant, inattentive, and unappreciative. Without a supervisor to determine performance, people may accuse each other of being lax and occasionally lash out at fellow team members they don't think are doing their jobs. It takes time for team members to accept responsibility for themselves and to trust others to be responsible as well.

When a self-managed team is formed, its members will face challenges adjusting to each other. It will take time for them to understand and accept the relationships created by the team. This is inevitable. These are problems every team will face—the bumps in the road.

States of Team Development

"Now it is time to describe all the stages of growth that routinely occur when groups deliberately attempt to form themselves into communities; pseudocommunity, chaos, emptiness, and community."

—*M. Scott Peck*

The development of human beings, whether as individuals or as groups, has fascinated psychiatrists and social scientists. Do we know how and why people and communities develop the way they do? No! But we do have some clues. People grow by learning. Learning is based on experience. Some experiences are created by people; some are products of the environment. Learning is motivated by the need to survive and to thrive. Unlearning is harder than learning. Learning is continuous. The problems teams face cause them to learn and grow.

These facts about learning help distinguish the four states of team development: *whoopee, whoa, well,* and *wow.* There is not a scientific study that confirms each of these states or names them. Knowledge of these states is based on what self-managed teams have learned, are learning, and have yet to learn. Note that these are "states" and not "stages": they do not necessarily appear in order and can reappear again and again. The important thing to remember about these states is that they happen. Then they can be recognized, addressed, and transformed. Another key point is that they are all necessary; no state is not better than another. Some may seem more pleasant and more fun, but all four are needed if growth is to occur. Table 20-1 describes these states.

Table 20-1 lists the states of mind that individuals and groups are in at any given moment on any given issue. Life and work are intertwined. This is especially true with self-managed teams because they encourage intimacy among team members. An entire team will never be in the same state at the same time. Most people function well in a couple of these states and poorly in others. This is a strength of teams. People compensate for each other and help the team maintain balance. Balanced learning is ultimately what leads to team growth. Understanding the states of team development helps team members anticipate the turns in the road.

Turn 1: Whoopee, This Is Fun!

A team has just been formed. Expectations are high. People are enthusiastic. The feeling of freedom and the sense of being in charge provide the new self-managed team with the energy needed to get started. During this state, team members will feel camaraderie with their teammates. The social aspects of team relationships will dominate work requirements. Team meetings are fun, and people look forward to playing their new roles.

Table 20-1. States of Team Development

Team State	Individual Issues	Relationship Issues	Necessary Evils
Whoopee, this is fun!	Unbridled enthusiasm; high hopes; we're free; we're in charge.	We're all friends; let's party; we'll work later; this is fun!	Energy boosting; sense of joy; good times to remember
Whoa, I want to go back.	Ominous responsibility; frustration; I can't change; I want to go back.	We can't do this; you're the problem; we want different teammates.	Reality check; stuff happens; everyone is different.
Well, how much farther?	This is hard work; boredom; I guess I could change some; I might make it.	When will we get there? I guess you're OK; maybe we can do this; dialogue requires listening.	Emptying of emotion with focus on tasks and tough changes
Wow, we're there!	I can contribute; my job means something; the changes I made are worth it.	Thanks for helping; we do better working together; look at our achievements; what's next?	Satisfaction; pride; togetherness; sharing of success

It is important for any group of people embarking on a journey to start with high hopes. The positive experience of a new beginning will be stored in the minds of team members. These memories will be crucial when the team faces the tough times to come.

Eventually, the good times will end, and the team will have to get to work. Some team members will want to stay in *whoopee* indefinitely, others will want to "get down to business," and many will gradually get bored and want to move on to something different. Here are some tips to remember when the team is starting out:

- Take time to build positive team experiences and have fun doing team-building exercises.
- Provide recognition for individuals in their new roles.
- Use this period to educate team members on skills such as conflict resolution and discipline to prepare for difficulties.

There is a truth that "all good things must come to an end." The first state of development for a self-managed team will end. Team members must remember this state and return to it periodically to recharge their enthusiasm.

Turn 2: Whoa, I Want to Go Back

Reality sets in. There is work to be done. Problems begin to surface. There is no longer a supervisor to supply all the answers. Common feelings are "They need to change, we can't" and "It's someone else's responsibility." Things don't happen as planned, and people get frustrated.

Every self-managed team comes to a point early in its development when members want to go back to the old system. They now realize how hard it is to be responsible for themselves and for the work of the team, to put aside their personal agendas and consider what others want to do. Many team members will want to have different teammates. Most teams will want to have a supervisor to solve their problems.

This state of team development brings out the worst in everyone. They will attack one another personally, get angry; it will be unpleasant. Is it necessary? Yes, because people are discovering their differences. The first step to resolving these differences is to recognize them. People who like to argue will want to stay in this state. Those who don't like conflict will want to avoid it. Most people will get exhausted from all of the bickering and will want to move on. The following tips will help the team understand this period of turmoil:

- Recognize that everyone is different and these differences are a source of strength for the team.
- It's OK to express opinions, but you must listen to and respect the opinions of others.
- The team coach must facilitate but resist the urge to solve problems.

Self-managed team members need to put their differences "on the table." The key here is putting them on the table and not on each other. Nothing worth having ever comes without a struggle. Team members will always have differences, and this state of team development will be revisited many times.

Turn 3: Well, How Much Farther?

Resolving differences is hard work. It requires listening and patience. During this state people begin to realize that to work together they must accept each other as they are. Individuals will experience a personal feeling of loss when they realize the old system is gone. The team will seem lethargic, and team meetings will be boring and poorly attended.

This state is the most difficult and the most crucial to team development. Everyone has a shadow side to their personalities as individuals, and self-managed teams will cast a collective shadow. These shadows are the weaknesses of the individuals and the team. Coming to grips with weaknesses is scary. Team members will realize during this time (even if they don't admit it) that they personally create most of their own problems. This realization is necessary if they are to understand that they also have the power to fix their own problems.

Somewhere in this state of malaise, team members will begin to listen to one another. Listening leads to caring. Caring leads to appreciation. Through the conversations that occur, team members will recognize that everyone on the team has talents to complement each other's weaknesses. There are a few natural martyrs who will thrive in this state. Those who don't like to express emotion will withdraw. But most people will welcome the opportunity to be understood and will want to understand how to grow. The tips below will help the self-managed team through this critical state:

- Be patient. People need time to think, share, and listen.
- Focus on the strengths of team members and recognize how people's skills complement one another.
- Invite people into dialogue. Don't force it on them.

This is the state of emptiness. Emotions from *whoopee* and *whoa* are drained. The fading of emotion prepares people to come together as a team and to focus on the work at hand. Teams that learn how to support each other during this state will create a nurturing system. This system will help the team during later periods of self-renewal when people are again wondering: Well, how much farther?

Turn 4: Wow, We're There!

Somewhere, sometime, when it's unexpected, the team arrives. Almost magically, people come together to work for a common purpose. Individual differences are put aside, and the self-managed team begins to function as a group of individuals whose strengths complement one another. Team members realize the contributions they make. They appreciate the contributions of their teammates. All the changes that have been made suddenly seem worth the effort. The team clicks, and there is great satisfaction in knowing that customers and patients are benefiting from their teamwork.

During this state of high performance, team members will thank each other for helping. People realize not only that collaboration is possible but that collaboration is natural. Pride and satisfaction will fill the spirits of the team. There will be a strong feeling of togetherness. People will share their successes and positive feedback from customers. Other teams will reinforce the sense of accomplishment experienced by the team. Team members will look at their achievements and start to think about what else they can accomplish.

How long does *wow* last? It varies, but it will start to wane. Unfortunately, some team members will get more credit than others, and egos will become inflated. Some team members will downplay the success as an accident. Many people will begin to tire as performing continuously at a high level drains their energy. Consider the tips below to help the team get the most out of this state:

- Celebrate the team's accomplishments as group.
- The coach needs to let top management know how well the team has performed and gain recognition for the team.
- Reflect on the steps taken to get to this level, and build on these for future team plans.

Success often comes when least expected. People need to take time to understand how much they can accomplish when they come together to work toward a common goal. Human beings naturally want to cooperate for the benefit of others. This is the truth that leads to *Wow, we're there!*

The Randomness of Development

"Anything can happen, child

ANYTHING can be"

—*Shel Silverstein*

Understanding that self-managed teams, like most organic systems, develop in a random manner is hard. The world of objects is Newtonian, and our habit has been to extend the Newtonian order to the rest of life—assuming predictable processes, smooth transitions, proportional reactions. Consequently, some people believe life follows patterns similar to the cycle of seasons: spring, summer, fall, and winter. While life often seems linear and sometimes even cyclical, the truth of the matter is that life is random. The worn-out phrase "There is nothing more constant then change" is the key to realizing that self-managed team development just happens.

A self-managed team may not start with *whoopee.* In fact, many people, especially management, start in *whoa.* This is why we don't have many self-managed teams. Teams that begin in *wow* and never experience *well* usually fall apart when they hit *whoa.* Those who never leave *whoopee* don't accomplish any work and eventually disband. It may sound like the odds are stacked against team development. They are—except for the fact that people naturally want to work together.

Does it matter where a team starts or what state it goes to next? Not really. The important point is that the team and its members need to know how to change and adapt. This is where the coach or facilitator can help. During the start-up process, someone needs to be available to offer the team some perspective. People and teams get can stuck like an old phonograph record that is scratched and keeps repeating the same few notes. Self-managed teams have flaws and will need an occasional nudge to get the rest of the music playing.

Every team member and every self-managed team will start in a different state. They will then move randomly—individually and collectively—to the other states of team development. This is not a problem. It is just the messy way of life. The curves on the road aren't arranged in a tidy oval: this is a grand prix.

The End of the Team

"What do I search for now?"

—*Shel Silverstein*

All self-managed teams will end. Some will end because the members find they can't work together as a team or because the work required did not need a team. Teams that are very successful may work themselves out of a job. Teams most commonly end as members leave to pursue other opportunities. Each time someone leaves or joins the team, the old team ends. A team with different members is not the same team.

Self-managed teams begin where they end. The old systems of hierarchy and bureaucracy were really teams. They were composed of people who had come together to do work. Granted, a few people tried to dominate the system. But in the end, the system changed, and people adapted to the new system. So it is with teams. Every time a team ends or changes members, a new team forms. The road ends at a new starting line.

Chapter Wrap-Up

Self-managed teams challenge people to live a paradox. They are to be individuals and team members—personalities meshed in complex relationships. As the individual team members negotiate their paradoxes, problems will arise. It is inevitable. Recognizing the states of personal and team growth is the starting point for dealing with the tough issues each team will face.

There will be periods of fun, fear, emptiness, and fulfillment in the life of every person and every team. People will not go through these states simultaneously or in any particular order. These states will happen. They are random. They are necessary. When a team can accept the randomness and respond to it, that team and its members will grow. Self-managed teams are at their most successful when they have problems—and take the responsibility for solving the problems themselves.

Suggested Reading

Peck, M. S. *The Road Less Traveled and Beyond.* New York: Simon & Schuster, 1997.

Chapter 21

Team Achievements and Celebrations

Chapter Preview

"Celebrations are definitely in order—people are very appreciative of being recognized and congratulated. The quarterly celebrations are useful in that they not only provide food (the key to every employees heart), but they also update the staff on what is occurring with other teams."

—*Laura Smith, heart services team, Mission+St. Joseph's Health System*

Humans have a basic desire for success and recognition. This chapter compares the feedback systems used in bureaucracies and self-managed environments. The impact of these systems on job performance is reviewed. The negative and positive implications of individual and team reward systems are discussed, including examples of team celebrations. The effects of these events on teams that are top performers and those that are struggling are reviewed, and a framework for developing a system of positive feedback that will result in ongoing individual and team growth is presented.

Chapter at a Glance

In this chapter, you will find

- Evidence that workers most want appreciation
- A resolution of the individual/team recognition dilemma
- Ideas for successful celebrations
- An argument that growth must be systematized

Appreciation and Motivation

"Appreciation of small steps leads to leaps over high hurdles."

Research by the U.S. Chamber of Commerce on "worker desire" revealed significant discrepancies between what employees wanted and what employers thought their employees wanted. Employers thought that the number one item desired by employees was good wages. This was actually fifth on the employee list. *At the top of the list for workers was "appreciation."* Employers, however, ranked appreciation eighth among their employees' desires. (See table 21-1.)

Why are employers so far off in their estimation of the importance of appreciation? The answer lies in the basic myths about motivation under which the hierarchies and bureaucracies of the industrial age operated. Industrial management assumed that workers work for money, taking no more pleasure or pride in the activity than an engine or an adding machine. Along with this putative lack of pride goes a lack of interest—workers don't care what the company does as long as they get their paychecks. That these myths persist today is borne out by the rankings in table 21-1. The only employee desire that employers underestimate more than appreciation is "feeling 'in' on things." Table 21-2 lists the myths, the corresponding truths, and implications for feedback systems that lead to high performance.

The acronym REST (Recognize, Encourage, Share, and Trust) emerges from table 21-2. Workers in the past did not have the opportunity for

Table 21-1. What Employees Want and What Employees *Think* Employees Want

Benefit	Employee Ranking	Employer Ranking
Appreciation	1	8
Feeling "in" on things	2	10
Help with personal problems	3	9
Job security	4	2
Good wages	5	1
Interesting work	6	5
Promotions	7	3
Management loyalty to workers	8	6
Good working conditions	9	4
Tactful disciplining	10	7

Source: This research was conducted by the U.S. Chamber of Commerce in 1986 and reprinted in the *New Age Journal*, April 1994.

Table 21-2. Myths and Truths about Motivation

Myth	Truth	Implication
People are lazy and only work to get a paycheck to meet personal needs.	People want to do their best and be appreciated for their contributions.	**Recognition** of talents, skills, and a "job well done" is the greatest incentive for personal growth.
Management knows what works best.	Workers know the most about their jobs.	**Encouraging** workers to find better ways to do their jobs promotes creativity.
Management is responsible for success; employees don't really care what happens.	Employees want the company to succeed, and they care about meeting customer/ patient needs.	**Sharing** responsibility for organizational success gives customers/ patients outstanding service.
Teams cannot be trusted with management information on operations and the budget.	Teams use information to make decisions that benefit customers and the organization.	**Trusting** teams to use information wisely leads to more information to plan for future success.

recognition, were not encouraged, had little shared with them, and were not trusted. Work was drudgery and having fun was frowned upon.

Self-managed teams need REST. They need to turn the traditional feedback loop on its head. Reprimands for mistakes are replaced with praise for what is done well. Control of work processes gives way to support for brainstorming on new methods. The rigid top-down model is replaced by an vision of partnership between workers, management, customers, and the community. Information is no longer hoarded by a few but is available to everyone to make the system work better. Appreciation is motivation.

Individual and Team Recognition

"The most recognized constellations are those in which all the stars shine bright."

Once management accepts the need to show appreciation, it faces another dilemma. Teams are made up of individuals and can only succeed when people perform well in their specific roles. Individuals who work together as a team need the support of team members to shine. So who deserves more recognition, the individual or the team? The answer is both. The dilemma is the solution: Teams require outstanding individual performance to meet the team's goals, and individuals require the support of the team to excel in their personal contributions.

Track and field is rarely considered a team sport. A track team is made up of athletes who specialize in events suited to their talents. But track meets are often won on the strength of points won in a relay race. The coach of a high school girls' track team knew this and had a unique way of preparing his team for the track season. The first three weeks of track practice were not held on the track, but on the cross-country course. The coach had the girls run Native American style for five miles each day.

Native Americans used to travel long distances through the woods by running together. They would run single file and take turns being the leader. New leaders sprinted from the back to the front of the line, allowing all the runners to take turns jogging while one was sprinting. The runner who was moving to the front was encouraged by those she passed.

The girls learned to work together using this method, building both strength and stamina, and running farther and faster than anyone could run on their own. When the track team finally got to the track, they mainly practiced handoffs for the relay events. The girls on this track team learned to depend on one another and cheered loudly for their teammates during both the individual events and the relays. At the end of each track meet, the girls would take a "victory lap" (even if they didn't win the meet) by running around the track Native American style as a team. The outcome for the season was that every girl earned enough individual points to get her varsity letter and the team did better in the conference standings than anyone thought possible.

A health care team is like a track team. It is made up of different professional disciplines who have specialized knowledge. One of the most common problems in health care is the "turf wars" that occur between professional groups. Some of the biggest breakdowns in patient care happen when one discipline fails to communicate and "hand off" the patient to a member of another discipline. This is not to suggest that doctors, nurses, pharmacists, and others should begin running through the halls of the hospital and taking turns in the lead. But it is amazing what happens when all caregivers begin to share the lead, encourage each other, and openly praise one another when positive patient outcomes are achieved.

Health care is a team sport. The health system works best when those providing care communicate freely with each other and cheer one another on in the race to meet the patient's needs. The success of the health care team depends on individual *and* team recognition, making all the stars in the constellation brighter.

Ideas for Celebrations

"Without celebration, work would seem like a run-on sentence with no pauses or punctuation."

—Brian Moore, planning team, Mission+St. Joseph's Health System

Surely people know intuitively when and how to celebrate! They don't. Knowing how to "party" is a skill, and it must be learned. Celebrating in the workplace has been discouraged in the past, and, as a result, few people understand what it takes to have a good time at work. The following tips serve as a starting point for organizing celebrations. Each team will discover what type of celebration works for its members. Celebrations should be planned to meet the specific needs of individuals, teams, and their environments.

Celebrate for a Purpose

There are many reasons to celebrate. These include reaching a goal, implementing a new system, recognizing individual contributions, welcoming new team members, or just having fun. When the celebration is announced, everyone should know why you are celebrating. The event will have focus, and the participants will know why they are there.

Schedule REST Breaks Regularly

Life and work are very busy. American culture rushes people from one activity to the next. People need regular intervals of REST to acknowledge the progress they have made and prepare for the next flurry of work. Children in school know when the marking period ends and when there will be days off to play. Adults need these endpoints as well. Don't forget to "stop and smell the roses."

Let Teams Plan the Party

How do you know what will make people happy? You ask them. One of the most common mistakes that top management makes is assuming they know what employees want. (We saw in table 21-1 that they didn't know at all.) It is not enough to involve staff in planning celebrations. Staff that are responsible for their own happiness will come up with creative and simple ideas to meet their needs.

Pep Talks Are Good, as Long as They're Short

The quickest way to turn an exciting event into a boring affair is for someone (especially management) to make a long speech. The most effective pep talks are given by team members. Ask team members to think of something or someone to recognize during the celebration, and then let them take turns sharing their appreciation.

Have Team Members Give the Reports

People want to publicly share their accomplishments. Employees want to know what is going on. A report from the person who has "been there, done that" is much more effective than a summary provided by a manager. It is especially effective to let team members give reports to senior management or the board of directors. The team's pride will shine through, and the feeling that the team's accomplishments are important to those at the top will spur the team on to higher goals.

Cheer Loudly!

The roar of the crowd is a great motivator. Actors and actresses live for the moment at the end of the play when the audience gives them a standing ovation. These moments of visible and audible recognition plant themselves in the minds of team members and reinforce the good things the team did to deserve the applause.

Top Management Simply Needs to Attend

The show belongs to those who put it on. Celebrations are for those whose accomplishments are being recognized. Top management is used to being in the limelight, and they must resist the urge to bask in it. Those at the top need to be present to demonstrate their support and appreciation. Just being there is what counts.

Give Teams a Budget to Get Away and Just Have Fun

Everyone likes to have a little "mad money" to spend. It doesn't take much, only $25 per person. These funds can be used to go out to lunch, go bowling, have a picnic, buy team T-shirts, take a rafting trip, or go to a ball game. The point is that it is the team's money and they have it to use whenever they want.

Make Sure the Celebrations Include All Shifts

Health care is a 24-hour operation. Celebrations need to include everyone. Night-shift employees appreciate it when the effort is made to accommodate their schedules. An even better idea is to provide coverage for them on their shifts so they can do something fun.

It's More Fun to Give Than to Receive

One hospital implemented a very popular on-the-spot recognition system. Management was given funds to award movie tickets, cafeteria passes, or gift certificates. One department of teams decided to give each team member $5 cafeteria passes. The only rule was that you had to give the pass to someone from a different team or department who had helped your team.

Those who got the most from this program were those who gave the passes away.

Celebrations can have positive and negative effects. Some teams will be propelled to higher achievements; others may feel intimidated by the success of others. The main thing to remember is to include everyone in the celebration. The worst feeling a person can have is that of exclusion. Make sure everyone is invited. If someone chooses not to attend, that is OK because it's his or her choice. All teams should be encouraged to give a report. Teams that don't have much to report and don't want to report should be allowed to pass once. They should not be forced to give a report. A team that is struggling needs help from its coach and other teams, but any meetings for this purpose should be kept separate from celebrations. Don't humiliate them. Experience has shown that people and teams want to do a good job and get recognition for it. Teams that are given a chance to wait for the next celebration to share their accomplishments generally respond by working hard so that they will have achievements to share.

Designing a Growth System

"It is a rough road that leads to the heights of greatness."

—*Seneca*

Implementing self-managed teams is hard work, as this book has stressed. But because the work is hard, the effort can be richly rewarded by personal and team growth. Like trees, people and teams grow in spurts. Each year the tree grows in a way that depends on the seasons and the changes in weather patterns it faces. The cross section of the tree's trunk reveals growth rings. These rings are not uniformly spaced because not every year is the same. Nevertheless, the tree grows, and as it grows its canopy of branches gets bigger. The branches are the visible evidence of growth. What is hidden is the vast expansion of the tree's root system. The roots provide nourishment and stability. The function of the roots is similar to the function of celebrations. Celebrations offer people a chance to renew their energy and reinforce the positive aspects of the relationships they have built. People and teams need to have a framework within which to pause and reflect on what they have learned and how they have grown.

Teams must plan systematically for growth. Table 21-3 lists some strategic considerations for such planning. Answering these questions will help teams develop a root system for individual, team, and organizational learning. Every person and every team wants to learn how to be better. Pausing to celebrate and REST can fuel new growth that draws on both the successes of the past and the lessons learned from mistakes. Celebrating is an important aspect of a system that encourages growth and satisfies the yearning for learning.

Table 21-3. REST: Something Every Team Needs to Do

Growth Ingredient	Strategic Considerations
Recognize	• How often do team celebrations need to be regularly scheduled? • What can be done to recognize individual contributions, either on the spot or at team meetings? • Ask teams and team members what kinds of "stuff" they would like to receive to recognize outstanding performance. • How much can be budgeted for celebrations?
Encourage	• How can teams be given positive feedback from management, other teams, and customers/patients? • Can a system be put in place to recognize good tries when things don't work? • What can be done to foster creativity and thinking outside the box? • How can team members and management "give each other a pat on the back"?
Share	• What kind of reports can teams give during celebrations to let others know what they have accomplished? • How can team accomplishments be shared with top management in person by the team? • What can top management do to communicate regularly with the teams on core values and organizational mission/vision? • How can team members and teams convey to top management their personal and team goals?
Trust	• What information is available to share with the teams on organizational performance? • How can information be shared in graphic form and displayed for teams? • What information do the teams need from top management to help them meet their goals and customer needs? • What information does top management need from the teams let them know how the teams are performing?

Chapter Wrap-Up

Appreciation is what employees want most. Self-managed teams defy the myths of hierarchical/bureaucratic organizations. People are motivated, not by money, but by recognition, encouragement, sharing, and trust. Getting people to work together starts with helping them recognize they are part of a team. Teams coalesce when team members support each other and celebrate their successes together. Growth is based on learning, and learning is based upon reflection. Celebrations provide a positive framework for reflection, helping teams learn by recognizing their achievements and contributions.

Chapter 22

Maintaining Team Excellence

Chapter Preview

"The most important measure of how good a game I'd played was how much better I'd made my teammates play."

—Bill Russell, Boston Celtics

When teams first get started, there is energy, enthusiasm, and the excitement of a challenge: "Going where few men have gone before." The team is motivated, management is interested and involved, and the organization is waiting to see what will happen. This level of energy and interest continues as the team learns new skills, struggles with new roles, and works to accomplish team goals. The first energy sapper comes when team members find that they do not have time for all they had planned to do and for all they would like to do. They must face their coworkers with the shame and embarrassment of not having done their part. This saps their interest and commitment. They become discouraged, and they seek someone to blame. The first place they look is to the monster that they created—self-management.

When team members find that self-management is hard work, often unrewarding, and a daily pressure, they consider abandoning it fast. They want to go back to the halcyon days when they had direct supervisors—not that life was any better with direct supervision, but expectations weren't so high, and they had someone to blame for everything that was going wrong, someone who was not themselves. It is a little like dating. When two people meet and are attracted to each other, their whole relationship develops a special glow, as they float along on the cloud of new love. However, six months to a year later, both parties are aware of each other's foibles, and neither is able to look at the relationship with quite the glow that they did at the beginning.

This chapter will help the team that wants to stay at the top with ideas for maintaining team energy and enthusiasm. It will help the team that is falling into the slough of despair identify the possible causes. This chapter includes characteristics of effective teams, common causes of team demotivation, and actions that teams can take to maintain their enthusiasm or regain their lost commitment.

Chapter at a Glance

In this chapter, you will find

- A detailed discussion of six characteristics of excellent teams
- A description of the most common causes of team failure and possible solutions
- Suggested resources for failing teams
- Hints on maintaining team excellence, once achieved

Characteristics of Excellent Teams

"When a team outgrows individual performance and learns team confidence, excellence becomes a reality."

—Joe Paterno, football coach, Penn State University

Since the early 1950s, authors and researchers have been investigating the characteristics of highly effective teams. The theory is that once this information is known, any work group can look at the characteristics, do a comparison, and adjust its behavior and performance to achieve excellence. It is assumed that this model for excellence will apply equally to all teams. Table 22-1 includes criteria from different authors on team excellence.[1] The criteria marked by asterisks are mentioned by at least three authors and will be discussed in detail below.

Shared Leadership

Shared leadership is the concept of sharing authority for decision making and sharing power on the team. Self-managed teams that hand over the power to one member or a small group of team members have given up the responsibility for thinking and analyzing. They have given up ownership of the outcome. They are in fact saying, "Your brain is more intelligent than all of our brains put together." Shared leadership is a fundamental concept of self-managed teams. It is one of the reasons that teams are so effective. It is the concept that by combining all of the team members' intelligences together, the team has a greater capacity for thinking and reasoning than any single person or any small, select group of people.

One tool that self-managed teams use to reinforce shared leadership is team roles. Once team members know that leadership is supposed to be shared, and they know that they will only hold the position or role that they are in for six months to a year, they operate more cooperatively and less like authority figures. They can perceive the disadvantages of acting like a boss or like someone with all the answers when another team member will soon hold their position.

Clear, Challenging Goals or Direction

Teams need to have a clear sense of direction. Clear goals keep the team from working in areas that are not important to the organization and not important to the team. Clear goals help the team become focused and efficient. When team members work on goals together, it draws them together and helps them function like a team. There is nothing like working alongside someone to accomplish something for building a sense of teamwork. Challenging goals help team members rise above petty differences to achieve a true sense of accomplishment.

Table 22-1. Criteria for Team Excellence

Team Characteristics	Wageman	Huszczo	Montebello and Buzzotta	Katzenbach and Smith	Becker-Reems and Garrett
*Shared leadership			√	√	√
*Clear challenging goals or direction	√	√	√		√
*Shared goals	√		√	√	√
Talented members		√			√
*Clear roles		√	√		√
*Systems and structure that support teams		√	√		√
*Effective communication		√	√	√	√
Feedback and support		√			√
External relationships		√			√
Respect for differences	√				√
Authority to make change	√				√
Rewards for team achievements	√	√			
Basic resources	√				
Team norms that promote strategic thinking	√				
Cooperative climate			√		
Ability to resolve issues			√		
Individual and mutual accountability				√	
Collective work product				√	
Commitment to learning					√
Focus on the customer					√
Measures performance directly				√	

*Mentioned by three or more authors.

Shared Goals

This criterion refers to the nature of team goals. They should not be goals that individual members of the team are expected to accomplish and that, put all together, become team goals. They are goals that require the input, involvement, and work product of the entire team. Shared goals give the entire team something to work toward and something to feel a sense of accomplishment about. When a whole group works and struggles to achieve a goal, they become cemented as a team. They learn more about one another and develop an appreciation for how the team is strengthened by the variety of skills, knowledge, and experiences present on the team.

Clear Roles

A team needs clear roles to provide structure to the team's functioning as well as to provide a clear delineation of responsibility. Team roles help the team distribute leadership responsibility. Roles let everyone on the team know what the team expects from them as a contributing member and what is expected of the rest of the team. The roles help the team get its work done; they help the team accomplish self-management.

Systems and Structure That Support Teams

When a team is formed, it is usually formed in an organization that has functioned in an hierarchical management structure. The policies and procedures and work systems are designed to be administered by a supervisor or director, or someone in a management-level position. Self-managed teams do not operate as hierarchies, and, therefore, they need systems and structures, policies, and procedures that support a team approach to management and support the concept of shared leadership.

Within a hierarchy, it is the manager who conducts the performance review, makes the hiring decision, and decides how the work will be done and who will get which assignments. The manager decides whether a change can be made, and when and how. The manager attends management meetings and receives management communication. When a self-managed team is formed, the human resources department needs to learn to work with a team structure. The team will hire, conduct performance reviews, make changes, and communicate to the rest of the organization; and the team will need to receive management-level communications.

Effective Communication

The area of effective communication is one of the most significant in achieving team excellence. Teams need to have open and honest discussions. They need opportunities to express their agreements and disagreements, to bring conflicts to the surface, and to explore how various members have reached the conclusions and beliefs they hold. The exchange of ideas is paramount to the success of a team. It is the opening of all the knowledge that the team possesses. Without a free flow of ideas and constructive conflict, teams would not be able to achieve much more than single individuals, or departments in which management makes all the decisions.

The six criteria for team excellence above provide the primary areas in which teams need to perform well in order to be truly successful. The other characteristics listed in table 22-1 are important, but there is no consensus among authors who have studied and worked with teams on how important these characteristics are. Teams should not exist just to be teams. They need a purpose, whether it is managing a function or serving a particular customer. Once the purpose of the team is clear, then the roles, structure, and systems tend to fall into place. It is the necessary interconnectedness of team members that makes teams different from work groups.

Causes of Team Failure

"When results don't turn out as expected, you and the other team members will need to master the art of forgiveness. Looking for someone to blame may mean abandoning the team's learning."

—*The Fifth Discipline Fieldbook*

Unfortunately, there are self-managed teams who, for some reason, never achieve true teamwork and are not successful in accomplishing their mission or goals. When a team faces failure, it can be for many reasons. Some of the reasons are problems within the team, such as problems of motivation, leadership and power struggles, communication and unresolved conflicts, self-confidence, and the education and skills of the team members.

Other reasons why teams fail are problems from outside the team. External problems arise because the organization does not know how to support the team or because the organization chooses not to support the team. In other cases, the team may lack support and feedback from management, the authority to make changes, or systems in the organization to support those changes. Teams struggle to perform well.

Internal Causes

The team is chugging along and all of a sudden it starts to cough and falter. The first place to look is internally. Team members may find that their own commitment, participation, and motivation are not at the level they need to be. They may find that their behaviors are contributing to the problems. Teams need to look internally at commitment, participation, and motivation distractions arising from external forces. Once internal causes are assessed, then teams can begin to remedy problem situations that lead to team failure.

Problems of Motivation It is a rare team that doesn't start out with a high level of motivation. However, if the team believes it has been forced to become self-managed and really doesn't want to do it, it will likely start out with a motivation problem. It is easy to recognize a team with a motivation problem. Team members never have time to attend meetings or work on team goals or projects. The team suffers from internal criticism, gossip, and backbiting. The team does not have celebrations and rarely stops to recognize its achievements. Team members are not providing input into decisions and don't care when decisions are made without their input. Individual team members fail to fulfill their roles, and work performance is mediocre. Anyone who is a member of a team exhibiting these signs of motivation problems will likely lose his or her own motivation in short order.

If a team starts out with a high degree of motivation, that is not a guarantee that the team will maintain the motivation over time. In fact, it is a characteristic of teams to pass through different states in which enthusiasm waxes and wanes throughout the life of the team. (See chapter 20.) A period when motivation is lacking is generally temporary and once recognized can usually be overcome. If the team begins a period of demotivation, it can be caused by a realization that the team had expectations that were too high. The team may have established a very aggressive schedule for accomplishing goals and implementing roles. When it sees that it is not progressing as it planned, the team can become discouraged and demotivated.

A related problem arises if the team is dealing with a number of external factors at the same time that it is learning to function as a self-managed team. For instance, within the Mission+St. Joseph's Health System in Asheville, North Carolina, newly formed pharmacy and respiratory therapy self-managed teams were learning how to be teams; becoming merged with a sister hospital department; consolidating policies, protocols, and procedures; and preparing for a Joint Commission accreditation visit all at the same time. It is a wonder that the teams were able to maintain their sanity, much less their motivation. However, teams do rise to a challenge, and that is one of the cures for a low level of motivation. Raise the bar. Ask the team to do even more. Give the team an exciting challenge, and they can usually achieve it and overcome motivation problems at the same time. A struggling team does not necessarily improve when the pressure is off.

One final contributor to the lack of team motivation is the team leader. If the team leader fails to be a cheerleader for the team and instead is adrift in his or her own world, the team senses a lack of commitment and sees a lack of involvement. When the team leader is neither committed nor involved and can't gather the energy to cheer the team on, this lack of enthusiasm and interest oozes out to the rest of the team and slowly erodes the entire team's enthusiasm.

What steps can a team take if it is facing motivation problems? First, the team should complete a fish-bone diagram, as displayed in figure 22-1. If the team completes a fish-bone diagram, they will uncover the contributing causes to their lack of motivation. They can address the most likely contributors, and motivation is likely to improve.

Figure 22-1. Fish-Bone Diagram for Motivation Problems

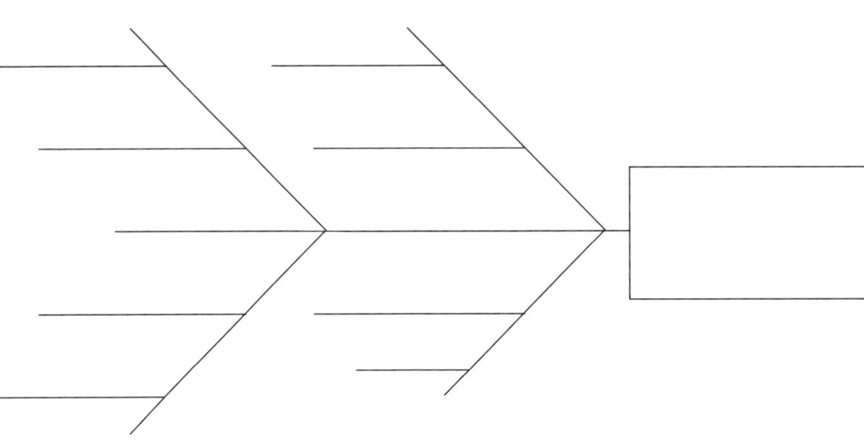

Problems with Goals and Direction Teams may fail because they don't have clear challenging goals or because they are not working on accomplishing their goals. Teams need to look inward when they are facing problems with goals. They can seek direction from outside the team, but if it is not provided, the team can easily identify goal topics—for instance, they can find opportunities to improve or change to better meet the needs of the customer—and those can become goals. Once the team has goals, the next step is to ensure that they are *team* goals and that they are challenging. A team goal is a goal that the entire team can work on, not a goal that just one or two people will strive to accomplish. A challenging goal is generally something new, or something difficult, that will stretch the team to perform at a higher level.

If the team has clear, challenging goals, then the next barrier is finding the time to work on the goals. Team members may have to adjust schedules, make a point to commit time to working on goals, postpone other activities to find time for goals, and so forth. Once time is found, the team can usually accomplish its goals. Another barrier to accomplishing a goal is that some team members may not have the knowledge or skill to complete their part of the goal project and may not want to admit that to the team. Either a fishbone diagram or a force-field analysis will lead the team to a correction when it is facing failure because it cannot accomplish its goals. A sample force-field analysis is displayed in figure 22-2.

Problems with Communication Teams may fail because they haven't found ways to communicate openly and with honesty. A team that is constantly beset with internal conflicts, anger, jealousies, power plays, and distrust will not be able to achieve high levels of performance. On the other hand, a team that moves smoothly from day to day with no conflicts or disagreements is not fully utilizing the diversity and creativity of its members. However, a team that has regular respectful but heated discussions and constructive disagreements has an environment that is conducive to a high level of team effectiveness.

Figure 22-2. Force-Field Analysis for Problems with Goals

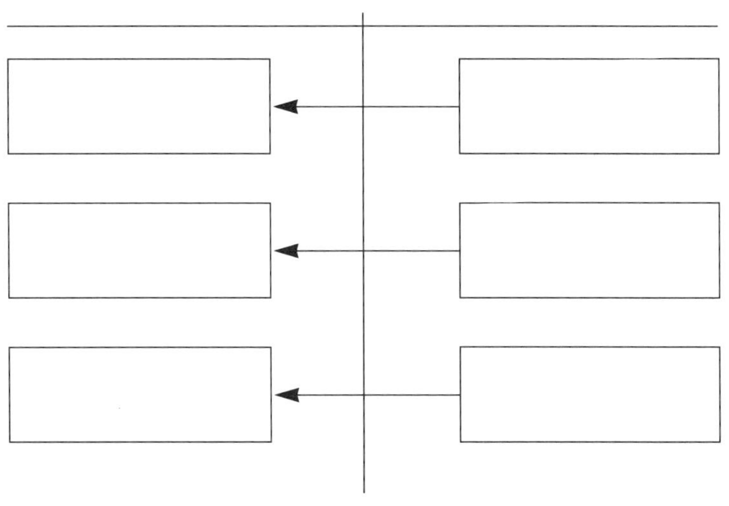

Problems with openness and conflicts can derail a team, but less obvious is the need for the team to communicate with people outside the team. Sometimes when teams form, the team members get so close and so tight together that they become isolated from others in the organization. This isolation can create barriers and cut the team off from the communication they need to integrate with the rest of the organization. When a team is isolated, it has difficulty knowing the appropriate direction to take, and it has difficulty maintaining positive relationships with customers and suppliers. These difficulties can become insurmountable barriers if they are not addressed in a timely manner.

How does a team overcome communication problems? First, it has to analyze what the problems are and what is causing them. Then, the team may need more education, new ground rules for behavior, or disciplinary action with one or more team members. Every problem that a team faces can be addressed and resolved, but first the team has to admit that it is having a problem.

Problems with Self-Confidence If a team has problems with self-confidence, it might be unwilling to admit that it is facing performance problems. Team members may not have high expectations for performance or teamwork. Team members may believe that borderline performance is the best they can achieve. Teams members may be so afraid of failing that they cannot discuss or address the performance issues that are staring them in the face. When a team has self-confidence problems, risk-taking behaviors are missing. The team does not try new things, change is not a frequent occurrence, and the team may isolate itself from interactions with customers and other departments. The team may not seek feedback from management on its progress.

To address problems of self-confidence, the team can make a point of identifying achievements on a regular basis. It can develop an inventory of team skills and team accomplishments. It can start asking for feedback from the organization in little bits from friends within the organization. Eventually confidence will build. A team without self-confidence may not fail, but it is unlikely that it will ever achieve true excellence.

External Causes of Team Failure

A team that is beset by problems from outside the team tends to draw together to try and overcome those problems. However, external problems, even though they are not as divisive as internal problems, are more destructive to the team's performance and its continued existence. The problems that a team faces from the organization can be grouped together in the category of level of support from the organization. Unless the team can depend on consistent support from the organization, it may eventually deteriorate to the point that it is not worth the time and effort that staff members are committing to it.

Problems with Support and Feedback from Management Although self-managed teams can survive for a long period without the support and feedback of management, eventually the lack of support and feedback can diminish the team's effectiveness and cause the team to lose heart. When a group decides to become a self-managed team, the commitment they make is substantial. For a minimum of six months, they are learning new ways of doing things, developing new skills, and taking on faith that the effort will produce a result that will be rewarding and better than the work environment that existed before.

In many organizations, a regular quarterly management feedback session is built into the team's systems. This session allows the team the opportunity of sharing its progress, goals, and achievements with management. Management uses this occasion to commend the team on its progress, and to relate to the team information and feedback that will help the team adjust its direction. Feedback from management not only gives the team much deserved praise, it also helps the team learn the new or changing priorities of the organization. Management feedback lets the team know what the leadership expects and how well it is progressing in meeting these needs.

When the team starts to feel abandoned or like no one in the organization really cares what it is doing or how it is doing it, team members lose their motivation, commitment, and willingness to step up to the challenges that their work environment presents. In short, they lose the reason for their existence as a team. If support and feedback are only given occasionally, the team can adapt. However, if they are nonexistent, the team will eventually dissolve.

Problems with the Authority to Make Changes At the outset, most self-managed teams are given the authority to manage the daily operations of their work areas. They then have the authority to make changes in how daily work is accomplished, the order of the work, and who is assigned to do what.

Most teams are given many other authorities, as described in chapter 3. Imagine this scenario:

> A self-managed team has just started and has two vacancies. It is a small team, and management is anxious to have the vacancies filled. The team receives education from the personnel department on how to select and hire new staff members and begins the lengthy process of interviewing candidates. Eventually, the team makes its selection. And then the team is told that the person they selected will not be hired because management prefers that someone else be hired.

The team suffers considerable disappointment, and its faith in management is shattered. Nonetheless, the team continues gamely on and with little interference, or support, from management is able to pull back together and make progress managing daily work and accomplishing goals. The team completes the development of its performance review system, shares the system with management, and is then told that, at least this year, supervisors will continue to do the team's performance appraisals.

To management, these midstream changes may not seem so important, and perhaps they ought to not devastate the entire team. However, when management either never gives authority to the team or gives it and then takes it away, the very soul of the team is destroyed. Most teams will be unable to continue their work with any commitment or dedication. Eventually, the team will disintegrate, and management may then say, "We knew this group wasn't ready to be self-managed" or "We knew self-management would never work."

Problems with Systems That Support Teams Self-managed teams will eventually fail if they do not have access to team-based systems. Self-managed teams need to be able to meet. If schedule and budget constraints keep the team from getting together, the team will be unable to use its most important communication, goal-setting, and problem-solving tool—the team meeting. Teams also need to be able to make consensus decisions, plans for the future, scheduling decisions, and hiring decisions. They need to be able to define their communication system and their measurement system, to focus on behaving like a team. If the team cannot have team-based systems, that means they must continue using a hierarchical system in which everything flows through the supervisor. If everything flows through the supervisor, then the team is not self-managed, by definition.

Resources for Failing Teams

"We had turnover problems and once vacancies were filled, we realized we needed to rebuild our team. We called on the human resource development department. They helped us get established originally."

—Debbie Vargo, dietitian team

A team will see warning signs if there are problems. Once the team starts to see a lack of interest through poor attendance at meetings, poor participation at meetings, failure to accomplish role or team assignments, failure to make progress on goals, continuous unresolved conflicts, backbiting, and formation of cliques, the team needs to take action. Certainly, the team should be looking at causes of problems long before it experiences the entire gamut of signals.

There are numerous resources both within and outside the organization that can aid and assist the team. Once the team has identified the probable causes of the problem, it can begin to seek help from internal experts. Most organizations have people from the human resources or human services field who can help, as well as people with knowledge about planning, finance, measurement, scheduling, and so forth. Teams can use external resources. They can contact local colleges and universities, use the library or Internet, and contact their professional organizations, authors, and other teams. There are many resources available if the team will use them.

How can the team address the problem if it is their own management? The best way is to gather facts and data and have an open discussion, not a blaming or accusing session. Perhaps management needs some education in self-managed teams and systems. Perhaps management is not aware of the inconstancy of its behavior. If the team keeps management informed of the problems it is dealing with and if management is involved in a dialogue or problem-solving session, management may be able to see ways of modifying their behavior to support the team. If open communication does not help, the next step is to follow the organization's problem-solving process, do nothing, or give up.

Any team can wallow in mediocrity for a time. Most teams when faced with lackluster performance will become dissatisfied and move in a new direction. The secret is to expect a lot from each other and not to accept mediocrity. The other half of the process for moving forward is to have the humility to admit that the team may not have all the answers, or all the resources, and to seek help from outside the team.

Maintenance of Team Excellence

"Things don't always go smoothly. However, when we think about returning to the previous supervisor-led management structure, we know we made the right decision. We are a very cohesive team!"

—Tina Barnes, One Day Surgery

Teams go through periods of superior cohesiveness and outstanding accomplishment. They reach crests of performance that are remarkable and hitherto unseen within the group that has become a self-managed team. It would be wonderful to sustain that high level of performance indefinitely, but is it possible? Most people who study groups and teams say no. It is very rare to find a group of employees who can work together at a constant level of high achievement and high camaraderie without something happening that diminishes their performance.

There are a few suggestions, however, that teams can use to keep them close to the top, almost all the time. Teams need to celebrate their successes. They need to take the time to stop and look at what they have accomplished, and to give themselves credit. They need to take the time to formally renew their commitment to the team, and to get their hearts reengaged in the mission of the team.

Teams need to request regular feedback and validation from the organization. There is one thing that is almost as satisfying as knowing you have done an excellent job, and that is when others know it, too, and commend you on your achievements. Teams that want to maintain a high level of excellence need to get regular confirmation from the organization.

Finally, to keep the team performing at the top, new challenges need to be introduced, before the team has finished its last set of achievements. In other words, there always needs to be a greater challenge on the horizon than the one the team is currently addressing. Teams gain energy from tackling projects and goals that are slightly more difficult than ones they have tackled before. They gain self-esteem and a fine sense of accomplishment when they do something that many thought was too difficult. They develop new skills, achieve personal growth, and attain a heightened sense of team spirit.

Chapter Wrap-Up

Although there is not a simple formula for success, researchers know that teams can be more effective if they have certain characteristics. The best teams will have shared leadership, clear and challenging direction, shared goals, clear roles, systems and structures that support teams, and effective communications. Self-managed teams that possess these qualities are more apt to perform at the highest levels of excellence.

Even teams that are aware of the criteria for team excellence can fail, however. They fail because they do not address internal problems—with motivation, goals and direction, communication and conflicts, and self-confidence. But as detrimental as these problems can be, once the team has identified them, the team can obtain resources to resolve them. They also fail because they are overcome by external forces that they cannot control or influence. Problems that arise in the external environment may have the more deleterious effect. If the team is unable to gain management's support, if its authority to make and implement change is only given lip service, and if the systems to support the team are not forthcoming, the team may fail in spite of all it tries to achieve.

Teams that have attained a superior level of performance are right to fear that they may not be able to hold on to excellence. Most teams find that their performance fluctuates over time, from very strong to somewhat mediocre and back to strong again. Teams that want to diminish the downward movements in performance can do so by taking time to celebrate their achievements and rekindle team enthusiasm and motivation, by getting regular feedback from management, and by continually seeking new and more difficult challenges. Excellent team performance is difficult to achieve, and even more difficult to maintain. There is no magic elixir.

Reference

1. R. Wageman, "Critical Success Factors for Creating Superb Self-Managing Teams," *Organizational Dynamics* 26, no. 1 (summer 1997): 49–61; G. Huszczo, *Tools for Team Excellence* (Palo Alto, CA: Davies-Black, 1996), p. 16; A. R. Montebello and V. R. Buzzotta, "Work Teams That Work," *Training and Development* 47, no. 33 (March 1993): 59–64; J. R. Katzenbach and D. K. Smith, "The Discipline of Teams," *Harvard Business Review* 71, no. 2 (March–April 1993): 111–20.

Chapter 23

Beyond Teams: Adapting to the Future

Chapter Preview

"Business is much more an enterprise of soul than of cents, much more a matter of empowering people than of making money. Money remains critical: no profit, no business. But the high road to profit clearly follows the path of relationships. A business organization will succeed to the degree that it is in the hands of people skilled in the *unquantifiable* abilities of loyalty and integrity, attending to the needs of others, and working for the good of the whole."

—*Bennett Sims*

Health care is in the midst of a transformation. This chapter examines the possible future environment for health care organizations and assesses the impact of mergers and managed care on self-managed teams. There are identifiable signs that signify when changes are needed in self-managed team structures, and the chapter provides steps for adapting teams to organizational changes. This chapter also describes how multidisciplinary networks of teams are forming in integrated health systems and discusses the impact of technology on the process of collaboration in virtual relationships. The chapter concludes with examination of the role of teams in emerging systems and how teams facilitate individual growth and contributions.

Chapter at a Glance

In this chapter, you will find

- Predictions about the future of health care
- A discussion of mergers and the transition to managed care
- Seven steps to adapt team structure to a changing environment
- A case example of a multidisciplinary network
- A description of the health care potential of electronic technology

The Future of Health Care

"Eventually, all of America's lesser problems will combine into one giant problem. The very survival of the society will feel at stake, as leaders lead and people follow. Public issues will be newly simple, fitting within the contours of crisp yes-no choices. People will leave niches to join interlocking teams, each team dependent on (and trusting of) work done by other teams."

—*William Strauss and Neil Howe*

Think back to the year 1897. Health care delivery was primitive by today's standards. Physician training was limited to the "cure" of common illnesses, and surgical procedures consisted of amputations and removal of bullets. Nursing had not developed as a recognized profession. Pharmacists mixed and prepared medicines based on the folklore of plant remedies. X rays and antibiotics had not been discovered. The hospital was a large building with wards where sick people went to have their suffering minimized while they waited to die.

Much has changed in the past century. Physician training with specialty residencies takes over 10 years. Nurses are responsible for complex technology, and caring has become a science. Medicines are now genetically engineered–based on molecular biology. A cadre of health professions, including laboratory technologists, radiology technicians, respiratory therapists, physical therapists, and genetic specialists, has evolved. The practice of medicine and large hospitals are now formed into complex integrated health systems. In 1897 few resources were available for the sick. Health care spending now accounts for over 15 percent of the national economy, and hospitals are the largest employers in many communities.

Will people in the year 2097 look back at 1997 and view our health care system as archaic, disorganized, and somewhat misguided? Perhaps. The next 10 years will be critical in the development of health care. By the year 2007 the United States will come face-to-face with the crisis that national and local leaders have been evading. Baby boomers will begin reaching the age of retirement and will anticipate the Medicare benefits to which they believe they are entitled. The dilemma of the next decade will be more people in need of health care than there are resources to provide for their care. Something will have to change, and these changes are beginning to occur. Health care is beginning to make a transition from a model based on curing sickness to one of maintaining health.

HMOs have been around since the building of railroads in the West. The underlying premise of the HMO is that it is better to keep workers healthy and on the job than pay for the cure of illness. The HMO concept started with individual companies and is now being transferred to the community setting with the advent of managed care and integrated health systems.

No one can anticipate the technological advances of the next millennium. What is known is that the current health system, with its disjointed redundancies, needs to become connected and efficient. The focus of health care spending needs to shift from heroic investments in life support for the terminally ill to the promotion of healthy lifestyles. The current health system requires social rather than technological change. Social change occurs when the behavior of people and the relationships between them change. Health care workers in the future will need to change their focus to prevention of illness. Multidisciplinary networks of health providers must be established and accessible to meet the needs of the public they serve. The future of health care is depends on linking resources to create a system that benefits the community.

Mergers and Managed Care

"The use of transition teams began at the time of Barnes-Jewish Inc.'s (BJI) formation, continued with BJI/Christian Health Services (BJC) merger, and was initiated again when Missouri Baptist Medical Center and St. Louis Children's Hospital joined BJC. The purpose of transition teams were to:

- coordinate efforts to support management and employees;
- plan for effective communications regarding the transition;
- make assignments for specific tasks related to handle the transition; and
- handle the identified issues proactively.

The teams were also enlisted to think of ways to instill pride and sense of being part of a winning organization."

—William M. Behrendt and Walter F. Klein

A senior vice president of a large community hospital recently was asked how his job was going. His response was "It's crazy, we are going through a merger and trying to take cost out of the system." Does this sound familiar? Most hospitals in many communities are facing the same two tasks:

1. Merge with their former competitor(s)
2. Reduce costs

All the merging and cost reduction is being done to "prepare for managed care." The health care market has changed. No longer is there an unlimited supply of resources from the government or insurance companies to pay for every night in a hospital, every test that is ordered, or every medication that is prescribed. The focus of managed care is managing costs. Those health care providers who cannot compete based on low cost will no longer be paid.

There is only one resource that enables hospitals and health systems to provide care and to manage cost. People. It is the frontline health care worker on whom the success or failure of the health system depends. The boards of directors and CEOs of hospitals work through the politics of mergers and then turn the task of merging over to the staff. New organizational charts for all the vice presidents are drawn, then the staff is asked to implement combined operations. A consultant is hired, a reengineering plan is announced, and then the staff is "challenged" to streamline the system. Every merger and cost reduction strategy conjured up by those at the top looks good on paper. But the responsibility for delivering patient care rests in the hands of those who come into contact with patients on a daily basis.

Health care workers generally respond to merger announcements and cost reduction plans with skepticism and fear. They are skeptical about the merger's success and fearful that it will be their jobs that are eliminated. What is at stake are the identities of the institutions being merged and the role that each person has previously played. In order for a new system to emerge, the old system must die. The greatest obstacle to establishing something new is that people want to keep doing what worked for them in the past. Mergers and cost management require a new culture, and people are threatened by the prospect of adapting to an unknown future culture. The transition to a new culture depends on two things:

1. The values people had in their old culture
2. Relationships based on shared values in the new culture

Self-managed teams facilitate cultural transitions. People who work in teams learn how to bring together diverse backgrounds and build relationships with others to accomplish a common purpose. A key to the success of mergers and managed care is the blending of cultures to increase efficiency and effectiveness.

Changes in Team Structure

"The single most important issue confronting leadership of collaborative organizations is how to pose problems and opportunities in forms that will elicit and inspire a collaborative response."

—*Michael Schrage*

Self-managed teams are in place. They are working, and customers are happy. Then it happens. It can come in several forms: the announcement of an organizationwide reengineering project, systemwide downsizing, reorganization of the top management structure, takeover by a competitor, or merger with another institution. Any of these external events will affect the structure of teams. The environment for teams will change. Attitudes of new leadership toward self-managed teams may be supportive, negative, or in most cases mystified. Teams will need to adapt.

The following steps are offered to help self-managed teams adapt to the challenge of working in a restructured environment:

1. *Gather data about the new environment.* Team members need to understand the driving forces that caused the organizational change and learn what the new organization's mission, vision, and values are going to be.
2. *Assess the perspective of the senior management on self-managed teams.* Open and honest dialogue with the new organizational leaders on their management philosophies is essential to enable the team to gauge what is expected of it and to educate top management about the team process.
3. *Review the current team mission, vision, values, and structure.* Before teams consider changes they must evaluate where they are and what they have been trying to accomplish.
4. *Talk to the team's customers.* This is a critical step. Customers will be affected by major organizational changes. In fact, customers may have been a driving force behind the change. Teams need to identify customers' future needs under the new structure.
5. *Develop strategies and alternatives for team structures and processes in the new environment.* Once the team knows the purpose of the new organization, the expectations of senior management, and future customer needs, the team members can plan for their future.
6. *Present the recommendations for team adaptations to contribute to the success of the new organization.* It is very important for the team to take the initiative and present its plan in a positive manner. People who step forward with action plans and a can-do attitude during periods of organizational turmoil are perceived as a help rather than a hindrance.
7. *Follow up at regular intervals and report on team progress.* Letting senior management and customers know that the team is adapting and achieving its goals to meet new expectations is essential to building confidence in the team process.

Rapid and disruptive organizational change is a sign of the times. Health care is going through a major upheaval. Self-managed teams that keep in touch with their environment and anticipate the needs of those they serve will be heroes. The worst thing people can do during a tumultuous period is complain about their predicament. The best thing people can do is ask, "How can I help?" Teams that provide solutions will save the baby when they drain the bathwater.

Multidisciplinary Networks

"The issue isn't teams; it's what kind of relationships organizations need to create and maintain if they want to deliver unique value to their customers and clients."

—*Michael Schrage*

Who is in charge? We all are. This rhetorical question and response summarizes the future of people who function as team members of virtual networks. There has always been an illusion of control in health care. Many people have thought the doctor was in charge, some have considered the hospital, some thought it was the insurance companies, and now a lot think it is up to government. Health care is everyone's responsibility, from the patient to the care provider to the payer.

Disease-based management is a new concept emerging in health care. Care for the patient is based on a continuum over the patient's entire life, rather than treatment of acute periods of illness. Many commercial health care providers and pharmaceutical manufacturers are developing disease-state management programs. These programs offer educational information for patients aimed at reducing hospital stays and increasing medication compliance. The commercially available programs are different from comprehensive community-based disease management systems. The commercial programs are a starting point, but they cannot build the complex connections required in a community to help individual patients with medical conditions lead normal lives.

Consider the care of the patient with diabetes. Diabetes is an extremely complex disease that affects 4 percent of the population and consumes over 16 percent of all the health care resources. In Asheville, North Carolina, a communitywide effort is underway to manage diabetes in a coordinated system called the Asheville Project. Patients, employers, physicians, pharmacists, nurses, dietitians, social workers, laboratory technologists, pharmacies, hospitals, diabetes education centers, and physician offices are all working together to help patients with diabetes. This effort grew out of a collaborative initiative by state pharmacy organizations and colleges of pharmacy. The original idea was to train community pharmacists to manage diabetic patients and then work with an employer to prove the cost-effectiveness of pharmacy-based education for the employer's patients with diabetes. This was not a novel idea and had been tried before in other states with very limited success. What made the effort in Asheville different? Self-organization and teamwork. The diabetes care system that emerged involved and connected all the parties listed above.

No one was in charge of the Asheville Project for diabetes care, but everyone contributed to its success. The employer took a risk and recognized the potential value of coordinated care for its employees. To encourage patients to participate, the employer offered to cover 100 percent of all employee expenses for diabetes medications, supplies, and education. The physicians agreed to help train the pharmacists and openly share medical information about the patients. Pharmacists gave up two weekends for intensive training and to change their pharmacy practices to provide counseling for the patients on a monthly basis. Educators from the Diabetes Center coordinated the training program for the pharmacists and established customized education plans for the patients. The laboratory staff came to special meetings with employees to draw blood work and run the tests free of charge. The patients agreed to become active participants in their care and to complete quality-of-life surveys to measure the impact of the project. Each person involved gave something. The end result is a self-organized communitywide network of people committed to improving the lives of patients with diabetes.

The future of self-managed teams in health care goes beyond the walls of a department, a practice, a hospital, or an integrated health system. Self-organized webs of caregivers emerge when people recognize the benefit of collaborative relationships for their communities. Health in the future will be supported by multidisciplinary networks that connect the system with dotted lines.

Changes in Technology

"Personal computers will become interpersonal computers. . . . The computer screen is now a shared space. . . . Conference rooms will evolve a technical infrastructure designed to support collaborative interaction—the active *sharing* of ideas, images, and thoughts rather than just their display. The room will be designed to augment the way teams interact with ideas—not just with individuals."

—Michael Schrage

The impact of digital communications and computer networks on our lives is almost incomprehensible. Some curse the very existence of beepers, cellular phones, voice mail, E-mail, and the Internet. Electronic communications at the speed of light have shrunk the world to a point where everyone on the planet can be connected instantly to anyone on the planet. More amazing is the fact that we have had these new tools for communication for less than 30 years. Try to imagine what life will be like in the year 2027.

Collaboration is a relatively new concept. Peter Drucker is recognized as the originator of the concept of modern management. However, "collaboration" does not appear in the index of any of Drucker's books. Collaboration will eventually replace the concept of management. Management is based on the illusion of control and order in systems based on Newtonian principles. Quantum physics and the science of self-organizing relationships demonstrate that life cannot be "managed." Systems emerge when people collaborate with each other. Collaboration is the process of creating and maintaining relationships for the benefit of all those involved and affected.

Merging the technology of the information age with the principles of collaboration is a key to the future. The range of connections that technology and collaboration make possible is limitless. This can be as simple as a writer who benefits from the word processor on a personal computer that simultaneously plays a pleasant-sounding compact disc to enhance the relationship of his creative senses. A more complex example is that of the entire world being connected by the electronic media to mourn the loss and celebrate the life of Diana, Princess of Wales. Technology can be used as a powerful tool to support collaboration that serves individuals, organizations, communities, and the world.

The Asheville Project took full advantage of technology to support the collaborative effort required to assemble and implement a complex network of diabetes care. Conference calls were used to make initial plans and introduce people from many locations to each other. Computer flowcharting software was used to develop shared models for care paths. Continuous E-mails to those involved created an electronic dialogue among all the participants. Drafts of training programs and forms to be used were faxed, revised, and refaxed. Beepers vibrated, and calls were returned instantly at critical points. Cellular phones allowed people to stay in touch from distant locations. The study data were maintained in computer databases, graphically displayed, and electronically converted into images to share with people across the state. The patients used "downloadable" glucometers so that the pharmacists could print out a monthly record of blood sugar levels. Many of these tools were taken for granted. If these tools had not been available, the process of collaboration would not have been possible.

Health care has had many medical technology breakthroughs. The most significant of these are yet to come. The next wave will not be new drugs, lasers, or bioengineering. Information-sharing technology in the form of computerized patient records, smart cards that carry patient histories, electronic image storage, and community databases will make the greatest impact on health care in the next decade. Health care workers from all disciplines will be able to share and update longitudinal care records to facilitate the lifelong health of patients. Technology is the tool that makes collaboration possible in virtual relationships.

Chapter Wrap-Up

Self-managed teams are not the end of organizational development. Teams are a bridge to the future. In chapter 1, self-managed teams were defined as "permanent, self-managed groups . . . who work together to produce a product or service." This definition implies that people on teams are employed by one organization to accomplish the goals of that organization. The health care system that is evolving is made up of many organizations, and health care workers serve multiple interests. The goals of each health care entity are subsumed by a shared purpose to improve the health of people in the community. Self-managed teams are making a transition to become self-organized networks of care providers. An emerging definition for these networks is "a virtual set of relationships between health workers who collaborate to serve the health needs of the community."

Self-managed teams provide an opportunity for people to learn the skills necessary to make the transition to the self-generating organizational systems of the information age. People on teams learn how to cocreate a shared mission. Practice gained in conflict resolution and compromise leads to an understanding of how to communicate through dialogue. Systems thinking is developed as employees are allowed to develop innovative work processes. Diversity in team composition demonstrates the value of blending differences to attain synergy. Recognition for personal achievement teaches people to appreciate the contributions of all members of the team. Self-managed teams serve as laboratories for people to experience and discover the path to individual and collective growth.

Health care is undergoing unforeseeable changes. The current trend of mergers and cost reductions is a precursor to new systems to provide health services that meet community needs. Self-managed teams provide a learning environment to blend cultures as the integration occurs in health systems. Multidisciplinary networks of providers are beginning to use the technology of the information age to collaborate in virtual relationships that support a continuum of patient care. Self-managed teams prepare people to contribute in the emerging systems of the future.

Suggested Readings

Behrendt, W. M., and W. F. Klein. "The Spirit of St. Louis: Merging Organizational Culture and Decision Making at BJC Health System." *Health Systems Review* 30, no. 4 (July/August 1997): 22–26.

Schrage, M. *No More Teams.* New York: Currency Doubleday, 1995.

Sims, B. J. *Servanthood.* Boston: Cowley, 1997.

Strauss, W., and N. Howe. *The Fourth Turning.* New York: Broadway, 1997.

Appendix

Facts about Actual Self-Managed Teams

Southeast: Dietitian Team

Organization Facts

Mission+St. Joseph's Health System
509 Biltmore Avenue
Asheville, North Carolina 28801

How long in existence: 100+ years

Type of business: Private acute care regional referral health system

Number of employees: 5,000

Date teams started at organization: 1992, in the housekeeping department; the dietitian team started in October 1994.

Why this team started: There was a vacancy in the clinical manager position; rather than fill the position, the department director gave the dietitians the option of becoming self-managed.

Champion for this team: Wil Bowler, director of food service

Team Facts

Structure

Department/service: Clinical nutrition services to patients served by the Mission+St. Joseph's Health System; contract services provided to nursing homes and a rehab hospital

Team structure, team roles, and role rotation: There is one health system clinical dietitian team. The team has 11 team roles: team coordinator, information systems, scheduler, diet manual/food service liaison, policies and procedures, quality management, continuum of care and marketing, resources and budget, education/training, human resources/celebrations, registered dietitian/registered dietetic technician liaison.

Primary customer of team: Patients

Number of people on team, types of jobs on team: There are 16 team members who fill the roles of dietitians and diet technicians.

Design and Boundaries

Design process: The original dietitian team was designed over a six-month period with the help of an internal facilitator from the human resources department. The current team is the amalgamation of two self-managed dietitian teams. The team accomplished its own design in team meetings and during a retreat. The design process took approximately four months.

Team meetings: Team meetings occur weekly for one and a half hours. Both team management business and clinical business are handled in team meetings.

Team boundaries: The team has the authority to manage daily operations, clinical workload, schedules, assignments, and performance reviews; it provides input into hiring and performs initial disciplinary discussions. The team does not fire or manage a budget.

Who team reports to: The team reports directly to Wil Bowler, director, food service.

Performance

Team performance measures: The team measures its performance by feedback from customers and success in meeting the Joint Commission's requirements.

Conflict resolution process: There is a three-member conflict group that includes the human resources role and two other members of the team. This group is available as a resource to anyone having a conflict. Initially, team members are expected to confront conflicts directly with the other party. If this method does not achieve a resolution, then any member of the conflict group may be contacted to help. If the conflict is not resolved, it goes to the full three-member conflict committee. There is a two-week follow-up to verify that the solution is adhered to.

Major achievements/accomplishments:

- Reduced turnover
- Systemwide nutrition screening process

- Consolidated/revised policies and procedures
- Team member cross-training
- Training and orientation program for new hires and diet technicians
- Conflict resolution process that does not include higher management

Celebrations: Occasional refreshments at team meetings, a catered lunch, creative posters commemorating special events, and novel ideas of recognition from one team member to another.

Training

Training: Meeting effectiveness, conflict resolution, goal setting, and communication skills. The team assesses education needs and receives training from in-house human resources staff.

Additional training planned: Training in giving and receiving feedback and in trust building. In addition, members of the team receive training from one another and at professional meetings and workshops.

Lessons Learned

Major hurdles overcome: The team has learned that things take longer when 16 team members are involved, that the responsibilities of self-management require new skills and take additional time, and that communication systems within the organization are not adjusted to the inclusion of self-managed teams.

What could be done differently in implementing the team: Some members of the team would like to receive additional compensation for assuming the responsibilities of self-management.

Changes that have occurred in how the team functions since starting: The team is less rigidly structured, less confusing, and more cohesive since it was first formed. Some of the roles have been modified.

Contact person: Dee Gabbard, team leader, 828-255-3649

Retirement Community: Southeast

Organization Facts

Givens Estates
Sweeten Creek Road
Asheville, North Carolina 28803

How long in existence: 19 years

Type of business: Methodist retirement community

Number of employees: 180

Date teams started at organization: 1996

Why teams started: Teams were created to fulfill a vision for a desirable and productive workplace.

The champion for these teams: Ken Partin, executive director, Givens Estates

Team Facts

Structure

Service: The Givens Estates retirement community provides a full range of services to its residents, including housing, meals, nursing care, maintenance, ground management, activities, transportation, worship, learning, gardening, and financial and operations management.

Team structure, team roles, and role rotation: The entire organization is structured in self-managed work teams. There are 13 teams that perform the various functions of the organization. Each team has the following roles: team leader, note taker, educator, human resources coordinator, quality improvement and personal touch coordinator, safety officer, and coach. Roles rotate every 12 months. Each person who fills a role is also a member of a role team. Within the role teams, goals are set for the roles, and staff learn how to function in their roles. Managers serve as chairs of the role teams.

Primary customer of teams: Residents

Number of people on teams, types of jobs on teams: Teams vary in size from 5 to 20 members. Jobs represented on teams range from nurses to food service workers, wait staff, resident services personnel, switchboard operators, and housekeeping staff.

Design and Boundaries

Design process: An expanded management team was formed to create the design. The management team met regularly to develop the structure, the management systems that the teams would use, and communication and reporting mechanisms.

Team meetings: Team meetings vary. Some teams meet as often as one hour per week. Other teams meet monthly. Meeting agendas are developed in advance of the meetings, and minutes are taken at each meeting and forwarded to administration. During meetings, daily operations issues are addressed as well as opportunities for performance improvement.

Team boundaries: Teams have the authority to manage daily operations, develop goals and plans, conduct 360-degree performance reviews, make decisions, and resolve problems with customers. They participate in hiring but do not have the authority to fire or manage budgets.

Who teams report to: Teams report to the director of the area in which they are located.

Performance

Team performance measures: Team performance measures vary depending on the type of team. All teams are expected to accomplish goals, meet or exceed customer needs, and implement quality improvements.

Conflict resolution process: There is a formal conflict resolution process that includes one-on-one confrontation, an active listening discussion and collaboration to resolve the problem. Unresolved conflicts are shared with the team. If the team is unable to come to a resolution, the conflict is referred to the supervisor or director.

Major achievements/accomplishments: The teams are in a learning process but have already accomplished much within the areas of their responsibility. Among the accomplishments are performance improvements, changes in work processes, and collaboration with other teams to resolve problems.

Celebrations: Teams are encouraged to celebrate. There is a quarterly meeting of all teams to review goals progress, accomplishments, and to celebrate achievements.

Training

Training: Team members and management have had general training on the concepts that underlie self-management. They have had specific training in meeting effectiveness, conflict resolution, decision making, and performance reviews.

Additional training planned: Additional training is planned in goal setting, performance improvement, hiring, discipline, customer service, and meeting effectiveness.

Lessons Learned

Major hurdles overcome: There have been five major hurdles that the teams are overcoming. One hurdle is adjusting to an organization structure of self-management. This has been a challenging transition for the staff and managers alike. Another hurdle is the time that it takes for staff to be self-managed. A third hurdle is involving the night shift in a meaningful way in self-managed team activities and responsibilities. Teams are dealing with the problem of attendance and participation at meetings: team members are busy caring for residents or are off work, and it is a challenge to keep them informed and to gain their input. The final hurdle is the staff turnover rate. It is difficult to continue to train new employees in how to be self-managed and fill team roles only to have them leave and having to start the training cycle all over with other new employees. The turnover rate has impeded the ability of some teams to become top performers as rapidly as they would like.

What could be done differently in implementing the teams: Initially teams were developed with a big picture approach. The managers were taught about teams and empowerment as well as the staff, but they were not given the tools or resources for creating the specific structures and systems that self-managed teams need in order to function effectively. The implementation would have gone more smoothly and would have taken less time if these tools and structures had been introduced right from the start.

Changes that have occurred in how the teams function since they started: Teams have more structure now than when they were started. In the beginning, they functioned like quality improvement teams, coming up with ideas for making improvements and helping implement the ideas. In the past year, teams have started assuming self-management responsibilities, and team roles have been created and implemented to assist in shared leadership and self-management.

Contact person: Allen Squires, chief financial officer, Givens Estates, 828-274-4800

Cross-Functional Team: Southeast

Organization Facts

Mission+St. Joseph's Health System
509 Biltmore Avenue
Asheville, North Carolina 28801

How long in existence: 100+ years

Type of business: Private acute care regional referral health system

Number of employees: 5,000

Date teams started at organization: 1992; the laundry teams started in February 1995.

Why these teams started: They were created to address productivity improvement and staff morale needs.

Champion for the teams: Graham Skinner, director, cooperative laundry service

Team Facts

Structure

Department/service: Laundry production, delivery, and pickup. The laundry processes in excess of 4 million pounds of laundry per year.

Team structure, team roles, and role rotation: There are three teams: Tunnel Rats—washing and drying; Rockin' Robins—ironing and distribution; and the Blues—folding. Each team has three roles: team leader, note taker, and timekeeper. Roles rotate every six months.

Primary customers of teams: Hospital patient care and surgery units

Number of people on teams, types of jobs on teams: There are approximately 12 members on each team. These members are all laundry workers.

Design and Boundaries

Design process: The design process took six weeks. The staff selected six representatives to serve on the design team. The design team met weekly to develop the team structure, roles, role rotation, ground rules, and performance expectations for teams.

Team meetings: Teams meet for one hour per week. The teams discuss issues relating to work flow, equipment, and supplies. Minutes are generally kept and issues facing the laundry staff are discussed. After these meetings, the team leaders discuss pertinent issues with the director and assistant manager. Occasionally the managers will attend team meetings.

Who teams report to: The teams report directly to Graham Skinner, director, cooperative laundry service.

Performance

Team performance measures: Team performance relates directly to productivity and the quality of the laundry service.

Conflict resolution process: If a conflict occurs between two team members, they are expected to try to resolve it between themselves. If they are unable to do that, they may involve the team leader. If the conflict is not resolved, they bring it to the director's or assistant director's attention for resolution.

Major achievements/accomplishments: The greatest accomplishment is meeting annual production increases of 10 percent with no increase in cost. Other accomplishments relate to the smooth functioning of the laundry. There is less stress, a more relaxed work environment, more cooperation, and fewer conflicts than in the past. Staff have a greater interest in the work and a greater feeling of professionalism in what they do. There has been the emergence of leadership and initiative in many staff members.

Celebrations: The teams celebrate with special meals, pizza parties, and ice cream. In addition, all team members receive team T-shirts.

Training

Training: Teams have received training in the concept of self-managed teams, expectations for team members, conflict resolution, communication, job description writing, 360-degree performance reviews, and safety.

Additional training planned: Each time new team leaders are selected, they receive training from human resources on their role and responsibilities. Other training programs will be offered as needs are identified.

Lessons Learned

Major hurdles overcome: The biggest hurdle is personality conflicts. Conflicts range from concerns about gossip to perceptions about willingness to share the workload. These conflicts are generally handled on a one-to-one basis in private. It seems that there will always be a need for an adjudicator. Conflicts have reduced in number and frequency, but they still occur.

What could be done differently in implementing the teams: The team needs someone on the floor to coordinate work flow. They might want to establish the position of team leader coordinator. The coordinator would help team leaders resolve issues relating to work flow and interpersonal conflicts.

Changes that have occurred in how the teams function since they started: Two major changes have been an increase in camaraderie among all staff and an increase in self-esteem. Team leaders have consistently demonstrated excellent performance in their roles.

Contact person: Graham Skinner, director, cooperative laundry, 828-255-3110

Outpatient Surgery Team: Southeast

Organization Facts

Mission+St. Joseph's Health System
Memorial Mission Hospital
509 Biltmore Avenue
Asheville, North Carolina 28801

How long in existence: 100+ years

Type of business: Health care organization

Number of employees: 5,000 in organization, 21 participate on One Day Surgery team

Date teams started at organization: 1992; One Day Surgery started in April 1996.

Why the team started: The team in the One Day Surgery Center started when there was vacancy for the manager's position. The staff met with the vice president and decided to try developing a self-managed work team.

Champion for the team: This idea was the collective effort of the One Day Surgery staff and was supported by their vice president and the director of human resource development.

Team Facts

Structure

Department/service: Preoperative and postoperative staff of an outpatient surgery center

Team structure, team roles, and role rotation: The team structure consists of eight key roles: coordinator/communicator, recorder, safety, scheduler, financial, human resources, quality, and educator. These staff members each have a "buddy" who works with that person to learn the functions and responsibilities of the position. This person is then ready to assume the key role the following year. There are two permanent roles that don't rotate yearly in this group—the educator and quality roles. They each have a buddy to assist them.

Primary customers of team: This team is part of a large health system and serves internal and external customers. Members of the team work with patients, physicians, and ancillary departments. They are also involved in strategic planning, task teams, and service lines within the health system.

Number of people on team, types of jobs on team: There are 21 staff members on the self-managed team. Each is a licensed nurse with specific clinical job responsibilities. Each key role team member also has specific responsibilities related to their role or their role as a buddy to another key role team member.

Design and Boundaries

Design process: The nursing team began after several months of preparation. The team used suggestions from other teams in health care and business and modified these to fit their needs. There was not a specific design for a nursing group. For the first year the team met twice a month. The team had to develop key processes, which required team review and vote. These meetings occurred in the early morning to accommodate operating hours.

Team meetings: The team now meets monthly for two hours. Subgroups meet as necessary for issues such as hiring and establishing policy and procedures.

Team boundaries: The management structure allows control of all aspects of our day-to-day operation, including staffing, budgeting, and hiring. The team performs peer review and conflict resolution. The team may begin the disciplinary process but is not allowed to terminate employees without assistance from the vice president.

Who team reports to: The team reports directly to a vice president.

Performance

Team performance measures: These include patient, staff, and other customer satisfaction survey results, using comparative Gallup results for the health system and their regional database.

Conflict resolution process: The team has an established process for conflict resolution that was established in the design process. This is facilitated by the human resources team role member.

Major achievements/accomplishments: Major projects include Joint Commission preparation and accreditation, improved customer satisfaction, and establishing and maintaining budgeted patient care hours. The team completed the development and implementation of nine new processes within the first year as a self-managed team.

Celebrations: The team celebrated surviving a year with a beach trip. They also have "secret sisters."

Training

Additional training: The team continues to read articles and material on self-managed work teams. Staff attend in-services on using E-mail, Word Perfect, budgeting, leadership, quality improvement, as well as other workshops. The team uses staff satisfaction surveys to look at ways to improve.

Lessons Learned

Major hurdles overcome: A major hurdle to establishing the team was the time needed to train staff in management functions, computer use, developing role responsibilities, and team processes. There were only a few staff members who were not supportive of the self-management concept and did not want to undertake a team role. They were supportive of other staff in the key roles.

What could be done differently in implementing teams: More education and preparation time prior to implementing the team, with emphases on effective communication and leadership skills.

Changes that have occurred in how the team functions since starting: In the second year, the team asked for volunteers for the key roles, rather than choosing through a random drawing of names as they did the first year. The team also made a change in a key role for the second year by combining the team coordinator and communicator roles. This allowed the team coordinator to be able to function more effectively in meetings and to better communicate with the team.

Additional comments: The team is very protective of the self-management concept and works hard to keep from being left out of communication loops. The team members are more confident in their roles and able to become active in health system leadership meetings.

Contact people: Dianne Hill and Anna Whitmire, One Day Surgery, Mission+St. Joseph's Health System, 828-255-3669

Management Team: Southwest

Organization Facts

Memorial Medical Center
2450 S. Telshor Boulevard
Las Cruces, New Mexico 88011-5076

How long in existence: 50 years

Type of business: Public acute care hospital

Number of employees: 1,400

Date teams started at organization: May 1997

Where teams started: Patient care services department directors

Why this team started: To provide coordination of the patient care services departments and to enhance the professional development of the department directors

Champion for the team: MaryAnn Aelmans-Digman, chief operating officer, Memorial Medical Center

Team Facts

Structure

Department/service: This management team provides leadership services to the ancillary departments that comprise patient care services. This group does not include nursing but does include all other clinical departments, including emergency care and surgical services.

Team structure, team roles, and role rotation: There is one management self-managed team in the organization. Team members fill nine roles. Three of the roles have two incumbents to provide continuity and to share the workload of those roles. The roles are team leader, record keeper, performance improvement coordinators (2), customer relations coordinators (2), finance coordinators (2), human resources coordinator, recognition and celebrations coordinator, and education and travel coordinator. There is also a team coach. Roles rotate every six months.

Primary customers of team: Physicians, patients, employees, the executive team, the chief operating officer, the board of directors, the community, and each other

Number of people on team, types of jobs on team: There are 11 team members who fill the following jobs: director, home health; director, emergency department; director, cardiovascular lab; director, imaging services; director and associate director, surgical services; director, respiratory care; director, pharmacy; director, rehabilitative services; director, materials management; director laboratory

Design and Boundaries

Design process: The management team met with a consultant for two days to get the process started, and then spent three months completing the design and related policies and procedures.

Team meetings: The team initially met weekly and is now meeting every two weeks. Meetings during the first six months focused primarily on developing the structure and systems for the team, communicating financial and customer service performance, finalizing team performance indicators, and reporting progress on team goals.

Team boundaries: The team is responsible for the effective management of the areas represented by the team. They have the authority to authorize operations expenditures up to $10,000. The team has the authority that a vice president in the organization has. If any team member is contemplating firing a staff member, the decision is reviewed with human resources, as well as the chief operating officer prior to its implementation.

Who the team reports to: The team reports directly to MaryAnn Aelmans-Digman, the chief operating officer for Memorial Medical Center.

Performance

Team performance measures: The team has established the following performance measurement areas: customer satisfaction, financial performance/cost reduction, and quality improvement. The overarching goal of the team is quality improvement.

Conflict resolution process: If there is a conflict between two team members, they are expected to discuss it between themselves and try to resolve it. If they are unable to resolve it, they then involve the entire team. If the conflict cannot be resolved by the team, it will then go to the chief operating officer.

Major achievements/accomplishments: The team believes its major achievements during its first six months are developing the structure, systems, policies, and procedures of the team; learning team roles; and developing true cohesiveness and interdependence as a team.

Celebrations: The team has regular celebrations and off-site parties. These parties/celebrations have been integral in improving team member cohesiveness.

Training

Training: The team has had training on what self-managed teams are and how to form them. They have also had training on financial topics, Joint Commission requirements, and performance improvement.

Additional training planned: The team would like more leadership development topics and additional training on team effectiveness.

Lessons Learned

Major hurdles overcome: One of the major hurdles the team has had to overcome is time. The meetings to form and design the team took more time than anticipated. Another hurdle that the team is dealing with is trust. There are different degrees of trust and different levels of participation on the team. The team has been hesitant about confronting team members.

What could be done differently in implementing the team: The team believes they would have been energized by tackling a significant performance improvement project early on. They also believe that they should have communicated more and earlier to the rest of the organization about the team, its purpose, and how it functions.

Changes that have occurred in how the team functions since starting: The team has become more effective in communicating and has developed a greater focus and more cohesiveness since it started.

Additional comments: It is very rare to find a cohesive management-level team. The team attributes its early success to the achievement orientation and the genuine desire to help and cooperate that each team member possesses.

Contact person: Paula Harty, administrative director, home health, 505-521-0750

Pharmacy Team: Southeast

Organization Facts

Mission+St. Joseph's Health System
Memorial Mission Hospital
509 Biltmore Avenue
Asheville, North Carolina 28801

How long in existence: 100+ years

Type of business: Health care organization

Number of employees: 5,000 in organization, 120 participate on pharmacy teams

Date teams started at organization: 1992; pharmacy teams started in 1995.

Why teams started: Teams started when the organization decentralized pharmacy services and individuals began to work in small groups or teams. Pharmacists no longer wanted to supervise; technicians and supportive help wanted more control over their jobs. The percentage of individuals covered under managed care was increasing, and the organization needed to respond quickly to change. Teams were initially formed with individuals from the inpatient and outpatient pharmacies and metabolic support services at Memorial Mission Hospital. Pharmacy teams were established at St. Joseph's Hospital when a partnership was developed between the two hospitals.

Champion for the teams: The director of pharmacy services was a strong supporter of the team concept prior to implementation. The director of human resources had written a book, *Self-Managed Work Teams in Health Care Organizations*, published by the American Hospital Association, and established teams in the housekeeping department at Mission. The pharmacy operations manager and pharmacy quality improvement coordinator worked with staff to implement teams.

Team Facts

Structure

Department/service: Pharmacy and metabolic support services

Team Structure, Team Roles, and Role Rotation: Each team has the same roles and elects a new leader, recorder, and reporter every four months. Roles for safety, quality, training, strategic planning, and cost rotate every 6 to 12 months. Team leadership is shared. Scheduling is accomplished by completing a shell with rotating weekend and evening shifts assigned. Time off is requested on a calendar with priorities giving to the sequence of requests. The completed shell is then given to the teams to fill in the required coverage.

Primary customers of teams: Teams are focused on different patient care service lines, such as surgery, pediatrics, heart services. There is a central pharmacy ("core") team that serves the decentralized pharmacy teams, and there are other support teams such as leadership, office, and purchasing.

Number of people on teams, types of jobs on teams: There are 13 teams, which have from 4 to 16 members. Teams have a different mixtures of all professionals within a department, depending on customers served. This includes pharmacists, pharmacy technicians, purchasing agents, secretaries, nurses, and dietitians. Some teams now include individuals from both Mission and St. Joseph's Hospitals.

Design and Boundaries

Design process: The teams used an eight-member design team to develop self-managed work teams. The design process took nine months. The design team initially met weekly for one hour each morning; as the process evolved, the design team averaged two meetings a month.

Team meetings: Individual teams meet when they need to, with scheduled and unscheduled meetings. The teams leaders meet twice a month as the department operations committee, and there is a weekly department staff meeting for information sharing. The team members in the quality and training roles meet monthly.

Team boundaries: The following were designated as responsibilities of the teams: make daily work assignments, keep daily records, schedule the staff, grant vacations/PTO, find relief for absences, authorize overtime, interview customers to identify needs, set customer service standards, monitor performance with customers, improve customer service, improve work systems and processes, schedule and conduct meetings, communicate, plan and set goals, assign goals and follow-up, monitor budget performance, work with suppliers, control absenteeism and tardiness and behavior, handle discipline, conduct performance reviews, write job descriptions, orient new employees, solve problems, hire and train employees, schedule celebrations, maintain equipment, keep work environment clean and neat, and plan celebrations. The leadership team's responsibilities include payroll, preparing the budget, allocating resources, preparing external memos, letters, and reports, firing employees, purchasing equipment, coaching and giving feedback on work, and communicating with upper management.

Who teams report to: The pharmacy leadership team includes the director of the pharmacy, who reports to a senior vice president.

Performance

Team performance measures: Each team establishes an average of three objectives with anticipated percentage completion rate using the "Plan, Do, Check, Act" process and records objectives with anticipated outcomes once every four months. Actual percentage completion rates are recorded with revised objectives and other improvements (if applicable) and results are reported at team celebrations every four months.

Conflict resolution process: If conflict develops between two members of the same team, the individuals are asked to immediately take time from work to discuss the issue face-to- face; if the conflict is not solved, the two individuals request a mediator (who may or may not be a coach); if the conflict cannot be solved, the administrative discipline process is implemented. If the conflict is between two teams, a representative from each team meets in an attempt to resolve the dispute (these individuals may have to consult with their respective teams to get consensus). If the conflict cannot be resolved, a coach (agreement of the choice of the coach must be by both teams) mediates a meeting with representatives from each team.

Major achievements/accomplishments: Pharmacy teams have gained a reputation for excellent service throughout the health system. Pharmacists are now being asked by physicians to develop pharmacy programs for their office practices and community outreach programs. The clinical role of the pharmacy has grown significantly with the transition to decentralized teams, and technicians are primarily responsible for drug distribution processes. A 360-degree performance improvement process has been established for each team member. The number of requests for pharmacy clinical consults has increased significantly. A major achievement the leadership team has accomplished has been shifting from traditional supervisory/leadership roles to the roles of a coach. New teams were also incorporated when Memorial Mission and St. Joseph's Hospitals combined into the Mission+St. Joseph's Health System. The team distributed a pharmacy team effectiveness attribute survey to measure how the staff feels about teams.

Celebrations: Every four months there is a celebration reporting team outcome reports, with drinks, cookies, brownies, and fruit. Each reporter presents his/her outcome report, and everyone applauds the results. There is also a designated amount of money for each team to meet off site for dinner and other activities to build trust and camaraderie among team members. This process has helped significantly with team bonding.

Training

Training: The teams had training on improving interviewing skills, the "Plan, Do, Check, Act" process, on the roles of individuals in conducting efficient meetings, and conflict resolution.

Additional training planned: Additional training is planned in the area of facilitation. "Teamliness" competencies for hiring, performance reviews, and conflict resolution are being established.

Lessons Learned

Major hurdles overcome: Some team members are assigned a role and do not perform that role. Many of the team members do not possess communication skills that will enable them to resolve conflicts with coworkers. Staff complain that the team concept takes a lot of time and that insufficient time is scheduled for these activities. Some individuals are more comfortable taking their concerns to a coach rather than taking responsibility for solving problems themselves. Considerable in-service is required to acquaint team members with interviewing skills and providing input in a team meeting. Competition between teams often develops.

What could be done differently in implementing teams: The design team needed to provide more upfront in-service on the responsibilities and functions of teams before implementation. A formal training program should have been established, with support from upper management. Personality profiles should have been used for team building to help team members understand the strength of the diversity of their membership.

Changes that have occurred in how teams function since starting: Teams interact directly with their customers (nurses, physicians, and patients). The coaches are viewed as supporters and not decision makers. Teams have taken direct responsibility for the hiring process. Considerable improvement has occurred with schedule coverage. Unscheduled absences have decreased dramatically, and teams cover for themselves when team members are unable to come to work. Team members have often stated they would find it very difficult to return to a traditional management structure; they like the freedom that the team environment provides. Teams increasingly concentrate on outcomes and understand that the process is their responsibility. The team wasn't planning to develop a leadership team initially but found they needed to follow the team process as developed by the design team just as carefully as the other teams in the department. There has been a real shift in thinking since the leadership team was formed; the team now explores opportunities for helping other teams accomplish their objectives using the team resources.

Contact person: R. Dean Strahm, pharmacy operations coach, 828-259-3755, fax 828-259-3462

Pharmacy Team: West Coast

Organization Facts

Huntington Memorial Hospital
100 W. California Blvd.
Pasadena, California 91109-7013

How long in existence: 102 years

Type of business: Health care organization

Number of employees: 2,300

Date teams started: 1994

Why teams started: The teams were started in response to restructuring in the organization when jobs were combined and levels of hierarchy eliminated; teams utilize the patient-focused care model.

Champion for the teams: The manager of the education department was the champion for teams; however, the idea was facilitated and pushed by the nurse in charge of patient-focused care.

Team Facts

Structure

Deparment/service: Pharmacy services

Team structure, team roles, and role rotation: The pharmacy teams consist of 10 pharmacy staff members (approximately 5 pharmacists, 4 technicians, and 1 intern). Pharmacists and technicians who work primarily in the same area, such as the IV additive room, were split up and put onto different teams. The team leader role rotates every three years. Teams meet monthly and generally address the same items of business to reach a consensus within each team. The five team leaders meet monthly with the coach to go over problem areas, to discuss items to address in team meetings, and to facilitate decisions.

Primary customers of teams: The primary customers of the pharmacy teams are physicians, nurses, and patients.

Number of people on teams, types of jobs on teams: There are 10 employees on each team. Each team has a team leader and a recorder.

Designs and Boundaries

Design process: The design team was done by the coach and took less than a month.

Team meetings: Generally the teams meet monthly in prescheduled conference rooms at noon. The leaders meet monthly with the coach in the coach's office.

Team boundaries: In general, most items dealing with the daily work processes are within the team boundaries except for budgets, firing, and written discipline. Though the teams do not hire their team members, the staff is involved in the hiring process. Oral discipline is handled by the team leaders; performance reviews, though not done strictly by the teams, are done by team members' working peers.

Who teams report to: Teams report to the coach—the department manager—who then reports to the vice president.

Performance

Team performance measures: Measured by accomplishments and decisions, such as work processes resolved, changed, and implemented.

Conflict resolution process: Conflicts are generally handled individually and privately, although not many incidents have occurred.

Major achievements/accomplishments:

- Improved order entry process
- Discharge prescription coordination
- Quality assurance program
- Implemented outsourced preparation of cardioplegia solutions
- Rewrote all job descriptions utilizing outcome statements
- Implemented attendance policy
- Implemented dress code policy
- Work schedule by team
- Multitude of changes in pyxis in terms of stocking, control, and procedures
- Peer review including review by MDs/RNs of pharmacists
- Improved turnaround time of outpatient prescriptions by IP/OP pharmacies
- Biannual pharmacy retreats, which greatly accelerated the decision-making process
- Utilization of the STP (Situation, Target, Proposal) for making good decisions
- Celebratory climate to recognize achievements
- Cross-training
- Pharmacy teams received the Leadership Award during employee recognition week

Celebrations: Generally through ice-cream socials during monthly staff meetings and group dinners during retreats.

Training

Training: The teams had little formal training in self-managed work teams. All pharmacy staff members are required to attend a five-day class entitled "Quest for Excellence" and a three-day seminar focusing on CQI, but not all staff have completed these courses.

Lessons Learned

Major hurdles overcome: Giving employees the feeling that they have a say in how, when, where, and who does the work. Another hurdle overcome was the feeling that the coach was calling the shots; the teams soon realized that they must express their ideas, thoughts, comments, and suggestions. In the beginning, team leaders had trouble finding time for preparation and meetings, and this was a major stumbling block to decision making, but holding retreats has increased the speed of the decision-making process.

What could be done differently in implementing teams: Having a design team and spending more time in the initial team-forming process. More frequent meetings, possibly every week for a shorter period of time, such as 30 minutes. Rather than each team addressing all the same items of business, assign each team a different item so they can formulate a recommendation that would then be taken to each team for consensus. Switch around team members and possibly team leaders on a regular basis.

Changes that have occurred in how teams function since starting: Improved dialogue and discussion. Some breaking down of walls—for example, between staff who work in the outpatient pharmacy and the inpatient pharmacy. Facilitation of cross-training improved relationships and understanding. There is an improved appreciation of the camaraderie established, especially compared to the departments who haven't gotten as far with self-managed teams.

Additional comments: The five teams leaders had an extreme commitment to the self-managed teams, including working overtime to compensate for the lean management structure.

Contact person: Glenn Y. Yokoyama, PharmD, pharmacy director, 626-397-5179, fax 626-397-5131

Physician Office Practice: Southeast

Organization Facts

Regional Surgical Specialists
16 McDowell Street
Asheville, North Carolina 28801

How long in existence: 16 years

Type of business: General surgery physician group practice

Number of employees: 10 office staff

Date team started: January 1997

Why teams started: There was a vacancy in the office manager position for the practice. Information about self-managed teams was discussed at the hospital in which the surgeons practiced. The office staff were competent, stable, and energetic. The physicians believed they could be an effective self-managed team.

Champion for the team: Randall Johnson, MD

Team Facts

Structure

Department/service: General surgery physician practice

Team structure, team roles, and role rotation: There is one self-managed team in the office. It contains all members of the office staff, and each member fills one of the ten team roles. The team roles are team leader, record keeper, quality improvement and data keeper, public relations, scheduler, educator, safety officer, human resources and policy and procedure coordinator, celebration coordinator, and purchasing and maintenance coordinator. Each role rotates every six months. Team members volunteer for roles. If more than one person volunteers for a role, names are placed in a hat and drawn to determine who fills the role. The team originally started with a three-month role rotation but found that the brief time in the role did not allow them the opportunity to learn their roles and accomplish something significant while serving in the role.

Primary customers of the team: The team identified patients, physicians, the licensing commission, and one another as important customers, with patients being the primary customer.

Types of jobs on team: There are office nurses, receptionists, medical secretaries, insurance secretaries, filers, billers and collections staff, a financial coordinator, and one nurse practitioner, who serves as the team coach.

Design and Boundaries

Design process: Since just one team was created in this physician office practice, the team designed itself during its first several meetings, with the help of an external facilitator.

Team meetings: Initially, the team met for one hour a week to accomplish the design. It later reduced the number of meetings to every other week for one hour. The team meets in the morning before the practice opens for the day. The team uses a detailed agenda that is prepared in advance by the team leader, with input from team members and the coach. The note taker takes the minutes and distributes them to all team members. The minutes are reviewed at the beginning of the next meeting.

Team boundaries: The team has the authority to manage all daily work, scheduling vacations and time off, goal setting and planning, purchasing office supplies, and maintaining the office facility. Any major equipment or technology purchase and structural repairs to the facility are reviewed with the physicians for approval or are initiated by the physicians. The team confronts problem behaviors within the team, but if they are not corrected quickly, refers them to the physicians for resolution. The team helps hire replacement staff but cannot fire anyone. The team establishes office performance standards, conducts patient satisfaction surveys, and monitors and reports office performance in areas such as waiting times, telephone access and responsiveness, and work flow.

Who the team reports to: The team reports directly to a physician.

Performance

Team performance measures: The team has established four performance measures:

- Waiting time for appointments
- Patient satisfaction with listening, courtesy, and responsiveness of staff
- Face sheet completion
- Work flow efficiency

Conflict resolution process: The team established a conflict resolution process that begins with a discussion between the two team members who are experiencing a conflict or concern. The team members follow a discussion outline that encourages active listening and collaboration to resolve the conflict. If the team members cannot reach a resolution, then the problem or issue is brought to the team for discussion and resolution. The team can utilize the team coach for assistance in conflict resolution.

Major achievements/accomplishments: Collaborating together, the team has reduced waiting times by adjusting scheduling procedures and bringing actual waiting time trends to the attention of the physicians; they have improved telephone answering, reduced questions about patient bills, learned how to function as a self-managed team, and learned how to effectively fulfill team roles; they have conducted patient satisfaction surveys, developed charts and graphs, and set goals and developed action plans for improvement.

Celebrations: The team celebrates the accomplishment of goals, meeting or exceeding quarterly performance measures, and becoming certified in CPR. They also celebrate birthdays; nurses', secretaries', and doctors' days; length of service; and role performance. Celebrations include dinners out, trips, and breakfast buffets.

Training

Training: The team has had training in meeting effectiveness and meeting leadership; how to develop a team mission, vision, and values; how to create goals and action plans; and how to make team decisions, resolve conflicts, hire and conduct performance reviews. The team has learned how to establish performance measures, monitor performance, and develop charts and graphs. They have learned how to develop work process flow diagrams and how to streamline work flow. They know how to develop a team report, write job descriptions, and conduct patient satisfaction surveys.

Additional training planned: Future training relates to learning more about the use of advanced office technologies, benchmarking, insurances, billing and coding for reimbursement, and disease entities.

Lessons Learned

Major hurdles overcome: The team has become a much more cohesive work group, less restricted by position and turf boundaries. Team members have learned to talk more openly about problems and concerns. The team has learned to value the different personality styles and to be less critical of differences. Individual team members have developed enhanced self-esteem by accepting the challenges of the team roles. Team members have learned how to adjust to the stress and time demands of their roles and have learned how to be better time managers. Team members see physician involvement and support as a necessity and hope to develop a greater "partnership" with the physicians as the team matures and the physicians develop greater confidence in the team's abilities.

What could be done differently in implementing the team: The team did not include or involve the physician assistants in communication about the team. They have since included them in the quarterly team reports. The team had an aggressive implementation schedule and believe that they could have benefited from taking more time in implementing the new roles and responsibilities.

What changes have occurred in how the team functions since starting: There has been a change in the role rotation schedule from a three-month schedule to a six-month schedule. There is a real change in the knowledge that team members have about how the office functions and how each job impacts the others. Team members also have an increased understanding of one another.

Additional comments: Team members have asked themselves each quarter whether they want to continue in self-management or return to having an office manager. The issues of the time it takes to be self-managed and the responsibility of managing the office come up each quarter. Although not unanimous, the team still feels strongly that self-management is providing them with valuable skill development and an unprecedented opportunity to lead and control the management of the office.

Contact person: Shirley Nesbitt, nurse practitioner and team coach, 828-252-3366

Hospital Preschool: Midwest

Organization Facts

Baptist Health
9601 Kanis Road
Little Rock, AR 72205-7599

How long in existence: 77 years

Type of business: Health care organization

Number of employees: 5,000 in organization

Date teams started: 1994

Why teams started: Teams were started as the result of a document known as the "Human Resource Plan." The intent of this document was to assess the current culture and to prepare the organization for changes that were anticipated on a national scale in health care. The plan recognized the human resources as the most valuable asset. It called for empowerment of staff, elimination of layers of management, and the creation of a culture that would support both. The "Human Resource Plan" was published in 1992. The formation of teams seemed to be the natural next step.

Where teams are: Currently teams exist in preschool, personnel, transcription, Baptist System Schools of Nursing and Allied Health, and respiratory. Teams will begin in 1998 in telecommunication, pharmacy, and network services.

Champion of the teams: Tom McCamery, vice president of human resources and author of the "Human Resource Plan," envisioned teams as the predominant structure within Baptist Health.

Team Facts

Structure

Department/service: Preschool

Team structure, team roles, and role rotation: The preschool consists of two sites and six subteams. Each subteam consists of a team leader, and the entire team has two coaches. Since inception of the team model, six management positions have been eliminated. This has occurred through natural attrition. The team leader position is rotated on an annual basis.

Primary customers of team: The work of each subteam is to care for children. The work varies from one subteam to the next based upon the age of the children in the group.

Number of people on team, types of jobs on team: The preschool employs 55 people. The largest subteam consists of 10 staff members.

Design and Boundaries

Design process: The model for the preschool was the work of a design team; the work was completed in 10 months.

Team meetings: Each subteam meets on a weekly basis for approximately one hour.

Team boundaries: The team boundaries are fairly broad. The team deals with all aspects of the business, such as ordering supplies, resolving customer concerns and complaints, scheduling, time off, interviewing, and conflict resolution among staff. The team has embarked on formal problem solving this year. The team receives and analyzes budget data and has involvement in the team members' evaluations via Team Trac.

Who team reports to: The coach

Performance

Team performance measures: The team has formal outcomes that are very specific, dealing with costs, enrollment, and customer satisfaction. These targets are predetermined and in written form prior to the end of the fiscal year. Each subteam develops a formal action plan for achieving success. The team receives timely progress reports on the outcomes and adjust their plans based upon the success of each outcome. Upon completion of the fiscal year, each subteam receives a bonus based upon the success with each outcome.

Conflict resolution process: Conflicts among team members are resolved at the team level. A facilitator can be utilized if desired or indicated.

Major achievements/accomplishments: The team has experienced a reduction of costs, as well as enhanced enrollment and customer satisfaction. The team has demonstrated concrete results in all three of the outcomes.

Celebrations: The team celebrates formally at the close of their fiscal year when team members receive their bonuses and recognize each subteam's outstanding player. Subteams also hold luncheons and give out gift certificates.

Training

Training: There was initial training on the team model implementation and team development.

Additional training planned: Additional training is planned for team leaders.

Lessons Learned

Major hurdles overcome: The biggest hurdle has been getting top-down commitment to the conversion process of team development.

What could be done differently in implementing teams: Providing additional training for the team leaders and allowing additional time for the coaches and team leaders to build relationships with team members.

Additional comments: The first five years are particularly challenging because the subteams go through various developmental phases, and each phase requires a different type of leadership.

Changes that have occurred in how teams function since starting: The team members have a higher level of satisfaction about their work. They have better attitudes because they have control over their work environment and realize that they do make a difference. They will quickly tell you that they would never want to return to a traditional workplace!

Contact person: Maureen W. Jones, Coach Baptist Health Preschool, 501-202-1946, E-mail mwjones@alpha-net.net

Cross-Functional Team: Southeast

Organization Facts

Mission+St. Joseph's Health System
509 Biltmore Avenue
Asheville, North Carolina 28801

How long in existence: 100+ years

Type of business: Private acute care regional referral health system

Number of employees: 5,000

Date teams started: 1992; the cross-functional team started in April 1996

Why this team started: The team was created to provide a special service to patients

Champion for the team: Nancy Righi, director, rehabilitation services

Team Facts

Structure

Department/service: Acute chronic and preventive wound care to patients in western North Carolina

Team structure, team roles, and role rotation: There is one cross-functional team with these seven roles: leader and team communicator, scheduler and purchasing coordinator, educator, QI coordinator, record keeper/human resources and physician relations coordinator, legal and safety coordinator, and budget and payor liaison. Roles rotate every six months.

Primary customers of team: Wound and potential wound patients

Number of people on team, types of jobs on team: There are 11 team members who fill the following jobs: certified wound care nurse, physical therapists, physical therapy assistants and technicians.

Design and Boundaries

Team meetings: The team meets weekly for one hour. At team meetings, clinical as well as team management issues are addressed.

Team boundaries: The team is responsible for daily operations, scheduling, hiring, firing, discipline, performance reviews, budget, and goal setting.

Who team reports to: The team reports directly to the vice president for outpatient services, Tim Johnston.

Performance

Team performance measures: The team uses a team assessment tool to help gauge team performance and team progress. The assessment is conducted about every six to eight months.

Major achievements/accomplishments: The team has developed positive feelings of trust, acceptance, and mutual regard. The team has utilized the organization's quality improvement process to create a new evaluation and assessment process and forms. It has developed new job descriptions, policies, and procedures. All of the team members have developed skills in their team roles, clinical roles, and in self-management.

Celebrations: Our celebrations invariably involve food.

Training

Training: The team has had training in meeting effectiveness, conflict resolution, communication, decision making, and safety.

Lessons Learned

Major hurdles overcome: One of the major hurdles the team had to overcome was lack of trust. The team was formed with members from different hospitals and different clinical specialties. These differences gave rise to differences in expectations. Team members also had different degrees of skill and experience in the areas that the team is responsible for.

What could be done differently in implementing the team: The team would have benefited from using a design team early in the process. It also would not have combined wound and enterstomal therapy services in one self-managed team.

Changes that have occurred in how the team functions since starting: The team experienced periods of frustration, anger, and general disarray as it tried to function as a blended team with enterstomal therapy but this has been alleviated since the two services were made into separate teams.

Contact person: Rose Spittle, team leader, 828-258-6830

Index